Gender Bonds, Gender Binds

Sense, Matter, and Medium

―

New Approaches to Medieval Literary and Material Culture

Edited by
Fiona Griffiths, Beatrice Kitzinger, and Kathryn Starkey

Volume 3

Gender Bonds, Gender Binds

Women, Men, and Family
in Middle High German Literature

Edited by
Sara S. Poor, Alison L. Beringer, and Olga V. Trokhimenko

DE GRUYTER

ISBN 978-3-11-112179-6
e-ISBN (PDF) 978-3-11-072919-1
e-ISBN (EPUB) 978-3-11-072925-2
ISSN 2367-0290

Library of Congress Control Number: 2021931823

Bibliografic information published by the Deutsche Nationalbibliothek
The Deutsche Nationalbibliothek lists this publication in the Deutsche Nationalbibliografie;
detailed bibliografic data are available in the Internet at http://dnb.dnb.de.

© 2022 Walter de Gruyter GmbH, Berlin/Boston
This volume is text- and page-identical with the hardback published in 2021.
Cover image: Konrad Fleck, *Flôre und Blanscheflûr*, Universitätsbibliothek Heidelberg, Cod. Pal. germ. 362, Bl. 54r.
Typesetting: Integra Software Services Pvt. Ltd.
Printing and binding: CPI books GmbH, Leck

www.degruyter.com

Essays in Honor of Ann Marie Rasmussen

Acknowledgments

This collection of essays is itself, of course, an acknowledgment of the great debt we, the editors and contributors to this volume, feel towards Ann Marie Rasmussen, who has been either a teacher, mentor, or cherished colleague to all of us, and for some, all of these things. However, there are also other debts that we would like to recognize here. The idea for the volume was hatched after a session held at the German Studies Association annual meeting organized by Katja Altpeter and Alison Beringer. The session was in celebration of the fifteenth anniversary of the publication of Ann Marie Rasmussen's *Mothers and Daughters in Medieval German Literature*. The idea for the session came from Katja and we thus owe her thanks for planting the seed that has grown into this volume. Thanks are also due to Katja for her contributions to the initial planning of the volume. Sara S. Poor wishes to thank her co-editors, Alison L. Beringer and Olga V. Trokhimenko for coming onto the editorial team midway through the process. We also owe a debt of gratitude to the National Humanities Center, where we were able to have one of our editorial meetings while Sara had a fellowship there. The peer reviewers of the volume, as well as one of the series editors, Kathryn Starkey, offered us insightful feedback, for which we are also grateful. Finally, we must thank all of our contributors, including our translators, not only for their outstanding work, but even more so for their patience, unwavering enthusiasm, and continuous support of this project.

Contents

Acknowledgments —— VII

List of Illustrations —— XI

List of Contributors —— XIII

Sara S. Poor, Alison L. Beringer, and Olga V. Trokhimenko
Introduction —— 1

Sara S. Poor
1   Peddling Devotion: Mothers and Daughters in Conversation Through Books —— 25

Mary Marshall Campbell
2   Why Siegfried Has to Die: Gender, Violence, and the Social Order in the *Nibelungenlied* —— 47

Olga V. Trokhimenko
3   "If You Are Desired, Then You Are Worthy": Mothers, Daughters, and Paradoxes of Femininity in the Middle High German Tristan Sequels —— 77

Katja Altpeter
4   Maternal Bonds in Konrad Fleck's *Flôre und Blanscheflûr* —— 103

Evelyn Meyer
5   Teaching a Daughter Sexual Desire and Love Lore: Herzeloyde's Mentorship of Sigune in Wolfram von Eschenbach's *Titurel* and Albrecht von Scharfenberg's *Jüngerer Titurel* —— 117

Ingrid Bennewitz
6   Mothers and Daughters Revisited: The Mother-Daughter Songs in the Context of the Later Neidhart Tradition —— 137

Andreas Kraß
7   Rivalrous Masculinities: Competing Concepts of Knighthood in Bernard of Clairvaux's Sermon *In Praise of the New Knighthood* and Hartmann von Aue's Novella *Gregorius* —— 161

Alison L. Beringer
8   A Fate Worse than Death? Virgil's "steinîn wîp" in Jans der Enikel's *Weltchronik* —— 177

Jutta Eming
9   Love and Disgust: Ambiguous Genres and Ambivalent Feelings in *Herzmäre* —— 199

Index —— 219

List of Illustrations

Figure 1.1 Family Trees Showing Relationship Between Agnes of Werdenberg and Elizabeth of Württemberg. © Sara S. Poor —— **32**

Figure 1.2 Paternosterer [Paternoster maker]; Stadtbibliothek im Bildungscampus Nürnberg, Amb. 317.2°, fol. 13r —— **36**

Figure 1.3 Rosary with dividing beads of chalcedony as paternoster markers, Inv.-Nr. R 940, Foto Nr. D25898 © Bayerisches Nationalmuseum München; Photo by Karl-Michael Vetters —— **37**

Figure 1.4 Gerard David. The Virgin and Child with Saints and Donor. Probably 1510. © The National Gallery, London. Bequeathed by Mrs Lyne Stephens, 1895 —— **38**

Figure 1.5 Joos van Cleve (1485–1540) and a collaborator. Crucifixion with Saints and Donor (1520), Metropolitan Museum of Art, New York, Bequest of George Blumenthal, 1941 —— **39**

Figure 1.6 Anonymous, 15th century. The Family of Jouvenel des Ursins. Paris, 1445–49. © RNM-Grand palais / Art Resource, NY. INV 9618. Photo: Gérard Blot —— **42**

Figure 6.1 Ms c, showing text with notes. Berlin, Staatsbibliothek zu Berlin – Preußischer Kulturbesitz, mgf 779, fol. 160v —— **143**

Figure 8.1 "Virgil's Revenge" Jans der Enikel, Weltchronik, Herzog August Bibliothek, Wolfenbüttel: Cod. Guelf. 1.5.2 Aug. 2°, fol. 143v
Photo: Herzog August Library, Wolfenbüttel —— **193**

List of Contributors

Katja Altpeter is Associate Professor of German at Lewis & Clark College. She has published on questions of gender and commerce and on representations of religious diversity in Konrad Fleck's *Flôre und Blanscheflûr*. She has also worked on female healing practices in *Tristan* and on representations of domestic violence in early modern German text and image. She has recently reoriented her research, teaching, and service towards the Environmental Humanities and investigates interspecies – especially human-animal – connections, ponders anthropocene pedagogy, strives to create decolonized, engaged, and emplaced learning environments, and serves her institution as Coordinator for Sustainability and Curriculum.

Ingrid Bennewitz is Professor of medieval German philology at the University of Bamberg. She received her PhD in German Studies, Musicology, and Philosophy at the Universities of Salzburg and Münster with a dissertation on the manuscript transmission of the Neidhart corpus (1985). She completed her habilitation in 1993, also at the University of Salzburg. Since being appointed to the chair in Bamberg in 1995, she has researched and published widely on the transmission and editions of medieval texts and their reception in the present day, as well as on medieval Gender Studies.

Alison L. Beringer is Associate Professor of Classics and General Humanities at Montclair State University in New Jersey. A German medievalist, she works on the reception of antiquity, and the materiality of late medieval and early modern German manuscripts and prints. She is the author of *The Sight of Semiramis: Medieval and Early Modern Narratives of the Babylonian Queen*. Her current research examines the depiction of statues in late medieval and early modern German literature, particularly *Meisterlieder*.

Mary Marshall Campbell is a doctoral candidate at Princeton University where she is completing a dissertation on violence as the means by which social order is en-gendered in the *Nibelungenlied*. The recipient of fellowships from the Fulbright Program and the German Academic Exchange Service (DAAD) as well as the University of Notre Dame, she has held lectureship positions at the University of New Hampshire and Princeton University. Her publications include "Sanctity and Identity: The Authentication of the Ursuline Relics and Legal Discourse in Elisabeth von Schönau's *Liber Revelationum*," which appeared in the *Journal of Medieval Religious Cultures*.

Jutta Eming is professor for medieval German literature at the Freie Universität Berlin. Her research interests include romances from the high to the late Middle Ages, genre theory and gender, emotionality, performativity, and premodern drama. She directs a project in the Freie Universität's special research center "Episteme in Motion" on "The Marvelous as a Configuration of Knowledge in Medieval Literature." Among her publications are *Funktionswandel des Wunderbaren: Studien zum 'Bel Inconnu,' zum 'Wigalois' und zum 'Wigoleis vom Rade'* (Trier 1999) and *Emotion und Expression: Untersuchungen zu deutschen und französischen Liebes- und Abenteuerromanen des 12.-16. Jahrhunderts* (Berlin/New York 2006).

Andreas Kraß is Professor of Medieval German Literature at the Humboldt University of Berlin where he directs a project on medieval German translations of Latin liturgical songs (online database: "Berliner Repertorium"). In addition, he is the director of the Research Center for the Cultural History of Sexuality where he administers a research project on the Naomi Wilzig Art Collection (Miami Beach) as well as a joint project on German Jewish literature of the 20th century together with the Hebrew University of Jerusalem. His recent publications include: "Meerjungfrauen: Geschichten einer unmöglichen Liebe" (2010) and "Ein Herz und eine Seele: Geschichte der Männerfreundschaft" (2016).

Evelyn Meyer is Associate Professor of German and affiliated faculty in the Center for Medieval and Renaissance Studies and the Women and Gender Studies Department at Saint Louis University. She has published essays on gender constructions in Hartmann von Aue's *Iwein* and *Erec*, Wolfram von Eschenbach's *Parzival* and *Titurel*, and on text-image relationships in *Parzival*. She has also co-edited two essay collections: *Changes of World View in Exile* (2010) and *Geschichten sehen, Bilder hören. Bildprogramme im Mittelalter* (2015). Her current book project explores visual story telling in *Parzival* illuminations, focusing on depictions of gender, race, and the other.

Sara S. Poor is Associate Professor of German Literature at Princeton University. In addition to numerous articles, she is the author of *Mechthild of Magdeburg and Her Book: Gender and the Making of Textual Authority* (Penn, 2004) and co-editor of two essay collections: *Women in Medieval Epic: Gender, Genre, and the Limits of Epic Masculinity* (Palgrave, 2007) and *Mysticism and Reform, 1400–1750* (Notre Dame, 2015). Her current research examines the relationship between gender and the production and circulation of devotional books in late medieval Germany.

Olga V. Trokhimenko is Professor of German at the University of North Carolina Wilmington. In addition to articles on gender, sexuality, and emotions in medieval texts, as well as on the function of proverbs in medieval and modern works (paroemiology), she is the author of *Constructing Virtue and Vice: Femininity and Laughter in Courtly Society (ca. 1150–1300)* (Vandenhoeck & Ruprecht, 2014). Her current research brings her ongoing interest in gender and sexuality to bear on high- and late-medieval comic narratives and on medieval proverbs.

Sara S. Poor, Alison L. Beringer, and Olga V. Trokhimenko
Introduction

One would be hard pressed to find a person today, in 2021, particularly a scholar, who has not heard of gender and feminist studies. Its methodology and vocabulary are so familiar, so widely applied in, and so deeply interwoven with numerous disciplines from literary criticism to history, cultural studies, and art history (to say nothing of social sciences like anthropology and sociology) that it is hard to imagine a time when terms such as "gender," "femininity," or "masculinity" sounded innovative or even radical. This collection of essays, *Gender Bonds, Gender Binds*, honors Ann Marie Rasmussen, a scholar whose book, *Mothers and Daughters in Medieval German Literature* (1997), appeared at a time when using this vocabulary to frame the argument of a study of medieval German literature was in fact a courageous act. The book was among the first studies in the field of medieval German literary criticism to use gender as a central category of analysis. 2017 marked the twentieth anniversary of this fascinating and deeply thorough analysis of several well- and also (at the time) lesser-known medieval German texts featuring mothers and daughters in conversations about love and/or sex. Yet, going beyond what German scholarship calls *Motivgeschichte* [thematic study], *Mothers and Daughters* did more than simply draw the reader's attention to the plight of female characters in premodern literary texts as the victims of patriarchal society. Its innovation lay rather in the author's willingness to examine the complexity of the workings of gender in these medieval texts. These workings become clear as *Mothers and Daughters* explores the literary depictions of women teaching each other how to be in the world not only as mothers, wives, and lovers, but also as public figures, professionals, and rulers of empires. Rasmussen's study also highlights the methods and strategies that women develop in order to transfer knowledge to one another. Put another way, it is a book about narratives of being a woman in a male-dominated culture and of producing and transmitting (often controversial and counter-cultural) knowledge in this culture.

In examining and unpacking these mother-daughter narratives, Rasmussen's path-breaking study deftly demonstrated the potential applications of cross-disciplinary theory for a range of medieval genres. Drawing from the then current feminist work on the psychology of the mother-daughter relation, and at the same time, grounding the adoption of terms and concepts from this work in a thorough understanding of the medieval historical and political context, *Mothers and Daughters* offered striking new readings of the following works: Heinrich von Veldeke's *Eneasroman*, the *Nibelungenlied*, *Kudrun*, Gottfried von Strassburg's *Tristan*, *Die Winsbeckin*, the poems of Neidhart, and the fifteenth-century dialogues known as *Stepmother and Daughter*.[1] Exposing the

---

[1] See below, Appendix A, for a complete Table of Contents as well as a full summary of the book.

ways that gender was both inflected and negotiated in the dialogic encounters between literary characters, these readings moved the study of gender roles in medieval German literature out of the realm of first wave feminism's focus on exposing patriarchal structures. In doing so, Rasmussen's new approach had the effect of opening doors for many to follow in her footsteps. One cannot therefore overestimate the impact of Rasmussen's *Mothers and Daughters* on medieval German studies specifically and on medieval studies generally.

While the objects of study in Rasmussen's book are medieval texts, the gender bonds and binds discussed continue to strike our present-day audience as unsettlingly familiar, which undoubtedly is why *Mothers and Daughters* continues to resonate so strongly in medieval German studies and beyond even now, more than two decades later.[2] This continued resonance was a significant motivation for this project. It seemed time not only to celebrate Rasmussen's achievement, but to explicitly carry it on. As the essays in the present volume demonstrate, the ideas and frameworks produced in 1997 remain relevant and have clearly inspired new generations of scholars, who apply these paradigms in an ever-wider range of texts, manuscripts, and cultural artifacts. Just as the mothers in the texts that Rasmussen studied tried to give their daughters tools with which to negotiate the contradiction-filled worlds of married life and courtship – at court, in the town, or in the country, Rasmussen's book also provides tools that help unpack gender bonds and binds visible in other narratives and historical contexts.[3] Finally, Rasmussen's study of medieval German mother-daughter discourses remains an important work in general for present-day readers as well: after all, understanding the longevity of patriarchy and its effects on human relations reminds readers how crucial the study of the past can be for the understanding of where we are as a society today.

The present volume serves as a tribute to this important milestone in medieval feminist studies[4] and even more so, to its extraordinary author, now at the height of her career, who has been either a teacher, mentor, or colleague (if not all three) to all the contributors of this volume. The essays feature new work on gender in medieval

---

[2] Since the publication of Rasmussen's study, scholarly interest in the topic of mothers and daughters has persisted across various fields. See, for example, Heller 2016; Sperling 2013; Kaldellis 2006; Davis and Müller 2003; O'Reilly and Abbey 2000; Bowers 1996. For a selection of recent work that engages specifically with Rasmussen's *Mothers and Daughters* and/or the articles growing out of this book project (Rasmussen 1996 and 2003), see Lienert 2019; Trokhimenko 2014; Bulang 2012; Buschinger 2012; Michaelis 2011; Dorninger 2008; and Classen 2007.

[3] See, for example, Hebert 2013 (English and French); Karras 1999 (English); Zimmermann 2009 (modern German literature); Feros Ruys 2005 (medieval Latin); Millet 2000 (Spanish); and Koller 2000 (Spanish).

[4] The idea for the volume emerged after a GSA panel celebrating the fifteenth anniversary of the publication of *Mothers and Daughters* organized by Katja Altpeter and Alison Beringer. The papers that became chapters one, two, and four, were first presented on this panel.

German literature that highlights the matter and media in which these bonds and binds appear and are negotiated. In this regard, the collection below could be seen as an extension of the tripartite methodology of *Mothers and Daughters*. Deftly engaging feminist theory, philology, and social history, Rasmussen's seven chapters taken together demonstrated how medieval fictions could "rehearse conflicting assumptions about medieval cultural norms" and "play out contradictions in medieval society at large" (222). They also showed not only how important social history can be for the interpretation of literature, but more significantly, how literature can provide insights into aspects of history that are not legible in the documents upon which historians generally rely (court records, wills, property transactions, genealogies). Rasmussen's chapters elucidate precisely how, for example, changes in aristocratic concepts of lineage and kinship left "a recoverable" and we might add material trace in the literary record (222). Taking inspiration from the methodology demonstrated in *Mothers and Daughters*, as well as its extension to the study of material objects in Rasmussen's more recent work on badges (for example, Rasmussen 2017), the essays below also examine medieval literature as material that can contribute otherwise elusive insights into the history of gender. While the majority of the essays use Rasmussen's arguments as starting points (though in varying ways),[5] several essays show Rasmussen's impact more indirectly, either by growing out of collaborations with her (Kraß), or connecting with Rasmussen's more recent work on materiality, insofar as they address how the representation of objectification functions in literature and its accompanying images or imagery (Beringer, Eming). All of the contributions, however, demonstrate what hardly seemed possible when *Mothers and Daughters* first appeared, namely the immense intellectual rewards of opening up medieval German literature and culture to an analysis that takes gender into account.

The first six essays take up Rasmussen's analysis of mother-daughter bonds and the binds to which relations between genders lead in a number of textual situations. For example, *Mothers and Daughters* begins with the account of a historical mother-daughter conflict about the daughter's refusal to marry the husband chosen for her and her subsequent rebellious choice of a Dominican convent as her preferred life path – rebellious because her mother would have preferred her to enter a different convent that was supported by the family and in a more traditional order. The first essay in the present volume, by Sara S. Poor, takes this example as its springboard, but examines a situation in which a daughter does enter the family affiliated convent. In this case, the daughter becomes abbess and her mother, the countess, appears to have helped the daughter in her efforts to reform the convent during the so-called "Observance Reform." Our access to this connection is not only

---

5 See also the notes to the chapter summaries in Appendix A.

through texts written long ago but rather through the medieval codices that were clearly transferred between the two women. Agnes von Werdenberg (c. 1400–c. 1471), the Countess of Oettingen from 1420 to 1440, gave her daughter Magdalena, the abbess of the Cistercian convent in Kirchheim am Ries from 1446–1496, at least six books of devotional readings. Five of the six books are marked explicitly as being owned by the abbess while being previously owned by her mother. In her essay, Poor discusses the evidence that these books provide of the ways that knowledge was transferred between noble mothers and daughters, and specifically, within the constraints of renewed enclosure.

With this context in mind, the essay turns to a specific text included in one of the books (Augsburg UB, III. 1. 4° 8) that is ostensibly about a set of rosary beads and their material make-up. In addition, the production and transmission of the text in this one codex points to other mother-daughter relationships: it was originally given to a contemporary of Agnes's, Mechthild, Countess of the Rhine Palatinate (1419–1482), on the occasion of her daughter's baptism. Mechthild was related by marriage to Agnes, which suggests how Agnes might have known about the text in order to have it copied into her compilation. In each of these cases, mothers are using written texts to transfer knowledge to their daughters. The rubric for the text, a spiritual dialogue between a princess and a "krämerin" [lady peddler] about the rosary, clearly encodes it as part of a young woman's education. Accordingly, the dialogue imparts much knowledge first about the way to pray with the rosary, and then, about the ways in which the various inherent powers of the precious stones on the rosary can influence the moral and spiritual state of the person using it to pray (or wearing it). A fascinating aspect of this text is that the knowledge, which the lady peddler claims to have acquired from learned writings and people, is delivered to the princess in an exegetical register by a common woman who is also, as a peddler, a liminal figure to both courtly and town society. Yet the text ultimately moves from the "outside" secular, perhaps more material world of the two countesses and the princess to the enclosed "inside," and supposedly more spiritual world of the cloistered abbess. As Poor argues, this is somewhat ironic given that the most significant part of the observant reform for women's houses was the reinforcement of the boundary between those two worlds through enclosure. Moreover, a further irony of the text in its monastic context is its implied and paradoxical message to the nuns reading it: wearing ornament itself can guard against the dangers of wearing ornament. Poor's essay unpacks this perplexing tangle of secular and sacred, this mix of devotional and conduct instruction, showing how we may discern women's agency in enterprises that nevertheless sought to constrain that agency.

While Poor's essay is informed by the historical material of the introduction to Rasmussen's book, Mary Marshall Campbell's essay deals with the *Nibelungenlied* (ca. 1200), the poem that is the focus of chapter two of *Mothers and Daughters*. In this essay, Campbell brings the lens of gender analysis to bear on the interpretation of Siegfried's courtship and death. While most scholars begin their readings from a position that the poem represents an amalgamation of divergent source and genre material – a mixture that explains various perceived inconsistencies in the plot – Campbell uses an analysis of gender and the social order depicted in the poem to show that the story is not inconsistent at all. In contrast to previous scholarship, which attributes Siegfried's death and collapse of the Burgundian dynasty to Siegfried's failure to fulfill his epic destiny (i.e., marry Brunhild), Campbell demonstrates that Siegfried fails to establish and maintain the proper patriarchal status quo because of his love for Kriemhild. That is, he fails because he subjects himself not only to Gunther (in order to win Kriemhild) but more significantly to Kriemhild herself.

Using Rasmussen's reading of the falcon dream as a starting point, Campbell shifts the focus from the mother-daughter dynamic itself in order to explore more thoroughly the context in which the pivotal dream conversation takes place. In addition, she expands the theoretical framework suggested by Rasmussen to the wider relations of power that are revealed in the early episodes of the narrative. The essay centers on the question of who is subject to whom, a question that the poem asks and considers through the sense of sight. If, upon the arrival of Siegfried in Worms, Siegfried asserts his superiority over Gunther and his men to their faces, he chooses nevertheless to subject himself to Gunther's sovereignty both in the geographically distant northern lands when he defeats the Danes and the Saxons on Gunther's behalf and in a more public and visible way when the bridal quest party arrives in Isenstein. Indeed, the primary conflict in the story is created by the contradicting social orders resulting from the viewing of Siegfried's gestures and behavior in several different settings. Campbell's deft readings of this aspect of the well-known poem offer new insights into its most discussed and contentious episodes. The real contribution of this essay, however, lies in its meticulous close readings of passages that are more often than not overlooked. Continuing the legacy of Rasmussen's work, Campbell's analysis of these details bears witness to the rich and provocative rewards of a nuanced focus on how social order is not merely constructed but also sensed through gender.

In the third essay in this cluster, Olga V. Trokhimenko takes Rasmussen's chapter four, which is dedicated to the relationship between Queen Isolde and her daughter Princess Isolde, the main heroine in Gottfried von Strassburg's monumental poem, *Tristan* (ca. 1210), as her starting point. These two Isoldes, it turns out, are not the only mother-daughter pair in the German Tristan tradition. The two sequels to Gottfried's unfinished work, one by Ulrich von Türheim (ca. 1240–1260) and the other by Heinrich von Freiberg (ca. 1300), mention another mother-daughter relationship, namely between Tristan's wife, Isolde of the White Hands, and her mother, the Duchess of Arundel, or Karsie. The essay thus grows out of the material fact that Gottfried's text is more often than not transmitted in manuscripts with either one or both of these sequels. Trokhimenko offers a detailed and compelling reading of these mother figures, who are conspicuously absent both in Gottfried's tale, which Ulrich and Heinrich claim to continue, and in Eilhart von Oberge's earlier rendition of the Tristan material, which is the declared source for the continuators. In the sequels, Karsie is similar to Gottfried's Queen Isolde; she is a powerful, secure, and respected wife and mother, who speaks on her husband's behalf, advises her son Kaedin, and makes important political and familial decisions. Trokhimenko shows, however, that there are telling differences between the two queens. Ulrich's Queen Isolde is more like Gottfried's powerful mother figure insofar as she is represented to be the true decision-maker in the family. Accordingly, her daughter Isolde of the White hands also has a more powerful and assertive role in the narrative, even turning from sweet maiden into an "übelez wîp" [evil woman] by the end. As Trokhimenko argues, Ulrich's text displays some ambivalence towards this version of femininity. While he has sympathy for both Isoldes, he nevertheless has them both fail precisely as a result of their assertiveness: "Isolde the Blond is on the wrong path, as is made clear by her trickery, narrow escapes, and her untimely death. Isolde of the White Hands is a wronged wife defending her rights, who by the end of the text turns into a cruel fury" – and this defense also comes to light as trickery. While Heinrich, on the other hand, has the Duchess give her daughter a "gift" of sorts, similar to the love potion in Gottfried's work, which is also intended to secure success in her forthcoming political marriage, he nevertheless makes the Queen and Isolde of the White Hands less assertive and independent. Indeed, as Trokhimenko shows, he seems to have much more sympathy for the second Isolde, whose attempts to follow the "rules" for comportment and accessibility to the suitor are both conventional and sincere. Yet Trokhimenko points out a poignant irony of this version: although Isolde of the White Hands does everything she is supposed to do in order to be desirable, she is nevertheless *not* desired and indeed, disappears from the end of the narrative (contrary to the source text by Eilhart, where she takes care of all of the aftermath of the lovers' demise). In other words, even though Heinrich seemed to want to promote a more traditional (passive, instrumental) ideal for women's behavior, his own narrative contradicts this desire insofar as it is still the assertive, transgressive woman, Isolde the Blond, who stands out and is remembered at the end of the narrative.

Katja Altpeter also writes about the success or failure of a generational relationship insofar as the parent is depicted as trying to ensure a secure future for their child within the framework of a political marriage. In her essay on the thirteenth-century love and adventure novel *Flôre and Blanscheflûr* by Konrad Fleck, Altpeter takes up Rasmussen's focus on the ways that dynastic interests and questions come to inflect or shape mother-daughter connections in order to work out the interplay between the two mothers of Flôre and Blanscheflûr and their relationships with their respective children (*Mothers and Daughters*, chapters three and four). In this rhymed couplet narrative, a Spanish king who fathers a child with his wife (the Queen, mother of Flôre) also brings into his household a female war captive (the unnamed mother of Blanscheflûr) who gives birth to a daughter on the same day that the Queen gives birth to a son. The text subtly insinuates that the king may have fathered both children and further complicates our reading of familial relationships by depicting in detail the women's friendship and the children's love for each other. The two women appear as friends, co-wives, and co-mothers. Their children are similar in looks and sensibilities and are repeatedly mistaken as siblings (but eventually become lovers and marital partners). In addition, the captive woman functions as the royal son's wet nurse. These complex family constellations are made more convoluted by the fact that the king's wife and son are Muslim while the captive woman and her daughter are Christian. Altpeter uses the distinction Rasmussen makes between a biological and genealogical background for the relationships to explain why the Queen is successful in separating the young lovers in contrast to the impotence and inaction of Blanscheflûr's mother. Despite the previous friendship based in biology (the bearing of children at the same time), the Queen is able to have Blanscheflûr sold into slavery, an act which ensures that her son Flôre would be available for a "better" (i.e., more politically useful) marriage. The Queen clearly wishes to strengthen the dynastic power of the royal line. She succeeds, at least at this juncture, because she has a genealogy (her own and that of her husband) that she can reference, whereas Blanscheflûr, a foreigner with no family attachments nor a husband at court, does not. According to Altpeter, "[t]he failure on the part of Blanscheflûr's mother to rewrite biology as genealogy is also what makes the mother-daughter relationship fade from the story's narrative or rather, never take a firm hold in it to begin with" (below, 114). This chapter also provides an answer to the question of why the efforts of the Queens in the Tristan narratives fail to secure their daughters' futures: rewriting biology as genealogy in a patriarchy tends to work better if you are a man.

The fifth essay turns to a foster mother-daughter relationship – that between Herzeloyde (mother to Parzival) and Sigune (Herzeloyde's niece) as it appears in Wolfram von Eschenbach's *Titurel* (ca. 1220) and Albrecht von Scharfenberg's *Jüngerer Titurel* (ca. 1260–1275). In her essay, Evelyn Meyer expands on Rasmussen's analyses of the mother-daughter conversations between the two Isoldes on the one hand and those in the didactic mother-daughter poems, *Die Winsbeckin* and *Stiefmutter und Tochter* on the other (chapters four, five, and seven respectively), situating Herzeloyde's and Sigune's conversations between these two models. Meyer's reading demonstrates how Herzeloyde's advice to Sigune does not follow the usual pattern of advice-giving for noble women and instead corresponds more closely, especially in Albrecht's version, to that found in stories of women of lower classes. Indeed, while as a young noblewoman Sigune could have expected to be advised by Herzeloyde about how and whom to love and/or marry, she gets no input in advance of falling in love and instead is faced with an explosive rant against a *minnedienst* [love service] that, in Herzeloyde's view, only brings suffering. The only practical advice that Herzeloyde imparts is grounded clearly in a more material, sensory context: namely that Sigune, being worn down by lovesickness, must quickly restore her physical beauty, as is proper for a young courtly lady generally.

In Wolfram's text, Meyer points out, this advice relates more to Sigune upholding her duties as a noble woman at court, one of which is to appear desirable to men. Albrecht's version on the other hand displays an interesting twist: Herzeloyde suggests to Sigune that it is *Sigune's* desire for her lover that will contribute to restoring her health and beauty. In other words, Albrecht's version emphasizes female sensual desire and agency in a more explicit way. Meyer's discussion of these subtle, yet obviously significant differences in the approach of these two works to the mentoring scene reveals that both authors might have been critical of the societal norm that defined women's worth only according to her desirability (whether that desire be due to the sensing of her noble status or her beautiful body). At the very least, Meyer suggests, they seem aware that the suffering caused by *minnedienst* was a very real manifestation of the contradictory and damaging demands it placed on the women involved.

The expression of female sexual desire that emerges tentatively in Albrecht von Scharfenberg's *Jüngerer Titurel* seems to have been a harbinger of things to come. As Rasmussen notes in the penultimate chapter of her book, the summer songs of Neidhart (as well as those authored anonymously in his style) also foreground the discussions between mothers and daughters about not only having sexual desire but also acting on it and enjoying sex. Ingrid Bennewitz's contribution to this volume takes up the invitation in Rasmussen's chapter to view this type of "Neidhart" song as a genre in and of itself and accordingly, undertakes an examination of the voluminous late medieval manuscript and early modern print transmission of "Neidhart" songs in order to see what changes or additions are made in the later manuscripts.

Paying particular attention to previously neglected songs and strophes that Bennewitz and her co-editors made available in their 2007 *Salzburger Neidhart-Edition*, Bennewitz brings to light several important observations about the changes in and the fluidity of material among the codices. A fertile example is a song transmitted in a parchment manuscript compiled in the late thirteenth century (R = mgf 1062), and then later included in a paper manuscript from the second half of the 15th century (c = mgf 779). In this later manuscript, the song has an additional seven strophes after the first eight. This additional material, connected thematically to the first part through the shared motif of the act of waiting, introduces a different version of a mother-daughter dialogue. Though recognizable as such, this version makes both subtle and more radical changes – for example, contrary to expectation, here it is the mother figure who bemoans that the daughter figure must wait to attend a dance (and thus to have a partner) while it is the daughter who argues that, although she lacks fine clothing, she still has her honor. As Bennewitz posits intriguingly, this role reversal results in the mother figure becoming a mouthpiece for "weibliche Selbständigkeit *in eroticis*" [female independence in (sexual) love matters]. Through her analysis of this song among others, Bennewitz affirms for the later Middle Ages the importance that Rasmussen ascribed to mother-daughter dialogues, positing that for this later period, too, the mother-daughter dialogues belong to the "Erfolgsmodell" [successful model] of Neidhart songs. The rich narrative variations found in the later examples of mother-daughter songs bear witness to the continual appeal and adaptation of this genre, as does the evidence of a new, hybrid form of transmission found in manuscript c, namely lyrics and music presented as one entity (Figure 6.1).

As these six opening essays demonstrate, Rasmussen's work on the mother-daughter theme provided rich new readings of canonical texts like Gottfried's *Tristan*, in addition to fertile ground for further study of mothers and daughters both in those texts (Campbell, Trokhimenko, Meyer, Bennewitz) and in others (Poor, Altpeter). From the analysis of mothers, daughters, and other family members in historical and fictional sources, our contributors have pointed to a number of different directions in which to follow Rasmussen's lead, all of which reflect the material turn in medieval studies in varying ways. But Rasmussen has not limited herself to the study of gender in mother-daughter tales (see Appendix B, Rasmussen Bibliography). Indeed, her work has ranged far and wide in the field of medieval gender studies. Accordingly, the last three essays in our volume turn to a varied set of topics, each relating to a different area of Rasmussen's research, as well as demonstrating the breadth and impact of Rasmussen's work.

Of course, tied up closely with ideals for how to be a woman were those for how to be a man. Andreas Kraß's study, growing out of a joint teaching and research project undertaken with Rasmussen from 2013–2015 (the "Rivalrous Masculinities Project"),[6] builds on the conclusions of a number of scholars that medieval society struggled to define what constitutes a man (Lees, et al. 1994; McNamara 1994; Stuard 1994; Karras 2003; Trokhimenko 2012). In her study *From Boys to Men: Formations of Masculinity in Late Medieval Europe*, for example, Karras observes that "no single form of masculinity [. . .] characterized the Middle Ages and even the later Middle Ages in Christian western Europe. Concepts of what it meant to be a man not only changed over time, they also coexisted and competed within any given medieval culture or even subculture" (2003, 3). In fact, the historian points out that it is more appropriate to speak of "masculinities" in the plural rather than the singular,[7] and offers three primary models of medieval masculinity: knightly, clerical, and urban craft worker. Andreas Kraß's reading of Hartmann von Aue's *Gregorius* and Bernard of Clairvaux's *In Praise of the New Knighthood* engages with the first two types, further complicating Karras's picture of the rivalry between the aristocratic courtly model and its clerical counterpart.

---

6 The project has also led to an edited volume. See Rasmussen 2019.
7 This becomes one of the three foundational claims of Rasmussen's *Rivalrous Masculinities* volume. The other two are "masculinity as an intersectional category of gender" and "medieval ways of thinking about gender as being incommensurate with modern assumptions about sex and gender based in heteronormativity" (xiii).

Kraß's findings go beyond the existing scholarship on the tensions between the knights and the clerics in that he expands the view that only the clerical model was perceived as dubious in regards to gender: as celibates, the clerics were excluded from the system of procreation and sexuality and therefore deemed to be insufficiently masculine, for which some historians have even coined the term "a third gender." Paradoxically, however, the knightly model could be criticized for its deficient masculinity as well. Indeed, as Kraß shows, Bernard criticizes courtly knights specifically because of what he sees as their effeminate behavior. Further, he uses this judgment as a defining foil to the "new" ideal of knightly masculinity he describes for the *milites Christi* [warriors of Christ] – the knights in the newly established Order of Templars, who focus their energies on the crusade enterprise in the Holy Land. Using their military might in the service of the expansion of Christianity, they avoid making themselves into women in the process – that is, they do *not* submit themselves to women's whims, wear fancy clothes, wear their hair in long, feminine tresses, or dress their horses in fancy gear.

Kraß rightly highlights Bernard's reliance on antithesis to make his points in contrast to the "more differentiated" rivalrous masculinities displayed in Hartmann von Aue's work. As Kraß shows, Hartmann contradicts the fundamentalist position that Bernard advocates insofar as he boldly restores the honor of courtly knighthood by turning the courtly man first into a monk, then a fallen landowner/knight, then into a saint (due to his heroic self-abnegation), and finally into the Pope. It seems as if, for Hartmann, a man might have any number of these masculinities at his disposal, but the best man is the one who manages to incorporate them all.

Alison L. Beringer's essay provides yet another fascinating depiction of what it means to be men and women, moving the discussion from the construction of ideals to the relationship between gender and the animate (or inanimate) body. As mentioned above, taking inspiration both from Rasmussen's assertions about the relevance of literature for an understanding of medieval ideology, as well as from her more recent work on material culture, Beringer chooses as her subject matter several episodes from the *Weltchronik* [world chronicle] of Jans der Enikel that feature the poet Virgil. In the medieval imagination, Virgil was primarily famous for his great poem about Aeneas (German, Eneas) and the founding of Rome. In addition, however, he was infamous for his powers as a magician (gained through a deal with seventy-two devils). In this chronicle, these powers become active in taking revenge on a married woman who refuses his sexual advances. On her husband's advice, the wife lures Virgil into a basket which she promises she will raise up to her chamber window during the night in order to fulfill his desire. Instead, however, in this well-known motif, she leaves the basket suspended in mid-air till the next morning, and the whole town sees Virgil hanging there in shame. Virgil takes revenge for this public humiliation in a most earthly and material way, by magically extinguishing all the fires in town. What is more, he ensures that the only way to light any future fires is to put a flammable torch up to the wife's rear end while she is poised on all fours on top of a pedestal (No one can claim that medieval literature is boring!). Certainly meant to be comic (the language of the passage suggests, of course, that the fire is produced by the wife's flatulence), the image is also a remarkable literalization of the idea of the instrumentalization of women. Here the woman becomes the actual tool that supplies fire to the town, and in so doing her "objectification" is complete.

Beringer's analysis helps us to see how Jans der Enikel uses the Virgil character to play with the various ideas associated with him – namely, his magical abilities, his way with words as a poet, and his connection to pagan religion. Turning a woman into a stone statue in an animalistic pose that spews fire from its ass (or at least into a figure who acts like this) is the perfect combination of all these qualities. The magic turns the flatulence into fire, his powerful words (and his blackmail) result in the statue-like pose, and the pagan custom of revering idols is mimicked in placing the statue-like woman on the pedestal, which the townspeople must respect (to get their fires lit). One wonders if this part of Jans der Enikel's narrative could be seen as a different type of comment on the situation of the instrumentalized woman thematized in many of the mother-daughter scenarios discussed in Rasmussen's book. That is to say, being a good wife here results in a (possibly comic) materialization of the fate of many good women in romance narratives who become mute and immobile. This wife is at least still visible, but only as a mockery of her position in life, as is depicted in Figure 8.1 below.

The volume concludes with an essay that connects both to Rasmussen's more recent work on the meaning of cultural objects, like pilgrim badges that represent individual body parts, as well as back to *Mothers and Daughters* in its use of feminist theories of psychology as a hermeneutic tool. Jutta Eming's rereading of Konrad von Würzburg's *Tale of the Heart* (*Herzmaere*) employs psychoanalysis to shed light on the mechanism of aggression in this fascinating account of how meaning is produced through human interactions with an object. She sees Konrad's tale as inhabiting the tradition of stories that entertain the reader through the use of shocking or scandalous elements. Be it the tale of the "Snow Child" sold by his own father or late-medieval *Maeren* about independent body parts having adventures of their own, the issues of power, violence, and gender come to the fore in these narratives. The *Herzmaere* is one such story, in which the audience is titillated and awed by the account of a lady tricked by her jealous husband into consuming the embalmed heart of her dead beloved. Traditionally read as a tale of love transcending all boundaries, akin to Gottfried von Strassburg's *Tristan*, this tragic narrative proves to have additional dimensions. By comparing Konrad's tale to similar stories, particularly one of Giovanni Boccaccio's novellas, Eming tackles some of the most gruesome and puzzling aspects of this Middle High German *Maere*, such as the lover's choice to send his embalmed heart to his lady, the husband's cruel decision to feed the heart to his wife, the wife's unwitting cannibalism, and her subsequent extreme emotional reaction to her transgression. The Freudian concepts of aggression and disgust expose the *Herzmaere* as also a tale about patriarchal domination, a battle between two men, where one "hijacks[s] the violent actions of [the] other and expand[s] on them," and a double assault on the female protagonist.

Yet Eming wisely points out the importance of this "also." That is, she refrains from claiming that this harsher reading suggested by what is going on with the posthumous "gift" of the heart is the only reading or even the dominant one for this text. Instead, she highlights the ambivalence of the narrative, due to its overall complexity, which is especially evident when compared to the later, more famous, yet much more simply told version by Boccaccio.

Eming's concluding remark that this later simplification is not the only example of medieval texts becoming abridged and leveled out in the later periods is telling. For the complexity and richness that Eming recognizes in the *Herzmaere* are characteristic of all of the medieval works discussed in this volume. Indeed, if there is a common thread to all the essays, it is precisely that what is revealed by a close, materially focused gender analysis is complex and not easily reduced to a platitude. Think of the woman religious reading about a princess who wards off the sin of wearing ornament by wearing ornament (Poor); or the insight that Siegfried, thought to be the greatest hero in the Germanic tradition, dies because of the contradictions inherent in both love service and kingship (Campbell); or the continuation of Gottfried's unfinished work in which the narrator seems to empathize with the woman who follows the constraining rules for her gender, but who is ultimately not remembered by the end of the tale (Trokhimenko); or the even greater level of failure of the mother-daughter plot when the mother is a foreigner who becomes dehumanized through enslavement in *Flôre und Blanscheflûr* (Altpeter). Further, we learn more of the complexities of love service in the prequels to *Parzival* in which Herzeloyde can only transmit the suffering it causes in her mentorship of Sigune (Meyer); and of the lasting interest in playing with the mother-daughter mentoring conversation for interesting results in the reception of the Neidhart songs (Bennewitz). Finally, we conclude in the last three essays with the multiple modes of masculinity available to male characters, all of which seem to be tried on by Hartmann's fascinating hero/saint, Gregorius (Kraß); and with material, yet at the same time imagistic explorations of the vulnerable position of women in medieval society that clearly read as both burlesque and sinister (Beringer, Eming). This variety and complexity speaks to the richness of the field as well as to the value added to this richness when using gender as a category of analysis. It is in this way that *Gender Bonds, Gender Binds* highlights the lasting contribution of Rasmussen's work, while at the same time making a vital contribution to the fields of gender studies and medieval German studies on its own.

Works Cited

Albrecht von Scharfenberg. *Jüngerer Titurel*. Edited by Werner Wolf. Berlin: Akademie Verlag, 1955.
Bowers, Toni. *The Politics of Motherhood: British Writing and Culture, 1680–1760*. Cambridge: Cambridge University Press, 1996.
Bulang, Tobias. "Inszenierungen höfischer Kommunikation im Roman um 1200: Poetologische Lektüren von Hartmanns 'Lunete' und Gottfrieds 'Brangäne'." *Euphorion* 106, no. 3 (2012): 277–98.
Buschinger, Danielle. "Mutter und Tochter in der Tristan-Tradition." In *Variationen des Tristan-Stoffes in diachroner Darstellung: Gesammelte Vorträge des Mainzer Tristan-Workshops, April 2011*, edited by Caroline Kolisang, 1–15. Amiens: Université de Picardie Jules Verne, 2012.
Classen, Albrecht, ed. *The Power of a Woman's Voice in Medieval and Early Modern Literatures: New Approaches to German and European Women Writers and to Violence Against Women in Premodern Times*. Berlin: De Gruyter, 2007.
Cramer, Thomas, ed. *Frauenlieder – Cantigas de amigo. Internationale Kolloquien des Centro de Estudos Humanísticos (Universidade do Minho), der Faculdade de Letras (Universidade do Porto) und des Fachbereichs Germanistik (Freie Universität Berlin): Berlin, 6. 11.1998, Apúlia, 28.-30.3.1999*. Stuttgart: Hirzel, 2000.
Davis, Isabel, and Miriam Müller. *Love, Marriage, and Family Ties in the Later Middle Ages*. Turnhout: Brepols, 2003.
Dorninger, Maria E. "Mutter- und Tochterbeziehung am Beispiel des Aeneasstoffes: Heinrich von Veldeke und Gottfried von Viterbo." In *Current Topics in Medieval German Literature: Texts and Analyses*, edited by Sibylle Jefferis, 23–54. Göppingen: Kümmerle, 2008.
Eilhart von Oberge. *Tristrant und Isalde: Mittelhochdeutsch/Neuhochdeutsch*. Edited and translated by Danielle Buschinger and Wolfgang Spiewok. Greifswald: Reineke, 1993.
Enikel, Jans. *Jansen Enikels Werke*. Edited by Philipp Strauch. Leipzig: Hahn'sche Buchhandlung, 1900.
Feros Ruys, Juanita. "Peter Abelard's 'Carmen Ad Astralabium' and Medieval Parent-Child Didactic Texts: The Evidence for Parent-Child Relationships in the Middle Ages." In *Childhood in the Middle Ages: The Results of a Paradigm Shift in the History of Mentality*, edited by Albrecht Classen, 203–28. Berlin: De Gruyter, 2005.
Gottfried von Strassburg. *Tristan*. 5th ed. Edited by Friedrich Ranke and Rüdiger Krohn. 3 vols. Stuttgart: Reclam, 1996.
Hebert, Jill. *Morgan le Fay, Shapeshifter*. New York: Palgrave MacMillan, 2013.
Heinrich von Freiberg. *Tristan und Isolde (Fortsetzung des Tristan-Romans Gottfrieds von Straßburg)*. Edited by Danielle Buschinger. Translated by Wolfgang Spiewok. Greifswald: Reineke, 1993.
Heller, Jennifer Louise. *The Mother's Legacy in Early Modern England*. New York: Routledge, 2016.
Kaldellis, Anthony, ed. *Mothers and Sons, Fathers and Daughters: The Byzantine Family of Michael Psellos*. Notre Dame, IN: University of Notre Dame Press, 2006.
Karras, Ruth Mazo. *From Boys to Men: Formations of Masculinity in Late Medieval Europe*. Philadelphia: University of Pennsylvania Press, 2003.
Karras, Ruth Mazo. "Sex and the Singlewoman." In *Singlewomen in the European Past, 1250–1800*, edited by Judith Bennett and Amy Froide, 127–45. Philadelphia: University of Pennsylvania Press, 1999.
Koller, Erwin. "Mutter-Tochter-Dialoge in 'cantigas de amigo' und bei Neidhart." In Cramer, *Frauenlieder – Cantigas de amigo*, 103–22.
Konrad von Würzburg. "Herzmaere." In *Novellistik des Mittelalters. Märendichtung*, edited and translated by Klaus Grubmüller, 262–95. Frankfurt am Main: Deutscher Klassiker Verlag, 1996.

Lees, Clare A., Thelma Fenster, and Jo Ann McNamara, eds. *Medieval Masculinities: Regarding Men in the Middle Ages.* Minneapolis: University of Minnesota Press, 1994.

Lienert, Elisabeth. "Antagonisten im höfischen Roman: Eine Skizze." *Zeitschrift für deutsches Altertum und deutsche Literatur* 147, no. 4 (2019): 419–36.

McNamara, Jo Ann. "The Herrenfrage: The Restructuring of the Gender System, 1050–1150." In Lees, *Medieval Masculinities*, 3–30.

Michaelis, Beatrice. *(Dis-)Artikulationen von Begehren: Schweigeeffekte in wissenschaftlichen und literarischen Texten.* Berlin: De Gruyter, 2011.

Miller, Maureen C. "Masculinity, Reform, and Clerical Culture: Narratives of Episcopal Holiness in the Gregorian Era." *Church History* 72, no. 1 (2003): 25–52.

Millet, Victor. "Der Mutter-Tochter-Dialog und der Erzähler in Neidharts Sommerliedern." In Cramer, *Frauenlieder – Cantigas de amigo*, 123–32.

Neidhart. *Neidhart-Lieder: Texte und Melodien sämtlicher Handschriften und Drucke.* 3 vols. Edited by Ulrich Müller et al. Berlin/New York: De Gruyter, 2007.

O'Reilly, Andrea, and Sharon Abbey. *Mothers and Daughters: Connection, Empowerment, and Transformation.* Lanham, MD: Rowman & Littlefield, 2000.

Putzo, Christine, ed. *Konrad Fleck: "Flore und Blanscheflur": Text und Untersuchungen.* Berlin/Boston: De Gruyter, 2015.

Rasmussen, Ann Marie. "Badges: Abzeichen als sprechende Objekte." In *Stimme und Performanz in der mittelalterlichen Literatur*, edited by Monika Unzeitig et al., 469–91. Berlin: De Gruyter, 2017.

Rasmussen, Ann Marie. "'ez ist ir g'artet von mir': Queen Isolde and Princess Isolde in Gottfried's *Tristan und Isolde*," in *Arthurian Women: A Casebook*, edited by Thelma Fenster, 41–58. New York: Garland, 1996. Reprint New York: Routledge, 2001.

Rasmussen, Ann Marie. "The Female Figures in Gottfried's *Tristan and Isolde*," in *A Companion to Gottfried's Tristan and Isolde*, edited by Will Hasty, 143–63. Columbia, S.C.: Camden House, 2003.

Rasmussen, Ann Marie. *Mothers and Daughters in Medieval German Literature.* Syracuse, N.Y.: Syracuse University Press, 1997.

Rasmussen, Ann Marie, ed. *Rivalrous Masculinities: New Directions in Medieval Gender Studies.* Notre Dame, ID: University of Notre Dame Press, 2019.

Schmidt, Friedrich. "Geistliches Gespräch zwischen einer Fürstin und einer Krämerin von einem Paternoster aus Edelsteinen." *Alemannia* 26 (1898): 193–229.

Sperling, Jutta Gisela. *Medieval and Renaissance Lactations: Images, Rhetorics, Practices.* Burlington, VT: Ashgate, 2013.

Stuard, Susan Mosher. "Burdens of Matrimony: Husbanding and Gender in Medieval Italy." In Lees, *Medieval Masculinities*, 61–71.

Trokhimenko, Olga V. *Constructing Virtue and Vice: Femininity and Laughter in Courtly Society (ca. 1150–1300).* Göttingen: Vandenhoeck & Ruprecht unipress, 2014.

Trokhimenko, Olga V. "'Believing That Which Cannot Be': (De)Constructing Medieval Clerical Masculinity in 'Des münches not'." *The German Quarterly* 85, no. 2 (2012): 121–36.

Ulrich von Türheim. *Tristan und Isolde (Fortsetzung des Tristan-Romans Gottfrieds von Straßburg) Originaltext (nach der Heidelberger Handschrift Pal. Germ. 360).* Edited and translated by Danielle Buschinger and Wolfgang Spiewok. Amiens: Publications du Centre d'études médiévales, 1992.

Wolfram von Eschenbach. *Titurel.* Edited and translated by Helmut Brackert and Stephan Fuchs-Jolie. Berlin: De Gruyter, 2003.

Zimmermann, Margarete. "Filiationen: Von schreibenden Müttern und ihren Töchtern." In *Generationen und Gender in mittelalterlicher und frühneuzeitlicher Literatur*, edited by Dina De Rentiis and Ulrike Siewert, 109–24. Bamberg: University of Bamberg Press, 2009.

Appendix A: *Mothers and Daughters in Medieval German Literature*

Table of Contents

Studying Medieval Mothers and Daughters (Introduction)
Part One:
Noble Mothers and Daughters: Conflicts of Sentiment and Power
1. Unruly Mother, Exemplary Daughter: The Construction of Female Power and Passion in Heinrich von Veldeke's *Eneasroman*
2. Exemplary Mother, Unruly Daughter: The Mother-Daughter Dialogue in the *Nibelungenleid*
3. Mother, Daughter, Foster Mother: The Politics of Lineage and the Socialization of Women in *Kudrun*
4. "In This She Takes after Me": Queen Isolde and Princess Isolde in Gottfried von Straßburg's *Tristan und Isolde*
5. "If Men Desire You, Then You are Worthy": The Didactic Mother-Daughter Poem *Die Winsbeckin*
Part Two:
Common Mothers and Daughters: Sexual Rebellion and Constraint
6. "I inherited It from You": The Mother-Daughter Poems of the Neidhart Tradition
7. "How A Mother Teaches Her Daughter Whoring": The Rhymed Couplet Text *Stepmother and Daughter*
Looking Back at the Middle Ages

Mothers and Daughters in Medieval German Literature

Summary

Because the first six essays in the present volume refer directly to chapters in *Mothers and Daughters*, we offer an account of this important study here. In seven chapters divided into two parts, Rasmussen's *Mothers and Daughters* analyzes the way that gender both frames and is negotiated in the fictional conversations between mothers and daughters about love in a selection of literary texts. Essential to this analysis is attention in each chapter to historical context. An introduction sets the stage for this historical approach by presenting the historical case of a mother-daughter conflict (Margaret of Courtenay and her daughter Yolande of Vianden) about the daughter's desire to enter a religious order instead of agreeing to a political marriage.[8] This historical case is then followed by an introduction to psychological

---

[8] For more on this case, see below, chapter one.

models of the mother-daughter relation, as well as a more general account of the nobility in the German Middle Ages, providing the terminology and tools for the analysis that follows.

As the Table of Contents suggests, part one of the study (chapters one through five) deals with texts about noble women and the conflicts between them concerning "sentiment and power." Rasmussen thus focuses the first chapter on Lavinia and her mother in Veldeke's *Eneasroman*. Analyzing the conversations between them about whom Lavinia should love and marry, Rasmussen highlights the intricacies of love, political power, gender identities, and, most importantly, gender hierarchy that come into play between the two characters. In a world where patrilineal descent is preferred, the strong, yet unnamed mother cannot be allowed to win in the struggle over Lavinia's marital fate. Instead, Rasmussen shows how the mother-daughter relation functions unexpectedly as a repudiation of itself, a repudiation that negates or interrupts the ability of that relation to be a means of knowledge transfer over time between women. This "secret that lies revealed – not concealed – at the heart of this story" is made clear by the death of the mother and the subordination of Lavinia to Aeneas, and thus to the patriarchal status quo (65).

Moving to the *Nibelungenlied* in chapter two, Rasmussen examines the conversation between Uote and Kriemhild, in which the mother interprets the daughter's famous falcon dream as foreshadowing Kriemhild's future encounter with heterosexual love. In contrast to the mother-daughter figures in chapter one, here Rasmussen shows that it is the daughter who does not conform to the expected gender role, transgressing from controlled object to out-of-control subject. Becoming a subject, however, means assuming a role that is socialized as male and this move is perceived as a threat in the world of the epic. For, as Rasmussen argues, Kriemhild's failure to heed social boundaries leads ultimately to her death.[9]

Shifting away from mother-daughter conversations centered on erotic love and the politics of marriage, chapter three takes as its focus the anonymous epic *Kudrun*, with its engagement with bilineal (adjacent to patrilineal) descent made evident in the depiction of both a mother-daughter and a "foster"[10] mother-daughter relationship. These two relationships are just one of the doublings in the *Kudrun* (another is the two main bridal quests, first of Kudrun's mother Hilde, and then of Kudrun herself), but because the two mothers are so radically different, the relation-

---

[9] Campbell, in chapter two below, examines the other side of this "coin," showing how Siegfried, the quintessential male subject, is refigured in the epic as feminine object, which is a disruption of the social order that also ends in death.

[10] Gerlint would be Kudrun's mother-in-law if Kudrun accepted Hartmuot's marriage proposal; Kudrun does not. Because Kudrun is subsequently taken hostage by Hartmuot and placed in the care of his mother, Gerlint assumes a type of guardianship similar to that associated with fostering in medieval literature. See 105.

ships provide extensive opportunity for the author to explore maternal strategies to socialize and educate (foster) daughters – and these daughters' response to such efforts. Despite the absence of analysis of a specific mother-daughter conversation, this chapter is full of material that foregrounds the mother-daughter relationship. For example, Rasmussen notes that Kudrun is far more frequently identified as her mother Hilde's daughter, than her father's, a significant detail which, according to Rasmussen, ensures that it is the mother-daughter relationship which remains uppermost in the reader's mind. Sometimes, Kudrun is called "Hagen's kin," but as Hagen is her *maternal* grandfather, this appellation subtly foregrounds that bilineal descent is significant for Kudrun (98–99).[11]

In addition to providing a foil for the supportive biological mother-daughter relationship, the cruelty of the foster mother also showcases for the reader the abuse of authority (101). Gerlint's behavior is marked as unacceptable by the text, but at the same time, it is predicated on her desire to increase her family fortune by ensuring that her son wins Kudrun as wife (an impossibility given the higher social status of Kudrun): Gerlint, then, is actively involved in issues of family allegiance and lineage. Kudrun has to endure – and overcome – Gerlint.[12] Further, Gerlint serves as a model of the type of female ruler Kudrun should *not* become. Indeed, as Rasmussen shows, Kudrun's experiences with Gerlint prepare her to become a "politically responsible woman" (111). Kudrun needs both mother figures: the one is exemplary in behavior, including as a female ruler, and gives Kudrun heroic lineage; the other forces her into experiences and suffering that demand patience and endurance of the young woman. Both mother-daughter relationships are critical to the formation of Kudrun as a wise ruler. That Kudrun becomes this at the end of the epic is shown by her arrangement of several marriages which result in alliances that benefit herself and her family and by her mother Hilde's arrangement of Kudrun's crowning as Herwic's queen.

Chapter four continues to explore matrilineal transfer by analyzing the mother-daughter relationship in Gottfried von Strassburg's take on the pan-European Tristan and Isolde story, *Tristan*. Here Rasmussen brilliantly examines the prominent female character, Queen Isolde of Ireland, who in her attempt to ensure her daughter Isolde's marital happiness, prepares the ill-fated love potion and thus sets in motion the tragic events of the story. The chapter presents Queen Isolde as a success story that her daughter fails to emulate.[13] The older Isolde has flourished in all aspects of

---

[11] Chapter four below invokes Rasmussen's analysis of lineage and gender.
[12] As Rasmussen convincingly argues, the endurance of that suffering is a choice that Kudrun makes, thereby "establish[ing] a new category for female behavior in which patience and endurance are *active* modes of existence" (110).
[13] This chapter has had the most impact on our authors below: see chapters three, four, and five for different takes on the mother/queens' attempts to secure their daughters' future success in love and political life.

her life: as a wife, as a mother, and as a powerful, knowledgeable, and skillful diplomat and politician, respected by her family members and the whole court. Consequently, her gift of the potion is meant to be "the gift of continuity between mother and daughter" (132) that would allow the younger Isolde (by ensuring love between her and her future husband, King Mark) to replicate her mother's success. Unfortunately, the demands of the inherited Tristan storyline require that the mother's efforts are in vain. And yet, as Rasmussen claims, the daughter is ultimately less different from her mother: the semblance between them paradoxically increases in the course of the tale so that by the end, the younger Isolde, now Queen of Cornwall, makes her mother's powers and knowledge truly her own (132).

The theme of knowledge transfer is continued in chapter five, which examines the didactic dialogue between a mother and a daughter – the thirteenth-century conduct text known as *Die Winsbeckin*. The conversation enacted in the poem reiterates the value of a woman in the patriarchal society that the elder Queen Isolde had recognized as well: she is valued not as a desiring subject, but rather as a desired object. As the poem states explicitly, "if men desire you, then you are worthy" ("so man gedenket ofte an dich / und wünschet dîn, sô bistû wert," *Winsbeckin*, st. 15, ll. 9–10).[14] This message becomes even more striking when the text is placed side by side with its male-voiced counterpart. A dialogue between a father and a son, *Der Winsbecke* prepares men to be active subjects in all aspects of their lives. The aristocratic identity that conduct literature helps to shape is, to use Rasmussen's words, "a cultural product, one that is realized through teaching, through education" (158). The mother in *Die Winsbeckin* constructs the social female identity as synonymous with sexual desirability, and even though the daughter initially scoffs at this proposition, she ultimately embraces it, acquiescing to her mother's wishes and promising to obey the rules of love (*minne*).

Part Two of Rasmussen's book turns to literature that represents "common mothers and daughters" and focuses on "rebellion and constraint" (161). Accordingly, chapters six and seven move away from "somber" genres such as epic and didactic literature and toward more light-hearted, comic texts, such as the *Sommerlieder* [summer songs] of Neidhart von Reuenthal and the rhymed couplet text known as *Stepmother and Daughter*. In Neidhart's songs (chapter six), the mother and the daughter know and share in each other's secrets in order to deceive men.[15] They are essentially versions of each other (188). Rasmussen claims that the mother-daughter relationship fails as "an apprenticeship in social conformity" (188), while succeeding as an apprenticeship of a sort of "secret society" that helps women to gain the upper hand in the patriarchy by duping men, deceiving husbands, and sharing secrets. The

---

14 The analysis referred to here is taken up by both Trokhimenko in chapter three and Meyer in chapter five below.
15 This chapter is the inspiration for the study offered in chapter six below.

mother-daughter connection in Neidhart's songs allows women what *Die Winsbeckin* denies them and what Queen Isolde's potion is meant to grant them (albeit in somewhat cruder terms) – namely agency through control over their own sexuality and pleasure.

Conversations about control over female sexuality and pleasure are also the subject matter of the *Stepmother and Daughter* dialogues analyzed in chapter seven. A tour de force demonstration of how philology and manuscript studies can be combined with historical evidence to produce particularly nuanced readings of medieval texts, this chapter examines three different yet contemporaneous versions of a mother-daughter conversation about sex. More specifically, the conversations revolve around how the daughter can profitably instrumentalize her desirability as a sexual object and thereby ensure her economic survival.[16] It is no accident that one manuscript calls the text "How a Mother Teaches her Daughter Whoring." The version here, which frames the narrative with an eavesdropping male narrator, allows for the mother to assert control over her reputation and honor through the stories she tells about herself as someone who has maintained the appearance of pre-marital virginity (while all along bearing 7 illegitimate children), a skill which she teaches the daughter in the dialogue. While the narrative frame concludes the tale with the narrator warning readers that all women are money-grubbing seducers and deceivers, as it were, the tale taken as a whole shows how conflicting notions of female honor can operate simultaneously and how these notions are informed by gender. A second version in a different set of manuscripts removes this ambiguity, as the mother places herself firmly in the dishonorable category, commanding her daughter simply to lie and cheat forever. Rasmussen makes sense of these differences with astute reference to contemporary regulations about licit prostitution in brothels versus illicit prostitution practices among the serving classes (housemaids, nurses, and the like). At the same time, she explains how the texts' generic qualities as rhymed tales that are satirizing conduct literature play into her readings. Finally, the chapter concludes with a third version that appeared in a late fifteenth-century broadsheet. With this account, Rasmussen brings her study full circle, as the daughter in this version (who unusually gets a name, Clärlein) repudiates her mother's even cruder "how to" on the exploitation of female sexual desirability. Recalling Lavinia's repudiation of her nameless mother in the *Eneasroman*, Clärlein claims she would rather die than "earn her bread this way" (216).

While readers may be inclined to look for an evolution laid out in these chapters, they will not find one. As Rasmussen notes regarding the variation evident just in the Stepmother material, all of the versions discussed in that chapter appeared in the same time-frame. The simultaneity of this varied material underscores one of

---

16 Meyer, in chapter five below, offers an interesting variation of this dynamic in a foster mother-daughter situation.

the main arguments of the book, namely that while fictional mothers and daughters "play out contradictions in medieval society at large," they do not offer one single recipe for how medieval authors understood and shaped ideas about gender (222). In Rasmussen's own words, "[s]tudying medieval mothers and daughters shows that feminist readings of the literature of the distant past can profitably seek not a grand synthesis on the issue of gender but rather the clusters of ideas about gender that arise and change over time" (223). Finally, the book makes no claim about the uncovering of an authentic women's voice, nor does it argue that women themselves embraced the often misogynistic hierarchies that constrained them. Rather, it provides a landscape of ideological complexity out of and through which female voices might have emerged (224).

Appendix B: Ann Marie Rasmussen, Bibliography

Books

(in press)	*Medieval Badges: Visual Communication and Community Formation*. Philadelphia: University of Pennsylvania Press, forthcoming.
2019	*Rivalrous Masculinities: New Directions in Medieval Gender Studies*. Ann Marie Rasmussen. University of Notre Dame Press.
2012	*Visuality and Materiality in the Story of Tristan and Isolde*, eds. Jutta Eming, Ann Marie Rasmussen and Kathryn Starkey. University of Notre Dame Press.
2010	*Ladies, Whores, and Holy Women: A Sourcebook in Courtly, Religious, and Urban Cultures of Late Medieval Germany, with Introductory Essays*, eds. and trans. by Ann Marie Rasmussen and Sarah Westphal-Wihl. Medieval Institute Publications: Kalamazoo, MI.
2002	*Medieval Woman's Song: Cross-Cultural Approaches*, eds. Anne L. Klinck and Ann Marie Rasmussen. Philadelphia: Univ. of Pennsylvania Press.
1997	*Mothers and Daughters in Medieval German Literature*. Syracuse, NY: Syracuse University Press.

Editor, Journal Volumes

2018	"Medieval Badges," *The Mediaeval Journal* 8.1, co-edited with Hanneke von Asperen (appeared 2019).
2016	"Medieval Media," *Seminar* 52.2, co-edited with Markus Stock.
2000	"Gender and Secrecy," *Journal of Medieval and Early Modern Studies* 30.1 (January).
1997	"Medievalism and Gender," *Medieval Feminist Newsletter*, vol. 23 (Spring).
1996	"Medievalism and Gender," *Medieval Feminist Newsletter* vol. 22 (Fall).

Articles

2019 "Medieval Symbols of Virtue and Mutual Devotion: Noble Dogs in Images, Badges, and Konrad von Würzburg's *Partonopier and Meliur*," in *Animals in Text and Textile: Storytelling in the Medieval World*, eds. Kathryn Starkey and Evelin Wetter, 227–44. Riggisberg: Abegg Stiftung.

2017 "Badges: Abzeichen als sprechende Objekte,"in *Stimme und Performanz in der mittelalterlichen Literatur*, eds. Monika Unzeitig, Angela Schrott, and Nine Miedema, 469–91. Berlin: De Gruyter.

2016 with Markus Stock "Introduction to Special Issue on Medieval Media," *Seminar* 52.2.

2016 "Materiality and Meaning: What a Medieval Badge Can Tell Us About Translation," in *Un/Translatables. New Maps for German Literatures*, eds. Catriona McLeod and Bethany Wiggin, 215–28. Chicago, IL: Northwestern University Press.

2016 "Babies and Books: The Holy Kinship as a Way of Thinking About Women's Power in Late Medieval Northern Europe," in *Founding Feminisms in Medieval Studies. Essays in Honor of E. Jane Burns*, eds. Laine E. Doggett and Daniel E. O'Sullivan, 205–18. Woodbridge: D.S. Brewer.

2016 with Heidi Madden, "Embedded Librarianship: Einbindung von Wissenschafts- und Informationskompetenz in Schreibkurse / Ein US-Amerikanisches Konzept," *BuB* (Forum Bibliothek und Information) 68.04: 202–5.

2015 "Problematizing Medieval Misogyny: Aristotle and Phyllis in the German Tradition," in *Verstellung und Betrug im Mittelalter und in der mittelalterlichen Literatur*, eds. Mathias Meyer and Alexander Sager, 195–220. Göttingen: V & R unipress.

2013 Reprint of "Moving beyond Sexuality in Medieval Sexual Badges," in *Nahrung, Notdurft, Obszönität*, ed. Andrea Grafetstätter, 125–54. Bamberg: Bamberg University Press.

2013 "Moving beyond Sexuality in Medieval Sexual Badges," in *From Beasts to Souls: Gender and Embodiment in Medieval Europe*, eds. E. Jane Burns and Peggy McCracken, 296–335. Notre Dame, IN: Univ. of Notre Dame Press.

2013 with Heidi Madden, "Hiding in Plain Sight: Print Literary Histories in the Digital Age," in *College and Research Library News* March 2013: 140–43. http://crln.acrl.org/content/current (accessed December 17, 2020).

2012 "Reading in Nuremberg's Fifteenth-Century Carnival Plays," in *Literary Studies and the Pursuits of Reading*, eds. Richard Benson, Eric Downing, and Jonathan Hess, 68–83. Rochester, NY: Camden House.

2012 "Wanderlust: Gift Exchange, Sex, and the Meanings of Mobility," in *Liebesgaben: Kommunikative, performative und poetologische Dimensionen in der Literatur des Mittelalters und der Frühen Neuzeit*, eds. Margreth Egidi, Ludger Lieb and Mireille Schnyder. Berlin: Erich Schmidt Verlag, 219–29.

2011 "Siegfried the Dragonslayer Meets the Web: Using Digital Media for Developing Historical Awareness and Advanced Language and Critical Thinking Skills," *Die Unterrichtspraxis* 44.1: 105–14.

2009 *Wandering Genitalia: Sexuality and the Body in German Culture between the Late Middle Ages and Early Modernity*. King's College London Medieval Studies, Occasional Series 2. London: Centre for Late Antique & Medieval Studies, King's College London.

2009 "War die Jungfrau wirklich in Nöten: Neue Forschungen zur Rolle der Frau im Mittelalter," *Merkur: Deutsche Zeitschrift für europäisches Denken* 63.7: 627–33.

2009 with Olga V. Trokhimenko "The German *Winsbecke, Winsbeckin*, and *Winsbecke* Parodies (Selections)," in *Medieval Conduct Literature: An Anthology of Vernacular Guides to Behaviour for Youths, with English Translations*, ed. Mark D. Johnston, 61–125. Toronto: University of Toronto Press and the Medieval Academy of America.

2006 "Masculinity and the Minnerede in Berlin mgo 186," in *Triviale Minne? Konventionalität und Trivialisierung in spätmittelalterlichen Minnereden*, eds. Ludger Lieb and Otto Neudeck, 119–38. Berlin: De Gruyter.

2006 "Visible and Invisible Landscapes: Medieval Monasticism as a Cultural Resource in the Pacific Northwest," in *A Place to Believe In: Locating Medieval Landscapes*, eds. Clare A. Lees and Gillian Overing. College Park: Pennsylvania State University, 239–59.

2005 "Subjektivität und Gender in der Märe *Die zwei beichten* (A und B)," in *Inszenierungen von Subjektivität in der Literatur des Mittelalters*, eds. Martin Baisch, Jutta Eming, Hendrikje Haufe, and Andrea Sieber. Berlin: Ulrike Helmer Verlag, 271–88.

2004 "Preserving the Pre-Modern: Cultural Studies and the Problem of Curtailed Memory," *German Studies Newsletter* 29.2: 29–39.

2003 "Emotions, Gender, and Lordship in Medieval Literature: Clovis's Grief, Tristan's Anger, and Kriemhild's Restless Corpse," in *Codierungen von Emotionen im Mittelalter / Emotions and Sensibilities in the Middle Ages*, eds. C. Stephen Jaeger and Ingrid Kasten. Berlin/New York: De Gruyter, 174–91.

2003 "The Female Figures in Gottfried's *Tristan and Isolde*," in *A Companion to Gottfried's Tristan and Isolde*, ed. Will Hasty. Columbia, S.C.: Camden House, 143–63.

2002 "Gendered Knowledge and Eavesdropping in the Late Medieval German Minnerede," *Speculum* 77.4: 1168–94.

2002 "Thinking through Gender in Late Medieval German Literature," in *Gender in Debate from the Middle Ages to the Renaissance*, eds. Thelma Fenster and Clare A. Lees, 97–111. New York: St. Martin's Press.

2002 "Reason and the Female Voice in Walther von der Vogelweide's Poetry," in *Medieval Woman's Song: Cross-Cultural Approaches*, 168–86.

2001 "Fathers to Think Back Through: The Medieval German Mother-Daughter and Father-Son Conduct Poems Known as *Die Winsbeckin* and *Der Winsbecke*," in *Medieval Conduct*, eds. Kathleen Ashley and Robert L. A. Clark, 106–34. Minneapolis: University of Minnesota Press.

2000 "The Crisis in the Humanities: Feminism, Medieval Studies, and the Academy," in *Medieval Feminist Forum* 29 (Spring 2000): 25–32. Reprinted in *Women's Studies at Duke University Newsletter* (Fall 2000): 2; 4–5; *Faculty Forum for Duke University* 12.4 (19. January 2001): 1–2.

2000 "Introduction, Special Issue on Gender and Secrecy," *Journal of Medieval and Early Modern Studies* 30.1: 1–4.

2000 "Medieval German Romance," in *Cambridge Companion to Medieval Romance*, ed. Roberta Krueger, 183–202. Cambridge, U.K.: Cambridge University Press.

1999 "Good Counsel for a Young Lady: A Low German Mother-Daughter Poem," in *Medieval Feminist Forum* 28: 28–31.

1997 "'Ich trug auch ledig siben chind': Zur sozialen Konstruktion von Weiblichkeit in der Minnerede 'Stiefmutter und Tochter,'" in *fremdes Wahrnehmen – Fremdes wahrnehmen*, eds. Wolfgang Harms and C. Stephen Jaeger together with Alexandra Stein, 193–204. Stuttgart: Hirzel.

1996 "Zur wissenschaftlichen Analyse von Müttern und Töchtern im Mittelalter: Margaret von Courtenay und Yolande von Vianden," in *Frauen: Weibliche Beziehungsgeflechte im Mittelalter*, eds. Hedwig Röckelein and Hans-Werner Goetz. *Das Mittelalter* 1.2: 27–37.

1996 "'ez ist ir g'artet von mir': Queen Isolde and Princess Isolde in Gottfried's *Tristan und Isolde*," in *Arthurian Women: A Casebook*, ed. Thelma Fenster. New York: Garland, 1996, 41–58. Reprint New York: Routledge, 2001.

1995 "Gender studies als Konzept disziplinärer Öffnung," in *Germanistik: Disziplinäre Identität und kulturelle Leistung, Vorträge des deutschen Germanistentags 1994*, 185–93. Frankfurt am Main: Beltz/Athenäum.

1994 "Woman as Audience and Audience as Woman in the Medieval German Courtly Lyric." *Exemplaria* 6.2: 367–84.

1993 "Bist du begehrt, so bist du wert: Magische und höfische Mitgift für die Töchter," in: *Mütter-Töchter-Frauen: Weiblichkeitsbilder in der Literatur*, eds. Helga Kraft and Elke Liebs, 7–34. Stuttgart: Metzler.

1992 "Feminismus in der Mediävistik in Nordamerika." *Mitteilungen des Deutschen Germanistenverbandes* 39 (Sept): 19–27.

1991 "Representing Woman's Desire: Walther's Woman's Stanzas in 'ich hoere iu sô vil tugende jehen' (L43,9), 'under der linden' (L39,11) and 'Frô Welt' (L100,24)," in *Women as Protagonists and Poets in the German Middle Ages: An Anthology of Feminist Approaches to Middle High German Literature*, ed. Albrecht Classen, 69–85. Göppingen: Kümmerle.

1991 18 entries for *Continental Women Writers*. Ed. Katharina M. Wilson. 2 vols. New York: Garland Press. SWITZERLAND (French-speaking): S. Corinna Bille (128–30), Anne Lise Grobêty (492–3), Ella K. Maillart (755–6), Yvette Z'Graggen (1377–80). SWITZERLAND (German-speaking): Cécile Ines Loos (739–41), Erica Pedretti (978–9), Vera Piller (989–9), Margrit Schriber (1125–6), Annemarie Schwarzenbach (1134–5), Regina Ullmann (1262–3). GERMANY: Katja Lange-Müller (695), Marianne Langewiesche (696), Herta Müller (886–7), Ilse Stach (1179). DDR: Renate Feyl (408), Rosemarie Fret (427), Monika Helmecke (544–5), Christa Müller (885–6).
Updated for 2nd edition (1996): Maillart, Piller, and Schwarzenbach.

1991 with Marilyn Migiel. "Francesco Petrarca, [Uber die Grisel. Ulm: Johann Zainer, 1474 or 1475], Rosenwald Collection 50; Goff P-404," in *Visions of a Collector: The Lessing J. Rosenwald Collection in the Library of Congress*, 68–70. Washington, D.C.: Library of Congress.

1989 "Women and Literature in German-Speaking Switzerland: Tendencies in the 1980s," in *Frauen-Fragen in der deutschsprachigen Literatur seit 1945*, eds. Mona Knapp and Gerd Labroisse. *Amsterdamer Beiträge zur neueren Germanistik* 29: 159–182.

1988 "Fredrik Böök and Georg Lukacs: Two Twentieth Century Claimants to the Goethe Legacy," *Orbis Litterarum* 43.2: 167–83.

Sara S. Poor
1 Peddling Devotion: Mothers and Daughters in Conversation Through Books

It is impossible to consider a mother-daughter relationship in the medieval German context without considering Ann Marie Rasmussen's ground-breaking monograph on this topic, *Mothers and Daughters in Medieval German Literature*.[1] Taking a number of exemplary fictional texts as her objects of study, she analyzes the "wider implications of the mother-daughter theme as a literary and cultural paradigm" (xi). The result of this analysis is the conclusion that the stories are neither uniform, nor fixed, but rather revealing of medieval culture's varied concerns about women on a number of levels. As Rasmussen relates:

> [Mother-daughter stories] embody tensions between what is innate and what is learned, between compliance and disorderliness, between conformity and rebellion, between collaboration and resistance. Whether arguing or agreeing, mothers and daughters in medieval German literature show us women in the process of performing cultural work that interrogates the vexed and contradictory, yet historically specific, scripts through which patriarchal ideals of womanhood take shape. (25)

Although the heart of the book focuses on fictional texts, Rasmussen begins her introduction with a historical narrative: the story of Margaret of Courtenay (d. 1270) and her daughter Yolande of Vianden (ca. 1231–1283), who rejected a planned marriage in order to take the veil in the Dominican order. As Rasmussen describes in the book, there was significant conflict surrounding this choice having to do with the mother's desire to secure a position of distinction and status for her daughter. That is, it was not necessarily the rejection of the marriage that was a problem, for, once Yolande rejected the offer of marriage, her mother quickly suggested Yolande enter the Cistercian order that the family patronized. However, Yolande was interested in joining the more recently founded and reform-minded mendicant Order of Preachers. The story of this choice and resulting mother-daughter conflict, as Rasmussen shows, is filtered through a hagiographical text written sometime after 1283 by Brother Hermann of Veldenz (d. 1307), *Das Leben der Gräfin Iolande von Vianden* (Meier 1889; Hermann 1995). Her analysis of this filter proves to be a fitting introduction to the narratives she analyzes in the rest of the book, which are also all male-authored texts, written in genres that have certain tropic requirements when

---

1 The author gratefully acknowledges the support of the National Humanities Center (NEH Fellowship and Josephus Daniels Fellowship of the Research Triangle Foundation) in 2017–2018, during which this essay was completed, as well as the generous comments of the audiences at the GSA, the University of Michigan Medieval and Early Modern Studies group, and the participants of the North Carolina Triangle Medieval Studies Seminar.

it comes to gender behavior and identity. Using a historical example – for, in addition to Brother Hermann's text there is historical documentation of Margaret's and her husband's extremely well-connected families – enables Rasmussen to make the point that fictional texts (or texts like Brother Hermann's that are filtered in some way) "*can contribute to women's history because they can reveal to us a great deal about the contradictions of medieval models for mothers and daughters*," contradictions that Rasmussen sees connected to the "real, historical circumstances of medieval women's lives" (13, emphasis mine).

Yolande's story is no doubt appealing to us, her modern audience, in part because of her decision to disobey, even rebel against the authority of her mother, who represents the establishment. This defiance can be seen as a sign not only of the contradictions of which Rasmussen speaks, but also of the agency that becomes visible as an effect of such contradictions. My understanding of agency and how to detect it is informed by recent work by Alisa Bierria on discerning agency in an environment of oppression.[2] Bierria roots her understanding of agency in philosophical accounts of intentional action in which "agentic action" refers to an act that is both initiated ("authored") and carried out according to the intention of an individual (Bierria 2014, 130). Bierria goes on to problematize the "reading" of agentic actions, noting that biases of the readers (in the case of her examples, cultural and institutional racial biases) change how the intention is read or perceived.[3] Reading the actions of black women with an awareness of the "structural and existential erasures of women of color" within which those actions are embedded can, Bierria suggests, "help us to better discern agentic action that is practiced by those subjects whose actions are defined away from them" (Bierria 2014, 130). In citing Bierria's work, I acknowledge that for women of color in the twentieth and twenty-first centuries, social and cultural readings of gender are inextricably linked with those of race, an issue that forms the core of Bierria's analysis. Moreover, I acknowledge that both of these terms – race and gender – were alien to the context of late medieval Germany. However, I find Bierria's formulations instructive and productive for thinking through how gender works in the story of these historical white women, Yolande and her mother. While they are not being socially read or constructed according to the category of race, their actions might nevertheless be said to be "defined away from them." Their story was read by Brother Hermann through the pattern of the lives of many saints, particularly those of antiquity, who chose conversion and martyrdom over forced marriage or concubinage to a non-Christian emperor. And it must be said that Yolande may herself have drawn meaning from seeing her actions in this light as well – in other words, for me to claim that Yolande saw her desire to be a Dominican as a moment of agency

---

[2] My thanks to Tala Khanmalek for alerting me to Bierria's work.
[3] Bierria cites the different readings or translations of the act of taking items from a grocery store during Hurricane Katrina as an example: news media reporting on whites doing this used the word "finding" versus reports of African Americans doing this used the word "looting."

would be anachronistic. I do not pretend to have access to medieval women's thoughts and plans. Rather, I argue here that the agentic action of a mother and a daughter can be glimpsed through a sensitive reading of the material culture of the late medieval devotional book and its contents and that this act of reading on our parts is an important task. My aim for this approach is to get a better sense of what women might have done, how they might have acted in this historical moment. But my hope is that this work might also give us insights into how to think about women's agency in other historical contexts in which their acts have been under erasure by social institutions, structures, and norms.

In this essay, then, I turn our focus to another response to the mother's advice, that is, to a daughter who follows it. Unlike Yolande, who defies her mother's ambition by choosing the poor Dominican order over the Cistercian order in which she has family money and affiliations, the noble daughter discussed below stays within this family sphere of influence, entering a Cistercian convent not only supported but also founded by her family. Like Yolande, however, this daughter also later becomes a leader of the house. Rasmussen acknowledges in her book the many other texts, particularly religious and devotional, that might be relevant to a consideration of mothers and daughters in medieval German literature and culture (xiii). My contribution here takes up the invitation implied in this acknowledgment by exploring evidence of a mother-daughter relationship in the late medieval material culture of devotion. For the story of these two women, Agnes von Werdenberg (ca. 1400–ca. 1471), the Countess of Oettingen from 1420 to 1440 and her daughter Magdalena, the Abbess of the Cistercian House in Kirchheim am Ries from 1446 to 1496, is accessible to us not through a hagiographical biography, but rather through an exchange of books.[4] Among the codices surviving from the Kirchheim convent library are six compilation manuscripts that were owned first by Agnes and then by Magdalena and the convent. As I will show, the story that emerges from these materials offers us another take on what Rasmussen describes as "the fundamental and perplexing issue underlying any literary or historical investigation of women: the conditions under which women in a patriarchal social order succeed or fail in transferring their knowledge and power to other women" (14).

In what follows, I will briefly discuss the situation of these codices, their production, and transmission so as to establish the mode of transfer between mother and daughter. In this case, the exchange seems to be connected to the daughter's efforts to promote the acceptance of observance reform in the Kirchheim convent. I then turn to a specific text included in one of the books ("Spiritual dialogue between a princess and a lady peddler about a rosary made with gemstones" [Schmidt 1898; Augsburg Universitätsbibliothek, III. 1. 4° 8, fol. 353r–403v]) that points to edificatory

---

4 The first section of this essay summarizes material I have published elsewhere. For the more detailed version, see Poor 2017.

knowledge transfer between women both in the circumstances of its transmission – it seems likely that Agnes acquired the text from a female relative – and in its content. Virtually no scholarly attention has been given to this short text, a dialogue in which the lady peddler holds forth about how to use a rosary and what the gemstones on this one mean. The text is thus explicitly about the transfer of knowledge and instruction from one woman to another. However, it presents us with a number of perplexing details: first, it is a low-born lay woman, a peddler, not a priest or monk, who delivers the largely religious information to the higher-born and noble princess; second, her discourse is clearly on the level of exegesis, offered in a series of short sermon-like monologues on both the paternoster and the rosary used to recite it, that is, not a discourse one would expect to come from a lady peddler; third, the knowledge conveyed appears to be about women's special need to suppress their "natural" and base inclinations (e.g., carnal desire) and as such, about the discipline and restraint required of women within the competing patriarchal orders of the noble home and cloister; and fourth, we know from the rubric in the manuscript that Carthusian monks composed the text, which clearly helps us make sense of the disciplinary tone, but does not explain why the source of this knowledge is figured as a common woman peddling junk on the road.

The discussion of the text in connection with the manuscript transmission allows us to consider the question of female agency from a number of different angles. This discussion allows us to see evidence of women acting independently in their constrained worlds even when they themselves are promoting those constraints.

1 Mother, Daughter, and Their Books

A brief perusal of catalogues of medieval manuscript collections in Germany, Austria, and Switzerland leaves no doubt that an exponentially larger number of German manuscripts survive from the fifteenth century than from any century before it.[5] Scholars generally agree that this increase in production can be directly connected to the so-called "Observance Reform" of the late fourteenth and fifteenth centuries, although there is some dispute about the extent of the connection.[6] As its name implies, the reform advocated a return to full observance of the monastic rule for religious houses in most of the religious orders of the day (except for the Carthusians). The most significant impact on women's houses was the reinforcement of enclosure. Renewed or increased isolation due to enclosure coupled with the compulsion and desire to be more observant were a large part of why more and more books of devotional

---

[5] For specific numbers, see Neddermeyer 1998.
[6] For information on the Observance Reform, see the essays in Elm 1989. For the debate about reform and literary production, see Williams-Krapp 1995 and Graf 1995.

material were being compiled and reproduced during this time. Women religious needed books of religious instruction and inspiration in order to be able to follow the new rules and become observant in a spiritual – that is, not just superficial – way.[7]

The books exchanged between Agnes and her daughter Magdalena must clearly be considered in this context. The first indication of the connection between mother and daughter comes from an ownership inscription. Four of the six books I have mentioned have an inscription either exactly like or very similar to the following:

> Daz buch gehort gen Kyrchen zü gebruch S[chwester]. Madalenen von Oettingen eptysin daselbs und ist fraw Agneßen von Werdenberg gewesen ir mütter selg.[8]

> [This book belongs to Kirchheim for the use of Sister Magdalena of Oettingen, Abbess of same, and it was Lady Agnes's of Werdenberg, her blessed mother.]

Magdalena's mother was the daughter of Count Eberhard III of Werdenberg, himself descended from a long line of counts of Montfort.[9] Agnes married the Bavarian Count Ludwig XI of Oettingen (1361–1440) in 1420. The family of Oettingen founded the Cistercian convent at Kirchheim in 1270 and it was a regular destination for daughters of the Oettingen counts, many of whom went on to serve as abbesses. Agnes's daughter became abbess in 1446 and, showing remarkable longevity, held this office for 50 years.

Coincident with what seems to have been a general family appreciation of books,[10] Countess Agnes probably commissioned and then donated or bequeathed at least four other books for her daughter's use, possibly five.[11] All of them are devotional compilations of German texts and as already mentioned, most of them bear the same ownership inscription indicating that the book had belonged to the Countess and was now the property of the convent, set aside for the use of the abbess, the

---

7 For an examination of how Observance affected women specifically, see Winston-Allen 2004.
8 Augsburg, Universitätsbibliothek, III. 1. 4° 8, inside front cover. All translations unless otherwise noted are my own.
9 On Agnes's family, see von Stälin 1856, 685–90; and Schnell 1984, 171–73.
10 The Oettingens also founded a Carthusian house in Christgarten and a Brigittine house in Maihingen. The Carthusians especially were known for their production and care of devotional writing. See Sexauer 1978; See also the annual journal *The Mystical Tradition and Carthusians* published by the University of Augsburg beginning in 1995. Subsequent abbesses of the convent, also coming from the Oettingen clan, followed suit – their names can be found in other surviving books from the Kirchheim collection: Margarethe von Oettingen (abbess from 1505–1535) commissioned a Latin Benedictine rule, Bayerische Staatsbibliothek, Clm 28306 (Glauche 1984, 84–85; and Schromm 1998, 38); Anna von Oettingen (abbess 1535–1545) owned a prayer book, which she left to the house, Augsburg, Universitätsbibliothek, III 1. 8° 46 (Schneider 1988, 617–18); and finally, a book of devotional texts with an ownership mark reading "Das buech gehert in die liberey" [This book belongs to the (Oettingen) library], Augsburg, Universitätsbibliothek, III 1. 2° 5 (Schneider 1988, 156–57; Schromm 1998, 31).
11 Augsburg, Universitätsbibliothek, III. 1. 2° 13, III. 1. 2° 32, III. 1. 4° 17, III. 1. 2° 36, III. 1. 4° 32.

countess's daughter. Since Magdalena was known to have been interested in facilitating observant reform (which likely was occurring between 1465 and 1473), it seems plausible that Agnes might have sent these particular books in response to a request for didactic material for the convent.[12] Arnold Schromm suggests further that the constellation of these books points to the possibility that Agnes, not Magdalena, was in fact the instigator of the convent's engagement with the observant reform (97). Whether or not the impetus for reform came from the mother depends to a certain extent on whether the books came to the convent as part of a bequest or were sent to the house while Agnes was still alive.[13] Whichever of these modes of transmission is the case, the fact remains that four of the six manuscripts in question date to between 1460 and 1466, suggesting that these books were certainly assembled and acquired during a period when the reform was either being considered or initiated.[14]

Although the evidence is more suggestive than definitive, the existence of these books and the fact that the convent librarians made a point of mentioning the previous owner with such deference do seem to point to a dynamic and significant relationship between the mother and daughter. In one scenario, the mother attempts to influence the actions of her daughter – whether for political or spiritual aims it is impossible to say for sure – and in the other, the daughter seeks assistance from her mother in her efforts to effect change. In either scenario, the evidence of female agency in the *absence* of mother-daughter conflict is noteworthy – suggesting a collaborative agency insofar as these two women are both acting and interacting through the transfer of knowledge in books.

2 The Gift of Guidance

While the evidence discussed thus far focuses on the transmission of whole books, the first manuscript I mentioned offers internal evidence of the transmission of knowledge through the exchange of single texts between female relatives. The penultimate text in this 404-folio compilation is described in the modern catalogue by Karin Schneider as follows: "Geistliches Gespräch zwischen einer Fürstin und einer Krämerin von einem Rosenkranz aus Edelsteinen" [Schneider 1988, 271; Spiritual

---

[12] Schromm quotes from a housebook from a neighboring convent in which a chaplain notes Magdalena's speaking to him about reform (Schromm 1998, 86–87). See also Cramer 1990, 165–77, who describes the sorry state of pastoral care in the fifteenth century leading to the rising importance of lay religious communities, culture, and textual production. It seems clear, though, that the lack of pastoral care also had this effect among the pious religious as well. The case of Agnes and her daughter gives us an example of how these spheres were in fact closely connected.
[13] For a more detailed discussion of the books Magdalena received from her mother, see Poor 2017.
[14] Of the other two manuscripts, one dates to the first quarter of the fifteenth century, and the other to 1453–1454.

Dialogue Between a Princess and a Lady Peddler About a Rosary Made of Gemstones].
The rubric in the manuscript reads quite differently, however:

> Diß hernach geschriben buochlin habend gemacht die kartauser zue dem guotterstain vnd habend es geschenckt mit dem pater noster der dar inn berürt wirt in ainem clainen kistlin zue totgaub der elteren von wirttenberg anno 1447 ze aurach. (fol. 353r)
>
> [The Carthusians of Güterstein made this little book written in the following pages and they gave it with the paternoster that is touched therein (this phrase refers to the rosary)[15] in a little box as a Godparent gift to the von Württemberg parents in the year 1447 in Aurach.]

Friedrich Schmidt has identified the von Württemberg parents, the recipients of the baptismal gift from the Carthusian monks acting in the role of Godparents, as Ludwig I of Württemberg (1412–1450) and his wife Mechthild, Countess of the Rhine Palatinate (1419–1482); the baptismal gift was for their new-born daughter Elizabeth (1447–1505). The Countess Mechthild was a contemporary of our Agnes (ca. 1400–ca. 1471) and more importantly, was related to her by marriage.[16] Mechthild's husband's aunt Elizabeth (whose name the new child shared) was married to Agnes's brother Johann II of Werdenberg (d. 1465). This made Agnes the sister-in-law of the young Elizabeth's great aunt, or in other words, also Elizabeth's great aunt by marriage (Figure 1.1). The dialogue, given as a kind of paternoster manual to Elizabeth's parents on the occasion of her birth ended up in the compilation that Agnes owned and gave to her daughter. The family relationship and the fact that Agnes and Mechthild were basically contemporaries suggests that Agnes might have gotten the text from Mechthild. The rubrication clearly indicates that the text was meant to help the parents educate their daughter. Its presence in Agnes's book, then, implies that Agnes may have chosen to include this text not only because she also had a daughter, but also because she knew her daughter, the abbess of a religious house, could then use the book for the edification of her own spiritual daughters in Kirchheim.

Scholars have pointed out that the source for the text could also have been a scribe called Johannes Kubach, who was a member of the Carthusian house at Güterstein mentioned in the rubrication. Bernard Schnell has connected this Johannes with the named scribe of the manuscript, "Johannes K" (Schnell 1984, 171–73). While one cannot be certain which avenue was the actual one without more definitive evidence, additional evidence from the Kirchheim library supports the greater likelihood of the family scenario. Another late fifteenth-century manuscript from the Kirchheim library bears a sixteenth-century ownership description that reads: "Düß buoch sampt andren vil schöner büechlin hand wir mit uns von Memmingen her gefüert, unser wirdige liebe müter und sch[western?] hands uns geben das wir gott für sy büttend" [fol. Iv; This book we brought with us from Memmingen along with many other beautiful

---

15 Winston-Allen 1997, 112.
16 On this Mechthild's well-known participation in late medieval literary culture, see Karnein 1995.

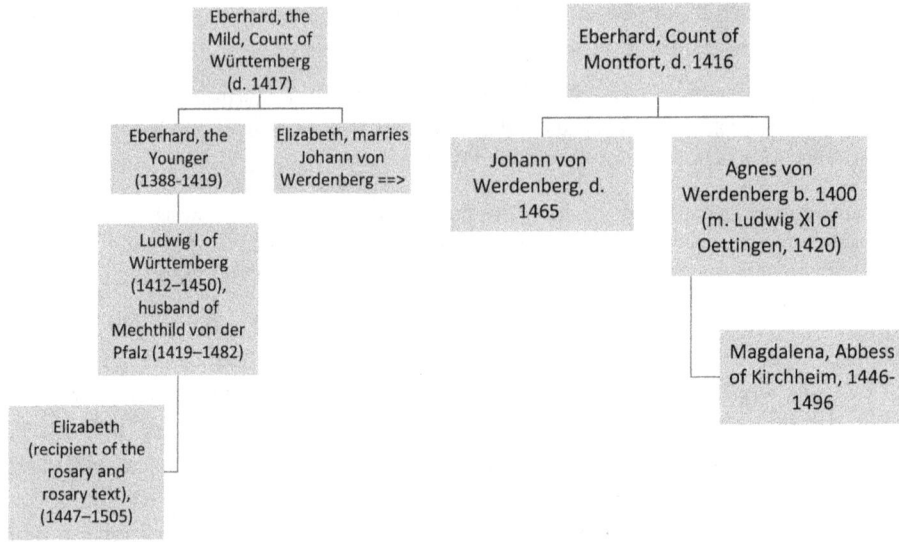

Figure 1.1: Family Trees Showing Relationship Between Agnes of Werdenberg and Elizabeth of Württemberg. © Sara S. Poor.

books; our worthy mother and sisters gave them to us so that we would pray for her].[17] Further, although from the seventeenth century, a book produced by a nun from a different convent for her biological sister, Anna Regina Meichlin, the abbess in Kirchheim (1688–1691), was so well-liked by the other sisters in Kirchheim that they commissioned at least another ten books from her (Schromm 1998, 41). These two examples only scratch the surface of the types of manuscript exchange taking place at this time. However, they are illuminating for this discussion insofar as they show a wider practice of inter-family book exchange.[18] In the context of this wider practice, then, the compilation containing the "Geistliches Gespräch," and the text itself, are clearly both functioning on a number of levels as part of a mother-daughter relation.

3 The Princess and the Lady Peddler

Anyone who works with manuscripts knows that when researching textual transmission, one sometimes overlooks or pays short shrift to the content of the texts

---

17 Augsburg Universitätsbibliothek, III. 1. 4° 30 (Schneider 1988, 314–18).
18 Already in the 1970s and 1980s, Karin Schneider made note of exchanges of books between women in connection with her cataloguing work (1975 and 1983). It has also been the focus of a number of more recent essay collections, for example, Blanton et al. 2017.

being copied and bound together. This next section demonstrates that attending to the contents serves to deepen the discussion raised by the codicological evidence in important ways. I therefore turn now to the lady peddler dialogue itself.[19] As will become evident, attention to the particulars of this unusual conversation raises important issues and questions for the larger discussion about the ways that knowledge (about patriarchy) is transferred between women.

The dialogue begins with a prologue that describes the usefulness of gemstones, which I paraphrase here: for the lady peddler, gems make money; noble young ladies and many men find pleasure and entertainment ("churzweil") in them; and clever "heathen" scholars, princes and princesses, other great noble lords, and wise men like them for their power and virtue. They also are known to heal many types of physical ailments. These positive qualities and powers come from God, of course, and the best way to get to God, who, as we know from the paternoster, is in heaven, is through prayer and the most useful prayer is the paternoster (especially for worldly persons who are not bound by an order to say the daily offices or to go to church). For this reason, it is useful to tell the story of a lady peddler who is carrying a paternoster (rosary) and a high-born princess (who is "mit tugenden, andacht und gnade von got begabt" [202; gifted by God with virtue, devotion, and grace]). The princess sees the rosary and wants to buy it: "als [sie] cluog von synnen sicht das paternoster, fragt sie [. . .] was das paternoster edels in im habe" [202; when she, clever of mind, saw the rosary, she asked what kind of noble value it had in it]. Showing a bit of good business acumen, instead of asking its price, she asks for an explanation of its value in terms of nobility.

After this introduction, topics addressed include what gems are on the rosary (big ones and small ones); what each type of gem does; literally how to use the rosary, that is what to do with it in your hands as you recite the prayer; an exegesis of the paternoster prayer; and basic moral instruction (for example, God answers no to every request in the paternoster if the person praying does not also help his neighbor [206]). Some of the dialogue's intriguing qualities are perhaps already apparent – it is clearly aimed at a worldly reader or listener, since the paternoster is explicitly said to be useful for those who are not professed to an order and therefore who are not *compelled* to say prayers many times a day.[20] The princess, who, we are told is not only clever but also already graced by God with virtue and devotion, expresses both gratitude and surprise at what she has heard, about which she confesses she has never thought at all. Intrigued, the princess asks for more. The lady peddler at this point delivers what can only be termed a treatise or sermon on the

---

19 Augsburg Universitätsbibliothek, III. 1. 4° 8, fol. 353r–403v; printed in Schmidt 1898, 201–29.
20 As Anne Winston-Allen notes in her comprehensive study of the rosary, "[a]s a devotional exercise, the rosary combined elements from three older kinds of meditations to create a new, more engrossing prayer that was particularly suited to the spiritual needs of the lay faithful" (Winston-Allen 1997, 4).

religious meaning and usefulness of the four gemstones – jasper, chalcedony, carnelian, and sapphire – and of the other objects strung together with the stones (e.g., a small crucifix). The treatise continues for seventeen printed pages.[21]

While basic rosaries were most often made with common materials like bone, wood, and glass, or even nuts or dried fruit, it is not surprising that other, more decorative or precious materials were used to make these prayer facilitators more like jewelry (See Figures 1.2 and 1.3). The list of materials from which beads were made is long: gold, silver, emeralds, rubies, diamonds, coral, jet, crystal, alabaster, pearls, lapis lazuli, polished or cut amber, ebony, marble, ivory, jade, mother-of-pearl, enamel, and porcelain. Already in the thirteenth century (in Europe), beads were well on their way to becoming a quintessential instrument of both devotion and dress ornament (Wilkins 1969, 46). All of these stones, but particularly the precious ones were thought to be apotropaic. The most common of these in the Middle Ages were amber and coral (Wilkins 1969, 47). This apotropaic quality is also what makes a rosary an appropriate gift for a god-child, and why one often sees strings of coral colored beads or jewels draped on infant Christ figures or hanging from the Virgin Mary's waist in paintings that include her (Figures 1.4 and 1.5).

Of course, we do not know what the rosary looked like that came in the little box along with our text. It seems safe to assume, though, that it was well-endowed with these semi-precious and precious stones. Similar to the coral, these stones were clearly also thought to be powerful in a number of different ways. And it is fascinating to see how the lady peddler, in explaining these powers, couches them all in good religious and moral instruction. Indeed, while there is plenty of practical devotional instruction in the text about precisely how to use the rosary, there is much more that is clearly moral. One especially striking example of this moral teaching helps us to see how a text purported to convey something about devotional prayer and meditation to a laywoman is also performing a specific kind of ideological work, particularly with regard to the instilling of misogynistic values. From the beginning of the long treatise on the gemstones, we learn that jasper signifies love, the good kind of love, the love that is life and that staves off damnation. But in signifying love, jasper also drives away fever and by that, according to the text, the lady means the heat and cold of fleshly desire:

> Jaspis vertreibt auch die febres, die böse hicze vnd kalte der vnlauttern flaischlichen bösen begierde, auch die *wassersucht* der geiczichait. Böse flaischlich begird ist gleich als ain inprünstig fewr, *das fewr verprent das claid, die vnlautter begirde verprennet die sele.* Die vnkeusch wollust wirt mit dem menschen geporen darvmb sollen wir sie in vnns wberwinden; wan ist es, das wir fürsichticlichen mit der sach vmbgangen, So sechen wir bald vnnsern veind vnd

---

[21] See also the discussion of conduct literature in Evelyn Meyer's contribution to this volume. The monologic quality of the lady peddler's discourse is striking because on the one hand, as Rasmussen has argued, "the authoritative voice is authoritative because it can and does hold forth without interruption" and on the other, the monologic authoritative voice that is usually male, belongs here to a common woman. See below, chapter five, 121n5, quoting Rasmussen 2001, 126.

wie wir im widerstan sollen vnd mügen in leichticlich wberwinden. Ist es aber, daz wir die wollust, die mit vnns geporen ist, nit wellen wberwinden vnd vnns geben zue andern lusten vnd flaischlichen begirden, so mögen wir sie kaum überwinden, vnd so wir mit vnns selb also gezwa[i]et seyen,[22] so werden wir verprent mit vnnserem aigen fewr, dann ain yedlich begird zuo ainer fremden frawen, die der man hat, Oder auch zuo ainem frömden manne oder chnaben, die die frawe hat, *sie seyent wer oder welches stats sie wöllen,* Ist ez, das die begird chompt bis zuo dem wollust vnd zuo dem gunste durch den willen, der das beslewsset. Die begird ist allzeit ain todliche sünd, wie wol es sey daz die wollust nit sey würcklich. Die fleschlich begir hat ir handhabung vnd ir ruo in der vncheuschhait in lindichait vnd in gezierde der claider in wbriger ruo des flesches vnd in müssiggaun. (213–14, emphasis added)

[Jasper also dispels fever, the evil heat and coolness of impure, fleshly, evil desire, and also the *dropsy* of avarice. Evil, fleshly desire is like a scorching fire, *the fire burns the clothing, the impure desire burns the soul.* Unchaste lust is born in men and for this reason we should try to overcome it, for if we tread carefully around this issue, then we soon see our enemy and we shall resist him and can overcome him easily. If, however, we do not want to overcome the lust that is born in us and we give ourselves to other lusts and fleshly desires, then we can hardly overcome it, and thus we would be consorting with ourselves in such a way, that we will be burned with our own fire, then every desire for an unknown woman that a man has, or also of an unknown man or boy that a woman has, *whoever they may be or from wherever they claim to be,* means that the desire becomes lust and pleasure through the will that decides this. Desire is always a deadly sin, even though it is true that lust is *not really real.* Fleshly desire has its manifestation and its resting place in licentiousness and listlessness and in *ornamentation of clothing* in the remaining resting place of the flesh and in idleness.]

In an earlier section of the text, the lady peddler makes a point of saying that the princess seems to be doing just fine in the way of presenting herself modestly and not showing evidence of falling into sin. Indeed, she is explicitly said to be *un*like princesses and "grosmechtige frawen" [great and powerful women] who with heavily ornamented clothing, ostentatious self-presentation and immodest behavior cause men to give themselves over to "böser unlautter begird" [211; evil impure desire]. Despite this fact, however, she is told again and again in the jasper section and in this passage about how terrible any behavior linked to desire can be. "Fleschlich begir," for example, "hat ir handhabung und ir ruo" [213; Fleshly desire has its manifestation and its resting place] in promiscuity, laziness, too much sleep, idleness, gluttony, and basically anything to do with the five senses, as in hearing impure words and songs, smelling really nice spices, seeing or looking at pretty young people, unseemly

---

22 The printed text has "gezwaret" here, but I suspect a misreading of an "i" as an "r" and thus, I read "gezwaiet." Lexer's Middle High German Dictionary defines "gezweien" according to a usage in courtly love lyric as modern German "gesellen" [to consort with someone, to have sex]. And the linked BMZ Middle High German Dictionary supplies this quote: "unz ich mich zuo der lieben gezweie" [until I am consorting with my beloved]. This meaning certainly seems to fit with the sentence context here, whereas "gezwaren" does not appear in any of the major dictionaries for Middle High German. http://woerterbuchnetz.de/cgi-bin/WBNetz/Navigator/navigator_py?sigle=Lexer&lemid=LG04417&mode=Vernetzung&hitlist=&patternlist=&sigle1=Lexer&lemid1=LG04417&sigle2=BMZ&lemid2=BZ01144 (accessed June 19, 2020).

Figure 1.2: Paternosterer [Paternoster maker]; Stadtbibliothek im Bildungscampus Nürnberg, Amb. 317.2°, fol. 13r.

Figure 1.3: Rosary with dividing beads of chalcedony as paternoster markers, Inv.-Nr. R 940, Foto Nr. D25898 © Bayerisches Nationalmuseum München; Photo by Karl-Michael Vetters.

Figure 1.4: Gerard David. The Virgin and Child with Saints and Donor. Probably 1510. © The National Gallery, London. Bequeathed by Mrs Lyne Stephens, 1895.

seeing or looking at parts of bodies or the whole body (214). And all of this behavior will bring on "wassersucht der geiczichait" or the dropsy of avarice. Dropsy, according to the text, is an ailment in which the more a person drinks, the more thirsty she becomes and this thirst is never sated.[23] Dropsy of avarice is clearly about unchecked desire, the moral here being: the more one succumbs to earthly desires, the more desire one has for earthly pleasures and for this reason, one will never be satisfied.[24]

---

23 In addition, the widely circulated (250 manuscripts across Europe) lapidary of Marbode of Rennes also lists fever and dropsy as the first two things that jasper counteracts (40–41). For a comprehensive study of the allegorization and use of gemstones in the Middle Ages, see Meier 1977, and also in this volume, on the healing of dropsy with gemstones, including jasper, 387–88.
24 "Dropsy," according to various dictionaries, is an old term for edema (swelling due to accumulation of water in the legs or other body parts; most often related to congestive heart failure). The

Figure 1.5: Joos van Cleve (1485–1540) and a collaborator. Crucifixion with Saints and Donor (1520), Metropolitan Museum of Art, New York, Bequest of George Blumenthal, 1941.

Jasper's power to fend off these evil tendencies is implicated in the profound moral disciplining the text undertakes. Everything is about restraint and limit – you cannot desire a man or a woman *regardless* of their social station or where they are from; giving in to sensual desire produces an irrepressible avarice that makes you both physically and spiritually sick; further, giving in to these desires, turning away from good works, makes you analogous to the calf or steer that is being fattened up for slaughter. The more useful animals, the ones to be kept, are kept alive,

---

term first appeared in the thirteenth century and goes back to the Greek "hydro" meaning water (Entries for "Dropsy" at "Medicine.net" and "OED").

being frugally fed and, of course, also confined. Confinement, deprivation, discipline, restraint are the ideal characteristics the princess should develop, all with the aid of the Lord's prayer and her rosary beads. The gems on the rosary are there not only to help remember the prayer and its exegesis (also given in great detail in the dialogue) but themselves help the carrier to achieve these goals, by virtue of the actual powers ("kräfte") that they possess.

The other three major stones do not receive as much explication as jasper, suggesting that the fight against desire for women is of paramount importance. However, these passages also offer interesting and somewhat contradictory approaches to devotional instruction. Chalcedony, a clear or black stone according to the text, although other medieval lapidaries mention several additional colors including, white, gray, blue, or brown (Rennes 1977, 43), signifies death or the consciousness of death ("todesgedechtnuss" [218]). Its power lies in that it reminds the wearer of death and its significance. Further, this consciousness drives all temptation to sin out of the heart because everyone knows that the last moment alive is the key to one's fate in the afterlife. If one dies in sin, one is doomed, whereas if one dies without sin, then the kingdom of heaven opens up immediately to the soul. Since death always comes unexpectedly, the constant consciousness of it should be a powerful deterrent to sin and a guarantor of heavenly access. The power of this stone thus gives a poignant meaning to the saying, "knowledge is power." An awareness of the ever-present possibility of death constrains the wearer of the jewel, helping her to conquer her more "natural" state which is receptive to the temptations of sin.

Carnelian, "plaich rott als wasser, dz in dem flesch gewesen ist" [221; pale red as water that has been in flesh], signifies confession. Its color comes from the association with flesh itself as well as with the shame felt in confession. This rather short section also talks about the conscience and its power to prevent sin, as well as the importance of remorse, which, if confessed properly, will dispel any anger the person might have felt. Indeed, the traditional medical application of carnelian is against anger and excess blood flow, particularly menstruation – "stellet allerlay pluot flusz nemlich der frewen" [203; stops all kinds of bleeding, particularly for women] (see also Rennes 1977, 60–61). As with the explication of jasper, the medical uses of carnelian are also understood figuratively as in "Carneol stellet den pluotfluss aller sünd, nemlich der unkeuschhait" [222; Carnelian stops the bloodflow of all sin, namely that of concupiscence]. Correspondingly, the association of the stone's color with bodily flesh is connected to a bodily response to sin, namely the blushing that accompanies feelings of shame. The princess is being taught through the metaphorical implications of the gem how to rein herself in; she is learning how to use negative emotions in the service of producing a higher level of self-reflection, one that is however always geared towards the suppression of that self.

Finally, sapphire, which according to C.W. King's commentary on Marbode of Rennes' *Lapidary* was the name for lapis lazuli until sometime in the thirteenth century when what we know as sapphire was found in volcanic deposits near Auvergne

(Rennes 1977, 41), represents constancy and peace. This stone has many "virtues" (222): it brings back peace that has been destroyed; it reconciles those who are in disputes; it helps a person resist bad habits; and it promotes modesty. Another interesting bodily association appears when we learn that it drives away sweat, which, it turns out, is caused by laziness in approaching good works. The implication is that one does not sweat if one approaches work with eagerness and energy (if only!). Sapphire also proves to be an antidote to poison, yet by poison, the peddler means gossip about a neighbor behind her back. We see the standard misogynistic stereotypes being checked off one by one. And finally, sapphire heals the eyes, which the lady peddler remarks are where haughtiness ("hoffart" [224]) appears, especially in women:

> Frewlin geren. . . Wir sehen geren hübsche und wppige ding vnd unnser grovste begird ist, das wir gesehen mügen werden und gelobt, Darumb zieren wir unns allermeist vnd mit allem fleisse vnder dem antlütz an der stirnen vnd umbedumb so wir aller last mügent. Sollichs legt diser stain ab, so man in recht prauchet. . . (224)
>
> [Ladies desire. . . we gladly see pretty and expensive things (things suggesting noble status?) and our greatest desire is that we might be seen and praised. This is why we adorn ourselves for the most part and with great effort under the face (and) on the forehead and all around it so that we are made open to any and all shame. This stone gets rid of all that, if one uses it properly. . .]

The focus put on the visage and the adornment placed around it is significant. There is plenty of evidence that ostentatious attire, whether in textile or jewelry form, was frowned upon by church authorities both inside and outside of religious orders. In her study of the symbolic background of European prayer beads, Eithne Wilkins mentions Dominicans who were forbidding lay-brothers (who needed the prayer counters because of their illiteracy) from giving "themselves airs by using excessively grand beads" (49). In the mid-fourteenth century, an Augustinian canon condemns the laity for wearing coral paternosters as necklaces, which in a Leipzig sumptuary law, were also forbidden for maid-servants to wear (Wilkins 1969, 49). The lady peddler follows suit, attributing to women the propensity for wearing ornament in order to encourage others to look at them.[25] This statement makes the peddling of this obviously precious and ornamental rosary all the more fascinating. It is the inherent (moral) power of the stone, however, that makes this palatable. Indeed, the most precious of the stones, the sapphire, is said to be able to heal the eyes, which is where the lady's sin is located – she wears ornament over and under her eyes (headdresses, garlands, crowns, necklaces) and the desire to be looked at involves the eyes of others connecting with hers. If the sight of a beautifully adorned visage creates a sinful

---

25 For examples of how "grosmechtige frawen" might have ornamented themselves around their faces, see the woman with the bejeweled headdress and jewel necklace in Figure 1.4, and also the two sisters wearing elaborate headdresses in the Jouvenel family portrait, Figure 1.6.

Figure 1.6: Anonymous, 15th century. The Family of Jouvenel des Ursins. Paris, 1445–49. © RNM-Grand palais / Art Resource, NY. INV 9618. Photo: Gérard Blot.

desire, the stone's presence will thus "heal the eye" by negating that desire. The connection between the "illness" and "cure" is clear.

For the nineteenth-century editor of the dialogue, Friedrich Schmidt, the gem lore in the dialogue represents the "period of superstition" that precedes the Reformation.[26] He sees potential sources for the gem lore here in Albertus Magnus's "De mineralibus," which relied heavily on a thirteenth-century text called "De virtutibus lapidum" sometimes anonymous, sometimes attributed to Arnoldus Saxo. Schmidt notes that the initial descriptions of carnelian, chalcedony, and sapphire are almost literal translations from the Saxo text (Schmidt 1898, 199). Leaving aside Schmidt's bias in his characterization of the gem lore as superstitious (and hence bad), we can see the monks manipulating what they knew as accepted natural philosophy in order both to appeal to the intended worldly readers, Mechthild and her daughter, Elizabeth, as well as to constrain them. They manoeuver beliefs about the stones' power, which as indicated in the prologue, were also useful to "world-wise, clever heathen scholars" (201) to support the proper devotional outlook and praxis in the young princess.[27]

Returning from this one text back to the level of the manuscript, let us consider the different modes of transmission and transfer in play here. Although the text in the manuscript is framed by the announcement that it was written by monks to be

---

[26] To support this view, Schmidt notes that the (purer and less superstitious) church fathers like Augustine, Jerome, and Bede do *not* mention the magical powers of gem stones when they explicate the Bible passages that mention them, although they clearly had the opportunity.
[27] Scholars of medieval magic note that "Western lapidaries were mainly based on the texts of Greek and Latin origin. This tradition was then greatly enriched by material coming from the Arabic world" (Lawrence-Mathers and Escobar-Vargas 2014, 54). See also Meier 1977.

given to a young woman at her baptism, readers might wonder about the choice to give the instructive voice not only to a lay woman, but to a common woman who was unattached to a religious community, who wandered about the countryside selling things, and who cites as her source in the prologue: "slechtem geschrifftlichen synnen" [204; simple/genuine scriptural meaning] as well as what she has heard from learned people. Readers might recall stories of knowledgeable queens, such as Queen Isolde in Gottfried von Strassburg's *Tristan* (ca. 1210), who concocts a magic potion in hopes of settling her daughter in a good (i.e., one in which she can act) marriage (Rasmussen 1997, 113–135); or Cleopes of John Metham's *Amoryus and Cleopes* (1449), who instructs her lover on how to defeat a dragon with the help of a magic ring, the power of gem stones, and a potion made from herbs and ground up stones (Metham 1974, 46–50).[28] But it is less common to see a lay woman present herself as a master of this type of knowledge. However, in a devotional context, such a depiction may be less surprising considering the well-loved tradition of tales about simple, unlearned folk teaching the socially elevated about God's word – Christ being the original example, of course.[29] Yet, it does seem significant not only that both speakers are female, but also that it is a woman teaching a woman about disciplining her body and her desires so that they accord with a religious rule laid down by men. The observant reform context is what ultimately makes sense of this seeming contradiction. One of the most effective strategies undertaken by reformers was to send women who had already accepted reform to houses that were still resisting. Reforms especially of women's houses were much more successfully implemented when women delivered the message and instruction as opposed to the male priests or chaplains.[30] It seems plausible that the monks who wrote the text might also have been thinking that an audience of noble women (princesses) would be attracted by the gemstones in the story (because, of course, as the text states, most princesses and great and powerful women are) and thereby be more receptive to the instruction about their power, even if that power is meant to help remove all earthly sinful impulses from their hearts and souls, to say nothing of confining them to a world of usefulness without pleasure. But perhaps their strategy backfires a little insofar as they are depicting two women of different classes acting independently in the world, that is, outside of the usual social spaces designated for women (home and cloister). Further, while the narrative frame of the dialogue is a consumer transaction, each figure is also depicted as active in the knowledge transfer: one is engaged in delivering moral instruction to the other, who in turn is taking part in her own instruction by asking questions that direct the instruction.

---

28 My thanks to Amy N. Vines, who alerted me to John Metham's text.
29 In the German tradition, a good number of this type of tale (the so-called "Eckhart legends") emerged surrounding the famed Dominican preacher, Meister Eckhart (d. 1328). Ruh 1980a, 350–54.
30 For a somewhat notorious example of a failed reform effort, see Cescutti 2004.

When we back up another step to the level of the manuscript transmission, we note first that among a wide variety of religious instructional texts, this manuscript also collects a short dialogic text called "Das Frauchen von 21 Jahren" [The Young Woman of One and Twenty] in which a young married woman teaches an experienced master of theology about true mystical practices – that is, another text in which a laywoman lays claim to a certain authority in passing on the knowledge of the divine.[31] Second, we remember that the book itself was exchanged between two women on either side of the cloister walls, thereby bridging the divide at a time when that division had become more strictly enforced.

The exploration of the material presented here – the exchange of books between mother and daughter, the exchange of texts between clerics and their spiritual "children," as well as between two mothers concerned with their daughters' education, and the exchange of knowledge between the lady peddler and the princess – has helped to highlight the complexity of the situation of women and their relation to the patriarchal structures in which they lived in the late fifteenth century. It seems clear that the reform movement afforded women multiple opportunities to be agents of their own education, even though this education often served the aims of those wishing to suppress and control them and the base characteristics attributed to them. A particular irony of the "Geistliches Gespräch" epitomizes how the contradictions inherent in these efforts to suppress women can sometimes backfire: the potential result of the lady peddler's advice is that the princess will not only buy the rosary beads but also take to wearing more of the colorful gemstones around her neck and headdress. For if criticized for adorning herself because "she wants to be seen and praised" (according to the text, a woman's greatest desire), she could reply with good reason that she is only helping her conscience to remember death, shame, and peace (chalcedony, carnelian, and sapphire), while fighting off the fever of excessive desire (jasper). In other words, the takeaway for the princess as well as for the medieval readers in Kirchheim may have been quite the opposite of the intention of the monks at Güterstein: that is, that the best protection against the dangers of wearing ornament was to wear them.

Works Cited

Bierria, Alisa. "Missing in Action: Violence, Power, and Discerning Agency." *Hypatia* 29, no. 1 (2014): 129–45.

Blanton, Virginia, Veronica O'Mara, and Patricia Stoop, eds. *Nuns' Literacies in Medieval Europe: The Antwerp Dialogue*. Turnhout, Belgium: Brepols, 2017.

---

31 Ruh 1980b; and on this narrative paradigm generally, Poor 2014.

Brother Hermann. *Brother Hermann's Life of the Countess Yolanda of Vianden*. Translated and with a Foreword by Richard H. Lawson. Columbia, SC: Camden House, 1995.

Cescutti, Eva. "*Et clausa et janua*: Maria von Wolkenstein, Nicolaus Cusanus und das 'richtige' Klosterleben." In *Fromme Frauen Devotione Feminile*, edited by Siglinde Clementi and Cecilia Nubola, 114–40. Innsbruck: Studienverlag, 2004.

Cramer, Thomas. *Geschichte der deutschen Literatur im späten Mittelalter*. Munich: dtv, 1990.

"Dropsy." *OED* (on-line subscription) (accessed December 18, 2020).

"Dropsy." *Medicine.net* (accessed March 15, 2018).

Elm, Kaspar, ed. *Reformbemühungen und Observanzbestrebungen im spätmittelalterlichen Ordenswesen*. Berlin: Duncker & Humblot, 1989.

Glauche, Günter, and Bayerische Staatsbibliothek. *Katalog der lateinischen Handschriften der Bayerischen Staatsbibliothek München: Clm 28255–28460*. Catalogus codicum manuscriptorum Bibliothecae Monacensis. Vol. 4, Part 8. Wiesbaden: Harrossowitz, 1984.

Graf, Klaus. "Ordensreform und Literatur in Augsburg während des 15. Jahrhunderts." In *Literarisches Leben in Augsburg während des 15. Jahrhunderts*, edited by Johannes Janota and Werner Williams-Krapp, 100–159. Tübingen: Niemeyer, 1995.

Karnein, Alfred. "Mechthild von der Pfalz as Patroness: Aspects of Female Patronage in the Early Renaissance." *Medievalia et Humanistica* 22 (1995): 141–70.

Lawrence-Mathers, Anne. *Magic and Medieval Society*. New York: Routledge, 2014.

Meier, Johannes, ed. *Bruder Hermann: Leben der Gräfin Iolande von Vianden*. Breslau: W. Koebner, 1889.

Meier, Christel. *Gemma spiritalis: Methode und Gebrauch der Edelsteinallegorese vom frühen Christentum bis ins 18. Jahrhundert*. Vol. 1. Munich: Fink, 1977.

Metham, John. *The Works of John Metham*. Edited by Craig Hardin. Millwood, N.Y.: Kraus, 1974.

Neddermeyer, Uwe. *Von der Handschrift zum gedruckten Buch: Schriftlichkeit und Leseinteresse im Mittelalter und in der frühen Neuzeit. Quantitative und Qualitative Aspekte*. 2 vols. Wiesbaden: Harassowitz, 1998.

Poor, Sara S. "Women Teaching Men in the Medieval Devotional Imagination." In *Partners in Spirit: Women, Men, and Religious Life in Germany, 1100–1500*, edited by Fiona J. Griffiths and Julie Hotchin, 339–65. Turnhout: Brepols, 2014.

Poor, Sara S. "The Countess, the Abbess, and Their Books: Manuscript Circulation in a Fifteenth-Century German Family." In *Nuns Literacies in Medieval Europe: The Antwerp Dialogue*, edited by Virginia Blanton, Veronica O'Mara, and Patricia Stoop, 341–65. Turnhout: Brepols, 2017.

Rasmussen, Ann Marie. *Mothers and Daughters in Medieval German Literature*. Syracuse, NY: Syracuse University Press, 1997.

Rasmussen, Ann Marie. "Fathers to Think Back Through: The Middle High German Mother-Daughter and Father-Son Advice Poems Known as *Die Winsbeckin* and *Der Winsbecke*." In *Medieval Conduct*, edited by Kathleen Ashley and Robert L. A. Clark, 106–34. Minneapolis: University of Minnesota Press, 2001.

Rennes, Marbode of. *Marbode of Rennes' (1035–1123) De Lapidibus, Considered as a Medical Treatise with Text and Commentary and C.W. King's Translation; Together with Text and Translation of Marbode's Minor Works on Stones by John Riddle*. Translated by C.W. King and John Riddle. Wiesbaden: Franz Steiner Verlag, 1977.

Ruh, Kurt. "Eckhart-Legenden." In *Die deutsche Literatur des Mittelalters: Verfasserlexikon*, 2nd ed., edited by Kurt Ruh and Wolfgang Stammler, 2: 350–54. Berlin: De Gruyter, 1980a.

Ruh, Kurt. "Die Fromme (Selige) Müllerin." In *Die deutsche Literatur des Mittelalters: Verfasserlexikon*, 2nd ed., edited by Kurt Ruh and Wolfgang Stammler, 2: 947–77. Berlin: De Gruyter, 1980b.

Schmidt, Friedrich. "Geistliches Gespräch zwischen einer Fürstin und einer Krämerin von einem Paternoster aus Edelsteinen." *Alemannia* 26 (1898): 193–229.

Schneider, Karin. "Beziehungen zwischen den Dominikanerinnenklöstern Nürnberg und Altenhohenau im ausgehenden Mittelalter, Neue Handschriftenfunde (Medium Aevum 31)." In *Würzburger Prosastudien II: Untersuchungen zur Literatur und Sprache des Mittelalters. Kurt Ruh zum 60. Geburtstag*, edited by Peter Kesting, 211–18. Munich: Fink, 1975.

Schneider, Karin. "Die Bibliothek des Katharinenklosters in Nürnberg und die städtische Gesellschaft." In *Studien zum städtischen Bildungswesen des späten Mittelalters und der frühen Neuzeit*, edited by Bernd Moeller, Hans Patze, and Karl Stackmann, 70–82. Göttingen: Vandenhoeck & Ruprecht, 1983.

Schneider, Karin. *Deutsche mittelalterliche Handschriften der Universitätsbibliothek Augsburg. Die Signaturengruppen Cod. I.3. und Cod. III.1*. Vol. 1. Wiesbaden: Harrassowitz, 1988.

Schnell, Bernhard. *Thomas Peuntner, "Büchlein von der Liebhabung Gottes."* Munich: Artemis, 1984.

Schromm, Arnold. *Die Bibliothek des ehemaligen Zisterzienserinnenklosters Kirchheim am Ries: Buchpflege und geistiges Leben in einem schwäbischen Frauenstift*. Tübingen: Niemeyer, 1998.

Sexauer, Wolfram D. *Frühneuhochdeutsche Schriften in Kartäuser Bibliotheken: Untersuchungen zur Pflege der volksprachlichen Literatur in Kartäuserklöstern des oberdeutschen Raums bis zum Einsetzen der Reformation*. Frankfurt am Main: Peter Lang, 1978.

Stälin, Christoph Friedrich von. *Wirtembergische Geschichte: Dritter Teil. Schwaben und Südfranken. Schluß des Mittelalters. 1269–1496*. Vol. 3. Stuttgart: J. G. Cotta'scher Verlag, 1856.

Wilkins, Eithne. *The Rose-Garden Game: The Symbolic Background to the European Prayerbeads*. London: Gollancz, 1969.

Williams-Krapp, Werner. "Observanzbewegungen, monastische Spiritualität und geistliche Literatur im 15. Jahrhundert." *Internationales Archiv für Sozialgeschichte der deutschen Literatur* 20, no. 1 (1995): 1–15.

Winston-Allen, Anne. *Stories of the Rose: The Making of the Rosary in the Middle Ages*. University Park: Pennsylvania State University Press, 1997.

Winston-Allen, Anne. *Convent Chronicles: Women Writing About Women and Reform in the Late Middle Ages*. University Park: Pennsylvania State University Press, 2004.

Mary Marshall Campbell
2 Why Siegfried Has to Die: Gender, Violence, and the Social Order in the *Nibelungenlied*

Broadly speaking, writing about gender and the *Nibelungenlied* has meant writing about women and their representation – about the extent to which and in what forms female figures wield power, about their agency or relative lack thereof, about their bodies and the construction of femininity.[1] At the same time, even as the centrality of the female figures in the poem has gone undisputed – with prominent scholar Hugo Kuhn going so far as to characterize the work as the "Frauenbiographie Kriemhilds" – gender nevertheless arguably remains a concern of peripheral importance in *Nibelungenlied* scholarship.[2] In the nearly five-hundred pages Jan-Dirk Müller dedicates to explicating and interpreting the literary-historical and socio-cultural rules he sees governing the world of *Nibelungenlied* in his seminal monograph, *Spielregeln für den Untergang*, to cite but one notable example, any significant account of gender is glaringly absent.[3] In contrast, through an analysis of Kriemhild's falcon dream and the dialogue with her mother the dream occasions, Ann Marie Rasmussen demonstrates that writing about the representation of female figures is key to making sense of the disorder into which the world is plunged at the epic poem's cataclysmic end. What is more, implied in her work, I suggest, is a conceptualization of gender as an analytical category whose relevance for interpreting the *Nibelungenlied* extends beyond a consideration of the relative importance of female figures – that is, the conceptualization of gender as a means of signifying relations of power in the story. Gender is a constitutive element of the *Nibelungenlied* and is, therefore, of central importance for the interpretation of the poem.

As I have already mentioned, Rasmussen's interpretation of the *Nibelungenlied* begins with Kriemhild's prophetic dream about a falcon she lovingly raises, only to be forced to witness helplessly as it is rent apart by two eagles, and the colloquy that follows between Kriemhild and her mother, Uote, about the dream's significance for the young princess. Whereas scholars have tended to devote their attention to the dream itself, Rasmussen shifts the focus to the conversation in which

---

[1] Notable examples of scholarship on gender in the *Nibelungenlied* include: Frakes 1994; Schausten 1999; Tennant 1999; Bennewitz 1995; Bennewitz 2001; Lienert 2003b; and Renz 2012.
[2] Kuhn 1980, 15. More generally, see, for instance, Schulze 1997b, 91–92; and Renz 2012, 2–5.
[3] J-D. Müller 1998. Sarah Westphal points out the absences in her review of Müller's book. Westphal 2002, 955.

Uote counsels her daughter in love's lore that it prompts.[4] In medieval German literature, such conversations represent a literary topos that functions as a nexus for the transfer of knowledge about female gender identity.[5] The knowledge that passes via this nexus from the experienced mother, Rasmussen explains, is meant to prepare her naïve daughter to assume a socially sanctioned form of femininity that corresponds to her class, and, as such, these dialogues serve to maintain the patriarchal social order (22–23). In keeping with convention, Kriemhild, the naïve daughter, resists her mother's instruction, but Uote, the experienced mother is ultimately proved right: Kriemhild does, in fact, become a wife. Importantly, inasmuch as her defiance of conventional feminine wisdom suggests "a will to seek her own path, a will toward self-definition, a resistance to the patriarchal order," the mother-daughter exchange prefigures Kriemhild's role in the total destruction to come (73). Drawing on Teresa de Lauretis's insights into myths, Rasmussen proposes viewing Kriemhild as the female obstacle to both of the epic's heroic male subjects (i.e., Siegfried and Hagen) – an obstacle who, with increasing obduracy, resists being subsumed under the role of object assigned to her in the patriarchal order. When, at the poem's end, Kriemhild is hewn to bits, she thus pays the price for violating the social order by having arrogated to herself the position of self-determining subject. In this way, Rasmussen concludes, Kriemhild's dream portends not only the fate of her future husband, Siegfried, but also her own: the symbol of falcon also refers to her (84).

In what follows, I take as my starting point Rasmussen's interpretation of Kriemhild as the female object who resists patriarchal order. Drawing upon the theoretical insights of Teresa de Lauretis, I show how, through an analysis of the representation of violence in the first half of the *Nibelungenlied*, gender difference is the means by which relations of subjection and dominance between the subjects and objects of that violence are signified. It is by means of gender that these asymmetric relations are represented because, I suggest, the social order in the world of the poem is based upon gender order – more specifically, a relationship of subjection of female/feminine to male/masculine. This relationship is made evident in the

---

[4] Examples of scholarship that disregard the importance of the mother-daughter dialogue include: Nordmeyer 1940; F. Schröder 1956; Frakes 1984; G. Müller 1975, 96–100; Ehrismann 1998, 20; De Boor 1953, 160; and W. Schröder 1968, 69–70. In his influential monograph on the *Nibelungenlied*, Jan-Dirk Müller even characterizes the two stanzas containing the dialogue as "diejenigen Strophen, die eine Reminiszenz an Veldekes *Eneit* enthalten, die für den Fortgang der Handlung aber irrelevant sind" [those stanzas containing a reminiscence of Veldeke's *Eneit*, which are, however, irrelevant for the continuation of the plot]. J-D. Müller 1998, 99.

[5] Rasmussen 1997, 23. In the book, Rasmussen considers representations of mother-daughter relationships more broadly, arguing that they can be viewed as "a source of profound connection or disconnection for women, a place where fears and anxieties about women's similarities and dissimilarities are acted out, an arena where women's strategies for learning to survive in a patriarchal social order find elemental representation." Rasmussen 1997, 18.

heroic figure of Siegfried for whom, I argue, becoming a king – that is, the male hero tasked with the work of creating distinction and difference and thereby establishing patriarchal order – depends upon conquering a bride – that is, establishing gender order by gaining mastery over the ultimate female object.[6] As I will demonstrate, that Siegfried will fail at this task begins to be legible in the scene of his arrival in Worms in the poem's third *aventiure*, and the consequences of that failure are evinced in the ambiguity concerning who is "undertân" [subject] to whom. That ambiguity only grows as the story unfolds. Even though Siegfried is successful in his quest for Kriemhild, his victory is also his defeat, for, in winning her as his bride, he succumbs to her as his ultimate female object. It is for this transgression of the patriarchal order that Siegfried must die – a fact made manifest in the representation of his death. In this way, Siegfried's death should be read as a "spiegelnde Strafe" [punishment that mirrors the transgression]. Moreover, I argue, "Siegfried's tragedy" does not stem "from his willful rejection of the woman who embodies this aspect of his destiny (i.e., Brunhild)," as Rasmussen, for example, argues it does (79). Instead, it is as a consequence of his transgression of the patriarchal order that he is supposed to uphold.

1 Distinction, Violence, and the Male Hero

That the social order in the *Nibelugenlied* is inextricably bound up with representations of gender and violence becomes apparent already in the poem's third *aventiure* and its portrayal of what happens when, on his quest to win Kriemhild as his bride, Siegfried arrives in Worms. By this point in the story, Siegfried has already been introduced in the second *aventiure* as the embodiment of courtly ideals. The son of King Siegmund of the Netherlands, he has been exemplarily schooled in the ways of the court. Moreover, all this attentive preparation has culminated in Siegfried's initiation into knighthood in a grand ceremony followed by a lavish feast, the details of which make up the bulk of the second *aventiure*. And yet to the chagrin of the land's noblemen, Siegfried has made it known that he is not yet ready to ascend the throne.[7] At the beginning of the third *aventiure*, Siegfried now turns his

---

6 By "patriarchy," I mean a historically specific, complex system by which women, in differing ways and through multiple and varying social institutions, have been subordinated to men of the same class, race, ethnicity, or other social group. See Bennett 2006, particularly 55–60 and 70–79.
7 Bartsch and De Boor 2002, Strophe 42, line 4, hereafter cited parenthetically as NL followed by strophe number and line numbers. Unless otherwise noted, all translations are mine with consultation of Hatto's English translation, as well as of the modern German renderings of Brackert, Grosse, and Heinzle.

mind to matters of "hôhe minne" [NL 47, 1; high love or courtly love].[8] His sights set on attaining "stæte minne" [NL 48, 2; constant love], he heeds the counsel of kinsmen and vassals in Xanten to pursue an affiance befitting his noble estate and makes it known: "sô wil ich Kriemhilden nemen, / Die scœnen juncfrouwen von Burgonden lant / durch ir unmâzen scœne" [NL 48, 4–49, 2; On account of her inordinate beauty, I shall take Kriemhild, the fair maiden of Burgundy]. Clad in the most princely of finery, Siegfried and a company of eleven men therefore set out for the Burgundian court to win the hand of a maid whom he knows only through tales of her legendary beauty. When Siegfried is greeted in Worms, however, these are not the stories to which he refers in response to Gunther's inquiry as to the purpose of his visit. "Mir wart gesaget mære in mînes vater lant," he tells Kriemhild's brother, "daz hie bî iu wæren (daz het ich gern' erkant) / die küenesten recken (des hân ich vil vernomen) / die ie künec gewunne; dar umbe bin ich her bekomen" [NL 107; I have heard told in my father's land – and I had to ascertain it for myself – that here, in your country, were to be found the most valiant warriors a king ever had. I heard this often; that is why I have come here.]. After explaining that he has heard imputed to Gunther a "degenheite" [warrior-spirit] excelling that of all other kings, he then declares: "[i]ch bin ouch ein recke und solde krône tragen. / ich wil daz gerne füegen, daz sie von mir sagen, / daz ich habe von rehte liute und lant. / dar umbe sol mîn êre und ouch mîn houbet wesen pfant" [NL 108, 1 and 109; I, too, am a warrior and am supposed to wear the crown already. I wish to bring to pass that it is said of me that I rightfully possess people and lands. For this, my honor and my head shall be the pledge]. Hereupon, Kriemhild's would-be suitor makes clear how he means to prove himself: "ich wil an iu ertwingen, swaz ir muget hân: lant unde bürge, daz sol mir werden *undertân*" [NL 110, 3–4, emphasis added; I intend to wrest from you everything you possess: lands and castles – all of it shall be *subject to me*]. Based on this initial exchange alone, it would seem that Siegfried has not undertaken his expedition to Worms for the purpose of wooing after all – and yet, as the audience well knows, he has. As Walter Haug has noted, the scene of the hero's arrival in Worms ranks chief among the interpretive challenges of the *Nibelungenlied* (Haug 1989, 298). Scholars have struggled to account for why Siegfried would court Kriemhild by challenging her brother to a duel in which both life and

---

[8] In his annotation to this verse, Grosse explains that the term designates a "zentraler Begriff der mittelhochdeutschen Minnelyrik; er bezeichnet die liebende Verehrung, die der Ritter einer Dame der höfischen Gesellschaft, deren hohes Ansehen außer Frage steht, entgegenbringt" [a central concept of Middle High German love lyric; it designates the loving veneration that the knight pays to the lady of courtly society whose high regard is beyond question]. Grosse 2002, 744–45, note to strophe 47. That said, the meaning of "hôhe minne" is clearly inflected in this context by "stæte minne" [constant love] in the following strophe, which, as Ehrismann points out, connotes conjugal love. Ehrismann 1975, 340. For a brief account of the meaning of "hôhe minne," see Bumke 2008, 516–29.

patrimony are at stake – but not a bride (Haug 1989, 298). In recent decades, most have sought an explanation for the implicit contradiction in the *Nibelungenlied* poet's melding of epic material and heroic tradition with the conventions and ethos of the courtly literature that was popular around the year 1200 when the poem was likely composed.[9] Instead of attempting to explain the inconsistency (away), I propose reading Siegfried's conflation of bridal quest with conquest as articulating a relationship between gender, violence, and kingship that is important for interpreting the poem as a whole. There is, I suggest, a reason that, in the same *aventiure*, the narrator uses the same word – *undertân* [subject] – to describe both the relationship that Siegfried would establish with Gunther through battle and the relationship that Siegfried will establish with Kriemhild through marriage: "Swaz man der werbenden nâch ir minne sach, / Kriemhilt in ir sinne ir selber nie verjach, / daz si deheinen wolde ze eime trûte hân. / er was ir noch vil vremde, dem si wart sider *undertân*" [NL 46, emphasis added; However many suitors were seen in pursuit of her affection, Kriemhild never admitted to herself in her own mind that she wanted any of them as a beloved. Still completely unknown to her then was he to whom she would later become *subject*].[10] Wooing here is equated to conquest, in that both entail the hero making an object *undertân* [subject] to him. In this way, I argue that, through the apparent gap in the narrative logic that emerges upon Siegfried's arrival in Worms, part of the "sex-gender system" that informs the fictional world of the poem begins to come into view and, with it, a way of understanding the story of the *Nibelungenlied* and its antinomies (de Lauretis 1987, 5).

Following Rasmussen's lead, I look to Teresa de Lauretis's theorization of the representation of violence and gender for a way of looking at this implied identity between courting and conquering.[11] In her essay, "The Violence of Rhetoric," de Lauretis posits two general kinds of violence that prevail in representations of violence: one "male," the other "female."[12] By this, however, she does not mean that

---

9 See, for example, Greenfield 1994, 184–85 and 190; G. Müller 1975, 98–101; Nagel 1977, 519–21; Jaeger 1985, 192–93; and, in an attenuated form, J-D. Müller 1998, 86.
10 Elisabeth Lienert has drawn attention to this passage at the beginning of the third *aventiure*, commenting that "*undertân*-werden und heiraten ist für Frauen offenbar dasselbe" [being made subject to someone and marrying is evidently the same thing for women]. Lienert 2003a, 149. See also Hasty 1998, 81, 88, and 92.
11 Rasmussen 1997, 77–80. Whereas Rasmussen draws upon de Lauretis's insights in order to explicate the poem's framing of the narrative positions of subject and object in terms of gender, I focus instead on the representation of gender and violence as a means of representing relationships in the poem.
12 De Lauretis 1987, ch. 2 "The Violence of Rhetoric," 42. Important to note is that, in this essay, de Lauretis's usage of "female/male" and "feminine/masculine" does not conform rigorously to the conventional association of the former with "sex" (i.e., a biological given) and the latter with "gender" (i.e., a social construct) in feminist thought. She describes, for instance, the subject of violence at one point as "masculine," and yet, in the very next paragraph, states that, in doing violence, he

the former is necessarily violence against a man and the latter violence against a woman, but rather that, through the representation of an act of violence, the "object is perceived or apprehended as either masculine or feminine" (de Lauretis 1987, 42). In other words, it is through the representation of violence that the object of that violence is differentially gendered masculine or feminine and the violence done to it understood as a kind of violence done to either a masculine or feminine object.[13] According to de Lauretis, the subject of violence is gendered in the process as well, but because "'man' is by definition the subject of culture and of any social act," the subject of violence, unlike the object, can only ever be "masculine" (de Lauretis 1987, 43). When violence is thus represented, the masculine subject of that violence is brought into relation with its object, whereby the relation established with the feminine object – regardless of whether it is "a woman, a man, or an inanimate object" – is one of "conquest, domination, and aggression"; while the relation with the masculine object is one characterized by "reciprocity" or "equality" (de Lauretis 1987, 42–43). For de Lauretis, "the representation of violence is inseparable from the notion of gender" not only because it is by means of gender that differential relationships between subjects and objects of violence are represented, but also because (the representation of) violence is a means by which gender relations are reproduced.[14]

What is more, it is violence upon a female object that de Lauretis sees as constitutive of myths, as is evinced in the corrective she offers to Jurij Lotman's theory of the origin of plot in which he postulates that the world of myth is populated by but two characters – the hero (or "mobile character") and the "immobile" "obstacle (boundary)."[15]

> In the mythical text, then, the hero must be male regardless of the gender of the character, because the obstacle, whatever its personification (sphinx or dragon, sorceress or villain) is morphologically female – and indeed, simply, the womb, the earth, the space of his movement.

---

is "constructed as human being and as male." De Lauretis 1987, 43. The reason for her relatively unconventional usage of these terms may lie in her understanding of the relationship between "sex," "sexuality," and "gender." This conceptualization receives relatively clear expression in a later essay where she contends that "distinguishing gender from sex and sexuality" is only "theoretically necessary," for "in social, subjective, and psychic reality, gender and sexuality are in fact interrelated." De Lauretis 2000, 160. In order to avoid any confusion as to my meaning, I have tried to adhere to conventional usage wherever possible.

13 The example de Lauretis offers here to illustrate the way in which both the object and the act of violence are gendered in representation is helpful. In the phrase "the rape of nature," she explains, "nature" is understood as "feminine" at the same time that "rape" is defined "as violence done to a feminine other." De Lauretis 1987, 42.

14 De Lauretis 1987, 33. Important for understanding de Lauretis's argument here is that she conceives of gender both as a "sociocultural construct" and a "system of representation which assigns meaning [. . .] to individuals in society." De Lauretis 1987, 5.

15 Lotman 1979, 167–68; and de Lauretis 1987, 43.

As he crosses the boundary and "penetrates" the other space, the mythical subject is constructed as human being and as male; he is the active principle of culture, the establisher of distinction, the creator of differences. Female is what is not susceptible to transformation, to life or death; she (it) is an element of plot-space, a topos, a resistance, matrix and matter.
(de Lauretis 1987, 43–44)

In her explication of Lotman's text, de Lauretis thus brings out the gendered and gendering violence at work in myth that Lotman's gender-neutral rhetoric obscures; and she does this in order to point up how both his scholarly discourse on myth and the discourse of myth itself produce "the object as female and the female as object" by bringing it/her into subjection to the subject – a subject who is thereby en-gendered as male and constructed as male (de Lauretis 1987, 45). It is, however, her analysis of myth that is of primary interest to me here – more precisely, her analysis of how, in performing acts of violence, the mythical hero is constructed as masculine and the object of his violence as feminine; and how, at the same time, it is through this violence that differences and distinctions are brought into being and social order thus established (de Lauretis 1984, 117–21). For de Lauretis, creating differences and distinctions is the principal work of the mythical hero, and, as she writes elsewhere, "the primary distinction on which all others depend is not, say, life and death, but rather, sexual difference."[16] Importantly, her analysis is not restricted to myths. Just as Lotman's theory pertains as much to what he calls the "modern plot-text" as it does to the mythological text, so too does de Lauretis's analytical approach apply as much to "fictional narrative" as it does to myths (Lotman 1979, 163–64; de Lauretis 1984, 117). As I will show in what follows, her account of how order is engendered in mythical texts through representations of violence which depend upon gender difference offers a way of making sense of not only the contradiction implied in the scene of Siegfried's arrival in Worms but also, more generally, the precipitous descent into disorder narrated in the *Nibelungenlied*.

2 Ambiguity 1: Siegfried's Arrival in Worms

When Siegfried rides into Worms and challenges Gunther to a duel, the violence he threatens would place the Burgundian lands and castles – and, by extension, the king who rules over them – into the same asymmetric relation of power in which a bride is (or, more precisely, should be) placed with respect to her husband. That is

---

16 De Lauretis 1984, 119. For de Lauretis, "sexual difference" also means "gender difference," for, as she posits in "The Violence of Rhetoric," "biological' sexual difference is the ground (in Pierce's term) of gender." De Lauretis 1987, 45. See also de Lauretis 2000, especially 159–70. I have nevertheless tried to hew to the distinction made between "sex" and "gender" in conventional usage.

also to say, in being made *undertân* [subject] to Siegfried (i.e., the subject), both conquered kingdom – together with its vanquished king – and wooed bride (i.e., the objects) are constructed as feminine; and, by the same token, Siegfried (i.e., the subject) is constructed both as "human being and as male" and as the hero.[17] However, and this qualification is crucial, the status of male hero that is conferred upon Siegfried through the violence he does is one that is shaped by historical context and inflected by the social class of the poem's contemporary audience: in other words, being made a hero in the *Nibelungenlied* means being made king. To the extent that Siegfried assumes the role of "the active principle of culture, the establisher of distinction, the creator of differences," he thus does so as a medieval ruler who establishes the distinctions and creates the differences upon which the patriarchal order is based (de Lauretis, 1987, 43). It is for this reason that it is only after he has won Kriemhild as his bride – which is also to say, after he appears to have constructed himself as the king – that Siegfried can return home, finally ready to accept the crown from his father.

It is also for this reason that the narrator's terse account of Siegfried's coronation and the transfer of royal authority it effects centers on the judicial powers with which the new king is endowed. According to that account, after formally declaring his son king, Siegmund then "bevalch im sîne krône, gerihte und ouch daz lant. / sît was er ir aller meister, die er ze rehte vant, / unt dar er rihten solde. daz wart alsô getân, / daz man sêre vorhte der schœnen Kriemhilden man" [NL 714; committed to him (i.e., Siegfried) his crown, his judicature, and, furthermore, his lands. From that time on, he was the lord (*meister*) over all those who appeared before his judicial court and where he had jurisdiction. Justice was carried out in such a way that fair Kriemhild's husband was greatly feared]. To become king is thus to become the land's supreme judge, and, by the same token, to wear the crown therefore consists in "rihten" – a polysemous verb whose meanings include "to judge," "to rule," and "to set to rights."[18] Not only does this conception of kingship find repeated expression throughout the poem,[19] but it is also consonant with the notion that prevailed at the time the *Nibelungenlied* was written that an ideal ruler was, above all else, the "oberster Rechtswahrer" [highest protector of justice] and therefore guarantor of order.[20] Significantly, as implied by the fear Siegfried strikes into the hearts

---

[17] De Lauretis 1987, 43. See also, de Lauretis 1984, 119.
[18] For the full range of meanings, see Lexer 1992, vol. 2, 433–35; and B. Hennig 2014, 258. For a legal-historical account of the meaning of "rihten" and how it developed over the course of the Middle Ages, see Kroeschell 1995, 147–51 and Köbler 1970, especially 101–13.
[19] Notably, for example, at NL 522–23.
[20] Kaufmann 1978, 1017. According to legal historian Hermann Krause, the medieval king's duty as a judge was equaled in importance only by his duty as a military leader. Krause 1952, 15. In addition to explaining the king's essential role in keeping "öffentliche Ordnung" [public order] by dispensing justice, literary scholar Joachim Bumke has also pointed out that the chaos that ensued in

of his subject in carrying out justice, "rihten" entails the use of – or, at least, the threat of – violence. In short, through the gendered and gendering representation of violence that informs Siegfried's conflation of bridal quest and conquest, we are given to understand that what makes a hero, what makes a king is his establishing of differences – differences between hero and obstacle, conqueror and conquered, and so on – all of which, according to de Lauretis's analysis of the hero, should be seen as fundamentally grounded in the difference between female and male. In this way, it makes all the more sense that, when describing how King Siegfried keeps order by making distinctions in his capacity as judge, the narrator refers to him as "der schœnen Kriemhilden man" [NL 714, 4; fair Kriemhild's husband].

Even before Siegfried announces his intention to depart for Worms, the narrator has already begun preparing his audience to see Siegfried's threat of violence as the act of a king in the making. His recounting of how Siegfried sets out on his expedition to woo Kriemhild comes directly on the heels of the narrator's account of the young prince's knighting. Historical documents and poetic works from the period alike attest to the widespread view of the ceremonial girting with the sword as a "Voraussetzung für das selbständige Handeln eines jungen Fürsten" [Bumke 2008, 319; precondition for a young prince's agency]. More specifically, a young prince's entrance into the knighthood is generally represented in those texts as a prelude to his first military campaign, his coronation, or his nuptials.[71] In the case of Siegfried, with his reference to the kingdom's magnates who would have gladly seen the prince ascend the throne, the narrator points out that Siegfried's knighting might have been followed by his coronation, were it not for the fact that "des engerte niht her Sîvrit, der vil wætlîche man" [NL 42, 4; Lord Siegfried, the very stately man, did not want it]. Despite the magnates' expectation that his coronation would follow his knighting, Siegfried is not yet ready to be king. Before he can wear the crown, he must first conquer a bride. That the audience is to understand this to be a necessary precondition for kingship can be inferred from what Siegfried himself proclaims just after arriving in Worms: "[i]ch bin ouch ein recke und solde krône tragen. / ich wil daz gerne füegen, daz sie von mir sagen, / daz ich habe von rehte liute und lant" [NL 109, 1–3; I, too, am a warrior and am supposed to wear the crown already. I wish to bring to pass that it is said of me that I rightfully possess people and lands]. Siegfried's bridal quest is as much about his conquest of Kriemhild as feminine object as it is about proving that he should rightfully wear his father's crown.

---

the wake of the death of Henry VI in 1197 moved poets of the time – perhaps most famously, Walther von der Vogelweide – to reflect on the meaning of law in their work. Bumke 2008, 34–35.
21 Bumke 2008, 318–23. Schultz stresses the significance of the knighting ceremony as a rite of passage into adulthood for the nobility. Schultz 1991, 534–35. Regarding the representation of the ceremony and attendant festivities more generally, see Marquardt 1985, 52–62.

3 Ambiguity 2: Hagen's Reports

As we learn when Hagen briefs Gunther on the heroic feats that Siegfried has already brought about, Kriemhild is not the first feminine obstacle that Siegfried has had to overcome. After receiving word that a group of twelve magnificently attired knights is approaching the court, Gunther summons Hagen, his fierce and trusty vassal, in the hope that he might be able to identify the unknown warriors. Based on the look of the strangers and what he has heard told of King Siegmund's son, Hagen surmises that Siegfried must be among them and offers Gunther a condensed account of two of Siegfried's past heroic deeds. Through the first, and longer, of Hagen's two reports, we learn how Siegfried has made himself lord of the Nibelungs and their hoard and taken possession of both the sword, Balmung, and Alberich's "tarnkappe" [invisibility cloak]. With the second, much shorter report, we are told that, after he slew a dragon and bathed in its blood, Siegfried's skin grew so horny that he is now impervious to the weapons of man. By way of Hagen's reports, we thus hear just enough about the storied exploits of Siegfried's past to know how he has come by all of the heroic attributes which will be essential to the plot of this story. However, I argue, the reports of youthful conquests should not be read as an attempt on the part of the anonymous poet to integrate the incongruous, yet indispensable vestiges of the "farbenreiches altheroisches Erzählgut" [colorful old-heroic narrative material] of Siegfried's literary-historical past with "seiner neuen höfischen Konzeption" [his new courtly conception] of the heroic figure – as modern scholars have often been wont to read them.[22] Instead, they frame our understanding of Siegfried's encounter with the ultimate feminine obstacle – for him, Kriemhild – and thereby allow us to see the significance of that encounter for social order at the same time that they make evident that social order depends upon gender difference in the world of the poem.

Hagen begins the first report by relating that, while out riding alone, Siegfried happened upon a throng of men that was gathered around the "[h]ort der Nibelunges" [NL 89, 1; hoard of the Nibelungs] which they had just carried out of a mountain cave. Having set the scene, Hagen then points up what was wrong with what the young prince saw: "nu hœret wunder sagen, / wie in wolden teilen der Nibelunge man. / daz sach der degen Sîvrit; den helt es wundern began" [NL 89, 3–4; Now hear told the remarkable tale of how the Nibelung men wished to divide it (i.e., the treasure). Siegfried, the warrior, saw this; the hero began to marvel at the sight]. The problem with the scene is that the two kings, Nibelung and Schilbung, are intent upon dividing up the treasure. Indeed, the division of the hoard is

---

[22] Here, I quote Bert Nagel, but it is an interpretation that recurs relatively frequently in the secondary literature, albeit with some variation. Nagel 1977, 517–18. See, for example, Bumke 1958, 262n1.

so significant that it bears repeated mention. Hagen points it out again for the first time two stanzas later when he relates how, after learning of Siegfried's presence and greeting him, the two kings "den scaz in bâten teilen, den wætlîchen man" [NL 91, 3; bade the stately man to divide the treasure for them]. In the very next stanza, Hagen emphasizes the division yet again. After limning the contours of the vast amount of gold and gems of which the hoard is composed, he namely reminds his listeners that "daz sold' in allez teilen des küenen Sîvrides hant" [NL 92, 4; all of it was supposed to be divided by the hand of bold Siegfried]. Despite the fact that Nibelung and Schilbung gave him "ze miete daz Nibelunges swert" [NL 93, 1; Nibelung's sword (i.e., their father's sword) as payment], the young prince could not carry out the task. It was this inability to divide the treasure that enraged the two kings, which, in turn, led Siegfried to strike them and their retinue of twelve giants down, before single-handedly vanquishing an army of seven hundred men and reducing the kings' fearsome vassal, Alberich, to submission. Importantly, Siegfried brought all of this about with Schilbung and Nibelung's father's sword, Balmung. Through Hagen's retelling of Siegfried's conquest of the Nibelungs, we are given to understand that what Siegfried chances upon at the foot of that mountain is a scene of patriarchal order in peril. King Nibelung, having presumably died, has been succeeded by his two sons, Schilbung and Nibelung. However, as is evinced through the symbols of the hoard and the sword, while they may wear the crown, Nibelung's two sons have nevertheless failed in their duty as kings to maintain the patriarchal order. To the poem's medieval audience, the hoard both symbolized royal dominion and evidenced its legitimate exercise (Schumann 1978, 243; Erler 1978, 111). When they heard that Schilbung and Nibelung were in the midst of dividing it, the contemporary audience thus understood them to be dissipating their patriarchal heritage and authority. The sword, like the hoard, belonged to the regalia, but it also bore added symbolic import in that the girding with the sword constituted a central part of a king's coronation (Hüpper 1990, 1572; Erler 1978, 110). What is more, thanks to its essential role in the knighting ceremony, the sword came to be emblematic of manhood for the nobility in the High Middle Ages.[23] Giving their deceased father's sword away thus suggests not only an abdication of patriarchal power but also an act of self-castration on the part of Schilbung and Nibelung. In slaying them and assuming their place as king, Siegfried dispatches the female obstacles that had threatened patriarchal order.

Hagen's second report is, by contrast, a single stanza in length: "Noch weiz ich an im mêre, daz mir ist bekant. / einen lintrachen den sluoc des heldes hant. /

---

[23] Hüpper 1990, 1571. To illustrate how endemic the association of the sword with masculinity was in medieval German culture I cite here two further examples. In legal texts, the portion of a deceased husband's estate that fell to his agates was referred to as the "Schwertteil" [sword share] or "Speerteil" [spear share]. Ogris 1990, 1574. In literature, centuries before Freud, medieval German poets frequently wielded swords as phallic symbols. See, for instance, Heiland 2015, 313.

er badet' sich in dem bluote: sîn hût wart hurnîn. / des snîdet in kein wâfen; daz ist dicke worden scîn" [NL 100; There is still more that I know about him. With his own hand, the hero slew a dragon. He bathed in its blood: his skin became like horn. Thence, no weapon penetrates him; this has been made manifest on many occasions]. Here, Hagen's pithiness is apt. The dragon is figured in medieval literature as the embodiment of otherness, the antonym of distinction and difference made incarnate.[24] In medieval saints' legends, when the dragon is not cast in the role of the Devil himself, it appears as the prefiguration of God's adversary (Hammer 2009, 229). While dragons are sometimes associated with the Devil in courtly and heroic epics as well, they are usually represented in these works as a threat to social order in this world, and any potential salvation-historical dimensions of this threat are, as a rule, not integral to the stories (Hammer 2009, 235–37 and 245–46). Despite the differences, hagiographical and secular discourses share a common conception of dragons as being opposed to rightly ordered humanity. This conception is evinced in both the language that poets use to depict dragons and their depictions of them. As Claude Lecouteux points out, there is as little agreement among medieval German poets with respect to the words they use to refer to dragons as there is concerning the details of their appearance.[25] The dragon can be called *wurm*, *tracke*, *slange*, *serpant*, *lintwurm*, *lintdrache*, *lint*, *unk*, *schozslang*, or *schußwurm*, and each of these terms, Lecouteux surmises, is likely meant to conjure up the mental image of a different serpent-like beast.[26] The conception of the dragon as an embodiment of disorder is manifest with particular vividness in the first detailed depiction of a dragon in Middle High German (ca. 1210 and 1220), which appeared in Wirnt von Grafenberg's *Wigalois*: the dragon we see here is, namely, a disconcerting assemblage of body parts abscised from a host of beasts both real and fabulous.[27] When we hear that Siegfried has killed a *lintrachen* [dragon] without any definite characteristics in a nondescript battle, we are thus being told that he has conquered an incarnation of the lack of distinction and difference. And, it is most appropriate that, through the impenetrability he acquires by bathing in the dragon's blood, Siegfried becomes a

---

24 Similarly, see Riches 2003, 200.
25 Lecouteux 1979, 13–19. More broadly, see Riches 2003, 200.
26 Lecouteux 1979, 13–19. With respect to the descriptions of dragons in heroic epic in particular, Christa Agnes Tuczay similarly observes that "die Heldenepik [vermittelt] nur eine sehr spärliche Kenntnis vom Aussehen der Drachen, lediglich die typischen Attribute werden immer wieder wie stehende Formeln wiederholt" [heroic epic conveys only a very scant knowledge of the appearance of dragons – typical attributes are merely repeated over and over again like a fixed formula]. Tuczay 2006, 177.
27 According to Lecouteux, onto a giant serpentine trunk, Wirnt von Grafenberg grafts body parts snatched from descriptions of a swordfish (*gladius*), a sawfish (*serra*), a basilisk (*basiliscus*), and a griffin; and, what is more, he brings his picture of the dragon, Pfetan, to life by likening individual parts or characteristics of the monster's body to those of a boar, a crocodile, a cock, a mule, a rotting eel, a bear, a peacock, and a steinbock. Lecouteux 1979, 23–29. See Wirnt von Grafenberg 2014, 5025–76.

kind of embodiment of heroic masculinity: his horn-hard integument physically differentiates him from the rest of the world at the same time that it enhances his prowess for making differences. In short, through Hagen's two reports, we see that what makes Siegfried a hero is that, through his use of violence in overcoming obstacles, he creates difference and establishes order. Equally significant, however, is that they also allow us to see that our apprehension of his creation of differences and establishing of order through violence is made possible by the fact that that violence is represented by means of a notion of gender difference which itself is predicated upon the dominance of male/masculine over female/feminine. Social order is predicated upon gender order in the poem, and it is therefore social order that is at stake when Siegfried faces the ultimate feminine obstacle: a beautiful woman and object of his love.

4 Who is Subject to Whom?

As foretold by Kriemhild's falcon dream, Siegfried does indeed succeed in his mission to take Kriemhild to wife. However, that does not necessarily mean that he overcomes her as his obstacle. On the contrary, I argue, insofar as, in his effort to attain Kriemhild, Siegfried actively subverts the social order that he is supposed to engender and maintain – he succumbs to her. As will become clear in the following discussion, it is his failure to overcome the female obstacle – which is also to say, his failure to (re-)establish patriarchal order – that precipitates his demise in the *Nibelungenlied*'s sixteenth *aventiure*.

That Siegfried will fail to master Kriemhild – and therefore fail to bring about patriarchal order – is signaled no sooner than he has challenged Gunther to defend the Burgundian throne in a duel. While the violence that he threatens would make him lord both over Burgundy as its king and over Kriemhild as her husband, Siegfried never actually follows through with that threat. Instead, an altercation between Siegfried and the Burgundians ensues, and just as it seems their incendiary words are about to set off open conflict, the thought of Kriemhild, "die hêrlîchen meit" [NL 123, 4; the lordly maiden], abruptly interposes itself, signaling a weakening of Siegfried's resolve. When, shortly thereafter, in response to Gunther's offer that "allez daz wir hân, / geruochet irs nâch êren, daz sî iu *undertân*, / und sî mit iu geteilet lîp unde guot" [NL 127, 1–3, emphasis added; everything that we possess shall be subject to you, and our lives and our goods shall be shared with you – provided you accept it according to honor], the hero becomes "ein lützel sanfter gemuot" [NL 127, 4; somewhat more well-disposed], Siegfried's threat of violence has been successfully averted, and his challenge to battle goes all but forgotten.

This scene has figured prominently in scholarship dealing with the representation of kingship and, more generally, power relations in the *Nibelungenlied*. For some scholars, Gunther's response to Siegfried's threat bespeaks a troubling weakness in Burgundy's ruler. Roswitha Wisniewski, for instance, has stressed the import of the literal meaning of Gunther's words, contending that his submissiveness in the face of Siegfried's aggression provides the first clear indication that he represents a "rex iniquus" [unjust king].[28] In the view of most critics, however, Gunther proves himself in this scene to be, to quote Siegfried Beyschlag, "der verantwortliche Herrscher" [the responsible ruler] whose words demonstrate both his conformance with expectations of him as a lord vis-à-vis his guest as well as his diplomatic acumen as king.[29] According to this view, Gunther's offer, as, for example, Jan-Dirk Müller has argued, should be construed as an expression of hospitality in the form of a "höfische Floskel" [empty courtly figure of speech] which has no real implications for his lordship (J-D. Müller 1974, 100). That said, in the medieval texts that scholars such as Beyschlag and Müller adduce in order to show that Gunther acts exemplarily with respect to custom, the circumstances under which those lords make ostensibly analogous utterances differ from those depicted in the *Nibelungenlied* in at least one crucial aspect: in those poems, the guest does not announce himself by declaring his intention to usurp his host's crown.[30] Context is, of course, determinative.

In this context, the interpretation of Gunther's offer as an unequivocal expression of hospitality is belied by the fact that his verbiage (i.e., "iu undertân" [subject to you]) echoes that of Siegfried when he had proclaimed that Burgundy's "lant unde bürge, daz sol mir werden *undertân*" [NL 110, 4, emphasis added; lands and castles –

---

28 Wisniewski 1973, 170, 172, and 186. Similarly, Hasty posits that, the juxtaposition of Gunther and his brothers' reaction to Ortwin and Hagen's expressed indignation shows that "the conciliatory attitude of the Burgundian kings amounts to acceding shamefully to Siegfried's demands without resistance." Hasty 1998, 83. For Gottfried Weber, Gunther's weakness is evidenced less in the content of his speech than in the fact that he dithers. Weber 1963, 67.

29 Beyschlag 1951/1952, 104. For similar arguments, see, for example, Reichert 2017, 10–11; Haug 1989, 298–99; and Murdoch 1998, 237–39. The case for Gunther's diplomatic prowess is perhaps most cogently formulated by Otfried Ehrismann, who characterizes Gunther's offer as a way by which, "ihm Gunther in der Formel der Gastfreundschaft das anbieten kann, was er ihm zuvor, mit der Kampfansage konfrontiert, verweigern mußte" [Gunther, using the formula of hospitality, is able to offer Siegfried that which he previously had to deny Siegfried when confronted with Siegfried's challenge to battle]. Ehrismann 1987, 119–20.

30 Beyschlag refers to Karl Hauck's study of ritual feasting in which Hauck adduces a scene from the eleventh-century Latin poem *Ruodlieb* to illustrate the benedictive function of the guest in literature of the tenth and eleventh centuries. While the words of greeting spoken by the host in the scene from *Ruodlieb* are reminiscent of those of Gunther, neither the red-headed guest nor his host is a king, which also means that their conflict does not concern the legitimacy of their respective kingship. Hauck 1950, 618; and Beyschlag 1951/1952, 104n29. Müller cites Constantine's welcoming of Rother in *König Rother*, but, while this exchange may involve two kings and Constantine's words may bear some resemblance to those of Gunther, Constantine's statement is, nevertheless, not a response to an explicit challenge to Rother/Dietrich's challenge to his kingship. Bennewitz, et al. 2000, lines 1275–87. See also J-D. Müller 1974, 100n37.

all of it shall be subject to me]. In fact, Gunther's words signify a problem that reverberates throughout the first half of the poem. This problem can be heard in Kriemhild's seemingly unmotivated assertion to Brunhild at the beginning of the fourteenth *aventiure* that "ich hân einen man, / daz elliu disiu rîche zu sînen handen solden stân" [NL 815, 3–4; I have a husband of such greatness that he ought to have dominion over all these kingdoms] – an assertion that Brunhild interprets as Kriemhild's claim that the lands of her husband, Gunther, should be "undertân" [subject] to Kriemhild's husband, Siegfried (NL 816, 3).[31] Importantly, it is Kriemhild's assertion that precipitates the heated quarrel between the two queens, which will, in turn, occasion Siegfried's murder. In the immediate wake of the queens' quarrel, this same problem can once again be heard in the otherwise inexplicable justification Hagen offers Gunther for eliminating Siegfried: namely, that "ob Sîfrit niht enlebte, sô wurde im undertân / vil der künege lande" [NL 870, 3–4; if Siegfried were no longer alive, then many kingdoms would be subject (*undertân*) to him (i.e., Gunther)]. In light of this broader context, what might be considered an unequivocally figurative expression of hospitality elsewhere assumes here significantly more equivocal meaning. What is communicated with the equivocality of Gunther's offer, I suggest, is that, because Siegfried's challenge to battle has gone unanswered, the question he raises with it remains unresolved: who is subject to whom and, therefore, who should be king? However, this ambiguity extends beyond Siegfried and Gunther. It also involves Kriemhild, for Siegfried's acceptance of her brother's offer cannot be understood in isolation from what it follows: the intervening thought of "die hêrlîchen meit" [NL 123, 4; the lordly maiden].[32] The fact that it is the thought of Kriemhild that diverts Siegfried from his course of conquest suggests that she represents the obstacle to his establishing his dominance in Worms. It is a suggestion made more emphatic through the narrator's description of Kriemhild as "hêrlich" – a word that literally means "equivalent to a lord" – implying that it is she who, at least in some sense, holds the power.[33] In short, the poem's third *aventiure* ends by raising the crucial question: who here is subordinate to whom?

---

31 While Jan-Dirk Müller points out that "Gunthers Angebot entspricht fast wörtlich Sîvrits Forderung" [Gunther's offer corresponds almost verbatim to Siegfried's challenge], he nonetheless overlooks its resonance with Kriemhild's statement at the beginning of the fourteenth *aventiure*. J-D. Müller 1974, 99. See also J-D. Müller 1998, 410–11. Conversely, Nagel asserts that Kriemhilds's provocative statement of praise for Siegfried contains a deliberate "Anklang an Siegfrieds frühere Provokation der Burgunden" [similarity to Siegfried's earlier provocation of the Burgundians], but he fails to hear in it the echoes of Gunther's offer. Nagel 1977, 473.
32 See G. Müller 1975, 100.
33 Voorwinden 2006, 281. Of note is that it is in the context of his analysis of "Siegfrieds Herrschaft" [Siegfried's lordship] that Voorwinden points out the semantic relationship between "hêrre" [lord] and "hêrlich" [lordly, magnificent, noble]. He overlooks the fact that the narrator applies the adjective to Kriemhild as well. Kriemhild's association with lordship is echoed mere stanzas later when the narrator refers to Kriemhild as "diu küneginne hêr" [NL 133, 3, emphasis added; the noble queen].

This question only grows more urgent after Siegfried's arrival in Worms, for the ambiguity that arises from his failure becomes more pronounced and its consequences more clearly dire as the story unfolds. Siegfried remains a whole year at the Burgundian court without even once laying eyes on Kriemhild, yet he pines for her all the same (NL 138). During that time, he repeatedly proves his worth as king through a series of heroic deeds which scholars have characterized as *minnedienst* [love service].[34] However, unlike conventional love service depicted in lyric love poetry and courtly romance, Siegfried's *minnedienst* to Kriemhild actually consists in service to her brother, Gunther.[35] Through it, I argue, the question of who is subject to whom receives poetic elaboration. Siegfried's first act of *minnedienst* comes in response to Gunther's appeal for military assistance in defending Burgundy against the Danish and Saxon forces that threaten to invade (NL 153–63).[36] On the one hand, in vowing that "iu sol mit triuwen dienen immer Sîvrides hant" [NL 161, 4; Siegfried shall always serve you (i.e., Gunther) loyally] and then fighting for him on the battlefield in Saxony, Siegfried plays the role of, to speak with Gernot Müller, "des zu *helfe* und *rât* verpflichteten Lehnsmannes" [G. Müller 1975, 104; the vassal obligated to help and to advise].[37] On the other hand, by leading the Burgundian knights into battle in Saxony while Gunther stays "bî den frouwen" [NL 174, 3; with the ladies] in Worms, Siegfried does the work of the king, eliminating the threat to patriarchal order in Gunther's kingdom by means of force.[38] After the army's triumphant return to Worms, the relations of power become even more ambiguous when we are reminded that Siegfried's military service to Gunther was also *minnedienst* to his sister. Despite his expressed desire to return to Xanten, the valiant hero who has just single-handedly captured both the Danish and Saxon king in battle now finds himself held captive in Worms by the hope that he might yet catch a glimpse of

---

34 See, for instance, Nagel 1977, 527 and Haustein 1993, 385.
35 See, for instance, J.-D. Müller 1974, 100–4 and Schultz 2006, 128–29.
36 Thomas Kerth, for instance, has asserted that his military service is "part of Siegfried's plan, and he means to exploit the debt the Burgundians owe him." Kerth 1986, 141. There is, however, no textual basis for imputing so much calculation to Siegfried's actions.
37 The kinds of service a vassal most commonly owed his lord were those of counsel and aid ("consilium et auxilium" or "Rat und Hilfe"). Reuter 1998, 644.
38 J.-D. Müller 1974, 101–2. That defending his lands on the battlefield belongs to the work of the king is implied in the text itself. For instance, when, at the end of the second *aventiure*, the narrator explains that, although Siegfried is not yet ready to wear the crown, "wolder wesen herre für allen den gewalt, / des in den landen vorhte der degen küen' unde balt" [NL 43, 3–4; as a bold and intrepid warrior, he wanted to be lord, defending against all the violent forces that he feared threatened the lands]. Regarding the role of the ideal king in the military defense of his kingdom more generally, see, for instance, Bumke 2008, 384–86; and Peters 1970, 101. More broadly, as the portrait of the Burgundian court that the narrator paints in the poem's opening *aventiure* implies, the qualities of physical strength, valiance, and warrior prowess are among those that an ideal king should possess in the world of the story. NL 4, 1; 5; and 8, 2. See Schulze 1997b, 144. Regarding the importance of the representation of the king as a warrior in the High Middle Ages, see Stieldorf 2015.

Kriemhild (NL 258 and 260). When, at the feast in celebration of victory in Saxony, Siegfried does finally get to see the fair maiden in person, hear her voice, feel her hand in his, and know the greeting of her kiss, he becomes so enthralled to "ir unmâzen scœne" [her inordinate beauty] that departing for his homeland is rendered all but impossible (NL 324, 1). Further compounding the ambiguity is the fact that Kriemhild's sway over Siegfried does not go unnoticed by her brothers who espy in it a vulnerability they can exploit (NL 272). It is, after all, because he recognizes the hero's affection as a vulnerability that Gernot counsels Gunther to have their sister greet him at the feast, explaining that, by means of her greeting, "wir haben gewunnen den vil zierlîchen degen" [NL 289, 4; we will have won the very magnificent warrior].

With Siegfried's next act of *minnedienst*, the question of who is subject to whom becomes explicitly thematized in the story itself. With the Saxon and Danish forces now vanquished, Gunther's mind turns to matters of love, and he sets his sights on winning the hand of Brunhild – the Icelandic queen with the strength of twelve men who is as famed for her beauty as for her brawn. According to the tales of her that Gunther has heard told, the man who succeeds in husbanding her must have the physical strength to beat her in "driu spil" [NL 327, 3; three contests]: spear-throwing, rock-hurling, and standing long jump. By losing even one of the three games, a suitor forfeits his head – a fate that has already befallen many a knight. In the face of this mortal danger, the Burgundian king once again turns to the hero for help. Led by Siegfried, Gunther's wooing expedition of four men sets sail for Isenstein. Just before they arrive, Siegfried enjoins Gunther, Hagen, and Dancwart to pledge that, with all their words and deeds at Brunhild's court, they will hew to a single storyline – namely that "Gunther sî mîn herre, und ich sî sîn man" [NL 386, 3; Gunther is my lord, and I am his vassal]. With this pledge, they all thus accept their respective roles in the deception they are about to stage at Siegfried's direction.

What the poem's audience had to infer from the portrayal of his arrival in Worms and his military service about the ambiguity surrounding who is subject to whom, they now see explicitly acted out in word and deed first before Brunhild and her courtiers in the ring at Isenstein and then for Brunhild in the royal bedchamber in Worms. This ambiguity is thrown into sharp relief by the dissonance that emerges between what the audience in the poem and the poem's audience can see in each of these scenes. On the one hand, not only does Siegfried once again play the part of the Burgundian king's vassal, but he also quite literally casts himself in the role for the audience in the poem. No sooner has the wooing party come ashore in Iceland than Siegfried's performance begins with his rendering of the *officium stratoris et strepae* [office of the bridle and stirrup] to Gunther: "[e]r habt' im dâ bî zoume daz zierlîche marc, / [. . .] unz der künic Gunther in den satel gesaz" [NL 397, 1–3; he held the magnificent charger by the bridle [. . .] until King Gunther was seated in the saddle]. With this symbolic gesture of subservience, Siegfried demonstrates to the viewing audience in Isenstein that they should receive him as the Burgundian king's vassal.[39] When making obeisance to Gunther nevertheless fails to prevent Brunhild from greeting him before the Burgundian king, Siegfried translates his subordination from gestures into words, responding to her salutation by declaring: "[v]il michel iuwer genâde, mîn vrou Prünhilt / daz ir mich ruochet grüezen [. . .] / vor disem edelen recken, der hie vor mir stât, / wand' er ist mîn herre" [NL 420; your grace is too great, my lady Brunhild, when you [. . .] deign to greet me before this noble warrior who stands here ahead of me, for he is my lord].[40] Siegfried continues to play the role of the dutiful vassal, vanquishing Brunhild for Gunther in the violent "spil" [contests] he wages against her in Isenstein and later in Worms. Crucially, it is thanks to his service that the audience in the poem – in the ring in Isenstein, Brunhild and her court; and in the bed chamber in Worms, Brunhild alone – can view Gunther as king (NL 432; 467, 4; and 665, 1–2).

On the other hand, while it too sees Siegfried act the part of Gunther's vassal, the poem's audience can also descry through the representation of the battles between Gunther and Brunhild that it is Siegfried – and not Gunther – who does the work of the king. This discrepancy between who seems to be superior and who should be superior is visualized for readers and listeners through Siegfried's use of the "tarnkappe" [invisibility cloak] in order to bring Brunhild into submission. It is in the ring in Isenstein that the hero first reaches for the cloak. Just as Brunhild's contests are about to commence, Siegfried approaches Gunther under its cover and quietly, so that no one else can hear, instructs him: "Den schilt gip mir von hende unt lâz mich den tragen, / unde merke rehte, waz du mich hœrest sagen. / nu hab du die gebære, diu werc wil ich begân [NL 454, 1–3; hand me your shield and let me wield it, and pay careful attention to what you hear me say. Now, you mime the deeds; I will do them]. Gunther complies, and while Brunhild and her retainers see Gunther throwing, hurling, and jumping to victory over the Icelandic queen, the poem's audience sees that it is really Siegfried who throws the throws, hurls the hurls, and jumps the jumps. The discrepancy is made apparent once again when Brunhild's "spil" [contests] resume in Worms and Siegfried once again dons the invisibility cloak before engaging her in conflict for a second time. Brunhild's confidence in Gunther's victory in Isenstein having been shaken because he has consented to his sister's marriage to Siegfried – a man who had represented himself as Gunther's vassal – she now balks at the Burgundian king's caresses on the night of their wedding. After Gunther's attempts to win his bride's maidenhead by force

---

39 This scene has been discussed extensively in the scholarship. Examples include: Schulze 1997a; Thelen 1988; Campbell 1997; J-D. Müller 1974; J-D. Müller 1998, 87–93, 140, and 258; Haustein 1993; and U. Hennig 1980. Regarding the historical and legal significance of the *officium stratoris et strepae*, see, for instance, Picot-Sellschopp 1998, 38–39 and Sellert 1993, 26–27.

40 Siegfried's equerry service fails to clearly signify his subordination not because the gesture itself is equivocal but because it is performed against the backdrop of signs and messages that contradict it. See Schausten 1999, 38 and Schulze 1997a, 37–39, especially n25.

result in her overpowering him, binding him hand and foot with her "gürtel" [NL 636, 2; girdle], and then leaving him hanging till sunrise from a nail on the wall, Siegfried slips on the invisibility cloak the following night, steals into the royal bedchamber, and violently breaks Brunhild's resistance so that "dô wart si Guntheres wîp" [NL 677, 4; she then became Gunther's wife]. The poem's audience is thus able to see that which the audience in the poem literally cannot: in the struggle with Brunhild, it is Siegfried – not Gunther – who proves himself lord.

As was the case for Siegfried's military service for Gunther against the Danes and Saxons, the ambiguity surrounding who is subject to whom that the representation of Siegfried's *minnedienst* engenders is heightened by the fact that it is in the service of Kriemhild that Siegfried plays the role of Gunther's vassal. However, unlike in that earlier episode, Siegfried's motivation need not be inferred, for he explicitly states it himself. Before the wooing party ever steps foot in Isenstein, King Siegmund's son makes plain not once, but twice that it is only on account of Kriemhild that he leads Gunther's expedition. He does so first when he agrees to Gunther's request for help, emphasizing that his agreement is predicated on one condition: "gîstu mir dîne swester, sô wil ich ez tuon, / die scœnen Kriemhilde, ein küneginne hêr. / sô ger ich deheines lônes nâch mînen arbeiten mêr" [NL 333, 2–4; I will do it if you give me your sister, the fair Kriemhild, a noble (*hêr*) queen. I desire no other reward for my troubles]. He then does so again when he bids Gunther, Hagen, and Dancwart to pledge to adhere to the storyline about his subordination just before they land on Icelandic shores. As if to forestall any confusion as to why he would conceive of and direct a play in which he casts himself in the role of a "küneges man" ["king's vassal"],[41] Siegfried reminds Gunther and his men, together with the poem's audience, of his reason: "[j]ane lob' ichz niht sô verre durch die liebe dîn / sô durch dîne swester, daz scœne magedîn. / diu ist mir sam mîn sêle und sô mîn selbes lîp. / ich wil daz gerne dienen, daz sie werde mîn wîp" [NL 388; This I pledge not so much out of affection for you as on account of your sister, the fair maiden. She is as dear to me as my own life and soul. I shall serve her gladly, so that she might become my wife]. It is for Kriemhild that Siegfried willingly plays at being "undertân" [subject to] her brother.

5 Gender, Violence, and Lordship

As I have shown, by having Siegfried and Gunther reprise the roles of vassal and king in the conquest of Brunhild, which they had played in the defeat of the Saxons and Danes, the narrator poetically elaborates the question of who is subject to

---

41 Importantly, this is the same Siegfried who, upon his arrival in Worms had contemptuously refused to fight Ortwin von Metz instead of Gunther on the grounds that "ich bin ein künec rîche, sô bistu küneges man" [NL 118, 3; I am a powerful king, while you are a king's vassal].

whom. Correspondingly, by recounting Siegfried's wooing of Kriemhild in such a way that it rhymes with Gunther's wooing of Brunhild, the narrator makes evident both why this question is significant with respect to patriarchal order in the world of the poem and how it should be answered. Scholars have long observed that the first part of *Nibelungenlied* is principally composed of "a bridal quest within a bridal quest," inasmuch as the success of Siegfried's quest for Kriemhild is made contingent upon that of Gunther's for Brunhild.[42] As Lynn Thelen, however, has demonstrated, the two princes' bridal quests do not merely interlock in the poem's plot; they also closely correspond to one another with respect to their narrative elements (1984, especially 144–48). In the case of each suitor, it is stories of the maiden's inordinate beauty that move the princely knight to embark on a perilous journey to win the hand of a foreign princess in marriage whom he has never met, let alone seen.[43] Each fair maid is the daughter of a deceased king, and both have, until now, resisted marriage, having dismissed many a knight as unworthy of her affection.[44] Both princes are counseled against pursuing their suit on account of the danger,[45] and attempts to dissuade them culminate in the tearful pleas of a female relative.[46] After each prince makes clear that he will not be deterred, it is, in both cases, that same female relative who leads a team of ladies in sewing the magnificent raiments the warriors wear on their bridal quest.[47] Before each knight sets off on his bridal quest, the possibility of raising an army for his campaign is mooted, and, in both cases, it is Siegfried who summarily rejects the proposal, insisting instead upon a wooing party composed of but a few warriors.[48] When both expeditions reach the princess's land, the wooers come "ûf den sant" [on the sand or shore] with their chargers.[49] Upon sighting the approaching wooing parties, trusted vassals well-versed in Siegfried's past exploits advise the land's sovereign that, despite having never laid eyes on him, they have reason to believe the storied hero to be among the approaching

---

[42] See, for instance, Andersson 1987, 84.
[43] Regarding the quest for Kriemhild, see NL 44–49. Regarding the quest for Brunhild, see NL 325–28.
[44] For Kriemhild, see NL 45–46. For Brunhild, see NL 327–28.
[45] In the case of Siegfried's quest, Siegfried's parents, in particular, do their best to dissuade him. NL 50–51. In the case of Gunther's quest, Siegfried plays the part of principal dissuader. NL 330.
[46] Siegfried's mother, Sieglind, and Gunther's sister, Kriemhild, assume those respective roles. NL 60 and 372–73.
[47] For Siegfried's quest, see 62–65. For Gunther's quest, see 354–66.
[48] For the quest for Kriemhild, Siegmund offers to raise an army, but Siegfried departs with only eleven men. NL 57 and 59, 1–2. For the quest for Brunhild, Gunther proposes an army, but Siegfried overrules him, and only four warriors sail to Isenstein. NL 339 and 341.
[49] For Siegfried's arrival in Worms, see NL 71. For Gunther's arrival in Isenstein, see NL 396. See also Thelen 1984, 147. This seemingly insignificant parallel is particularly striking, I suggest, because there is no explicit mention in the text of Siegfried and his companions sailing from Xanten to Worms.

party of men of fearsome mien, and both exhort their liege to therefore receive the strangers hospitably.[50] In each case, the wooing consists in a kind of "Kampfwette" [wager of battle] in which both the suitor's "êre" [honor] and "houbet" [head] are explicitly at stake,[51] and, accordingly, both Siegfried and Gunther must prove themselves in battle in order to win their bride.[52] Finally, not only do both wooers succeed in winning their bride, but they are also married on the very same day in Worms.

It is, however, through a crucial difference with respect to the "Kampfwette" [wager of battle] that the significance of the rhyming of the two bridal quests becomes apparent: in the case of Siegfried's, the battle goes unfought upon his arrival in Worms; whereas, in the case of Gunther's quest, it is fought, beginning in Isenstein and then ending in Worms. The fact that the narrative elements of Siegfried's bridal quest so closely parallel those of Gunther and, moreover, that it is through the very same "Kampfwette" – that is, the one against Brunhild in which Gunther appears to fight, but Siegfried invisibly does the fighting – that both quests end in the suitor winning his bride suggests that Gunther's quest for Brunhild is both a repetition and conclusion of that of Siegfried for Kriemhild. As such, the battle Siegfried fights for Gunther against Brunhild tells us how we are to understand the battle he does not fight against Gunther when he first rides into Worms. It tells us, I argue, by making the relationship between gender, violence, and lordship, which remains implicit in the third *aventiure*, more explicit: being king is predicated upon overcoming the ultimate female obstacle. As is suggested in Siegfried's bridal quest, wooing in Gunther's quest for a bride also means conquest – something that is made clear when Brunhild first concedes defeat in Isenstein, proclaiming to her kinsmen and vassals, "ir sult dem künic Gunther alle wesen undertân" [NL 466, 4; you shall all be subject to King Gunther]. Just as in Siegfried's quest for Kriemhild, the wooer in Gunther's quest must prove himself worthy to be king by conquering the "die hêrlîchen meit" [the lordly maiden] – his heart's beloved and ultimate female obstacle.[53] This Brunhild herself makes explicit when, after being violently subdued, she

---

50 Upon Siegfried's arrival in Worms, Hagen advises Gunther. NL 86. Upon Gunther's arrival in Isenstein, it is an unnamed courtier who counsels Brunhild. NL 411.
51 In Worms, Siegfried lays down "mîn êre" [my honor] and "mîn houbet" [my head] as the "pfant" [wager]. NL 109, 4. In Isenstein, Brunhild warns Gunther that "die êre und ouch den lîp" [both your honor and your life] are at stake in her contest. To her warning, Gunther replies: "mîn houbet wil ich verliesen, ir enwerdet mîn wîp" [I am willing to lose my head if you do not become my wife]. NL 425, 1 and 427, 4 respectively. See also Weigand 2006, 250–51.
52 In Siegfried's quest, he marries only after having first led Gunther's army to victory over the Danes and Saxons and then having bested Brunhild in her "Kampfwette" [wager of battle]. Crucially, it is, however, by vanquishing Brunhild that Siegfried wins Kriemhild as a bride. In Gunther's quest, he wins Brunhild's hand only after she has been vanquished in her contests. NL 139–264; 326; and 423, 2–3.
53 The same epithet is used to refer to both Kriemhild and Brunhild. See, for example, NL 123, 4 and 675, 4.

concedes defeat for the second time in the royal bedchamber in Worms, crying out in pain: "künic edele, du solt mich leben lân. / ez wirt vil wol versüenet, swaz ich dir hân getân. / ich gewer mich nimmer mêre der edelen minne dîn. / ich hân daz wol erfunden, daz du kanst vrouwen meister sîn" [NL 678; noble king, let me live! I will more than atone for all that I have done to you. I will never again refuse to submit to your noble love. I have truly experienced that you know how to master a woman]. For Siegfried, however, overcoming Brunhild, "die vil hêrlîchen meit" [NL 675, 4; the lordly maiden] for Gunther only throws into sharp relief that he has succumbed to Kriemhild, the "die hêrlîchen meit" [NL 123, 4; the lordly maiden]. By playing the role of Gunther's vassal and thereby making Gunther (seem to be) the king, Siegfried – who clearly proves that he should be the king – subordinates himself in the eyes of the poem's audience. But, crucially, it is not Gunther to whom he subordinates himself. Because it is on account of "die hêrlîchen meit" [the lordly maiden], Kriemhild, that he casts himself into the role of her brother's subordinate, it is she to whom he subordinates himself. It is for this reason that, after taking Brunhild's "guldîn vingerlîn" [gold ring] and "gürtel" [girdle] as trophies of the conquest in the royal bedchamber, Siegfried later "gab iz sînem wîbe; daz wart im sider leit" [gave them to his wife – for this he would later be sorry].[54] He has succumbed to the ultimate feminine obstacle – his heart's beloved, Kriemhild.

6 Making Sense of Siegfried's Death

That it is for this trespass against the patriarchal order that Siegfried must die is reflected in the narrator's depiction of his death. Through it, I argue, the hero's death can be viewed as a "spiegelnde Strafe" in that it conforms to the principle that, to quote Heinrich Brunner, the legal scholar who coined the term, "[d]ie Strafe selbst soll sagen, warum sie verhängt wird" [the punishment itself should say why it was imposed].[55] A "spiegelnde Strafe" speaks of the transgression for which it is imposed poetically, signifying it by means of metonymy or metaphor for the viewing

---

54 NL 679, 3; 680, 1; and 680, 3.
55 Brunner 1892, 588. See also His 1920, 356–58 and Kaufmann 1990, 1761–63. In contrast to other legal scholars who insist on their being different, Ebert argues that the "spiegelnde Strafe" is a kind of *lex talionis* [law of talion] – that is, the principle of punishment encapsulated in the expression "an eye for an eye." Ebert 1987, 401. See also Günther 1889, 240 and 262. Weigand has also characterized Siegfried's death as a "spiegelnde Strafe," writing that "Siegfrieds Betrug in der Kampfwette zieht nämlich eine reale Schuld nach sich, die seine Tötung für mittelalterliche Zuhörer der Geschichte objektiv gerechtfertigt erscheinen lassen mußte. Die Überwindung Siegfrieds durch List kann man im Verständnis der Zeit durchaus als 'spiegelnde Strafe' für seinen eigenen, listigen Betrug auffassen" [Weigand 2006, 257; Siegfried's deception (of Brunhild) in the wager of battle entails real guilt which must have made his killing seem objectively justified for the story's medieval

audience through and on the transgressor's body and in the scene of the punishment's execution.[56] In the case of the *Nibelungenlied*, the representation of Siegfried's death communicates both that he dies for a transgression and that his transgression consists in his love for Kriemhild. This understanding is communicated through the symbol of the linden tree – the tree under whose sprawling umbrage Siegfried is dealt the mortal blow (NL 972, 1 and 977, 3). In medieval Germany, the linden tree commonly served as the venue for a community's judicial proceedings, and because disputes were so regularly settled and judgments so often spoken under its branches, the tree came to stand for legal order.[57]

But the linden tree does more than merely signal that Siegfried's death should be understood as a punishment for a transgression – it also adumbrates the nature of his transgression. At the same time the tree figures justice in medieval German culture more broadly, it also appears in medieval German lyric and narrative poetry as the "tree of love" (Hatto 1954, 195). In the scene of Siegfried's death, the linden's link to love is reinforced by the fact that it is surrounded by "klê" [NL 976, 3; clover] and "bluomen" [NL 988, 1 and 998, 1; flowers] and that under the cover afforded by its spreading branches is a "brunnen kalt" [NL 969, 2; cold spring]. The linden tree, the cool shade, the refreshing water of a spring, and the meadow of clover dotted with flowers – they are all elements typical of the *locus amoenus* [pleasant place or

---

listeners. The overcoming of Siegfried by means of cunning can be understood, for all intents and purposes, as a "spiegelnde Strafe" (punishment that mirrors the transgression) for his own cunning deception]. While I agree that Siegfried's death represents a "spiegelnde Strafe," I nevertheless disagree with Weigand's analysis of the transgression that Siegfried's punishment reflects. Crucially, he fails to show how what he considers to be the hero's transgression – namely, his deception of Brunhild – is reflected in the scene of his death.

56 To cite but a few examples, perjurers often forfeited the hand with which they had sworn not to bear false witness; in many regions, counterfeiters were boiled alive, for just like "der Fälscher durch das Sieden die Münzen verändert hat, so sollte er auch durch das angewendete Mittel sein Leben einbüssen und 'wieder' gesiedet werden" [Günther 1889, 244; the counterfeiter altered coins by means of boiling, so too should he forfeit his life by the same means that he employed and be boiled again]; in one region, a bigamist was hewn in two so that each of his wives could receive her literal half of the husband they shared (Günther 1889, 262); and, according to many medieval German legal codes, liars and slanderers had to strike themselves "aufs Maul" [Günther 1889, 260; on the mouth]. See also Kaufmann 1990, 1762 and Ebert 1987, 400. A particularly amusing example is that of the punishment that was imposed in some regions on the fraudster "der mit beschisz umbgangen" [Gierke 1871, 52n182; who swindles (more literally: traffics in shit)]: the offender was placed in a bucket and then either dangled over a pool of excrement or lowered down into it. See also His 1920, 356.

57 Kramer 1971, 774–75; Grimm 1899, 415–17; and Rudloff 1890, 81. For a broad overview of the linden tree's historical role in German legal culture as well as an inventory of significant "Gerichtslinden" [judicial linden trees], see Lenzing 2005. Judicial lindens can also be found in medieval German literature. To cite but one example, it is under a linden tree that the lord of the ant castle crawls into the ear of the lion king in order to redress the latter's transgressions against the social order. Heinrich der Glichezaere 1984, 1293. See Widmaier 1993, 135.

pleasance], a literary topos commonly employed as a setting for scenes of love.[58] The tree of love, however, holds significance for Siegfried beyond the fact that it is below its umbrage that he is killed: as we were told in the preceding *aventiure*, it was under the branches of a linden that Siegfried was bathing in the dragon's blood when a leaf landed "zwischen die herte" [NL 902, 3; between his shoulder blades], leaving him with a vulnerable spot on his back. In the context of his death being set in a *locus amoenus*, that linden-leaf-shaped spot now suggests that it is on account of love that Siegfried is penetrable. And when, in describing Siegfried's death, the narrator recounts how Hagen "schôz in durch das kriuze, daz von der wunden spranc / daz bluot im von dem herzen vaste an Hagenen wât" [NL 981, 2–3; shot him through the cross (sewn on his clothing) such that his blood gushed from his heart, bespattering Hagen's clothes], he gives the audience to understand that, if it is on account of love that Siegfried is penetrable, it is on account of his love for Kriemhild – and, by extension, Kriemhild as his love – that he is now penetrated. For Kriemhild is implicated in her husband's transgression not only in that the linden-leaf-shaped spot refers to Siegfried's heart, which, in turn, also stands metonymically for her.[59] Equally as important, it was Kriemhild who not only revealed to Hagen where her husband's vulnerable spot was, but also directed Hagen's aim by sewing the cross on his clothing to mark it (NL 901–905).

That is, however, only half of what the representation of Siegfried's death has to say. Through the instrument that is thrust into the linden-leaf-shaped spot between his shoulders, it also tells the audience that, with his love for Kriemhild, the hero has violated the patriarchal order. Siegfried is struck by a "gêr" [spear] – a weapon that, by 1200, had become the "charakteristische[] Angriffswaffe des Ritters" [characteristic assault weapon of a knight] and that, together with the sword and crown, served as a chief "symbol der herrschergewalt" [symbol of sovereign power].[60] A means by which the ruler established and maintained order through violence, the spear was thus a symbol of not only lordship but also masculinity.[61] Its association with masculinity in particular is underscored by its use in medieval German literature as a symbol or metaphor for the penis.[62] Importantly, it is with his own oversized spear that Siegfried is slain – the same spear described as being endowed with a

---

[58] Ehrismann 1987, 150; and Brinker-von der Heyde 2003, 126. Ehrismann and Brinker-von der Heyde, however, attach little significance to the fact that the scene of Siegfried's death is represented as a *locus amoenus*: for them, it merely throws into sharp relief the odious perfidy of Hagen's act. Regarding the topos of the *locus amoenus* more generally, see, for example, Curtius 1942, 230–31.
[59] Regarding the symbolic significance of the heart and its conflation with the heart's beloved, see Hödl and Lauer 1989.
[60] NL 2002, 980, 3; Bumke 2008, 221 and H. Schröder 1890, 27. See also Meynert 1868, 57–58.
[61] In her analysis of Hartmann's *Erec*, Dorothea Klein, for instance, highlights the significance of the spear as a symbol of masculine power and patriarchal lordship. Klein 2002, 446.
[62] Brinker-von der Heyde 1999, 60. The spear's popularity as a phallic symbol is particularly well attested in Middle High German *Mären* [fabliaux or novellas]. Heiland 2015, 93.

massive head that is "wol zweier spannen breit, / der zuo sînen ecken vil harte vreislîchen sneit" [NL 73, 3–4; a good two spans wide with very fearsome cutting edges] which the hero had carried with him upon his arrival in Worms to conquer Kriemhild. It is particularly telling that Siegfried – the same Siegfried who had made himself a hero by restoring patriarchal order to the land of the Nibelungs when he dispatched its two kings with their own sword – is now himself dispatched with his own spear. Like Nibelung and Schilbung, he too has failed in his duty to establish and maintain the patriarchal order. It is likewise telling that, having been stripped of his sword and spear, Siegfried – the same Siegfried who had made himself into the embodiment of masculinity by slaying a dragon and bathing in its blood under a linden – is now himself slain under a linden and the surrounding flowers are bathed in the blood gushing from his wound (NL 988).[63] Just as overcoming a female obstacle made him a male hero, succumbing to the ultimate female obstacle – that is, to his heart's beloved – has not only rendered him impotent but also made him a female obstacle. In sum, what the *Nibelungenlied's* audience is told when the narrator relates how Hagen penetrates Siegfried's vulnerable spot with his hefty spear is that the hero must die as a female object because he has violated the patriarchal order.

Works Cited

Primary Sources

Heinrich der Glichezaere. *Der Reinhart Fuchs des Elsässers Heinrich*. Edited by Klaus Düwel, Katharina von Goetz, Frank Henrichvark, and Sigrid Krause. Tübingen: Max Niemeyer Verlag, 1984.
König Rother. *Mittelhochdeutscher Text und neuhochdeutsche Übersetzung*. Edited by Ingrid Bennewitz, Beatrix Kroll, Peter K. Stein, and Ruth Weichselbaumer. Translated by Peter K. Stein. Stuttgart: Philipp Reclam, 2000.
Das Nibelungenlied. Edited by Karl Bartsch, Helmut de Boor, and Siegfried Grosse. Translated by Siegfried Grosse. Stuttgart: Philipp Reclam, 2002.
Das Nibelungenlied. Mittelhochdeutscher Text und Übertragung. Edited and translated by Helmut Brackert. 2 volumes. Frankfurt am Main: Fischer Taschenbuch Verlag, 1979.
Das Nibelungenlied und die Klage. Nach der Handschrift 857 der Stiftsbibliothek St. Gallen. Edited and translated by Joachim Heinzle. Berlin: Deutscher Klassiker Verlag, 2015.
The Nibelungenlied. Edited and translated by A. T. Hatto. New York: Penguin Books, 1969.
Wirnt von Grafenberg. *Wigalois: Text, Übersetzung, Stellenkommentar*. 2nd ed. Edited by J.M.N. Kapteyn, Sabine Seelbach, and Ulrich Seelbach. Translated by Sabine Seelbach and Ulrich Seelbach. Berlin: De Gruyter, 2014.

---

[63] Just as spears can stand for penises in medieval German literature, wounds can be metaphors for vaginas. The association between wounds and vaginas is also attested by *Mären* [fabliaux or novellas]. Heiland 2015, 82. For a more general discussion of the gendering of wounds in medieval literature, see McCracken 2003.

Secondary Sources

Andersson, Theodore M. *A Preface to the* Nibelungenlied. Stanford, CA: Stanford University Press, 1987.
Bennett, Judith M. "Patriarchal Equilibrium." In *History Matters: Patriarchy and the Challenge of Feminism*, by Judith M. Bennett, 54–81 and 172–79. Philadelphia: University of Pennsylvania Press, 2006.
Bennewitz, Ingrid. "Chlage über Kriemhild. Intertextualität, literarische Erinnerungsarbeit und die Konstruktion von Weiblichkeit in der mittelhochdeutschen Heldenepik." In *6. Pöchlarner Heldenliedgespräch. 800 Jahre Nibelungenlied: Rückblick – Einblick – Ausblick*, edited by Klaus Zatloukal, 25–36. Vienna: Fassbaender, 2001.
Bennewitz, Ingrid. "Das *Nibelungenlied* – Ein 'puech von Chrimhilt'? Ein geschlechtergeschichtlicher Versuch zum *Nibelungenlied* und seiner Rezeption." In *3. Pöchlarner Heldenliedgespräch. Die Rezeption des* Nibelungenliedes, edited by Klaus Zatloukal, 33–52. Vienna: Fassbaender, 1995.
Beyschlag, Siegfried. "Das Motiv der Macht bei Siegfrieds Tod." *Germanisch-Romanische Monatsschrift* 33 (1951/1952): 95–108.
Brinker-von der Heyde, Claudia. "Hagen – *valant* oder *trost* der Nibelungen? Zur Unerträglichkeit ambivalenter Gewalt im *Nibelungenlied* und ihrer Bewältigung in der *Klage*." In *Der Mord und die Klage: Das* Nibelungenlied *und die Kulturen der Gewalt. Dokumentation des 4. Symposiums der Nibelungenliedgesellschaft Worms e.V. vom 11. bis 13. Oktober 2002*, edited by Gerold Bönnen and Volker Gallé, 122–44. Worms: Verlag Stadtarchiv Worms, 2003.
Brinker-von der Heyde, Claudia. "Weiber-Herrschaft oder: Wer reitet wen? Zur Konstruktion und Symbolik der Geschlechterbeziehung." In *Manlîchiu wîp, wîplîch man: Zur Konstruktion der Kategorien "Körper" und "Geschlecht" in der deutschen Literatur des Mittelalters. Internationales Kolloquium der Oswald von Wolkenstein-Gesellschaft und der Gerhard-Mercator-Universität Duisburg, Xanten*, edited by Ingrid Bennewitz and Helmut Tervooren, 47–84. Berlin: Erich Schmidt Verlag, 1999.
Bumke, Joachim. *Höfische Kultur: Literatur und Gesellschaft im hohen Mittelalter*. Munich: Deutscher Taschenbuch Verlag, 2008.
Bumke, Joachim. "Sigfrids Fahrt ins Nibelungenland: Zur achten *aventiure* des *Nibelungenliedes*." *Beiträge zur Geschichte der deutschen Sprache und Literatur* 80 (1958): 253–68.
Brunner, Heinrich. *Deutsche Rechtsgeschichte*. Vol. 2. Leipzig: Verlag von Duncker & Humblot, 1892.
Campbell, Ian R. "Siegfried's Vassalage Deception Re-Examined." *Neophilologus* 81 (1997): 563–76.
Curtius, Ernst Robert. "Rhetorische Naturschilderung im Mittelalter." *Romanische Forschungen: Vierteljahrsschrift für romanische Sprachen und Literaturen* 56 (1942): 219–56.
De Boor, Helmut. *Die höfische Literatur: Vorbereitung, Blüte, Ausklang, 1170–1250*. 7th ed. Vol. 2 of *Geschichte der deutschen Literatur von den Anfängen bis zur Gegenwart*, edited by Helmut de Boor and Richard Newald. Munich: C.H. Beck, 1953.
De Lauretis, Teresa. *Alice Doesn't: Feminism, Semiotics, Cinema*. London: Macmillan Press, 1984.
De Lauretis, Teresa. *Technologies of Gender: Essays on Theory, Film, and Fiction*. Bloomington, IN: Indiana University Press, 1987.
De Lauretis, Teresa. "Gender, Body, and Habit Change." In *Pierce, Semiotics, and Psychoanalysis*, edited by Joseph Brent and John Muller, 159–75. Baltimore, MD: The Johns Hopkins University Press, 2000.
Ebert, Udo. "Talion und Spiegelung im Strafrecht." In *Festschrift für Karl Lackner zum 70. Geburtstag am 18. Februar 1987*, edited by Wilfried Küper, Ingeborg Puppe, and Jörg Tenckhoff, 399–422. Berlin: De Gruyter, 1987.

Ehrismann, Otfrid. "Siefrids Ankunft in Worms: Zur Bedeutung der 3. *aventiure* des *Nibelungenlieds*." In *Festschrift für Karl Bischoff zum 70. Geburtstag*, edited by Günther Bellmann, Günter Eifler, and Wolfgang Kleiber, 328–56. Cologne: Böhlau Verlag, 1975.

Ehrismann, Otfrid. *Nibelungenlied: Epoche – Werk – Wirkung*. Munich: C. H. Beck, 1987.

Ehrismann, Otfrid. "'ze stücken was gehouwen dô daz edele wîp': The Reception of Kriemhild." In McConnell, *A Companion to the* Nibelungenlied, 18–41.

Erler, Adalbert. "Herrschaftszeichen." In *Handwörterbuch zur deutschen Rechtsgeschichte*, edited by Adalbert Erler et al. 2: 109–13. Berlin: Erich Schmidt Verlag, 1978.

Frakes, Jerold C. "Kriemhild's Three Dreams: A Structural Interpretation." *Zeitschrift für deutsches Altertum und deutsche Literatur* 113, no. 3 (1984): 173–87.

Frakes, Jerold C. *Brides and Doom: Gender, Property, and Power in Medieval German Women's Epic*. Philadelphia: University of Pennsylvania Press, 1994.

Gierke, Otto. *Der Humor im deutschen Recht*. Berlin: Weidmannsche Buchhandlung, 1871.

Greenfield, John. "Lyric Love and the Epic Hero: Notes on Siegfried's Wooing of Kriemhild in the *Nibelungenlied*." *Revista da Faculdade de Letras: Línguas e Literaturas* 11 (1994): 181–90.

Grimm, Jacob. *Deutsche Rechtsalterthümer*. Edited by Andreas Heusler and Rudolf Hübner. 4th ed. Vol. 2. Leipzig: Dieterich'sche Verlagsbuchhandlung Theodor Weicher, 1899.

Grosse, Siegfried. Commentary to *Das Nibelungenlied*, edited by Bartsch, Karl, Helmut de Boor, and Siegfried Grosse, 719–935. Stuttgart: Philipp Reclam, 2002.

Günther, Louis. *Die Idee der Wiedervergeltung in der Geschichte und Philosophie des Strafrechts: Ein Beitrag zur universal-historischen Entwickelung desselben*. Vol. 1, *Die Kulturvölker des Altertums und das deutsche Recht bis zur Carolina*. Erlangen: Th. Bläsing's Universitätsbuchhandlung, 1889.

Hammer, Andreas. "Ordnung durch Un-Ordnung: Der Zusammenschluss von Teufel und Monster in der mittelalterlichen Literatur." In *Monströse Ordnungen: Zur Typologie und Ästhetik des Anormalen*, edited by Achim Geisenhanslüke, Georg Mein, and Rasmus Overthun, 209–56. Bielefeld: Transcript Verlag, 2009.

Hasty, Will. "From Battlefields to Bedchambers: Conquest in the *Nibelungenlied*." In McConnell, *A Companion to the* Nibelungenlied, 79–93.

Hatto, A. T. "The Lime-Tree and Early German, Goliard and English Lyric Poetry." *The Modern Language Review* 49, no. 2 (1954): 193–209.

Hauck, Karl. "Rituelle Speisegemeinschaft im 10. und 11. Jahrhundert." *Studium Generale* 3 (1950): 611–21.

Haug, Walter. "Höfische Idealität und heroische Tradition im *Nibelungenlied*." In *Strukturen als Schlüssel zur Welt: Kleine Schriften zur Erzählliteratur des Mittelalters*, edited by Walter Haug, 293–307. Tübingen: Niemeyer Verlag, 1989.

Haustein, Jens. "Siegfrieds Schuld." *Zeitschrift für deutsches Altertum und deutsche Literatur* 122, no. 4 (1993): 373–87.

Heiland, Satu. *Visualisierung und Rhetorisierung von Geschlecht: Strategien zur Inszenierung weiblicher Sexualität im Märe*. Berlin: De Gruyter, 2015.

Hennig, Beate, ed. *Kleines mittelhochdeutsches Wörterbuch*. Berlin: De Gruyter, 2014.

Hennig, Ursula. "Herr und Mann – Zur Ständegliederung im *Nibelungenlied*." *Montfort: Vierteljahresschrift für Geschichte, Heimat- und Volkskunde* 32, no. 3/4 (1980): 349–59.

His, Rudolf. *Das Strafrecht des deutschen Mittelalters*. Vol. 1, *Die Verbrechen und ihre Folgen im allgemeinen*. Leipzig: T. Weichler, 1920.

Hödl, Ludwig and Hans Hugo Lauer. "Herz." In *Lexikon des Mittelalters*. 4: 2187–89. Stuttgart: Metzler, [1977]–1999.

Hüpper, Dagmar. "Schwert." In *Handwörterbuch zur deutschen Rechtsgeschichte*, edited by Adalbert Erler et al. 4: 1570–74. Berlin: Erich Schmidt Verlag, 1990.

Jaeger, Stephen C. "The Clerical Rebellion against Courtliness." Chapter 9 in *The Origins of Courtliness: Civilizing Trends and the Formation of Courtly Ideals, 939–1210*. Philadelphia: University of Pennsylvania Press, 1985.

Kaufmann, Ekkehard. "König." In *Handwörterbuch zur deutschen Rechtsgeschichte*, edited by Adalbert Erler et al. 2: 999–1023. Berlin: Erich Schmidt Verlag, 1978.

Kaufmann, Ekkehard. "Spiegelnde Strafe." In *Handwörterbuch zur deutschen Rechtsgeschichte*, edited by Adalbert Erler et al. 4: 1761–63. Berlin: Erich Schmidt Verlag, 1990.

Kerth, Thomas. "Siegfried's Theatrical *liste*." *Amsterdamer Beiträge zur älteren Germanistik* 24 (1986): 129–61.

Klein, Dorothea. "Geschlecht und Gewalt: Zur Konstruktion von Männlichkeit im *Erec* Hartmanns von Aue." In *Literarische Leben: Rollenentwürfe in der Literatur des Hoch- und Spätmittelalters. Festschrift für Volker Mertens zum 65. Geburtstag*, edited by Mattias Meyer and Hans-Jochen Schiewer, 433–63. Tübingen: Max Niemeyer Verlag, 2002.

Köbler, Gerhard. "Richten – Richter – Gericht." *Zeitschrift der Savigny-Stiftung für Rechtsgeschichte: Germanistische Abteilung* 87, no. 1 (1970): 57–113.

Kramer, Karl-Sigismund. "Dorflinde." In *Handwörterbuch zur deutschen Rechtsgeschichte*, edited by Adalbert Erler et al. 1: 774–75. Berlin: Erich Schmidt Verlag, 1971.

Krause, Hermann. *Kaiserrecht und Rezeption*. Heidelberg: Carl Winter Universitätsverlag, 1952.

Kroeschell, Karl. "Haus und Herrschaft im frühen deutschen Recht." In *Studien zum frühen und mittelalterlichen deutschen Recht*, edited by Karl Kroeschell, 113–55. Berlin: Duncker & Humblot, 1995.

Kuhn, Hugo. "*Tristan, Nibelungenlied*, Artusstruktur." In *Liebe und Gesellschaft*, edited by Wolfgang Walliczek, 12–35 and 179–80. Stuttgart: J. B. Metzlersche Verlagsbuchhandlung, 1980.

Lecouteux, Claude. "Der Drache." *Zeitschrift für deutsches Altertum und deutsche Literatur* 108, no. 1 (1979): 13–21.

Lenzing, Anette. *Gerichtslinden und Thingplätze in Deutschland*. Königstein im Taunus: Karl Robert Langewiesche Nachfolger Hans Köster Verlagsbuchhandlung KG, 2005.

Lexer, Matthias. *Mittelhochdeutsches Handwörterbuch*. 3 vols. Stuttgart: S. Hirzel, 1992.

Lienert, Elisabeth. "Gender Studies, Gewalt und das *Nibelungenlied*." In *Der Mord und die Klage: Das* Nibelungenlied *und die Kulturen der Gewalt. Dokumentation des 4. Symposiums der Nibelungenliedgesellschaft Worms e.V. vom 11. bis 13. Oktober 2002*, edited by Gerold Bönnen and Volker Gallé, 145–62. Worms: Verlag Stadtarchiv Worms, 2003a.

Lienert, Elisabeth. "Geschlecht und Gewalt im *Nibelungenlied*." *Zeitschrift für deutsches Altertum und deutsche Literatur* 132, no. 1 (2003b): 3–23.

Lotman, Jurij M. "The Origin of Plot in the Light of Typology." Translated by Julian Graffy. *Poetics Today* 1, no. 1/2 (1979): 161–84.

Marquardt, Rosemarie. *Das höfische Fest im Spiegel der mittelhochdeutschen Dichtung (1140–1240)*. Göppingen: Kümmerle Verlag, 1985.

McConnell, Winder, ed. *A Companion to the* Nibelungenlied. Columbia, SC: Camden House, 1998.

McCracken, Peggy. *The Curse of Eve, the Wound of the Hero: Blood, Gender, and Medieval Literature*. Philadelphia, PA: University of Pennsylvania Press, 2003.

Meynert, Hermann. *Geschichte des Kriegswesens und der Heerverfassungen in Europa*. Vol. 1, *Vom frühen Mittelalter bis zur Einführung der Feuerwaffen*. Vienna: Beck'sche Universitäts-Buchhandlung (Alfred Hölder), 1868.

Müller, Gernot. "Zur sinnbildlichen Repräsentation der Siegfriedgestalt im *Nibelungenlied*." *Studia Neophilologica: A Journal of Germanic and Romance Philology* 47, no. 1 (1975): 88–119.

Müller, Jan-Dirk. "Sivrit: künec – man – eigenholt. Zur sozialen Problematik des *Nibelungenliedes*." *Amsterdamer Beiträge zur älteren Germanistik* 7 (1974): 85–124.

Müller, Jan-Dirk. *Spielregeln für den Untergang: Die Welt des* Nibelungenliedes. Tübingen: Max Niemeyer Verlag, 1998.

Murdoch, Brian. "Politics in the *Nibelungenlied*." In McConnell, *A Companion to the Nibelungenlied*, 229–50.

Nagel, Bert. *Staufische Klassik: Deutsche Dichtung um 1200*. Heidelberg: Lothar Stiehm Verlag, 1977.

Nordmeyer, George. "Source Studies on Kriemhild's Falcon Dream." *Germanic Review* 15 (1940): 292–99.

Ogris, Werner. "Schwert." In *Handwörterbuch zur deutschen Rechtsgeschichte*, edited by Adalbert Erler et al. 4: 1574. Berlin: Erich Schmidt Verlag, 1990.

Peters, Edward. *The Shadow King: Rex Inutilis in Medieval Law and Literature, 751–1327*. New Haven, CT: Yale University Press, 1970.

Picot-Sellschopp, Sabine. "Stratordienst." In *Handwörterbuch zur deutschen Rechtsgeschichte*, edited by Adalbert Erler et al. 5: 37–40. Berlin: Erich Schmidt Verlag, 1998.

Rasmussen, Ann Marie. *Mothers and Daughters in Medieval German Literature*. Syracuse, NY: Syracuse University Press, 1997.

Reichert, Hermann, ed. "Einleitung zum Textteil." In *Das Nibelungenlied: Text und Einführung nach der St. Galler Handschrift*, 3–41. 2nd ed. Berlin: De Gruyter, 2017.

Renz, Tilo. *Um Leib und Leben: Das Wissen von Geschlecht, Körper und Recht im* Nibelungenlied. Berlin: De Gruyter, 2012.

Reuter, Timothy. "Vasallität." In *Handwörterbuch zur deutschen Rechtsgeschichte*, edited by Adalbert Erler et al. 5: 644–48. Berlin: Erich Schmidt Verlag, 1998.

Riches, Samantha J.E. "Encountering the Monstrous: Saints and Dragons in Medieval Thought." In *The Monstrous Middle Ages*, edited by Bettina Bildhauer and Robert Mills, 196–218. Toronto: University of Toronto Press, 2003.

Rudloff, Karl. "Die Linde in Geschichte und Dichtung." *Zeitschrift der Gesellschaft für Beförderung der Geschichts-, Altertums-, und Volkskunde von Freiburg, dem Breisgau und den angrenzenden Landschaften* 9 (1890): 78–92.

Schausten, Monika. "Der Körper des Helden und das 'Leben' der Königin: Geschlechter- und Machtkonstellationen im *Nibelungenlied*." *Zeitschrift für deutsche Philologie* 118 (1999): 27–49.

Schröder, Franz Rolf. "Kriemhilds Falkentraum." *Beiträge zur Geschichte der deutschen Sprache und Literatur* 78 (1956): 319–48.

Schröder, Heinrich. *Zur Waffen- und Schiffskunde des deutschen Mittelalters bis um das Jahr 1200: Eine kulturgeschichtliche Untersuchung auf Grund der ältesten deutschen volkstümlichen und geistlichen Dichtungen*. Kiel: Verlag von Lipsius & Tischer, 1890.

Schröder, Werner. "Die Tragödie Kriemhilts im *Nibelungenlied*." In *Nibelungenlied-Studien*, edited by Werner Schröder, 48–156. Stuttgart: J.B. Metzlersche Verlagsbuchhandlung, 1968.

Schultz, James A. *Courtly Love, the Love of Courtliness, and the History of Sexuality*. Chicago: University of Chicago Press, 2006.

Schultz, James A. "Medieval Adolescence: The Claims of History and the Silence of German Narrative." *Spectrum* 66, no. 3 (1991): 519–39.

Schulze, Ursula. "Gunther sî mîn herre, und ich sî sîn man: Bedeutung und Deutung der Standeslüge und die Interpretierbarkeit des *Nibelungenliedes*." *Zeitschrift für deutsches Altertum und deutsche Literatur* 126, no. 1 (1997a): 32–52.

Schulze, Ursula. *Das Nibelungenlied*. Stuttgart: Reclam, 1997b.

Schumann, P.E. "Hort." In *Handwörterbuch zur deutschen Rechtsgeschichte*, edited by Adalbert Erler et al. 2: 242–43. Berlin: Erich Schmidt Verlag, 1978.

Sellert, Wolfgang. *Recht und Gerechtigkeit in der Kunst*. Göttingen: Wallstein Verlag, 1993.

Stieldorf, Andrea. "Das Bild vom König als Krieger im hochmittelalterlichen Reich." In *Der König als Krieger: Zum Verhältnis von Königtum und Krieg im Mittelalter, Beiträge der Tagung des Zentrums für Mittelalterstudien der Otto-Friedrich-Universität Bamberg (13.–15. März 2013)*, edited by Martin Clauss, Andrea Stieldorf, and Tobias Weller, 23–64. Bamberg: University of Bamberg Press, 2015.

Tennant, Elaine C. "Prescriptions and Performatives in Imagined Cultures: Gender Dynamics in *Nibelungenlied* Adventure 11." In *Mittelalter: Neue Wege durch einen alten Kontinent*, edited by Jan-Dirk Müller and Horst Wenzel, 273–316. Stuttgart: S. Hirzel Verlag, 1999.

Thelen, Lynn. "The Internal Source and Function of King Gunther's Bridal Quest." *Monatshefte* 76, no. 2 (1984): 143–55.

Thelen, Lynn. "The Vassalage Deception, or Siegfried's Folly." *Journal of English and Germanic Philology* 87, no. 4 (1988): 471–91.

Tuczay, Christa Agnes. "Drache und Greif – Symbole der Ambivalenz." *Mediävistik: Internationale Zeitschrift für interdisziplinäre Mittelalterforschung* 19 (2006): 169–211.

Voorwinden, Norbert. "*Ich bin ouch ein recke und solde krône tragen*: Zur Legitimation der Herrschaft in der mittelalterlichen Heldendichtung." In *8. Pöchlarner Heldenliedgespräch: Das Nibelungenlied und die europäische Heldendichtung*, edited by Alfred Ebenbauer and Johannes Keller, 275–94. Vienna: Fassbaender, 2006.

Weber, Gottfried. *Das* Nibelungenlied: *Problem und Idee*. Stuttgart: J.B. Metzlersche Verlagsbuchhandlung, 1963.

Weigand, Rudolf Kilian. "Frau und Recht im *Nibelungenlied*: Konstituenten des zentralen Konflikts." *Archiv für das Studium der neueren Sprachen und Literaturen* 243 (2006): 241–58.

Westphal, Sarah. Review of *Spielregeln für den Untergang: Die Welt des* Nibelungenliedes, by Jan-Dirk Müller. *Speculum* 77, no. 3 (2002): 953–55.

Widmaier, Sigrid. *Das Recht im* Reinhart Fuchs. Berlin: De Gruyter, 1993.

Wisniewski, Roswitha. "Das Versagen des Königs: Zur Interpretation des *Nibelungenliedes*." In *Festschrift für Ingeborg Schröbler zum 65. Geburtstag*, edited by Dietrich Schmidtke and Helga Schüppert, 170–86. Tübingen: Niemeyer Verlag, 1973.

Olga V. Trokhimenko

3 "If You Are Desired, Then You Are Worthy": Mothers, Daughters, and Paradoxes of Femininity in the Middle High German Tristan Sequels

It is no secret that medieval literature abounds with strong, willful, and determined female characters, be they damsels of courtly romances, the haughty and inaccessible "*minne*lady" of the love lyric, wise and at times conniving queens of the epic, unruly wives of *Mären* [short rhymed couplet narratives] and *Schwänke* [comic tales], or female saints, unshakable in their determination. Feminist scholarship continues to study such female figures as both a reflection and a critique of the patriarchal social order. Of course, when a woman crosses the boundaries of what is considered to be womanly behavior, forgets her duty of proper submission to her husband by taking power and authority into her own hands, or, worse still, if she dares to employ physical force toward a man, to presume to occupy a position of a "woman on top," she is treated as a notorious "übelez wîp" or "valandinne" [evil woman; female devil], like Kriemhild in *The Nibelungenlied*. Her punishment for such audacity can be intra- or extra-textual and restores a traditional gender hierarchy. But what about the seemingly socially compliant, submissive model of femininity? One would expect that such behavior would be extolled and promoted, particularly where the institution of marriage is concerned. The Griselda-like type of a suffering, but ever-patient, wife clearly pulled at the heartstrings for at least some medieval and early-modern audiences; and yet it appears that however consistent with the Church's teachings about wifely submission to the husband's authority, the passive model of female behavior was not without controversy.

Isolde of the White Hands, a secondary character of the medieval Tristan stories, is frequently described by modern scholars as a model wife, for whom medieval authors have much compassion (Buschinger 1993, 61; Chinca 1997, 108). That medieval poets and audiences must have felt at least a degree of sympathy toward the neglected virginal spouse who remains obedient and compliant despite the unfairness done to her is easy to imagine; and yet, to say that this heroine is treated with invariable kindness would be an oversimplification. As the 2010 study by Ute Nanz demonstrates, despite her being a secondary character, Isolde of the White Hands is a rather complex and ambivalent figure (Nanz 2010, 301; also Gibbs 2003, 261–284).[1] This ambivalence goes beyond her tragic lie at the end of the story that signals her sudden personality

---

[1] As Ruthmarie H. Mitsch points out, Isolde of the White Hands has been ignored or glossed over by the scholarship (Mitsch 1994, 75). Indeed, despite numerous studies mentioning her, the heroine

change and her unexpected transformation from an all-enduring victim into a jealous wife. Rather it is closely connected to the individual authors' attitude toward Tristan and Isolde's adulterous passion and to their views of marriage, love, and gender. For example, in Ulrich von Türheim's and Heinrich von Freiberg's late thirteenth-century versions of the Tristan legend, all female characters, particularly the two Isoldes, undergo what may be called taming, which in Heinrich's case in particular means a return to the ideal of compliant, normative femininity. Heinrich's approach appears to be predicated on the pervasive demand that women be virtuous and desirable at the same time, a principle best summarized by Alice A. Hentsch in her study of medieval conduct literature for women: "A woman should know how to make others desire her" (1975 [1903], 47).[2] The ambivalence of Isolde of the White Hands has much to do with reinforcing this maxim: she is desirable and beautiful, and yet she is not desired and as such, has little value in the universe of the text.

In all versions of the Tristan legend, it is Isolde the Blond who serves as a natural contrast to the White-Handed Isolde: lover versus wife, adulterous versus loyal, active versus passive, first love versus second love, Isolde versus "the other Isolde."[3] Whatever attitude individual authors may have toward Tristan's illegitimate liaison, whatever censures the lovers' tribulations or dishonesties incur, the Irish Isolde is nevertheless the memorable one who gets everybody's preference, sympathy, and love, particularly in the end.[4] She is a beautiful and desirable woman, desired and admired by her husband Mark, by Tristan, and by anybody who sees her. In contrast, Isolde of the White Hands often fades out of the text and of everybody's memory, a truly *minor* character, despite her major, fateful role in her husband's life.

Two texts, however, create yet an additional foil to the poor "other Isolde": it is her own mother, the Duchess of Arundel, who appears only in Ulrich von Türheim's (ca. 1240) and Heinrich von Freiberg's (ca. 1290–1300) sequels to Gottfried von Strassburg's (ca. 1210) unfinished torso. She is conspicuously absent in both the prequel that the two poets claim to continue and in Eilhart von Oberge's earlier take on the legend (ca. 1170–1175), which they actually use to complete their respective tales.[5] Like Gottfried's Queen Isolde, the duchess is a successful aristocratic

---

herself has not in fact been studied thoroughly until recently. Notable exceptions are the studies by Nanz (2010) and Trokhimenko (2011).
2 "Une femme doit savoir se faire desirer." All translations in this essay are mine, unless specifically indicated otherwise.
3 In scholarship on the Tristan legend, it is common to refer to Isolde of the White Hands as "the other Isolde." On the two Isoldes see Mitsch 1994; Mälzer 1991; Rabine 1980, esp. 33; Schausten 1999; Thomas 2003. The feminist analyses by Rasmussen 2003, Altpeter-Jones 2009, Moi 1999, and Trindade 1996 all consider only Ulrich's and Heinrich's predecessors.
4 Even the Breton Isolde's brother Kaedin, whose honor is wronged no less than hers by Tristan's behavior, readily accepts the Irish Isolde's superiority over his sister.
5 Cf.: "Bei Eilhart war diese Figur völlig bedeutungslos für das Handlungsgeschehen" [Mälzer 1991, 239 n10; For Eilhart this character was of no importance whatsoever for the plot development]. The mother

woman and an example of all that her daughter fails to become – a respected wife, a loving and loved mother of the family, and a shrewd advisor and politician.[6]

This paper takes a long overdue look at this unexpected and mostly ignored secondary character. It does so through the lens offered by Ann Marie Rasmussen in her path-breaking 1997 study of mother-daughter relationships in the medieval German tradition in order to examine the purpose of this new mother figure in the two Middle High German Tristan sequels. As such, the following discussion will consider the continuities and discontinuities that exist between the mother and her daughter in Ulrich's and Heinrich's epics, and the extent to which understanding the duchess contributes to a better understanding of the character of her daughter, Isolde of the White Hands, the most important "minor" character of the Tristan legend.[7]

1 "Seek your father's advice, and your mother's as well. This is proper": How a Noblewoman Wields Her Power

When Tristan leaves Cornwall for good and lands in Brittany in the duchy of Arundel, all of the texts in the Middle High German tradition introduce us to the family of the local noble ruler, comprised of the duke himself, his son Kaedin (or Kehenis in Eilhart's text), and his lovely daughter and Tristan's future wife, Isolde of the White Hands. In Eilhart's and Gottfried's texts, Kaedin understands Tristan's usefulness to himself and quickly befriends him. He needs the latter's military prowess to keep his enemies at bay, and for this reason decides to create a permanent alliance with the hero by giving him his beautiful sister in marriage (EvO 6344–6365; GvS 19088–19102). However, in Ulrich von Türheim's and Heinrich von Freiberg's continuations of Gottfried's poem, some of the strategic planning comes not only from the male heir, but also from his mother, the duchess, who in Heinrich's text is called

---

is mentioned briefly and only once in the "Bold Water" episode in Eilhart (EvO, vv. 6382–6387). Gottfried von Strassburg does not mention the mother at all. To differentiate between different Tristan-texts, I use the following abbreviations: EvO for Eilhart von Oberge's *Tristant und Isalde* (1993); GvS for Gottfried von Strassburg's *Tristan* (1996); HvF for Heinrich von Freiberg's *Tristan und Isolde* (1993); and UvT for Ulrich von Türheim's *Tristan und Isolde* (1992). Hereafter quotations from these texts will be cited parenthetically with the appropriate abbreviation followed by line numbers.

6 On the character of Queen Isolde see Rasmussen 1997, 113–35, esp. 119–33; Rasmussen 2000; Rasmussen 2003; Classen 2002; Classen 2007.

7 NB: The original Middle High German for the first half of the following subtitle is: "Habe es dines vaters rat / unde diner muter, daz ist guot" (UvT 94–95). The second half of the subtitle is an allusion to the subtitle in Rasmussen's chapter on Gottfried's Queen Isolde, which reads "How a Noblewoman Wields Political Power" (1997, 119). For a summary of this chapter, see above, Appendix A, following the Introduction.

Karsie. One may wonder why this secondary character should have been developed, as it seems, by Ulrich von Türheim, and then later further modified by Heinrich, who knew and used this version in addition to the two earlier poems by Gottfried and Eilhart.[8] Both sequels make the duchess reminiscent of Gottfried's Queen Isolde: she is a fulfilled, powerful, secure, and respected wife and mother, who speaks on her husband's behalf, advises her son Kaedin, and makes important political and familial decisions. She is also the mother who, similarly to Gottfried's Queen Isolde, tries to secure a good future for her only daughter, to guarantee that her life as a married woman will be that of respect and love.

Of course, Ulrich as well as Heinrich fall short when compared to Gottfried's masterful handling of Queen Isolde.[9] The episodes involving Duchess Karsie in both works are not as elaborate and poetically crafted as those in their famous prequel; and yet, there is a striking resemblance between the two women's respective situations, their access to power, their influence and how they wield it, and, in Heinrich's case, even in their relation to their daughters, the point which I will address below. Both poems present the duchess as a driving force in the family, a decision-maker, and a valued advisor, although of the two, it is Ulrich's version that does so much more explicitly and forcefully. Having decided to forget his lover in the embraces of another woman, Tristan asks her brother Kaedin to help him secure her hand in marriage. He sends his friend off to talk to the parents and gives him the following instruction: "Habe es dines vaters rat / unde diner muter, daz ist guot" [UvT 94–95; "Seek your father's advice and your mother's as well. This is proper"]. However, when Kaedin goes to fulfill his mission, he surprisingly does not address the head of the family:

> Hine ginc do Gahedin
> zu sinen gelieben allen drin,

---

8 Gibbs says it is not certain that Heinrich knew Ulrich's version, but there is evidence that he did, e.g., his correction of Isolde's behavior in the Petitcriu-episode (2003, 277). There are several other episodes that may also be read as Heinrich's indirect engagement with Ulrich's text. Other scholars agree with my opinion that Heinrich knew and responded to his predecessor, just like he did to Eilhart, whom he also does not mention (Buschinger 1993, 62–63; Nanz 2010, 222–23, 229; Sedlmeyer 1976, 263 and 302).

9 Common criticism of the sequels includes: "so blatantly not Gottfried von Strassburg"; "little ability to emulate [Gottfried] or – more significantly – to demonstrate an awareness of his true purpose"; "complete reversal of Gottfried"; and standing Gottfried "on his head" (Gibbs 2003, 273–75, 281). Thomas Kerth sees Ulrich "struggling with two models to produce an independent writing, but inferior to each" (as quoted in Gibbs 2003, 275); while Wetzel calls Ulrich's sequel "die klägliche Fortsetzung" [the pitiful sequel] (1993, 75). At the same time, Peter Strohschneider (1991) and Christopher Clason (2006) consider it altogether unfair to compare either Heinrich or Ulrich to Gottfried and offer instead to treat the two later texts as independent works. Gibbs joins Strohschneider in believing that perhaps the two later poets' aim "was not to reach the end but to delay the ending by means of a completely new process of narration" (2003, 273–74). For a detailed summary of critical responses to both later epics also see Gibbs and Johnson 1997, 373–74.

da er si bienander vant.
mit vuge sprach er so zehant:
"ich bin da her zu iuh comen
unde han Tristandes mut vernomen
unde gar anz ende erkunnet.
er bit, daz ir im gunnet
Ysot, miner swester, ze e.
er giht, er welle iemmer me
gerne hie bi uns bestan.
nu soln wir in geniesen lan,
daz er uns wol gedienet heit
unde durh uns ritterlichen streit.
a hi! wan hat nirgen ritterschaft
ane prise also groze craft,
als diu Tristandes hat?"
(UvT 117–33)

[Then Kaedin went to his loved ones, all three of whom he found sitting together. He at once spoke with decorum: "I have come to you, for I have heard and found out all about Tristan's intentions. He begs you to give him in marriage Isolde, my sister. He says he wishes to remain with us forever. Now we must show our gratitude to him for all the knightly service he rendered us. Oh, where have knightly deeds ever earned such great praise as those of Tristan?"]

Even more surprisingly, the reply he receives comes not from his father but from his mother who does not simply make a decision about establishing a profitable and prestigious marriage in order to secure a champion of great fame for her daughter, but sees much farther than her son politically. She instantly calculates that an alliance with Tristan means subjugation of one of their archenemies, Count Riol, an allusion to Eilhart's epic:

"Wol dir, reine selic man!"
sprach diu süeze herzogin.
"vil lieber sun Kaedin,
sit ez dir wol behaget,
wir suln Ysot, die claren maget,
geben Tristande.
bestat er in dem lande,
wir sin iemmer me genesen,
unde muz Riol der grave wesen
mit vorhte under dinem vanen."
(UvT 136–45)

["Bless you, you pure noble man!" said the sweet duchess. "My dear son Kaedin, since it seems right to you, let us give Isolde, the pure maiden, to Tristan. If he remains in our lands, we will be forever safe, and Count Riol will be compelled by fear to serve under your banner as well."]

Where Kaedin thinks of one person, however grand, and of the prestige that comes with having such a hero at his court, his mother foresees an immediate and specific benefit that would guarantee her land peaceful existence. To prove her acumen as an outstanding politician even further, Ulrich's duchess wants to seal the deal as soon as possible, so as not to allow such an opportunity to slip through her fingers:

> "daz getane ist daz getane.
> ich bin in dem wane,
> biz daz dinc ist ungetan,
> so mag ez vil wol zegan.
> sa zehant als ez geschicht
> sone mag ez danne erwinden niht.
> ganc, brinc Tristanen her.
> er vindet al sine ger."
> (UvT 153–60)

[Only what is done is truly done. I truly believe that while something is not completed, it may very well fall apart; but as soon as it happens, one can no longer undo it. Go and bring Tristan here, for he will find everything he desires.]

In this passage, the duchess refers to a public oath, a binding oral contract in the presence of all, which Tristan would never be able to break afterwards without losing his honor. Her words are also an admonition that his marriage ties should not be taken lightly, for by attaching himself to Isolde of the White Hands, Tristan binds himself to her and her whole family for life. The mother demands that Tristan remain in Arundel until his death: "ir muzet aber beliben hie bi uns / iemmer biz an iuwern tot" [UvT 188–89; But you will have to remain here with us forever, until your death]. One may wonder if this stipulation should be read as a simple wish to secure the hero's continuous support or as a mother's sensing that Tristan would turn out to be a bad husband and break his oath because of his love for another woman.[10] Ulrich's text does not offer us this specific insight; and yet ironically, the duchess' words do function as a prediction in the long run, since, although Tristan leaves several times to see his lover after his marriage, he ultimately dies in Arundel with (and because of) his wife. Noteworthy in this scene is the fact that Tristan's reply to the duchess does not at all address this sobering stipulation of hers; he behaves rather nonchalantly, simply responding that he will gladly take Isolde as his wedded wife ("ich will gerne nemen Ysot / unde iemmer elichen haben" [UvT 190–91]), and later even makes a joke during the ceremony, provoking everybody's laughter (UvT 197–99). The duchess, however, is in no mood for joking and insists

---

10 Tristan's liaison with Isolde the Blond appears to be widely known in the world of the epic, since Isolde of the White Hands reproaches him for it on their wedding night. Cf. UvT, 362–73.

on completing this important business as soon as possible, thus showing the presence of mind that Ulrich clearly admires by calling her clever ("cluc"):

> "herre, so lat den eit iuh staben,"
> sprach die herzoginne cluc.
> daz heiltum man dar truc,
> dar uffe swur sich Tristan
> Ysot zeim elichen man.
> (UvT 192–96)

> ["My lord, so let us hear you swear an oath," said the clever duchess. The monstrance was then brought in, on which Tristan swore to become a husband to Isolde.]

It is no surprise that Ulrich describes his heroine as "cluc." Her intelligence becomes so much more evident when compared to her husband's behavior.[11] The duke is shown to employ his authority in Ulrich's text only once, following the famous "Bold Water" episode, in which the truth about Tristan's avoiding his spousal responsibilities finally comes to light thanks to his wife's involuntary indiscretion.[12] Kaedin, who heard it, consults both parents about the best way to proceed, addressing himself, as usual, first to his father and then to his mother: "sime vater selt erz zehant / unde siner muter dar zuo. / 'waz woltir, daz ich dar umb tu?'" [UvT 460–62; He told his father about it at once, and his mother, too, asking: "What do you wish me to do?"]. This time the narrator does not specify which of the two parents actually responds; however, the reader familiar with Ulrich's text can recognize the duchess' voice in the almost legalistic precision of the ensuing instructions and the clarity of her thinking:

> "da soltuz dinen vriunden clagen,
> mannen unde magen.
> Tristan soltu vragen,
> waz er meine da mite.
> vil gesellecliche in bite,
> daz er sinen muot wandele
> unde baz Ysoten handele.
> si daz ers niht tuge,
> sun, ob dich daz muge,
> daz la den luten wesen schin."
> (UvT 464–73)

---

[11] In her study of the Isolde characters in the Tristan tradition, Mälzer points out the unusual forcefulness of Ulrich's duchess' character and calls her "die gegenüber dem Ehemann und Bruder der Isolde II dominierende Figur" (1991, 239 n10).

[12] In the "Bold Water" episode (UvT 374–518; HvF 3757–95) the horse that Isolde of the White Hands rides steps into a pool, sending a sprinkle of cold water under the woman's undergarments. The shock of it causes the woman to laugh and make a surprising comment about the water being bolder than her husband Tristan. When pressed, Isolde admits that despite being married for a long time, she still remains a virgin.

[You should complain about this to your friends, your vassals and your kinsmen. You should also inquire of Tristan what he means by this. Ask him in a very friendly way to change his mind and treat Isolde better. Should he refuse, my son, then let all know that it offends you deeply.]

Had these words belonged to the father, they would have been inconsistent with his sudden expression of unrestrained, albeit justifiable, public display of animosity toward Tristan several verses later. When Kaedin and Tristan come to ask for permission to leave Karke, so that Tristan could defend himself by showing Kaedin the insuperable beauty of Isolde the Blond, the duke rebukes Tristan scornfully in public and even threatens to punish him by death:

"da mit kumt er [Tristan] niht abe,
ine heiz im tun den tot.
er hat mich unde dich unde Ysot
an eren gar geschendet,
unser hohe vroude erwendet.
dez muz im sterben nahen."
(UvT 724–29)

[He [Tristan] will not get away with it: I will send him to his death! He has deprived me, you, and Isolde of honor and our lives of joy. For that his death is drawing nigh.]

It is only with the help of his daughter that the duke's honor and reputation of a just sovereign are saved. Such a simplistic response to the situation and a desire for immediate vengeance contrast unfavorably with the above-mentioned suggestions of the duchess that prove her political and psychological astuteness. The prompt yet careful outline of legal steps that would make Tristan's crime public and thus secure their kin's and vassals' support in case of a future retribution, coupled with the emphasis on restraint and need to convince Tristan to begin treating his wife as he ought to, showcase the duchess' talents as a diplomat who thinks both long- and short-term.

However impressive this noblewoman may be, it is important to remember the limits of political authority for women. As Rasmussen observes in her analysis of Queen Isolde, although the woman may be "rich, wise, beautiful, witty, and perceptive, her access to political power is predicated solely on the esteem and love with which her husband the king regards her. She cannot exercise power publicly unless he loves and trusts her enough to command it" (Rasmussen 1997, 128). Susan Mosher Stuard emphasizes that if women exerted any power at all, they derived it from their intimacy with and access to the male ruler (quoted in Rasmussen 1997, 129).[13] Ulrich's text gestures toward this reality. The duchess is clearly loved and respected by her male relatives: it is *her* advice that is truly sought, although on the surface the advice formally solicited is that of her husband or of the two of them as a couple.

---

13 The same point is made by Rüdiger Schnell in his more recent study. See Schnell 2004.

The character herself is depicted as keenly aware of the limitations constraining her behavior as a female member of the household, albeit a wise and respected one: she proves herself to be as skillful a politician within her own family as in external affairs. In her argument, she cleverly appeals to her son's ego, pointing out that an alliance with Tristan will benefit *him* directly, for the subdued enemy will have to fight under *his*, Kaedin's, banner. Although she is the one in charge of all decisions in the engagement episode and is the *only* person who speaks in almost 100 verses (UvT 117–210), the text also reflects her subordination over and over again by consistently mentioning her husband first.[14] That power and influence of such women as Queen Isolde and Duchess of Arundel is limited and to some extent even ephemeral is supported by the words of Isolde of the White Hands in Ulrich's text. Even though it is the mother who arranges everything in her presence,[15] Isolde as a dutiful daughter expresses her obedience only to *her father's* will, thus suggesting that the duchess was acting as a mouthpiece of the duke, to whom authority truly belongs:

> Tristan schimlichen sprach,
> davon zelachene in geschah:
> "juncvrouwe, welt ir nemen mich?"
> "spreche ich nu, here, 'nein ich',
> daz were *mime vater zorn.*
> des ist ez besser verborn.
> *swaz wil min vater,* daz wil ich."
>   (UvT 200–3, emphasis added)
>
> [Tristan said jokingly, which made all of them laugh: "My lady, would you take me?"— "My lord, if I were to say 'no,' it would cause my father's anger, so I'd rather avoid it. Whatever my father wills, that is my will as well."]

Ulrich von Türheim is known for portraying characters who "speak," either vocally or with their bodies, and his treatment of the "herzogine" is consistent with his overall approach (Trokhimenko 2011). His successor, the Bohemian poet Heinrich von Freiberg creates a narrative that is starkly different. As Margarete Sedlmeyer points out: "Unzureichend wäre es [. . .] sicherlich, Heinrich ausschließlich als Bearbeiter oder 'Korrektor' Ulrichs von Türheim zu verstehen. Er benützt wohl dessen Fassung und distanziert sich gleichzeitig auch von ihr . . . [. . .] [Er] folgt in ungefähr einem Zehntel seines Werkes Ulrichs Handlung" [Sedlmeyer 1976, 263; It would certainly be insufficient to see Heinrich exclusively as a person who reworks and 'corrects'

---

14 Also cf.: "Tristanen wol enphiengen / *der wirt, die wirtin* unde Ysot" [UvT 174–75; *The host, the hostess,* and Ysot received Tristan well]; "*vater unde muter* des vrouten sich" [UvT 204; *father and mother* were happy about that]. Emphasis added.
15 For additional instances when the duchess speaks, see: "Ysot ir mutter do gebot / daz si Tristanen gruzte" [UvT 176; Isolde was then ordered by her mother to greet Tristan]; "done sprach die herzogin san" [UvT 183; The duchess then spoke at once]; "die wirten sprach ze Tristan" [UvT 205; the hostess spoke to Tristan].

Ulrich von Türheim. He does make use of the latter's version and yet simultaneously distances himself from it. [. . .] About one tenth of his work actually follows Ulrich's plot].[16] In addition to their respective lengths of 6890 vs. 3730 verses, the two epics differ in their overall ethos and, as a result, in their treatment of the leading characters. Writing at the royal court in Prague during its cultural revival, the Bohemian poet cannot conceal his enthusiasm for knightly life and courtly values (McDonald 1990, 55; Bumke 2000, 195; Spiewok 1993, 145). Heinrich portrays Tristan as a splendid courtly hero whose chivalric adventures offset his failings in love. To Gottfried's and Ulrich's understanding of passion this author prefers a more conventional view of love and marriage and has been described as "the voice of the self-assured moralist" (McDonald 1990, 55) whose text "is marked [. . .] by the hostile encounter of heroic action and amorous passion" (Deighton 2004, 111). Returning to chivalric romance in Heinrich's case means a return to chivalric values, particularly the disciplined courtly body, and to a traditional view of gender relations. In his depiction of the duchess, whom he names Karsie, Heinrich seems at first glance to follow Ulrich's model. Like his predecessor, he presents her as a well-bred, respected, loved, and intelligent noblewoman, whose advice is solicited and treasured; and like Ulrich he maintains male preeminence by always mentioning Karsie second to her husband Lovelin: "Wir han gehort, wie Tristant / in Arundele daz lant / zu dem herzogen quam, [. . .] / den man da nante Lovelin. / Karsie hiez die herzogin" [HvF 85–90; We have heard how Tristant came to the land of Arundel, to the duke, whose name was Lovelin; the duchess was called Karsie].[17] However, this is where the similarities between the two works end, for Heinrich reinforces gender hierarchy much more forcefully than Ulrich.

Heinrich's romance is undoubtedly superior in a poetic sense; it incorporates character descriptions and the conventions of courtly protocol, something that Ulrich does not do. His duchess is described through a series of standard epithets as pure and free of all falsehood ("die reine, valsches vrie" [HvF 447]); her relationship with her husband and her son is given a touch of softness: the two parents sit like two doves "bie ein ander" [HvF 382–83; next to one another]; and Kaedin kneels in front of his parents as he addresses them (HvF 394–97). And yet these seeming markers of respect curiously coincide with Karsie's much diminished authority. In a striking reversal of Ulrich's text, where, although both parents are appealed to, the decision and all actions come only from the duchess, Heinrich's Kaedin speaks to his mother first. However, this approach proves to be not much more than a bow to courtly etiquette: "sin mut vrut und guter / und sine zucht im

---

16 See also Buschinger 1993, 60.
17 See also, the following additional examples: "ich [Kaedin] lege dines herzen kur / minem vater gerne vur / und dar zu miner muter" [HvF 371–73; "I [Kaedin] will tell my father as well as my mother about your heart's choice"]; and "der herzoge und die herzogin" [HvF 427; the duke and the duchess].

daz gebot" [HvF 396–97; His cleverness and goodness as well as his upbringing told him to do so]. In fact, Kaedin orders his sister to leave so that he can speak to his *father* in private, which he indeed does by presenting his arguments to the duke alone (HvF 382–93, 398–407).

In Heinrich's text the political authority and decision-making rest with male characters; in their turn, women are left to busy themselves with the spheres of love and marriage. While it was Ulrich's "herzogine" who provided brilliant reasoning for forming an alliance with Tristan, Heinrich gives this function to Kaedin: *he* is the one who advises his parents to grant his friend's wish and provides support for this strategy, while the noble couple rejoices in hearing this news (HvF 408) and Karsie merely inquires about the origin of the idea (HvF 410–14). Once Tristan arrives, he is formally welcomed into the family by the father (HvF 494–500), who promises to share his rule with him. Karsie is allowed to notify her daughter of their joint decision and later to inquire about Tristan's intentions but only in what concerns love: "Die herzogin Karsie / die kusche, wandels vrie, / nam ern Tristanden [. . .] / und vraget in in den ziten, / ob ez were der wille sin / um die botschaft, als Kaedin / het geworben wider sie" [HvF 481–89; Duchess Karsie, the chaste and honest, took Tristan [. . .] and asked him if the news that Kaedin had brought them expressed his free will]. It is easy to see how the character of the "herzogine," whom Heinrich could have borrowed only from Ulrich is reshaped to fit a much more traditional courtly gender stereotype. The political authority and the diplomatic astuteness of Ulrich's duchess are transformed and channeled into what might have been perceived as a more proper outlet – that of love and marriage, the traditional prerogatives of women.[18]

2 Like Mother, Like Daughter? Continuities and Discontinuities between Mothers and Daughters

"The mother-daughter relationship is about the production and transmission of knowledge about women between women: about bodily pleasure and pain, [. . .] about self-love and self-loathing" observes Ann Marie Rasmussen in her study on this topic (1997, 15). This study as well as much of feminist theory views the mother-daughter relationship as a key factor in how women acquire gender identity in a patriarchal society. Literary representations of mother-daughter interactions are what Rasmussen calls "culturally conditioned narratives" about the choices older and

---

[18] A similar gendered division in spheres is found in medieval conduct discourse, best represented by the two *Winsbecke* poems. See Rasmussen 1997, 136–59; Rasmussen and Trokhimenko 2009; and Trokhimenko 2014, 105–11.

younger women have in a patriarchal social order and about the "scripts, the stereotypes, the roles through which these stories can be told" (1997, 18). One such script is an equation of female identity with a sexual identity, "a sociosexual" identity, to borrow Rasmussen's term, that "depends on the woman's becoming an attractive and compliant object of male desire," and imposes on her an unsatisfiable requirement of being virtuous and accessible at the same time (Rasmussen 1997, 23).[19]

Both Tristan sequels provide ample examples of women's instrumental function. As mentioned above, Ulrich's approach to the Duchess of Arundel is consistent with the historical evidence that shows that an aristocratic woman's success or limitations always depended on the will of her male partner (Mälzer 1991, 29–30; Rasmussen 1997, 128–30; Rasmussen 2003, 145). And yet, in the universe of his text the duchess sets a powerful example to her daughter, Isolde of the White Hands, of what it means to be a successful noblewoman. Her behavior in Ulrich's epic has been described in the scholarship as unusual in its forcefulness (Mälzer 1991, 239).[20] As Rasmussen points out, the mother reproduces in her daughter "the same kind of female identity that the mother herself has acted out, or is in the process of acting out" (1997, 118), and indeed the two distinguishing features of this character in Ulrich's text are conspicuously her intelligence and her pride. In fact, Nanz (2010, 175) observes that they are the very first characteristics the poet points to in Tristan's future wife by describing her as *ffier unde also cluc* [UvT 321; proud and so clever].[21] Even though this daughter's fate turns out to be starkly unlike her mother's, the former replicates the latter in her readiness to express herself, as well as in her ability to think legalistically and to act quickly. Conspicuously, it is the White-Handed Isolde who convinces her father to give up his vengeance once her marriage is revealed to be a sham. When the enraged duke wishes to kill Tristan, no matter what arguments his son-in-law offers and no matter what defense his own son Kaedin and Tristan's trusted friend Kurvenal

---

19 Thelma Fenster similarly observes that "Arthurian literature itself often reveals some of these same tensions: its earliest avatar, medieval romance narrative, suggested woman's desirability but could nonetheless cast woman's desire as a problem" (1996, XIX). Also see Trokhimenko 2014, Ch. 3–4.

20 Cf. also note 10: "Die Herzogin ist in dieser Szene die gegenüber dem Ehemann und Bruder der Isolde II dominierende Figur: sie gebietet ihrer Tochter, sich Tristan gegenüber entsprechend höfisch zu verhalten (U. 176ff.); sie setzt die Bedingungen für dei Eheschließung fest (Tristan muß bis zu seinem Tod in Karke bleiben) und läßt Tristan einen Eid darauf schwören (183ff.; 192f.); und schließlich segnet sie die Brautleute im Bett (212ff.)" [In comparison to her spouse and to Isolde II's brother, the duchess is the dominant figure in this scene: she commands her daughter to behave in a courtly way with Tristan (U. 176ff.); she sets the conditions for the marriage (Tristan must remain in Karke until his death) and compels Tristan to swear an oath to that effect (183ff; 192f.). Finally, she is the one blessing the newly married couple in bed (212ff.)] (Mälzer 1991, 239).

21 There are, of course, also more traditional epithets as well, referring to Isolde's beauty, goodness, and purity, such as "süez," "clar," "wolgetan," "guot," "rein" [UvT 101, 140, 731; UvT 320, 811; UvT 394, 455; UvT 112, 278, 310, 391, respectively].

mount on his behalf, it is the young Isolde who settles the affair. She tells her father not to sacrifice his honor to anger and vengefulness and, remarkably, the hitherto outraged man yields:

> done sprach diu magt Ysolde,
> die suze wiz gehende:
> "Tristan ist ellende.
> ez ist laster, der im iht tuot.
> vater, verkere dinen muot
> unde beganc dekeine schande." [. . .]
> "Tohter, swas dich dunket gut,
> des wil ich dir niht versagn."
> (UvT 736–41, 750–51)

[Then the sweet maiden Isolde of the White Hands said: "Tristan is a stranger here; it would be shameful if anything were to happen to him. Father, change your mind and don't commit an infamy." [. . .] "Daughter, whatever seems good to you I will not deny you."]

Albeit for one brief moment, Ulrich's Isolde of the White Hands approaches her mother in manifesting her ability to think quickly, clearly, and strategically, and argue persuasively.

This is not the only example of the second Isolde's ability to strategize and to think juridically. With the exception of her involuntary revelation in the Bold Water episode (UvT 374–473), this character is shown to plan her actions. At the end of the tale, she cunningly secures herself a helper, a merchant's wife, who has to notify her of the arrival of her rival, Tristan's lover Isolde the Blond (UvT 3367–71); but even before it comes to this cruel revenge, examples of her strategizing abound. After her unsuccessful first night, it is Isolde of the White Hands herself who makes a decision to perform as a married woman by putting on a married woman's headdress; and before confronting Tristan about his failure as a husband, she carefully thinks everything over.[22] She also gives her husband an ultimatum as to how long she is willing to tolerate his refusal to pay his marital debt:

> nu hore, lieber Tristan [. . .]
> din herze mich niht meinet
> als ez ze rehte solde.
> ez ist diu blunde Ysolde,
> die diz gebot geboten hat.
> daz dinen eren misse stat. [. . .]
> gerne wil ich liden die geschiht
> biz an daz gesprochen zil.
> mit vlize ich ez dar heln wil,

---

[22] "eines nahtes si gedâhte, daz si dô vollebrâhte" [UvT 333–34; One night she thought of what she then carried out].

> daz ez niemer wirt gesagt,
> biz daz daz jar sich hat vertagt,
> biz da hin wil ichs lazen sin.
>   (UvT 353, 360–64, 368–73)

["Now listen, my dear Tristan. Your heart doesn't love me as it rightly should. [. . .] It is the blond Isolde who has mandated this oath so detrimental to your honor. [. . .] I am willing to bear with your story until the appointed time. I will take pains to conceal it, lest it becomes known before a full year has run out. Until then I am willing to let it be."]

The passage reveals the Breton Isolde to be not at all as naïve and gullible as she might appear. Her strong warning to Tristan demonstrates her knowledge of his ongoing infatuation with her namesake and her awareness of what is due to her. Ulrich's romance is essentially a tale about the Second Isolde's rights, which is reflected in its language, in its constant repetition of the word *reht*. It is not surprising that in her rebuke, Isolde II also evokes the language of rights and honor.

At the conclusion of the epic, one of the text's editions allows a possibility of Isolde of the White Hands arguing and defending her spousal rights until the very end, at Tristan's bier, even though by then her character has clearly lost the audience's sympathy in favor of Tristan's lover Isolde the Blond (Trokhimenko 2011, 212–13). Unlike her mother, who was lucky or shrewd enough (or both) to learn how to use the institution of marriage to her advantage in order to gain political influence, Isolde of the White Hands is trapped by it. And yet, as the text shows, she is not at all a completely compliant and voiceless object of homosocial exchange. Despite her vilification at the conclusion of the work, one must acknowledge that whether sympathetic or vengeful, Ulrich von Türheim's Isolde of the White Hands is consistently shown attempting to obtain at least some control over her marriage throughout the story. Together with her forcefulness and readiness to speak, this drive to obtain control constitutes the true continuity between her and her mother.

In her study, Rasmussen demonstrates how woman's instrumental function can become "a convention to be defied or a model to be subverted" (1997, 118). Even though clearly intended (and having intended herself) to be "an attractive and compliant object of male desire," Isolde of the White Hands in Ulrich's epic does not fit this mold (Rasmussen 1997, 117).[23] And yet, her case is not a repudiation of this convention; on the contrary, it is to some extent its reaffirmation. The achievements of such women as Duchess Karsie and Queen Isolde show that female intelligence must be properly channeled and supported within marriage in order to increase the woman's own and her family's honor. In contrast, in the case of "the other Isolde" the inability to become an object of male desire leads to everybody's

---

[23] Also see Nanz's description of Isolde of the White Hands as neither a loving nor a sympathetic character in Ulrich: "weder als liebende noch als bemitleidenswerte Figur" (2010, 302).

destruction.[24] Although Ulrich von Türheim is sympathetic toward the tragic adulterous love between Tristan and Isolde the Blond, as becomes evident in his plea to God to take mercy on the two protagonists' souls (UvT 3653–57), his approach to Isolde of the White Hands is to some extent that of a cautionary tale about femininity, sexuality, and marriage.

The connection between female desirability and life success is shared and is made even more conventional in Heinrich von Freiberg's version of the Tristan-story. Heinrich's Isolde the Second is a poster child for the instrumental function of women, for the ideology that sees women as attractive and compliant objects of male desire. One might even say that she is an example of this ideal taken to the extreme. Yet it is also possible to see this character as pointing to tensions within this model.

As Heinrich's handling of the Duchess of Arundel illustrates, this poet tones down his female characters in order to make them correspond to a much more traditional image of courtly femininity (Trokhimenko 2011, 213–26). His depiction of the maiden of Arundel is consistent with this overall tendency. The Second Isolde is as a model courtly woman, endowed with all stereotypic attributes: chaste and wise ("kusche," "wise" [HvF 445]), beautiful and lovely ("wunnenclich" [HvF 664]), and always carries herself with propriety ("in zuchten," "zuchticlich" [HvF 607 and 928–29, respectively]). Strongly reminiscent of Enite, the exemplary wife in the Hartmann von Aue's popular medieval romance *Erec*, this Isolde is introspective, self-critical, self-sacrificing, perfectly good-mannered, and willing to conceal her own pain and disgrace from others.[25] It is her own behavior, not her husband's, that she first examines and questions on her disastrous wedding night (HvF 815–21). Despite the slight, she remains supportive of Tristan's honor and even approves of his abandoning her for a while, so that he can improve his knightly repute (HvF 1494–1510). In short, this Isolde is not at all outspoken or rebellious, but extremely compliant, non-confrontational, passive, pliable, and meek.

Similar to Ulrich's *Tristan*, there is a connection between the mother and the daughter in Heinrich's work; but if in the earlier sequel it was due to similarity in their personalities, this version of the Tristan story adds one more important element to their relationship and to our modern understanding of the Breton Isolde's character. In Heinrich's epic, we get a glimpse of Karsie's shaping of her daughter's identity in adherence to her instrumental function. The Bohemian poet is commonly

---

[24] Nanz points out that Tristan in Ulrich's work does not at all care for Isolde of the White Hands (2010, 177).

[25] After her unsuccessful nuptials, Isolde's behavior is said to reveal nothing to the onlookers: "an ir geberden nicht erschein, / weder daz megetliche nein / noch daz wipliche ja. / si gebarte tugentliche da, / sie konde mit zuchten uber sen, / ob ir waz icht od nicht geschen" [HvF 873–78; Her behavior confirmed neither the maidenly "no" nor the womanly "yes." She conducted herself virtuously; and if anything or nothing at all had happened to her, she was able to ignore it graciously].

commended for his deep familiarity with contemporaneous courtly and clerical discourses and his particular effort to approximate his predecessor Gottfried von Strassburg (Nanz 2010, 221; Sedlmeyer 1976, 303). The description of Isolde's behavior on her wedding night, greatly expanded in Heinrich's *Tristan*, is in perfect compliance with the scripts of femininity found in high-medieval conduct texts, such as the thirteenth-century treatise *Die Winsbeckin* (ca. 1210–1220), for example.

One important function of noble mothers in medieval fiction is that of attending to their daughters' upbringing and guiding them into a proper marriage (Rasmussen 2003, 144). This is what the wise mother in *Die Winsbeckin*, as well as Gottfried's Queen Isolde, and Heinrich's Duchess Karsie do. *Die Winsbeckin* lays out the exact requirements for female comportment most likely to attract and secure male attention:

> Wis liebiu tohter wol gemuot
> daz doch der zuht die sinne pflegen [. . .]
> mahtu die tugent uf gewegen
> dir wirt von mangem werden man
> mit wunschen nahen bi gilegen
> soltu mit sælden werden alt
> zuo der schoene die du hast
> durh dich verswendet wirt der walt.[26]

[Beloved daughter, be even-tempered, so that your mind governs your modesty. [. . .] If you can rise in virtue, then many a worthy man will lie with you in his dreams. If you are to grow old with good fortune together with the beauty you already possess, then forests will be laid waste on your account.]

The image of a forest of knightly spears broken in the young maiden's name in tournaments "sustains the idea of male active desire fueled by exemplary passive feminine beauty" and reinforces the message that "socially sanctioned, demure, virtuous, asexual feminine conduct arouses male lust" (Rasmussen 1997, 142). Male desire therefore determines female social value, warns *Die Winsbeckin*: "So man gidenchet oft an dich / und wunschet din so bistu wert" [*Winsbeckin* 17, 9–10; If someone thinks of you often and desires you then you are valuable].

Heinrich's Isolde of the White Hands is a fascinating example of not only trying to implement *Die Winsbeckin*'s dictum and but also of its failure. As Rasmussen's work illustrates, the notion of desire in many courtly and conduct texts can be "clearly identified with men's sexual appetites: love is male desire that a woman attracts and excites by displaying exemplary passivity in the face of male action" (1997, 142). The Breton Isolde is socialized by her mother to be a beautiful, compliant,

---

26 *Winsbeckin*, 15, 1–10. *Die Winsbeckin* will be cited parenthetically by strophe and line numbers; it is quoted and translated according to Rasmussen and Trokhimenko 2009. For a detailed analysis, see Rasmussen 1997, 142.

and non-confrontational object of admiration, desire, and exchange, whose lack of agency is consistently emphasized by the narrator: she is *led* to Tristan (HvF 664–66) and literally *laid* down in her husband's arms by her mother (HvF 669–71). While after the wedding her counterpart in Ulrich's text puts on a married woman's wimple on her own initiative, Heinrich's heroine yet again allows others to define her status and her fate: her mother does it for her.[27] Hers is the tale of intra- and extra-textual objectification, not of rights (*reht*). Heinrich's text suggests that Isolde's mother Karsie is the person from whom she learns this behavior. Heinrich's narrator emphasizes the intimate friendship and trust that exist between the mother and the daughter by calling Karsie her daughter's "trut" [literally "beloved"], the person the young Isolde loves and cherishes the most (HvF 849). It is her words that Isolde thinks of and tries to implement on her wedding night in order to increase Tristan's passion (HvF 683–740). Before her new husband approaches her, the maiden wraps her legs in her chemise ("pfeitel") and presses her knees to her stomach in what appears to be a fetal position (HvF 698–713), thus creating what the narrator calls a fortification ("eine veste") out of her own limbs (HvF 728–33). She does so not because of fear of sexual intercourse, but rather because she acts *als ir muoter het erzogen* [HvF 731; as her mother had taught her, emphasis added]. The goal of showing some reticence before final surrender is both to convince Tristan of her maidenly modesty and to titillate him:

> sie dachte: "ob ein gelustel
> von herzen Tristande gat,
> daz er dich minnenclich bestat,
> do vindet er dich ouch bie wer.
> ob ich mich eine wile ner
> vor im durch megetlichen pris,
> der junge suze Permenis
> her nach mich habet deste bas."
> (HvF 714–21)

[She thought: "If Tristan has desire in his heart to attack you in an amorous way, he will find you prepared to defend yourself. If I resist him for a while for the sake of my maidenly glory, the young sweet man of Parmenia will only love me more for it."]

The mother has clearly taught her daughter how to recognize and manipulate male desire according to the rules of courtly society. Isolde's behavior and Karsie's instructions are in compliance with a passage in *Die Winsbeckin* about proper courting ritual

---

27 Cf: "diu reine, suze maget Ysot, / slouf in wiplich gewant; / ir houbt si vil schone bant / durh den gewunlichen site" [UvT 310–13; The pure sweet maiden Isolde slipped on a married woman's clothes and bound her headdress beautifully according to custom]; "sie [Isolde's mother Karsie] nam Tristandes wane brut / und leget ir riche cleider an, / als sie beste mochte han, / und bant sie nach der briute site" [HvF 850–53; Karsie took Tristan's supposed wife, dressed her richly in the best clothes she could have, and bound her headdress according to the custom of married women].

between men and women, in which female resistance is presented as a necessary and anticipated part of protocol:

> Ez ist komen her in alten siten
> vor manegen iaren unde tagen
> daz man diu wip sol guetlich biten
> und lieplich in dem hertzen tragen
> so sullen si zuhticlich versagen
> oder aber ze sinneclich gewern.
> (*Diu Winsbeckin* 22, 1–6)

> [It has long been the custom, from many days and many years ago, that men woo women nicely and bear them tenderly in their hearts. And women are meant to decline with true modesty or to fend them off so wisely]

As in most medieval literary representations of mothers and daughters, the socialization and the sexualization are inextricably linked here. Isolde's behavior reveals her awareness that a courtly woman must be both virtuous and seductive at the same time. Her display of modesty makes her both chaste and erotic; her self-constructed "veste" calls to mind the image of the closed garden (*hortus conclusus*), a popular trope in medieval discourse on virginity, thus emphasizing her virtue and purity.[28] The reference to the woman's shift or chemise as one of the components of "veste" contributes to the Second Isolde's eroticization. The chemise is an undergarment that simultaneously conceals and points to the presence of a naked female body. The message sent is that this fortress wants to surrender, and the closed garden invites Tristan to break in.[29]

As Rasmussen points out, "Mothers and daughters talk about sex. [. . .] The mother teaches her daughter love lore. In so doing she reproduces a female sphere of activity, initiates her daughter into the patriarchal social order" (1997, 22–24). Or, put another way, "[t]he only 'commodity' [the woman] possesses in patriarchy [is] her sexuality, her desirability, her instrumental function" (1997, 134). Heinrich's *Tristan* is yet another text where this happens. In teaching her daughter about exciting through resistance in order to make the new husband love and appreciate his

---

[28] Cf. "A garden enclosed is my sister, my spouse; a spring shut up, a fountain sealed" (Song of Songs 4:12). The function of this trope in the medieval *Virginitätslehre* is discussed in Kelly 2000, 11.

[29] The narrator sexualizes Isolde of the White Hands by calling her a "noezel", a diminutive of "nôz" [an animal], which suggests her animal instincts, thus echoing the misogynous belief in female sexual insatiability: "ei, wie wol bedâchte daz / der minne ein menschlîch noezel! / sie lac an einem kloezel / zu samme gedrücket / und minneclîch gesmücket in megetlîchem ruome" [HvF 722–27; Oh, how cleverly did Love's little human animal devise this! She lay there so lovely, adorned in her maidenly glory, all curled together around a little lump]. At the end of the passage, the narrator slyly laments the fact that the pure silk shift was left intact by Tristan's hand ("nicht wart zurizzen" [HvF 734–41]). For a detailed discussion of clothes in courtly romance see Burns 1993; Schultz 1997, 91–110. Nanz also draws a comparison to the "Minneburg"-motif [love castle] here (2010, 236–37).

bride even more, Duchess Karsie shares with her a strategy that perhaps had worked in her own case and allowed her to secure for herself a position of respect and relative influence. One can therefore draw a parallel between her and Gottfried's Queen Isolde. Both women share with their daughters something that is meant to facilitate their married life: for Queen Isolde, it is the love potion; for Heinrich's Karsie it is her advice about attracting the husband. Considering Heinrich's tendency to imitate Gottfried, it would not be surprising that the later poet's depiction of the mother-daughter relationship would be reminiscent of his predecessor's approach. If Ulrich's duchess resembles Queen Isolde in her wisdom, political acumen, and decisiveness, Heinrich's does so in providing a "gift" for her inexperienced daughter that is meant to give her "a measure of control" over her instrumental function (Rasmussen 1997, 128). Like that of the love potion, the point of her advice is manipulation of love. It is, of course, true that Heinrich does not share Gottfried's overall ideology and morality; neither does he achieve the same level of sophistication and poetic mastery. His duchess' "gift" is a far less complex device than Gottfried's magic draught; and yet both are intended to secure, at least partly, the young woman's success in her forthcoming political marriage and in this way to replicate her mother's destiny as a woman and a wife of an appreciative husband. Conspicuously, in both cases, the gift fails, highlighting the limitations imposed on women by the patriarchal system.[30]

Like the mother in *Die Winsbeckin*, Heinrich's Karsie has seemingly taught her daughter how to be successful within patriarchy. The "other Isolde's" behavior throughout the text, until the very end of the tale, is nothing short of perfect. Indeed, some scholars see in her the "Idealtyp des tugendhaft erzogenen jungen Mädchens" [Nanz 2010, 233; ideal type of the young maiden raised to be virtuous]; and yet her perfection fails to produce the expected results. Her response to Tristan's long tale about his lack of interest is willing submission and complete self-denial: "ob ich maget / blibe biz an minen tot, / dar umb gelide ich nimmer not. / lat mich sin, als ich nu sie" [HvF 1098–1101; Even if I remain a virgin until my dying day, I will never suffer on that account. Let me remain as I am now]. Isolde of the White Hands lives with her husband in what appears to all to be complete harmony, except that he continues to fail in paying her his marital debt until the very end of the story (HvF 11190–222); and yet, despite all of this self-sacrifice and compliance, she does not earn any respect either intra- or extra-textually. In Ulrich's version, Tristan openly acknowledges his wrong-doing toward his wife ("durh got solt tu varn lan, / swas ich dir leides han getan. / ich erkenne wol mine schulde" [UvT 833–35; You should forgive me for the love of God whatever hurt I may have caused you. I recognize my offense]), but not so in Heinrich's. In Ulrich's version, Kaedin confronts Tristan at once, revokes his friendship until the latter proves his innocence (UvT 519–21), and

---

30 On the role of the love potion and the intentions of Queen Isolde in Gottfried's *Tristan*, see Rasmussen 1997, 129.

the whole family is ready to act immediately against their son-in-law. In Heinrich's, however outraged or hurt Isolde's brother appears to be in the Bold Water episode, when he hears about his sister's plight, his anger and even feeling of dishonor quickly give way to male bonding. The woman is first silenced by Kaedin who orders her not to disclose her and her family's shame to anybody (HvF 3816–17) and then is further degraded by her brother's curiosity, who wishes to see her rival. The irony of the situation cannot be lost on Heinrich's audience: Tristan's excuse for mistreating his wife and glorifying his lover Isolde the Blond only confirms Kaedin's dishonor. And yet the latter forgives the misdeed remarkably quickly because he likes Tristan (HvF 3888–91). The alliance between the two men is threatened but quickly restored; and as long as they are assured of their reciprocal loyalty and friendship, the woman's dishonor loses its urgency. Kaedin's desire to see with his own eyes the wondrous beauty of his brother-in-law's mistress overcomes his sense of shame and injustice done to his own kin, and makes him willing to put his family honor on hold: "zwar, so sol die swester mein / nicht gar lange wessen maget" [HvF 3994–95; Well, my sister would not have to remain virgin for long], he reasons. The wise woman of *Die Winsbeckin* warned her own daughter that male desire and societal approval are closely connected and that, to use Rasmussen's words, "to be lusted after *does* increase a woman's honor" (Rasmussen 1997, 143). Isolde of the White Hands is not desired and, as a consequence, she is not valued. The needs of men and the bonds between them supersede the damage done to the woman and the shame resulting from it.

Finally, Heinrich's approach to his Second Isolde is starkly at variance with the view popular in modern scholarship that the poet treats his heroine with great sympathy. The woman, initially described as "wise" [wise], is shown to be childish, first in the Bold Water episode and particularly so at the very end of the story, after which she is simply disposed of.[31] She continues to be self-sacrificing and simple-minded, taking good care of her wounded husband and planning no revenge. There is no strategy to her actions; in fact, the poet eliminates the very possibility of her having an accomplice such as the merchant's wife in Ulrich's text, bribed by the Second Isolde to notify her of the arrival of the ship carrying her husband's lover. It is Tristan's trusted friend Curvenal who is sent instead to fetch Isolde the Blond in Heinrich's work.[32] The wife's own consistently good and meek nature, her

---

[31] In Heinrich's work, the splash of water and Isolde's unguarded revelation are not the horse's fault, but the consequences of her own simple-minded curiosity and wish for flowers (HvF 3757–65). For an analysis of this passage, see Trokhimenko 2011, 217–20.

[32] Even though the motif of jealousy, so prominent in Ulrich, is mentioned, it is also downplayed thanks to Heinrich's vague and non-committal "I don't know": "doch enweiz ich, ob siz müete, / daz der halptôte Tristant / nach jener Îsôten hête gesant, / der blunden ûz Irlande" [HvF 6365–71; Yet I do not know whether it bothered her that half-dead Tristan had sent for the other Isolde, the blond one of Ireland].

proclaimed readiness to remain "the way she is now" even until death, and the fact that her marriage does get consummated shortly before Tristan's demise all preclude the interpretation of her vengefulness.³³ The Breton Isolde merely blurts out the fateful words about the color of the sail without thinking and regrets them at once: "Ysot gar jemerlichen schre: / 'ich han geschimpfet, Tristan! / der segel ist wiz, den ich da han / uf dem mer aldort gesehen!'" [HvF 6400–403; Isolde wailed: "It was only a joke, Tristan! The sail that I have seen in the sea is white!"]. Her impulsive, rash behavior and her immediate and sincere sorrow make her a more sympathetic figure than her calculating counterpart in Ulrich's text, and yet they also downgrade her to the status of a foolish child who futilely tries to correct what she has done and deserves to be harshly chastised for her misbehavior:

> ez were ir ernst oder ir schympf,
> ez waz ein torisch ungelimpf,
> daz im von ir die warheit
> in diser not nicht wart geseit. [. . .]
> waz sie gerief, ez waz geschehen,
> und waz sie weinens gepflac,
> her Tristan al da tot gelac.
>   (HvF 6389–92, 6404–6)

[Whether in earnest or in jest, it was a foolish mischief on her part not to tell him the truth in his need. (. . .) Cry all she may, it has already happened; and however much she wept, my lord Tristan lay there dead.]

If in the end of Ulrich's text, Isolde of the White Hands regains some degree of autonomy (albeit for the first time and of a gruesome kind) and acts, Heinrich deprives his heroine of it by taking away premeditation and jealousy and by characterizing her as thoughtless and immature.³⁴ Her punishment, both intra- and extra-textual, is her disappearance. For the audiences inside and outside of Heinrich's tale, she is totally supplanted at her own husband's bier by the attention given to her namesake and competitor, Tristan's lover Isolde the Blond who came to die with him. The true value of Isolde of the White Hands in Heinrich's epic is ultimately revealed in the narrator's final ode to Tristan, in which she is virtually equated with the dog Petitcriu (HvF 6465–80), another sweet, adorable, and compliant pet won by Tristan for consolation (Trokhimenko 2011, 225–26).

Encumbered by the tensions stemming from the contradictions between the story he has to tell, his own desire to turn the Tristan tale into a more traditional courtly romance, and his traditional, Christian view of love and marriage, Heinrich

---

33 Both in Ulrich's and Heinrich's texts, Tristan does fulfill his spousal duties close to the end of the story (UvT 3090–3102; HvF 5967–72).
34 Eilhart, like Heinrich, also calls Isolde's lie foolish: "an aller schlacht falschait / sprach sü so tumlichen" [EvO 9606–607; Without any evil intention, she spoke foolishly].

von Freiberg creates a paradox of Isolde of the White Hands: she is a beautiful, perfect, and submissive wife, intended to have the audience's and the narrator's sympathy for her plight, who is nevertheless actually treated as worthless – by her husband, by her relatives, and by the narrator. "Lat mich sin, als ich nu si" is clearly not the future that maiden Isolde's mother had in mind for her; rather she wished her daughter to have a future that would have replicated her own, one of love, influence, and respect. The Second Isolde's complaisance and willing surrender of her rights are meant to illustrate her obedience and submission to her husband, expected of her according to the actual feudal practices and the church teachings; and yet in her case they do not secure her joyous existence. On the contrary, they, ironically, ensure her unhappiness and failure and lead to her husband's demise.

3 Some Conclusions

The Middle High German Tristan tradition presents three possible scripts of femininity in a patriarchal society: the one represented by a socially successful mother (be she Queen Isolde of Gottfried's text or the Duchess of Arundel/Karsie in the sequels) and the other two by the two Isoldes. Of the three, only the first one is consistently treated as unambiguously positive. The paths associated with the young Isolde of the White Hands and her namesake Isolde the Blond are viewed as ambivalent and at times clearly negative. It is no wonder, for the mother characters in Gottfried's, Ulrich's, and Heinrich's texts are examples of a relative success within patriarchy. They are women who are wise, astute, respected and trusted by their husbands to make important decisions and at times even speak on their behalf in public. In contrast, neither of the two Isoldes succeeds in replicating her respective mother's fate. Even though Gottfried's sympathy for the main female protagonist of the tale, the Irish beauty Isolde the Blond, is unswerving and unquestionable, "her life makes a sham of wifely obedience, of women's subordination to their husbands. [. . .] Princess Isolde experiences love as a force that is irreconcilable with the normative social and sexual order" (Rasmussen 1997, 130). It is not known with how much sympathy Gottfried would have treated her namesake, the Breton Isolde, whose story he never told to its end, but the demands of the shared tale require that her plight be a sad one, of a wife abandoned, a woman scorned. In the final part of his unfinished torso, however, Gottfried appears to take pity on Isolde of the White Hands. He presents her as a lovely and sweet maiden, used, as expected, to establish and maintain homosocial ties between her brother Kaedin and her future husband, Tristan. She is encouraged to act seductively, but as she eventually inflames Tristan's passion with her charms, she also becomes more and more emotionally involved herself (GvS 19225–39, 19342–51). Although Gottfried's Second Isolde is also spurred into action by her male relatives pursuing their own goals, this episode is less about coercion and more about the attraction that develops between the maiden of Arundel and the protagonist of story. That is why Tristan's tortured monologue (GvS 19424–548) about being torn between the two Isoldes is so poignant. The agency of the Second Isolde stems from Love, from her true love for Tristan. For this reason, there is only one mother in Gottfried's tale, Queen Isolde of Ireland. She sets the force of love into action, and there is no need for another one.

As for the continuators of Gottfried's tale, Marion Gibbs has justly pointed out that both of them "did considerably more than continue" (Gibbs 2003, 281). Ulrich and Heinrich introduce the second mother figure into the story, the mother of the Breton Isolde. In both of these epics, the Duchess of Arundel takes on some features of Gottfried's Queen Isolde, although coming nowhere close to the complexity of the latter in her depiction. The character of the "herzogine" and her relationship with her daughter in Ulrich von Türheim's text are not very developed, which is consistent with his overall style. However, his duchess resembles Queen Isolde in her strength of character and her skill as a politician and a diplomat. She wields the same command in her own family and is granted the same respect as her Irish counterpart. Although the traditional gender hierarchy is recognized by all and formally acknowledged, it is the duchess who ultimately rules and decides, establishes feudal ties, and makes legal and familial arrangements for her daughter. Such a strong mother suits and corresponds to the depiction of a strong-minded and strong-willed daughter. Ulrich's Isolde of the White Hands threatens her ineffectual husband, plays a role of a married woman not out of complaisance but as a part of a strategy, and, finally, takes her revenge. And although she becomes less likable as her rebellion against Tristan comes to its tragic denouement, there is strength and power to her character in this version of the story. One can say that the scripts of femininity represented by the First and the Second Isoldes are both ambivalent. Ulrich's sympathy for the unfortunate lovers that makes him write a story for the "rehte minnere" [UvT 3629; true lovers] does not obscure his apprehension of their union: Isolde the Blond is on the wrong path, as is made clear by her trickery, narrow escapes, and her untimely death. Isolde of the White Hands is a wronged wife defending her rights, who by the end of the text turns into a cruel fury. Both Isoldes fail in replicating their mothers' success as politicians, wives, and women of honor.

Things appear to be more clear-cut in Heinrich von Freiberg's take on the Tristan story, at least intra-textually. He follows Ulrich's suit in creating a second mother, a positive example, who somewhat resembles both her counterpart in Ulrich's text and Gottfried's Queen Isolde. Like the latter, Duchess Karsie is shown to inculcate her daughter with her instrumental function in the patriarchal society and attempts to "give her a measure of control over it" (Rasmussen 1997, 129), a "gift" meant to ensure love, which will fail. However, the important function of the mother in the sequels, particularly in Heinrich's text, is to help us see the paradox of the daughter. If Heinrich has no scruples about voicing his disapproval of Isolde the Blond, he appears to be very sympathetic toward Tristan's wife. His Isolde of the White Hands is the character who satisfies all the requirements of feminine comportment, emphasized in medieval conduct literature, and is both accessible and virtuous; and yet while being desirable, she is not desired and is treated as a minor character by everybody, including Tristan, her family, the narrator, and the poet himself. Her depiction in the sequels is the illustration of Gibbs' point that the two Tristan sequels are not actually sequels, but rather they are their own versions of the Tristan legend. Ulrich is drawn to the active, perhaps wicked, side of Isolde of the White Hands, which he finds in Eilhart's version.[35] This active side of the heroine no longer exists in Heinrich's version, which borrows from Eilhart's the idea of unpremeditated foolishness,[36] but then goes a step further by depriving Isolde the Second of the agency she has in Eilhart's account, of allowing her to take things into her own hands, to rule and make arrangements for Tristan's burial (EvO 9684–89). Heinrich's Isolde of the White Hands simply fades away into the background, grieving, submissive, unheard, and unseen. If it is true that Heinrich intended for his readers to see "the other Isolde" as an alternative to the adulteress Isolde the Blond, his strategy was not very successful, for it is the lover who draws attention to herself both inside and outside the tale, while the dutiful wife vanishes. The two sequels are therefore ambivalent in their treatment of femininity: despite their overall tendency of curtailing the expression of their female characters, it is their outspoken and robust heroines who are not easily forgotten. In this, they correct the statement of the wise mother in *Die Winsbeckin*: the woman is worth something in the courtly world when she is thought of and desired, but she will be thought of only if she herself is active.

Works Cited

Primary Sources

Eilhart von Oberg. *Tristrant und Isalde. Mittelhochdeutsch/Neuhochdeutsch*. Edited and translated by Danielle Buschinger and Wolfgang Spiewok. Greifswald: Reineke, 1993.
Gottfried von Strassburg. *Tristan*. 5th ed. Edited by Friedrich Ranke and Rüdiger Krohn. 3 vols. Stuttgart: Reclam, 1996.
Heinrich von Freiberg. *Tristan und Isolde (Fortsetzung des Tristan-Romans Gottfrieds von Straßburg)*. Edited by Danielle Buschinger and translated by Wolfgang Spiewok. Greifswald: Reineke, 1993.

---

[35] Ulrich has definitely sharpened the discussion between the two Isoldes at Tristan's bier. In Eilhart's version, Isolde the Blond merely tells the wife that she has loved Tristan longer and therefore has a right to be at his side. She also asks Isolde of the White Hands to move aside (EvO 9585–88; 9650–59).
[36] A moment of inconsistency in Eilhart's storytelling: Isolde of the White Hands both finds an accomplice to report to her about the color of the sail (like in Ulrich) (EvO 9585–88) and blurts out the fatal words in naïve thoughtlessness and "without evil intention" (like in Heinrich).

Rasmussen, Ann Marie, and Olga V. Trokhimenko, ed. and trans. "The German *Winsbecke, Winsbeckin*, and *Winsbecke* Parodies (Selections)." In *Medieval Conduct Literature: An Anthology of Vernacular Guides to Behaviour of Youths, With English Translations*, edited by Mark D. Johnston, 61–125. Toronto: University of Toronto Press, 2009.

Ulrich von Türheim. *Tristan und Isolde (Fortsetzung des Tristan-Romans Gottfrieds von Straßburg), Originaltext (nach der Heidelberger Handschrift Pal. Germ. 360)*. Edited and translated by Danielle Buschinger and Wolfgang Spiewok. Amiens: Publications du Centre d'études médiévales, 1992.

Secondary Sources

Altpeter-Jones, Katja. "Love Me, Hurt Me, Heal Me – Isolde Healer and Isolde Lover in Gottfried's *Tristan*." *German Quarterly* 82, no. 1 (2009): 5–23.

Bumke, Joachim. *Geschichte der deutschen Literatur im hohen Mittelalter*. Munich: DTV, 2000.

Burns, E. Jane. *Bodytalk: When Women Speak in Old French Literature*. Philadelphia: University of Pennsylvania Press, 1993.

Buschinger, Danielle. "La composition et le sens du *Tristan* de Heinrich von Freiberg." In Buschinger and Spiewok, *Tristan-Studien*, 57–63.

Buschinger, Danielle and Wolfgang Spiewok, eds. *Tristan-Studien: Die Tristan-Rezeption in den europäischen Literaturen des Mittelalters*. Greifswald: Reineke, 1993.

Chinca, Mark. *Gottfried von Strassburg: Tristan*. Cambridge, UK: Cambridge University Press, 1997.

Clason, Christopher R. "Gottfried's Continuator Ulrich von Türheim: Epistemology and Language." *Tristania* 24 (2006): 17–36.

Classen, Albrecht. "Die Mutter spricht zu ihrer Tochter: Literarhistorische Betrachtungen zu einem feministischen Thema." *The German Quarterly* 75, no. 1 (2002): 71–87.

Classen, Albrecht. "Women Speak up at the Medieval Court: Gender Roles and Public Influence in Hartmann von Aue's *Erec* and Gottfried von Strassburg's *Tristan and Isolde*." In *The Power of Woman's Voice in Medieval and Early Modern Literatures: New Approaches to German and European Women Writers and to Violence Against Women in Premodern Times*, edited by Albrecht Classen, 69–103. Berlin: De Gruyter, 2007.

Deighton, Alan, "Ein Anti-Tristan? Gottfried-Rezeption in der 'Tristan'-Fortsetzung Heinrichs von Freiberg." In *Deutsche Literatur des Mittelalters in und über Böhmen II: Tagung in České Budějovice/Budweis 2002*, edited by Václav Bok and Hans-Joachim Behr, 111–26. Hamburg: Verlag Dr. Kovač, 2004.

Fenster, Thelma S., ed. *Arthurian Women: A Casebook*. New York and London: Garland, 1996.

Fenster, Thelma S. "Introduction." In Fenster, *Arthurian Women: A Casebook*, xviii–lxiv.

Gibbs, Marion. "The Medieval Reception of Gottfried's *Tristan*." In Hasty, *Companion to Gottfried von Strassburg*, 261–84.

Gibbs, Marion and Sydney Johnson. *Medieval German Literature*. New York: Routledge, 1997.

Hasty, Will, ed. *Companion to Gottfried von Strassburg*. Rochester: Camden House, 2003.

Hentsch, Alice A. *De la littérature didactique du Moyen Âge s'adressant spécialement aux femmes*. 1903. Genève: Slatkine Reprints, 1975.

Kelly, Kathleen Coyne. *Performing Virginity and Testing Chastity in the Middle Ages*. London: Routledge, 2000.

Mältzer, Marion. *Die Isolde-Gestalten in den mittelalterlichen deutschen Tristan-Dichtungen*. Heidelberg: Winter, 1991.

McDonald, William C. *The Tristan Story in German Literature of the Late Middle Ages and Early Renaissance: Tradition and Innovation.* Lewiston: Mellen, 1990.

Mitsch, Ruthmarie H. "The Other Isolde." *Tristania* 15 (1994): 75–83.

Moi, Toril. "'She Died Because She Came Too Late . . .': Knowledge, Doubles, and Death in Thomas's *Tristan*." In *What is a Woman? And Other Essays*, edited by Toril Moi, 422–50. Oxford: Oxford University Press, 1999.

Nanz, Ute. *Die Isolde-Weißhand-Gestalten im Wandel des Tristanstoffs: Figurenzeichnung zwischen Vorlagenbezug und Werkkonzeption.* Heidelberg: Winter, 2010.

Rabine, Leslie W. "The Establishment of Patriarchy in *Tristan and Isolde*." *Women's Studies* 7 (1980): 19–38.

Rasmussen, Ann Marie. "*ez ist ir g'artet von mir:* Queen Isolde and Princess Isolde in Gottfried von Strassburg's *Tristan and Isolde*." In Fenster, *Arthurian Women: A Casebook*, 41–58.

Rasmussen, Ann Marie. *Mothers and Daughters in Medieval German Literature.* Syracuse, NY: Syracuse University Press, 1997.

Rasmussen, Ann Marie. "The Female Figures in Gottfried's *Tristan and Isolde*." In Hasty, *Companion to Gottfried von Strassburg*, 137–57.

Sedlmeyer, Margarete. *Heinrichs von Freiberg Tristanfortsetzung im Vergleich zu anderen Tristandichtungen.* Frankfurt am Main: Lang, 1976.

Schausten, Monika. *Erzählwelten der Tristangeschichte im hohen Mittelalter: Untersuchungen zu den deutschsprachigen Tristanfassungen des 12. und 13. Jahrhunderts.* Munich: Fink, 1999.

Schnell, Rüdiger. "Macht im Dunkeln: Welchen Einfluß hatten Ehefrauen auf ihre Männer? Geschlechterkonstrukte in Mittelalter und früher Neuzeit." In *Zivilisationsprozesse: Zu Erziehungsschriften in der Vormoderne*, edited by Rüdiger Schnell. et al., 309–29. Cologne: Böhlau, 2004.

Schultz, James A. "Bodies That Don't Matter: Heterosexuality Before Heterosexuality in Gottfried's *Tristan*." In *Constructing Medieval Sexuality*, edited by Karma Lochrie, Peggy McCracken, and James A. Schultz, 91–110. Minneapolis: University of Minnesota Press, 1997.

Spiewok, Wolfgang. "Zur Überlieferung der *Tristan*-Fortsetzung Heinrichs von Freiberg." In Buschinger and Spiewok, *Tristan-Studien*, 145–54.

Strohschneider, Peter. "Gotfrit-Fortsetzungen: Tristans Ende im 13. Jahrhundert und die Möglichkeiten nachklassischer Epik." *Deutsche Vierteljahrsschrift* 65 (1991): 70–98.

Thomas, Neil. "Duplicity and Duplexity: The Isolde of the White Hands Sequence." In Hasty, *Companion to Gottfried von Strassburg*, 183–201.

Trindade, W. Ann. "Nouvelles perspectives sur le personnage d'Iseut aux Blanches Mains." In *Tristan – Tristrant: Mélanges en l'honneur de Danielle Buschinger à l'occasion de son 60-ème anniversaire*, edited by André Crépin and Wolfgang Spiewok, 521–30. Greifswald: Reineke, 1996.

Trokhimenko, Olga V. "'And All Her Power Forsook Her': Female Bodies and Speech in the Middle High German Tristan Continuations." *Journal of English and Germanic Philology* 110, no. 2 (2011): 202–28.

Trokhimenko, Olga V. *Constructing Virtue and Vice: Femininity and Laughter in Courtly* Society *(ca. 1150–1300).* Göttingen: Vandenhoeck & Ruprecht unipress, 2014.

Wetzel, René. "Tristan in Böhmen: Die südostmitteldeutsche Überlieferungsinsel von Gottfrieds *Tristan* im Kontext der böhmischen Gesellschafts- und Bildungssituation und der Minne-Ehe-Kasuistik im 13.-15. Jahrhundert." In Buschinger und Spiewok, *Tristan-Studien*, 165–81.

Katja Altpeter
4 Maternal Bonds in Konrad Fleck's *Flôre und Blanscheflûr*

The textual material that constitutes the focus of this essay is the thirteenth-century Middle High German love and adventure novel *Flôre und Blanscheflûr* by Konrad Fleck, a to date largely neglected piece of Middle High German literature and culture. Together with Rudolf von Ems' *Der guote Gêrhart*, it counts as one of the first German texts to depict its protagonist as a valiant and honorable merchant. With extant versions in Spanish, Italian, Greek, French, Dutch, English, Norwegian, Icelandic, Danish, Swedish, Middle High and Middle Low German, its story belongs among the most popular literary motifs in medieval and early modern Europe. Its adaptation history extends almost uninterrupted from the late twelfth into the twentieth century. And yet, *Flôre und Blanscheflûr* has attracted relatively little attention among German medieval scholars.

Marion Gibbs and Sidney Johnson (1997) point to the lack of a modern German edition of the work and the complete absence of an English translation of Fleck's text as potential factors leading to the critical oversight of *Flôre und Blanscheflûr* to this date (322).[1] Although Gibbs and Johnson point out that the text may lack the "tragic grandeur" (320) of, for example, the story of two other well-known lovers, Tristan and Isolde, and may suffer from a "lack of impact . . . due to the modest stature of its principal German narrator [i.e. Konrad Fleck]," (320) they also warn that the text should not be – as is commonly the case – "dismissed as a rather bland little tale of young love," and assert that it "warrants closer attention than it has so far received" (322).[2]

At first sight, the story of the children's developing affection for each other looks charmingly sweet: born on the same day – Flôre to a Muslim queen, Blanscheflûr to her Christian lady-in-waiting – the two children lovingly smile at each other while still in their cribs. In growing up, they attend school together where they are introduced to the literature of love, which gives them the means to express their feelings for each other. Flôre's father's decision to separate the innocent lovers and sell Blanscheflûr to the Orient is not too perturbing, since we – the audience – have already been told that Flôre and Blanscheflûr will live happily ever after and will one day be grandparents to Charlemagne.

---

[1] The recently published new critical edition of *Flôre und Blanscheflûr* by Christine Putzo (2015) promises easier access to the text for students and scholars, and advocates persuasively for the promise of renewed and invigorated engagement with Fleck's work.
[2] On the persistence of the "Verniedlichung des Romans" [the trivialization of the text], see Putzo 2015, 28–30.

The focus of the present essay is not so much the sweet relationship between the young lovers, however, but instead the two mother-child relationships that occupy a prominent role at the beginning of Fleck's tale. In addition, the present essay investigates the connection between the two mother figures in the text. Even though Flôre and Blanscheflûr are originally portrayed as quasi-identical and sibling-like, their differences become more pronounced throughout the course of the narrative. Interestingly, the development of these differences happens in conjunction – and this will be a primary focus of this essay – with the development of differences in each respective mother-child relationship. We notice for example that the figure of Flôre's mother gains prominence – both vis-à-vis her offspring and in the text overall – while the figure of Blanscheflûr's mother becomes increasingly more irrelevant to her daughter's well-being and eventually fades completely from the text. This movement in diametrically opposed directions coincides with an increased distance and alienation between the two women who earlier on in the text – throughout their pregnancies and respective childbirth experiences – are inseparable, appearing as both co-wives to the King and co-mothers to Flôre and his beloved Blanscheflûr.

As I hope to show, Ann Marie Rasmussen's work on mothers and daughters – and specifically Rasmussen's focus on the ways in which dynastic questions shape mother-daughter relationships – provides the critical tools to unpack the dynamics of initially pronounced sibling similarities, strong affective ties between the two mothers, and similarities in the two mother-child relationships, as well as the eventual undoing of those same similarities and affective ties. As shall become evident, dynastic concerns constitute the key catalyst for the establishment and dissolution of the friendship between the two mothers in Fleck's tale as well as the unfolding of each respective mother-child relationship. Let us begin then by examining Flôre and Blanscheflûr's bond with each other, the friendship their mothers enjoy, and the respective mother-child relationships.

As the narrator reports, the children:

> wurden geboren an einem tage
> in einem hûse ze einer stunt;
> daz ist wizzentlîche kunt,
> eine amme zôch sie beide. . .[3]
> (lines 348–51)

[were born on the same day / in the same house at the same hour, / that is well known, / one wet nurse raised them both.]

---

[3] All quotations are taken from Putzo's (2015) edition of the text and hereafter will be cited parenthetically. All translations are my own.

They also look almost identical and they behave identically. The children's similarities and identical birthdates suggest to an audience that Flôre and Blanscheflûr are quasi-siblings. In fact, they bear resemblances usually found only in twins. Always close and never to be separated ("ungescheiden aller dinge" [line 600]), they establish a friendship while still in their cradles ("vriuntschefte pflâgen, / dô sie in den wagen lâgen" [line 601]), then become "schuolgenôzen" (schoolmates [line 645]) and finally (very young) lovers. Hand in hand, they walk to school together (line 675–76) and are generally inseparable.

Flôre und Blanscheflûr, however, are also part of an interesting and seemingly unconventional family dynamic which links their respective mothers in a symbiotic co-mothering dynamic and – seemingly – an erotic triangle with the Queen's husband. King Fênix has taken Blanscheflûr's mother, a French woman of Christian faith and a stranger whom he has captured in battle, under his wing. She has lost her husband in battle and is already pregnant at this point. And yet, the way in which King Fênix obtains Blanscheflûr's nameless mother is reminiscent of a bridal quest.[4] In reading King Fênix's "claiming" of her, one gets the impression that when he takes her from the battlefield and abducts her to Spain, he considers her war booty and his own personal gain. As the narrator describes it, he truly relishes this particular reward of war and conquest:

> den künic dûhte der gewin
> an der vrouwen daz beste
> (lines 444–45)

[The king considered the acquisition / of the woman the best]

I would like to contextualize this further in order to support the contention that Fênix's procurement of the Christian woman has the characteristics of sexual conquest. King Fênix is Muslim, and the passage describing the abduction of the Christian

---

[4] During a bridal quest, a man ventures out in hopes of finding a wife. Typically, the questing man needs to overcome an obstacle, as the wife he desires is either unwilling or strictly guarded by a male relative who objects to the union. Many bridal quest tales include a conversion narrative (with either future husband or wife converting to Christianity). Scholars distinguish between two patterns of bridal-quest narratives: one "in which a bride is abducted by means of force or battle," and another in which "the bride is wooed by means of disguise and guile" (Bornholdt 2005, 4 (following the distinction suggested by Frings 1939–40, 306–21)). Bridal quest tales can be found in early Germanic texts and are prevalent in Middle High German minstrel epics (*Spielmannsepen*). One might argue that *Flôre und Blanscheflûr* offers both types of bridal quest. King Fênix abducts the French woman after a battle. Much later in the tale, his son Flôre ventures out to retrieve (and eventually marry) Blanscheflûr by employing disguise and cunning. On the topic of bridal quest, see Bornholdt 2005 and Bowden 2012. On the topic of Christian/Saracen dynamics in bridal quest narratives, see Kohnen 2014.

woman suggests that he shares the insatiability vis-à-vis women that the text also ascribes to another prominent adult male Muslim figure in the text, the Babylonian *amiral* (i.e. ruler), to whose court Blanscheflûr will later be sold as a slave. The text marks the amiral's behavior as strange and alienating. Part of his alien and alienating manners resides in his desire for excess, both material/fiscal and amorous/sexual. Thus the amiral is cited for collecting excessive customs duties ("ungevüeger zol" [line 3382]) and for his excessive desire for women. Instead of being devoted to one woman, the amiral holds seventy women captive in his tower of maidens. He marries a new wife each year after cruelly murdering the previous year's wife, lest she marry another man after him.[5] The depiction of the amiral's otherness conforms to contemporaneous western stereotypes of the Oriental and Muslim ruler who was imagined as a cruel despot prone to excess and especially to sexual aberration. The text, in other words, avails itself of descriptions that would have resonated with a medieval audience familiar with stereotypical "attributions to Muslims of limitless enjoyment and unarrestable desire, of sexual deviation, of powers of seduction, of madness, of disorder, and of idolatry" (Uebel 2005, 30) that characterized Muslims as "violent and lustful" (Tolan 2002, 149) and as lecherous "from the soles of their feet to the tops of their heads" (Fidentius of Padua, quoted in Tolan 2002, 211).

Flôre's father, the Muslim King Fênix, shares the amiral's penchant for anger. His ardent desire to capture and bring home Blanscheflûr's Christian mother suggests that he also shares in the amiral's penchant for sexual excess. The suggestion that King Fênix takes the Christian woman to sate his sexual desire, combined with the fact that Blanscheflûr's mother and his own wife give birth in the same house and on the same day to sibling-like children give the impression that Blanscheflûr's mother plays the role of co-wife to the Muslim wife who awaits King Fênix at home, and that King Fênix is the putative father of both children.

Both the children's similarities that make them appear as though they are siblings, twins even, and the putatively triangular erotic dynamic between the King, his wife, and the Christian woman he brings to his court, are suggestive of an untraditional and unconventional family situation that pairs both women as co-wives and possibly co-mothers. In addition, and more importantly, the two women establish a close emotional bond based on their shared experience as mothers. Let us examine then how the relationship between the two women is formed, what characterizes it, and how it is eventually undone.

---

[5] I have suggested elsewhere (Altpeter-Jones 2003, 193–97) that his behavior bears all the marks of excess outlined in Georges Bataille's 1985 "The Notion of Expenditure."

As the King begins to dispense war booty in compensation for services rendered to him during his military expedition, he also distributes to his wife her portion of the war gains:

> dô wart der küniginne
> diu kristenvrouwe vür ir teil;
> des wart sî stolz unde geil.
> (lines 504–6)
>
> [Then the Christian woman became / part of the Queen's possessions. / The Queen was elated and happy.]

Interestingly, the Queen does not treat the gifted woman as a slave. Instead, the women immediately begin a warm and close friendship.

> sî was ir liep und des wart schîn:
> sî hiez sî willekomen sîn.
> sî gnâdete alsô sî kunde
> der küniginne. sâ ze stunde
> die vrouwen sî müede sach
> und vuorte sî an guot gemach
> in ir kemenâten.
> die vrouwen hübeschlîchen tâten
> und kusten sî besunder.
> (lines 507–15)
>
> [The Christian woman was dear to the Queen, that was obvious. / The Queen bid her welcome. / She in turn thanked the Queen as best she could. / Shortly thereafter, the Queen saw that the lady was tired and led her promptly to a place of comfort in her bedroom. / The women were courteous with each other and kissed one another sweetly.]

It is quite obvious that the Queen immediately takes a liking to the Christian woman. She welcomes her new companion, and the Christian woman thanks the Queen as much as possible in light of the existing language barriers. The Queen, realizing that the Christian woman is exhausted, quickly takes her to a "guot gemach" [place of comfort]. The women behave according to courtly decorum and kiss each other sweetly. Eventually, the Queen gives the Christian woman permission to live according to her Christian religion and traditions ("daz ir diu künigîn verhancte / ze lebende nâch der kristenheit" [lines 524–25]). The two women are, the text tells us, inseparable: wherever the Queen sits, the Christian woman always sits right by her side ("wan swâ diu küniginne saz, / sô saz bî ir diu kristæne" [lines 530–31]). In addition, the Queen is so charmed by the captive's sweet language, that she asks her to instruct her in French ("sî bat sich franzois lêren" [line 537]).

Clearly the two women have a close and intimate relationship. The Queen likes the Christian woman, and – perhaps recognizing her plight in a strange and foreign country – shows kindness towards her by welcoming her, allowing her to practice her religion, and being willing to learn her language. The Queen is open to the other woman's background and culture and shows an interest in the Christian woman's heritage (her language). Both women show courtly respect for each other and they are constantly around each other. They are inseparable. All of this suggests that they practice a form of friendship and fellowship, a friendship or fellowship of women, we might say.

Nowhere in the text is the notion of a fellowship of women more evident than in the two women's parallel, in fact, exactly simultaneous dates of conception, pregnancies, and experiences of childbirth. The Queen notices one day that her Christian friend is pregnant ("und sach wol daz sî truoc" [line 562]). Both realize that they conceived ("worden kindes haft" [569]) at exactly the same time ("an dem selben zil" [line 568]). At this point, Fleck tells us that both rejoice on realizing "der vrömeden geselleschaft" (line 570), an expression we might translate as "friendly or loving bond with a stranger."[6] The concept implied in their earlier accommodating behavior is here explicitly termed a friendly and copacetic bond, community, friendship – even love. Their parallel pregnancies are the ultimate symbol of this fellowship or bond. Elated by the news, the two women calculate their coinciding due dates, then indeed give birth on the same date ("der selben zîte" [line 580]; "nider kâmen beide sant" [line 597]), and also recover in tandem ("dô die vrouwen gebâren / und alsô glîch genesen wâren / beide ze einer stunde" [lines 589–91]).

The friendship between the two women becomes a close bond and fellowship because they endure their specifically female experience – pregnancy, childbirth, and recovery – together. This is, in other words, a fellowship based on common biology. The women's bond is later echoed in the children's sibling-like similarities. However, the bond between the two women, despite its seemingly strong affective ties, disintegrates later on in the tale as the women's roles especially vis-à-vis their offspring shift. The women's sweet *geselleschaft*, based on the common biological experience of motherhood and reinforced textually by the suggestion that they are co-wives to the King and co-mothers to their sibling-like children, disintegrates as the children grow up. Why might this be so?

"At its most basic," writes Ann Marie Rasmussen (1997), "the mother-daughter relationship is a genealogy, grounded as a metaphor in biological and physiological process, made meaningful through individual, social, and cultural investment" (14). According to this observation, the mother-daughter relationship is a genealogy that creates narrative out of biology. This narrative of genealogy is made meaningful through individual, social, and cultural investment. It is, I believe, precisely this dynamic of transforming or rewriting biology into genealogy which initiates shifts

---

6 According to Benecke, Müller and Zarnke ([1854–66] 1990) gesellschaft means "freundliches verbundensein, . . ., gemeinschaft, freundschaft" (friendly bond, . . . community, friendship). Lexer ([1876] 1970) translates the term as "freundschaftliches beisammen- oder verbundensein, freundschaft, liebe" (copacetic being with or bond, friendship, love).

in the relationship between the two women and their children, and in the prominence the text assigns to each woman and her relationship with her offspring.

Interestingly, the text is silent on what happens with the mothers from the time the children are born and the women begin to recover from the hardship of pregnancy and childbirth to the time when Flôre's parents perceive the children's amorous relationship with each other as dynastically inopportune. At this latter point, both mothers reappear on the stage, but this time with vastly different roles and in a rather conflictual relationship. Flôre and Blanscheflûr are now of marriageable age. With regard to the women's function, biology has been replaced by social and dynastic strategizing as the primary modus operandi that defines and circumscribes the activities of the two mothers. From here on out, the Muslim Queen gains in prominence while the Christian woman's position becomes negligible within the tale's plot structure. Each woman's role in this dynamic is tied to the way in which she relates to her offspring and the way in which she transforms biology – biological motherhood – into genealogy – or what we might call the social functions of motherhood in this tale. The Muslim Queen is successful in doing so, the Christian woman is not.[7]

The relationship between the parents and their children becomes conflictual as the royal family's dynastic prospects come into focus, represented here first and foremost – as is to be expected – by the marital prospects of the royal couple's son. "Marriage was often used instrumentally, as a tool for securing political alliances while keeping wealth, influence, and power within the noble class," writes Rasmussen (1997, 116). Indeed, King and Queen are wildly preoccupied with their son's future marital prospects. At this point, the Queen emerges as superbly adept in reading and squelching her husband's anger about Flôre and Blanscheflûr's tender bonds. So distraught is the King that he considers having the girl killed. The Queen, however, manages to dissuade him from this idea. In so doing, the Queen shows awareness of the public implications should her husband kill the girl for dynastic reasons.

While the King acts out of anger, the Queen functions as advocate for a pragmatically oriented approach to the perceived problem, which takes into consideration social and political realities and consequences. She counsels with wisdom, strategic foresight, and a clear sense for the political significance of seemingly private actions. In appeasing both her husband and her people, she demonstrates her abilities as an astute strategist within the private and public sphere. The wife makes sure that the private translates most appropriately into the political:

> wan uns müese widervarn
> beidiu laster und schande,
> swenn man in dem lande

---

[7] Both gender and class or social status play a role in this divergence in complexly intersectional ways, the exploration of which would take us too far afield here. This topic is developed further in Altpeter-Jones 2003, especially in chapters two, three, and six.

> diu mære begunde sagen,
> daz wir ein maget heten erslagen.
> (lines 924–28)

[Because we would suffer / both dishonor and shame, / if people started telling a story in this country / that we had killed the girl.]

At times it appears as though the Queen is concerned primarily with her son's physical and emotional well-being, as though her "taking care of things" is a kind of purely maternal care based on affective ties. As she and her husband hatch plans to sell Blanscheflûr and concoct the lie that Blanscheflûr has died in Flôre's absence, the Queen worries that in a worst-case scenario, Flôre – upon hearing of Blanscheflûr's supposed death – might attempt to commit suicide. Her focus here is clearly on the well-being of her son, and her thoughts are articulated in the language of affective ties, love, and caring. Yet they are simultaneously inflected by the language of dynastic positioning and priorities. This becomes apparent when the Queen expresses her fear about a possible suicide attempt by her son as fear for the well-being of "Flôre unser erbe" [1931; Flôre our heir].

That the Queen values empire over emotions is evident, also, in the cool strategizing she practices in disposing of the girl, Blanscheflûr. While she twice prevents Blanscheflûr's killing, she does not hesitate to have her sold into slavery (which, after all, might be synonymous with or even worse than a death sentence). The reason for this is that Blanscheflûr ostensibly stands in the way of a proper, and dynastically opportune marital match for their son. "In the feudal world, powerful kin meant political clout," writes Rasmussen (1997, 10). Without any kin to speak of, Blanscheflûr essentially has no clout and thus no value. In other words, the girl is sacrificed in order to protect the royal family's dynastic goals. Blanscheflûr's needs and the needs, worries, and hardships of her mother are tossed aside, never even mentioned, while dynastic issues are clearly foregrounded.

The King gives his wife full permission to proceed "mit den kinden beiden" (with both children) as she sees fit (2489). This go-ahead functions as a sign of the King's recognition of his wife's abilities: he trusts that his wife has the acumen to take care of these dynastically important matters. That clearly both parents, mother and father are in charge when it comes to making decisions about their offspring's future is evident also when Flôre, ready to embark on his mission to rescue Blanscheflûr, announces his decision to them *both* and asks both for permission to venture on his journey:

> unde gie ze sînem vater
> unde sîner muoter; dô bater
> urloubes von in beiden;
> (lines 2577–79)

[And he went to his father / and to his mother: he asked / permission of them both.]

Both parents are, we observe, clearly decision makers and permission givers.

What we see in these examples is that the Queen, previously characterized primarily by means of her biology – through a focus on the time leading up to the birth of her son, the birth itself, and the ensuing recovery – has now evolved into an influential political strategist who ensures that her child's future and with it the future of her political realm will be secured.

Ann Marie Rasmussen writes in her book that in many of the texts she examines, we see an aristocratic mother guiding her daughter into "a marriage that will reinforce valuable political and economic alliances for her family and provide wealth and prestige for the daughter herself" (14). In *Flôre und Blanscheflûr* interestingly, Flôre's mother attempts to do precisely this . . . but, in this case, for her son.

While the Queen thus appears in a new and mature role of political strategist, Blanscheflûr's mother is relegated to a secondary and ancillary role – a role, importantly, that gives her no authority over her daughter, instead assisting in her daughter's potential demise. Witness, for example, the Christian woman's role when King and Queen decide to send Flôre off to Muntôre so that he might forget about his Christian lover. The parents fabricate a double lie: their current but elderly tutor can no longer teach the children due to his advanced age, they claim, and therefore Flôre has to go to Muntôre for instruction – first lie. Blanscheflûr cannot go, because – second lie – her mother is sick and only the daughter can take appropriate care of her:

> diu maget müeze hie bestân,
> mit ir siechen muoter umbe gân
> . . .
> wan nieman enpflæge ir
> sô getriuwelîche wol
> als ein kint sîner muoter sol.
>   (lines 1003–8)

> [The girl must remain here, / and take care of her sick mother / (. . .) because nobody will nurse her / as faithfully and well / as a child will her mother.]

Thus Blanscheflûr's mother's impotence vis-à-vis her daughter's future and well-being is aptly represented through her fabricated sickness and helplessness. In addition, mother and daughter are both portrayed as being relegated to the realm of the body: the mother's body is said to be ailing, and Blanscheflûr is conscripted into nursing this ailing body. While Flôre's mother has transcended the realm of the body (conception, pregnancy, childbirth, recovery), Blanscheflûr and her mother remain caught in it.

When the King and Queen's ploy to distract Flôre in Muntôre fails, Blanscheflûr's mother is pulled into a second deceptive plot, this time as an active participant. Thus she is the first person at Fênix's court who apprises Flôre of his lover's (staged) passing. Blanscheflûr's mother is frightened when Flôre visits her quarters asking for his girlfriend. Yet, she plays her role without hesitation. "I don't know where she is," she answers initially (line 2150), then elaborates that Blanscheflûr has passed away as God has ordained (lines 2157–58). When Flôre loses consciousness from sadness, the Christian woman begins to cry and wail:

> als diu kristæne dô gesach,
> daz im von leide wart so wê,
> sî begunde weinen unde schrê
> eine jæmerlîche stimme
> (lines 2172–75)

[When the Christian woman saw, / how he suffered in pain, / she began to cry and scream / in a pitiful voice.]

What is interesting here is that the text depicts how Blanscheflûr's mother cries and screams when she sees Flôre suffer but is completely silent on the mother's reaction to her own daughter's disappearance (which for all practical purposes is a kind of death sentence!). Why does Blanscheflûr's mother reappear in the text only now, when Flôre's emotions and well-being are at stake? Why does the text gloss over her grief at having lost her daughter, her one and only child? Are we to assume that she did not grieve, recognizing perhaps that the prerogative of dynastic preservation outdoes all other potential principles guiding social interactions? Or that, being for all practical purposes still just a dispossessed slave at the King's court, this was to be expected? Did she recognize from early on, that she could never lay full claim to her child? Or is she just being a good, compassionate, self-sacrificing Christian woman? Perhaps we should not try to psychologize this and instead simply acknowledge that to Fleck, the mother-daughter relationship has become sufficiently secondary and, in fact, so negligible as to drop out of the narrative altogether. The loss of significance is, I would argue, directly related to a lack of genealogical significance in the mother-daughter relationship.

In contrast to the relationship of mother and son in this tale, which is characterized primarily in terms of dynastic concerns and the parents' primary impetus to ensure genealogical certainty, the mother-daughter relationship lacks this concern. In fact, Blanscheflûr bemoans exactly this when she reasons why a relationship between her and Flôre is impossible. She articulates the fact that she has no genealogical currency and is thus valueless in a dynastic system whose primary function is to establish opportune family ties in order to uphold lineage:

> wir sîn geborn ungelîche,
> wan er ist eines küniges kint,
> sô enweiz ich wer mîn mâge sint,
> biderbe oder smæhe.
> mich wundert wie mir geschæhe.

ich bin ir aller ungewert,
wie wære ich sîn dan wert?
          (lines 1794–1800)

[We are born unequal; / he the child of a king, / and I don't know who my kin are, / if they are highborn or low. / I wonder what might happen to me. / I am without guarantee ("ungewert," ohne Gewähr) to them, / how could I thus be worthy of him?]

And while Flôre's mother is concerned for the wellbeing of her son as "erbe" [heir], Blanscheflûr bemoans specifically that all she has inherited from her mother is that woman's bad luck:

sî begunde unsælden vruo[. . .]
die ich erbe mit unheile.
          (lines 1188; 1193)

[She encountered bad luck early on, . . . / which I in my misfortune inherit.]

The word "erben," here used as a verb, echoes the Queen's concern for her son as her "erbe." Yet the contrast to the Queen's interest in her offspring as somebody who will guarantee ongoing dynastic success and a lasting genealogy is quite obvious here. While the Queen is concerned that her son might commit suicide, Blanscheflûr here wishes herself dead. And the only thing she has inherited thus far, she complains, is her mother's unhappy circumstances.

What is apparent, then, is that Blanscheflûr lacks a genealogically valuable background, and thus appears deprived of both history (she says that nobody knows who her family is which effectively deprives her of an intelligible past) and telos (she wonders but cannot foresee what might become of her). Perhaps the fact that the King wants to have her killed and that King and Queen together pretend that she has died is an indication of precisely this lack of telos. Importantly, the mother-daughter relationship is therefore here characterized by absences: the only thing Blanscheflûr's mother has bequeathed to her daughter is a *lack* of opportune and meaningful family ties (a lack of genealogy) and thus a lack of any value – being worthless. Both translate into an uncertain future.

What we see, too – and here I am closing the circle back to the earlier quote from *Mothers and Daughters* about the mother-daughter relationship being a genealogical narrative based on biology – is a breakdown in the mother-daughter dynamic: the mother-daughter relationship depicted here fails to replace biology with genealogy. Genealogy is missing in this mother-daughter relationship and therefore these family ties do not seem to be worthy of ongoing detailed depiction. They become negligible. Where Blanscheflûr's mother fails, then, is precisely with respect to her expected role of being able to rewrite biology as genealogy. She fails to be able to produce a genealogical narrative and as such, she appears valueless – *ungewert* like her own daughter – in the production of the tale's own narrative. Superfluous, she exits the tale and the mother-daughter relationship ceases to play a role.

Rasmussen's analysis of mother-daughter relationships in medieval German literature thus provides a potent explanatory model for elucidating why *Flôre und Blanscheflûr* initially depicts the women's respective mother-child relationships as running parallel, but then as diverging as the children mature. Rasmussen's thesis that the mother-daughter relationship is grounded in both biology and genealogy constitutes the linchpin in my own analysis of the mother-child relationship in *Flôre und Blanscheflûr*. Importantly, Rasmussen's model also elucidates the transformation in the mother-to-mother relationship in Fleck's tale. What connects the two women initially is a bond forged over a shared biological destiny. What later tears apart this initially symbiotic relationship is one woman's successful rewriting of biology into genealogy and the other woman's inability to do so. In other words, motherhood – in this case the biological aspects of motherhood – is what initially forges a bond between the two women, but it and its secondary, but ultimately more important function – to ensure genealogical success – is also what ultimately undoes the bond of jointly experienced motherhood.

The failure on the part of Blanscheflûr's mother to rewrite biology as genealogy is also what makes the mother-daughter relationship fade from the story's narrative or rather never take a firm hold to begin with. The mother-child relationship gains narrative footing only in so far as it manages to rewrite biology as genealogy (i.e. in the relationship of Queen to son). Where it fails to do so, this relationship is glossed over or drops from the story line altogether (as is the case for the relationship of Blanscheflûr and her mother).

As Rasmussen (1997) remarks, "[m]other-daughter stories are thus about power, about the social construction of relationships of domination and subordination as they inflect relationships between men and women and between women themselves. . . . They can reveal the assumptions about women's power, women's sexuality, and women's relationships to one another upon which patriarchal order rest. Mother-daughter stories are about the schism between women that the power relations of patriarchy create" (14). We clearly see this schism between women in the relationship of Blanscheflûr to her mother. Without a meaningful and valued currency within a feudal dynastic system, mother and daughter lack the "glue" that attaches one woman to the other. Their relationship is fated to disappear, the story of their bond fated to dissipate. The same is true for the relationship of the co-mothers. The bond that exists originally – despite religious and cultural differences, and linguistic incompatibility – crumbles as the biologically maternal morphs into the feudal and dynastic maternal, as it enters, we might say, the realm of patriarchal order.

Works Cited

Altpeter-Jones, Katharina. "Trafficking in Goods and Women: Love and Economics in Konrad Fleck's *Flôre und Blanscheflûr*." PhD diss., Duke University 2003.
Bataille, Georges. "The Notion of Expenditure." In *Visions of Excess: Selected Writings, 1927–1939*, edited and translated by Allan Stoekl, 116–29. Minneapolis: University of Minnesota Press, 1985.
Benecke, Georg Friedrich, Wilhelm Müller and Friedrich Zarncke. *Mittelhochdeutsches Wörterbuch*. 3 vols. Leipzig: 1854–66. http://woerterbuchnetz.de/cgi-bin/WBNetz/wbgui_py?sigle=Lexer&mode=Vernetzung&lemid=LG02934#XLG02934 (accessed December 17, 2020).
Bornholdt, Claudia. *Engaging Moments: The Origins of the Medieval Bridal-Quest Narrative*. Berlin: De Gruyter, 2005.
Bowden, Sarah. *Bridal-Quest Epics in Medieval Germany: A Revisionary Approach*. London: igrs books, 2012.
Frings, Theodor. "Die Entstehung der deutschen Spielmannsepen." *Zeitschrift für deutsche Geistesgeschichte* 2 (1939–40): 306–21.
Gibbs, Marion E. and Sidney M. Johnson. *Medieval German Literature: A Companion*. New York and London: Garland, 1997.
Kohnen, Rabea. *Die Braut des Königs: Zur interreligiösen Dynamik der mittelhochdeutschen Brautwerbungserzählungen*. Berlin: De Gruyter, 2014.
Lexer, Matthias. *Mittelhochdeutsches Handwörterbuch*. 3 vols. Leipzig: 1872–78. http://woerterbuchnetz.de/cgi-bin/WBNetz/wbgui_py?sigle=Lexer&mode=Vernetzung&lemid=LG02934#XLG02934 (accessed December 17, 2020).
Putzo, Christine. *Konrad Fleck 'Flore und Blanscheflur': Text und Untersuchungen*. Berlin/Boston: De Gruyter, 2015.
Rasmussen, Ann Marie. *Mothers and Daughters in Medieval German Literature*. Syracuse: Syracuse University Press, 1997.
Tolan, John Victor. *Saracens: Islam in the Medieval European Imagination*. New York: Columbia University Press, 2002.
Uebel, Michael. *Ecstatic Transformation: On the Uses of Alterity in the Middle Ages*. New York: Palgrave Macmillan, 2005.

Evelyn Meyer
5 Teaching a Daughter Sexual Desire and Love Lore: Herzeloyde's Mentorship of Sigune in Wolfram von Eschenbach's *Titurel* and Albrecht von Scharfenberg's *Jüngerer Titurel*

> Mothers and daughters talk about sex. Such dialogue, a literary convention reaching back to classical literature, characterizes the mother-daughter relationship as a sexual alliance between women. It takes as its bodily and social point of departure the daughter's sexual maturation, for the daughter's sexual maturation marks her transition to female adulthood. The mother teaches her daughter love lore. In so doing she reproduces a female sphere of activity, initiates her daughter into the patriarchal social order, and prepares her daughter for the role that awaited virtually all sexually active medieval women: motherhood. [. . .] Medieval adolescent daughters in these texts are taught the rules and protocols of female gender identity from their mothers in an overtly didactic, pedagogical manner.
> – Ann Marie Rasmussen, *Mothers and Daughters* (1997, 22–23)

From the thirteenth century onward, vernacular conduct literature flourished throughout medieval Europe and over time enjoyed ever-widening numbers and circles of readers.[1] It is found all over medieval literature appearing during many centuries and in many literary genres, such as conduct books, lyric poems, verse, epic, and romances. Most conduct books describe proper etiquette at court and sought to systematize a society's codes of behavior, thus functioning as guides of proper behavior for their readers. Yet as the later Middle Ages are also a period of great flux in which religious practices, class structures and political identities changed, these books, as argued by Kathleen Ashley and Robert Clark, also serve the purpose of being "a guide for literate readers to negotiate new sets of social possibilities" (Ashley and Clark 2001, x). Roberta L. Kruger also notes this and writes:

> Transmitting the precepts of classical ethics, Christian piety, and savvy behavior in a variety of forms, these books [i.e. conduct books, E.M.] conserved and rewrote the rules for good living to reflect changing socio-historical realities and to reach new audiences within different linguistic, geographical, and social contexts. As their production moved from royal and aristocratic courts to bourgeois households, conduct books played a major role in the spread of literacy, in cultural education, and in social mobility. (Krueger 2009, ix)

---

[1] I would like to thank Gretchen Arnold, Arline Cravens, Georgia Johnston, Colleen McCluskey, Angela Smart, and Constance Wagner, members of the St. Louis University Women's and Gender Studies Research Group, who read and commented on earlier versions of this essay.

Thus, while conduct literature by its nature develops slowly, absorbs, and transmits traditional teachings, it also contains and/or creates space for new interpretations of traditional teachings, a place to debate them, and to transform them. In the German vernacular tradition, the focus of this essay, we find texts that were written explicitly as conduct literature, such as Thomasin von Zerclaere's *Der Wälsche Gast* (ca. 1215–1216), Hugo von Trimberg's *Der Renner* (ca. 1290–1300), "Spruchdichtung" [didactic verse],[2] or *Die Winsbeckin* and *Der Winsbecke* (both ca. 1210–1220). However, parental advice-giving scenes, be those with biological or foster parents, are common in courtly literature and epics – where they likely functioned discursively as conduct literature – such as in Wolfram von Eschenbach's *Parzival* (ca. 1220), Wolfram von Eschenbach's *Titurel* (ca. 1220), which was continued and expanded by Albrecht von Scharfenberg as *Jüngerer Titurel* (ca. 1260–1275), Gottfried von Strassburg's *Tristan* (ca. 1210–1215), and the *Nibelungenlied* (ca. 1200).

Ann Marie Rasmussen expertly analyzes key mother-daughter didactic conversations in her groundbreaking study *Mothers and Daughters in Medieval German Literature* (1997) (e.g., those in *Die Winsbeckin*, the *Nibelungenlied*, and *Tristan*) but did not include those in *Titurel* or *Jüngerer Titurel*, namely the didactic conversations between Herzeloyde and her niece Sigune, perhaps because their relationship is not a biological mother-daughter one. Instead theirs is a kinship relationship of aunt and niece. However, Herzeloyde stands in as Sigune's mother throughout her life, as she fosters Sigune after Sigune's mother Schoysiane died at her birth and her father placed her under Herzeloyde's guardianship. Therefore I will refer to their conversation as one between a mother (figure) and daughter, in which Sigune can expect to be mentored and instructed by Herzeloyde as if she were Herzeloyde's own daughter. Rasmussen convincingly shows in *Mothers and Daughters* that "[t]he medieval world did not have one set of beliefs, attitudes, and expectations towards women and the roles they played as mothers and daughters. Rather, it produced different, often conflicting, models" (Rasmussen 1997, 13). Furthermore, she shows how literary mother-daughter conversations about sex and love lore are shaped differently based on genre and class. In texts that feature noble women, these conversations about love focus on directing the young woman towards a heterosexual marriage, marriage negotiations which tend to converge with political issues, for a noble woman's choice of marriage partner was usually about political alliances forged between men. In contrast, literary texts that feature lower class or peasant women tend to discuss choices of sexual activity and sexual partner and cover a broad range of possibilities.[3] My particular interest here lies in female mentorship,

---

[2] All translations are my own, unless otherwise noted.
[3] See the individual chapters in Rasmussen's book, and also her introductory overview (Rasmussen 1997, 22–25).

the specific teaching and advice given to the young Sigune by Herzeloyde and how Wolfram and Albrecht break with one "model" of literary convention of courtly conduct advice sometimes found in other contemporary examples. Such conversations between the knowledgeable mother and inexperienced daughter mostly take place *before* the daughter falls in love and experiences erotic desire. The daughter usually is instructed about the inevitability of heterosexual love resulting in marriage; what love is; and how her external beauty makes her desirable to a man, and that therein lies her worth. In this essay, I will focus mostly on the didactic conversation between Herzeloyde and Sigune in *Titurel* and *Jüngerer Titurel*, which does not follow this pattern. In order to draw out the unique features of this particular conversation, I will make comparisons to *Die Winsbeckin*, as well as brief references to the counterpart male mentorship conversation in *Titurel* and *Jüngerer Titurel* between Gahmuret and his foster son and squire Schionatulander, and the "pseudo"-didactic conversation between the young lovers Sigune and Schionatulander.

In the didactic conversation between Herzeloyde and Sigune in *Titurel* and *Jüngerer Titurel*, as I will argue, the noble mother figure refuses to teach the daughter about love, conventional behavior, and expectations to secure an appropriate husband; instead she complains bitterly about the suffering caused by linking *minne* [(courtly) love] to chivalry. This conversation is far more about Herzeloyde's pain and frustration with her own *minne*-suffering than instruction about love and sexual desire for the young noble lady, although sexual desire and a woman's agency or passivity do feature strongly in this conversation as well. By instructing Sigune more about the figurative flipside of the coin, namely that *minne* can and usually does cause suffering and that suffering is bound up in sexual desire, the effect of Herzeloyde's instruction on Sigune must be one of caution. In *Titurel*, the conversation about sexual desire more closely follows the model Rasmussen describes for noble women, which focuses on making the noble girl desirable to men for marriage. The conversation about sexual desire in the *Jüngerer Titurel* shifts more towards the style of conversations of lower class women, which focus on being in control of and proactive about one's sexual desires. The *Jüngerer Titurel* generally accords with this conversation as found in *Titurel*, but there are significant differences in the depiction of the figure Herzeloyde which show, as we shall see in what follows, that Albrecht von Scharfenberg intentionally reshapes both Herzeloyde's character and the message she delivers to Sigune.

Wolfram in *Titurel* and Albrecht in *Jüngerer Titurel* break with the literary tradition, in which, as Alexander Sager states, "dem Liebesgespräch zwischen den Hauptfiguren zuerst ein Lehrgespräch über die Liebe mit dem Vormund vorangeh[t]" [Sager 2003, 269; the love talk between the two main figures is preceded by a didactic conversation with the guardian about love]. Here the instructional conversations between parental figures and youths come after the two lovers, Schionatulander and Sigune, have confessed their love for and to each other, thus having taught themselves what *minne* is without guidance. Sager writes:

> Denn es gelingt Schionatulander und Sigune in ihrem Gespräch, am *anevanc ir gesellschefte mit worten* (Str. 73,1 f.), unter eigener Motivierung und aus eigener Kraft die richtige Sprache zu finden und ihre Beziehung in die richtige Form – die des Minnedienstverhältnisses – zu bringen.
> (Sager 2003, 279)

> [At the "beginning of their relationship with words" – at their own initiative and under their own power – Schionatulander and Sigune are successful in their conversation and are able to find the right language and put their relationship into the right form – that of love service.]

Although including some of the conventions of female advice-giving conversations, (e.g., the inexperienced Sigune has to ask what *minne* is, and she initially resists love and being bound to a man through *minne*), the key difference here is that neither of the youths is instructed by a parent. Therefore, these parental advice-giving conversations are less about what *minne* is than they are, for the young couple, about obtaining their elder's approval of their choice in *minne*-partner. They also offer little to no advice about proper conduct for courtly lovers.

Gahmuret immediately understands his foster son Schionatulander's suffering as caused by lovesickness, because he knows from personal experience both the joy and suffering caused by love as well as its bodily effects, especially the loss of one's healthy glow and the paling of one's skin (T 95 // JT 769).[4] He implores him to give up his secret and if Schionatulander refuses to reveal his secret to him, he will violate the principles of "triuwe" [loyalty] and "stæte" [steadfastness] (T 102, 2 and 4 // JT 774, 2 and 4). Schionatulander confesses his love for Sigune out of a sense of honor and responsibility, but also reminds Gahmuret of his responsibility towards him, to help him cope with Sigune's strong power over him, because he, Schionatulander, has served him well (T 105–106 // JT 778–779). Theirs is a conversation of equals, where both are bound to each other by duty and responsibility. Schionatulander gives up his secret and Gahmuret gives him advice, namely that the only way to heal his lovesickness is to earn her *minne* through *minnedienst*. Men do not overcome lovesickness by transforming themselves into beautiful and desirable objects, but instead by continuing to perform chivalric deeds, only this time in the service and honor of their chosen "minnedame" [lady love]. Their honor is bound up in successful chivalric deeds, proper courtly behavior and political activity appropriate for the dominant masculine role; and therein lies the emphasis of male (-voiced) advice conversations. *Minne* only plays a small role in the advice boys are given by their fathers or male mentors, whose roles in medieval society are far more varied

---

[4] I will cite primarily from Wolfram's *Titurel* (T), but also list the corresponding strophe and line numbers in Albrecht's *Jüngerer Titurel* (JT) for reference, unless there is a significant and noteworthy difference in meaning and wording in the text of *Jüngerer Titurel*, in which case I will cite both texts separately.

than those available to women, as they span the chivalric, political, social, courtly, religious, private, and public realms. They are active participants in public life and educated accordingly. The conversation between Gahmuret and Schionatulander follows the model of father-son didactic conversations: they cover the complexity and multifaceted roles and responsibilities that men in secular society have. Marriage and *minne* are discussed to a far lesser degree than in female advice conversations.[5]

Despite the fact that Schionatulander and Sigune keep their love secret, Herzeloyde and Gahmuret should have been aware of the young lovers' suffering long before they are, for it has gone on "ze lange" [T 114, 2 // JT 790, 2; too long]. Only when the symptoms of lovesickness literally stare them in the face do they take notice. Sigune's eyes are red and wet like a dew-covered rose, her mouth and her face are marked by her inner suffering, which is caused by intense longing for her beloved (T 115 // JT 791). While Sigune's inner suffering is mentioned, the narrator draws our attention largely to her diminished beauty, as does Herzeloyde later on in her advice to Sigune. By contrast, the narrator describes Schionatulander's lovesickness by noting both internal and external effects on him: lovesickness strips him of all his heart's joy (T 88, 4 // JT 762, 4), he loses his high spirits and endures such deep pain that it would be more pleasant for him to be dead (T 89, 2–4 // JT 763, 2–4); as a result, he becomes too weak for battle (see T 90 // JT 764). Externally, his perfect appearance also changes: his skin and his bright eyes, which had made his appearance attractive, have lost their brightness and shine (T 94 // JT 768). Lovesickness here is presented as a gendered difference: in a man it can have much more devastating effects, because it renders him too weak for battle. Thus he is unable to fulfill his male responsibility within knighthood to defend those in need, society and its values, the political system, and Christianity. In a woman, while she too suffers internally, it "only" makes her less beautiful, and thus less desirable to a man.

Herzeloyde notices that something is amiss with Sigune in her red and wet eyes, and the sorrow clearly marked in her mouth and face (T 115 // JT 791). She feels concerned about Sigune and immediately remembers her own intense suffering caused by her *minne* for Gahmuret, but then makes the assumption in *Titurel* that Sigune's

---

[5] Rasmussen describes the father-son conversation in *Der Winsbecke* as primarily a monologue in which the father "earnestly advises his son on rules for virtuous, god-fearing worldly conduct." After the son's objections, "the father closes with prayer-like praise for the spiritual retreat from the world he and his son are undertaking." "The structure of the poem as a monologue is challenged, but ultimately sustained. Because the father's voice dominates the poem, a structural link between authority and monologue is maintained as a communicative strategy: the authoritative voice is authoritative because it can and does hold forth without interruption" (Rasmussen 2001, 111 and 126). Here, as in the Gahmuret-Schionatulander advice conversation, the topics included are broad, covering many a topic from public and private lives, religion, knightly responsibilities, virtues and their applicability to daily life, and proper conduct towards and appreciation of virtuous women generally. Marriage to and love for a woman are only briefly mentioned in strophes 8–9 of *Der Winsbecke* (see Rasmussen and Trokhimenko 2009, 61–125).

suffering must be caused by not feeling comforted by her (i.e. Herzeloyde), nor by her own (i.e. Sigune's) kinsmen who are so far away (see T 117, 2–3), and in *Jüngerer Titurel* that she may not obtain help, for she may not feel comforted by loved ones and all of Herzeloyde's kinsmen (see JT 792, 2–3). The only reason for Sigune's affliction that Herzeloyde can imagine is loneliness and homesickness, not the pains of *minne*.

Herzeloyde, unlike Gahmuret, does not react favorably to Sigune's plight and she does not provide the expected mentorship, advice, instructions, and words of wisdom for the presumably "unwise" Sigune. Instead, she exposes her to an explosion of her own anger about the negative consequences of *minnedienst*, her paranoia about Queen Anflise's revenge for stealing Gahmuret away from her, and she refuses to acknowledge Sigune's suffering caused by lovesickness. Her own suffering caused by Gahmuret's absence does not make her empathetic towards Sigune's plight. Instead, throughout this conversation Herzeloyde fluctuates between anger and some paltry attempts of mentoring Sigune in proper courtly conduct in matters of sexual desire and love. Likewise, she fluctuates between speaking with a private voice expressing her own opinions about *minne* and its effects and with a representative, public voice on behalf of courtly society describing courtly love, *minnedienst* and a woman's gendered role in it. Despite the reversal in the temporal order of didactic parental and lovers' conversations, Sigune can nonetheless anticipate being advised by Herzeloyde about "expectations, gender roles, and proper behavior in courtly society [. . .] around the topic of love, more specifically, around sexual desire and courtly norms of controlling it" (Trokhimenko 2008, 492–93)[6] for Herzeloyde has served as Sigune's surrogate mother throughout her life. Yet as we will see, Sigune receives little practical advice because Herzeloyde suffers from her husband's absence, as she tells Sigune at the beginning of this conversation: "[. . .] ich truoc ê alze vil ander riwe, / der ich phlac hin nâch dem Anschevîne" [T 116, 2–3 // JT 792, 2–3; Until now, I had too much other pain/sorrow, which I endured, longing for the Anschevin].

At this point, Herzeloyde grudgingly begins to deal with Sigune whose suffering she finally acknowledges and shows some compassion for in *Titurel*: "Ellendiu maget, nu muoz mich *dîn ellende* erbarmen" [T 118, 1; Homeless maiden, now I must have compassion for *your abandonment*, emphasis mine), thus again solely placing the emphasis on the cause for Sigune's affliction on her being an orphan. Sigune is indeed an "ellendiu maget," brought to her aunt's court after the death of her mother and thus abandoned by her father, who immediately in his grief foreswore not only the life of chivalry (T 22, 4), but also courtly love (T 23, 4) and thereby the possibility to provide Sigune with another mother within an immediate family context. Most noble children grew up with their families, but fosterage was

---

6 Though Trokhimenko describes this for the Winsbeckin's daughter, these topics are representative for mother-daughter advice conversations.

particularly common for royal children, as their parents travelled often in their roles as Kings and Queens and therefore could not provide a stable upbringing for their offspring. However, most children spent the early years growing up in their family, and were only moved into fosterage after they reached approximately 7 years of age (Orme 2001, 55–56). While fosterage of noble boys is more common – Schionatulander, for example, was fostered early on by Queen Anflise (see T 129, 1 // JT 807, 1) – it is rare for girls (Slitt 2018), yet in Sigune's case, it was necessary, after the death of her mother, to be raised by her maternal aunt.

However, "ellende" and "ellendiu maget" do not solely address homelessness, as Herzeloyde does, but more broadly convey affliction, including that caused by lovesickness, as is the case here with Sigune. Thus, both Wolfram and Albrecht primarily convey in this statement, that Sigune is "ellende," miserable, on account of the unaccustomed effects of pain her love for Schionatulander causes her and not just her homesickness. Despite the obvious symptoms of lovesickness, Herzeloyde nonetheless fails to identify them, nor is she moved towards sincere compassion for her niece's plight, despite the fact that Herzeloyde is suffering from a similar form of lovesickness herself. Instead, she intentionally mistakes Sigune's suffering as caused by her homelessness and by being a foreigner in Herzeloyde's lands, thus choosing to focus on only one aspect of Sigune's "ellende" – the one that afflicts her less, if at all, at that moment. In the *Jüngerer Titurel*, where the figure Herzeloyde is generally even less compassionate towards Sigune's plight, she demands that Sigune show her compassion, as she says instead: "Ellende maget schone, nu můstu *mich* erbarmen!" [JT 794, 1; Homeless/Afflicted, beautiful maiden, now you must show *me* compassion! emphasis mine]. Here, Herzeloyde is presented as more concerned with her own reputation and situation than that of her distraught niece. The implication is that Herzeloyde's unhappiness takes precedence over Sigune's. While Herzeloyde's words in the rest of the strophe are almost identical in both texts, this opening line reveals a sharply different characterization of the figure Herzeloyde in the Albrecht version of the narrative that is maintained throughout these parallel conversations.

Both responses by Herzeloyde are puzzling, for Sigune's "ellende" [homelessness] had not been a problem at all according to the narrator, and secondly, Herzeloyde herself suffers from that which Sigune suffers: lovesickness, making such a misinterpretation of the signs and situation implausible. As a matter of fact, both narratives tell us: "diu küngin wart innen mit herzen schrîck, waz Sigûne dolte" [T 114, 4 // JT 790, 4; The queen noticed with fright in her heart what Sigune suffered from]. She knows that Sigune suffers from lovesickness, but her words reveal "daß Herzeloyde die Wahrheit der *minne* nicht wahrhaben wollte" [Sager 2003, 283; that Herzeloyde does not want to accept the truth of *minne*], in addition to her own ambivalence towards *minne*, which causes her to have great difficulty assuming her representative role towards her charge ("ihre repräsentative Rolle gegenüber ihrem Mündel zu übernehmen" [Sager 2003, 282]). Herzeloyde's response, therefore, can only be interpreted as a clear indication of how much she does not want to deal with courtly love and the expectations surrounding it, and instead seeks other plausible reasons for Sigune's unhappiness, namely her homelessness at her aunt's court. Only in that area is she willing to do everything "daz dîn kumber swinde" [T 118, 3; so that your pain/sorrow will disappear], yet not for love. Pain caused by loneliness in a foreign country moves Herzeloyde deeply, but lovesickness does not (see T 117–118).

Despite Herzeloyde's willful blindness to it, Sigune's secret is now out in the open, her lovesickness mapped onto her body for all to see. Sigune thus has no choice but to reveal that which she had guarded so carefully from the public for quite some time. She puts her faith in Herzeloyde, for the latter had cared for her with tender love like a mother and therefore, she now turns to this mother figure for advice, expressing her need for help and naming the area in which she seeks advice. Sigune says:

> "Dînes râtes, dînes   trôstes, dîner hulde
> bedarf ich mit ein ander, sît ich al gernde nâch friunde iâmer dulde,
> vil quelehafter nôt. daz ist unwendec.
> er quelt mîne wilde gedanke   an sîn bant. al mîn sin ist im bendec."
> (T 121 // JT 797)

[I am in need of your advice, of your comfort, of your favor, all of them together, for I endure sorrow, much excruciating affliction, (I who am) filled with longing for my friend/my beloved. That cannot be undone. He fetters my untamed thoughts to his bonds. My entire mind is firmly attached to him/is compliant to him.]

Sigune initiates this conversation in the tradition of a didactic conversation between a mother and daughter, looking for instruction on how to conduct herself appropriately in the ways of courting her "vriunde" [beloved], and to cope with her mind that is "al gernde" [full of longing] and her "vil quelenhafter nôt" [excruciating affliction]. However, the "sît ich al gernde nâch friunde iâmer dulde, vil quelehafter nôt" [for I endure sorrow, much excruciating affliction, (I who am) filled with longing for my friend/my beloved] is syntactically not as straight forward as it may seem at first and as I translated it above. "al gernde" [full of longing] can syntactically be connected with "nâch friunde"[for the beloved], i.e., Sigune deeply longs for her beloved, yet it can also be read as creating a difference between the two: she is "al gernde" [full of longing] and also suffers excruciating affliction and pain caused by the lover. In one, he is the object of her longing, in the other, she longs to be free of the pain he causes her by trapping her in unwanted *minne*. Sigune's "wilde gedanke" [untamed thoughts] likewise take on a double meaning, for they can be both about her sexual desire for her beloved, and her fury for having been trapped in *minne* against her will.[7] She expects and can expect to be advised by her aunt about how to cope with desire and sexual

---

7 Likewise, Brackert's and Fuchs-Jolie's commentary on this line in Wolfram's *Titurel* 2003, 231.

longing, about proper courtly conduct for courting, and about courtly norms of controlling sexual desire, and this is what Sigune asks of her aunt. At the same time, Sigune also asks about being released from this unwanted torment of having been trapped by *minne*, which is fettering her freedom to act and forces her into acting as a *minnedame*. She continues by adequately describing her restlessness, how she stands by the window, the tower, or even by the sea, to look for him; in search and hopes of news from her beloved, who makes her go from feeling very cold (T 126, 2) to so hot as if she lay "in dem gnaneistenden viure, // sus erglüet mich Schoynatulander" [T 126, 2–3; in a crackling fire, thus Schionatulander causes me to glow from heat/passion].[8]

Herzeloyde does not know that the lovers' talk between Schionatulander and Sigune has already taken place and therefore needs to assume that Sigune has to be instructed, at least further than she would have been up to this point as a young courtly lady. Sigune has some knowledge of what is expected of her, as Sager convincingly argues in his book *minne von mæren*, for already at the age of five, Sigune was attuned to her future life as courtly lady and *minnedame*, even if her knowledge at that time came primarily from words, literature, and role playing.[9] One would expect that like the other literary mothers mentioned earlier, Herzeloyde would instruct the younger woman in the ways of *minne*, especially on how to be a *minnedame*, how to maintain her honor and virtue despite her sexual desires now awakened, and how to cope with the negative impact of *minne* on her mind and body, with lovesickness caused by separation, and with the inability to act freely. Yet Herzeloyde does no such thing and instead explodes into outright rage accusing Anflise of putting these words into the young Sigune's mouth as an outlet for her (Anflise's) own anger and in order to take revenge on Herzeloyde:

> "'Ôwe', sprâch diu küngîn,   'dû redest nâch den wîsen.
> wer hât dich mir verrâten?   nû fürht ich der Franzoysæren küngin Anphlîsen,
> daz sich habe ir zorn an mir gerochen.
> al dîniu wîslîchen   wort sint ûz ir munde gesprochen.
>
> Schoynatulander   ist hôch rîcher fürste.
> sîn edelkeit, sîn kiusche   getörste doch nimer genenden an die getürste,
> daz sîn jugent nâch dîner minne spræche,
> op sich der stolzen Anphlîsen   haz an mir mit ir hazze niene ræche.
> Si zôch daz selbe kint, sît ez   der brust wart enphüeret.'"
>   (T 127, 1–129, 1 // JT 805, 1–807, 1)

---

8 Kurt Ruh notes that the fire of love belongs to the original and widely used metaphors of love language during the Middle Ages, yet Wolfram only makes use of it twice in his entire oeuvre, once in *Parzival* to describe Jeschute's red, hot, and desiring lips, and here in *Titurel* to describe the intensity of Sigune's love, which seized her so violently (see Ruh 1989, 509–10).
9 See Sager 2006, Ch. 2, especially 35–37; and Sager 2006, Ch. 3, especially 66–68, and 77–81.

["Alas," said the queen, "you speak like an experienced person: Who betrayed you to me? Now I fear that the Queen of the French, Anflise, has taken her revenge on me in her fury. All your wise words come from her mouth.

Schionatulander is a noble and powerful lord. His nobility, his chaste courage never would dare to be so audacious, that because of his youth he would ask for your *minne*, had not the hatred of the proud Anflise wanted to take revenge on me in her spitefulness. She raised this very child [i.e., Schionatulander] since he was weaned."]

The intensity of Herzeloyde's anger and her paranoia about Anflise's revenge are puzzling and make little sense. Neither *Titurel* nor *Parzival* contain anything in the story that gives a stamp of credence to Herzeloyde's paranoia; after all, Anflise quietly bowed out after Herzeloyde legally enforced her rights of marriage over Gahmuret.[10] Furthermore, according to the expectations of courtly society, it was anticipated that Sigune marry. Therefore, Herzeloyde should have assumed that everything was developing according to plan and social expectations. Her anger is thus remarkable and a totally unexpected reaction, causing us to pause and contemplate it.

We have to turn to Wolfram's *Parzival* and Herzeloyde's marriage claim over Gahmuret for a possible explanation. Herzeloyde wanted to choose her own husband and for that reason set up a tournament; the winner would have to marry her. When Gahmuret tried to avoid this marriage, Herzeloyde legally enforces her rights, disrespects his marriage to Belakane on religious grounds, and forces him to marry her. Wolfram created Herzeloyde as a figure who does not play by the rules nor conduct herself according to courtly expectations of women, but instead sets the terms for her marriage by claiming the right to choose for herself. She is and needs to be in charge, yet despite her best efforts, she never gains full control over Gahmuret. He is not subsumed by *minne* as Herzeloyde is, and has a fierce independent streak of his own: he makes his consent to this marriage contingent upon her granting him a monthly leave to participate in tournaments. While he could not avoid this marriage to Herzeloyde, he resists submitting to her control. His monthly absence, be it for tournaments or other chivalric duties, proves to be another source of Herzeloyde's anger. She is angry that Gahmuret subjects her to intense forms of lovesickness, and demonstrates the limitations of her control and power. As Herzeloyde did not conduct herself according to courtly love conventions in the context of her own marriage to Gahmuret, it is consistent that she does not transmit the expected advice about love, for that would imply a betrayal of her strong conviction that women should have control over their own fate in choice of marriage partner and marriage itself. *Minne* requires women to occupy the passive role and Herzeloyde managed to circumvent this "law" of love when she was "won" by Gahmuret. It seems that Herzeloyde is angry because Sigune is falling into the courtly love tradition, from which

---

10 See esp. *Parzival* 86, 29–89, 2; 94, 1–96, 10; and 97, 13–98, 14.

Herzeloyde herself has broken away.[11] Herzeloyde, therefore, chooses not to teach Sigune the "normal code" because of what she did herself. This is further evidence that this is not a normal didactic conversation between a mother and daughter, but instead a conversation about "schon vollendete Liebestatsachen" [Sager 2003, 269; already settled love matters], about Herzeloyde's anger because her own bid for agency in love, though initially successful (she does win Gahmuret), has failed (she loses him to chivalry).

Interestingly, Sigune remains silent until the end of this conversation, thus behaving very differently from the Winsbeckin's daughter, where

> the mother and daughter speak and respond to one another, each representing a different point of view on courtly love. Their voices, though distinct from one another, are completely intertwined. [. . .] [T]he dialogue structure of *Die Winsbeckin* makes it closely resemble debate or dispute literature. [. . .] The daughter is neither a passive recipient of her mother's teachings, nor is her role limited to making a single, decisive interruption. Instead, the daughter asks questions, suggests topics, redirects the conversation, challenges her mother, and expresses respect and love, as well as indignation, anger, and fear.[12] (Rasmussen 2001, 126–27)

Sigune seems to see no need to please her aunt. She seems to sense, whether intuitively or otherwise, that no one can reproach her for her *minne*-relationship with Schionatulander despite his and her youth, an argument Herzeloyde utilizes herself to dissuade Sigune from participating in *minnedienst*. Wolfram even emphasizes the fact that because it is a *Kinderliebe* [love between youths] (see T 46, 3 // JT 709, 3) that it is the more "lûterlîche" [pure] and that no one in the world will find any "truopheit" [T 46, 4 // JT 709, 4; impurity/blemish] in their love (Ruh 1989, 505). As a matter of fact, as Sager notes, there is not even any social or personal reason which requires them to keep their love secret as they do (Sager 2003, 267). They are perfectly suited to each other according to courtly norms and expectations. Sigune listens to her aunt's response as Herzeloyde works herself towards granting her approval of this relationship. This is Sigune's ultimate goal, namely "daz ich den Grâharzoys vor al der werld nu mit urloube sô minne!" [T 136, 4 // JT 814, 4; that I now have the permission to love the Graharz in front of the entire world!][13]

With some of her anger spent, Herzeloyde does begin to give Sigune *some* advice, but does so in sharp contrast to the Winsbeckin. The Winsbeckin explains courtly virtues to her daughter by means of specific examples and practical advice,

---

[11] For the same reason, Herzeloyde removes Parzival from courtly influences after he is born and withdraws to the wasteland of Soltane.
[12] For further analysis of the mother-daughter conversation in *Die Winsbeckin*, see Trokhimenko 2004, 327–50; Trokhimenko 2008, 490–505; Rasmussen 1997, 136–59; Rasmussen and Trokhimenko 2009, 61–125; and Classen 2007, 159–86.
[13] These are the final words spoken in the first fragment of *Titurel*, thereby making them perhaps even more eminent.

e.g., that wild glances mean that a woman's eyes dart about immoderately and that she would be perceived as conducting herself without proper measure, which would be harmful to her reputation (see WB 7), or that after *minne* strikes the daughter, "mahtû ein kiuschez herze tragen / des muostû lop und êre hân" [WB 27, 3–4; if you want to have a pure heart, then you must receive praise and honor for it]. Most importantly, however, she tells her daughter "sô man gedenket ofte an dich / und wünschet dîn, sô bistu wert" [WB 15, 9–10; if a man thinks often of you and desires you, then you are worthy]. Being desirable to a man and desired by him is what ultimately makes women matter in the context of *minne*, but this also reveals that love as sexual passion is defined in terms of male desire (Rasmussen 1997, 139; Trokhimenko 2004, 334). Herzeloyde, however, does not focus on courtly virtues at all and only on restoring bodily beauty and erasing the physical markers of lovesickness. Wolfram's Herzeloyde is fairly matter of fact in this advice:

> "gap si niht durch triegen den rât, der dich hât als unsanfte gerüeret,
> du maht im, er dir vil fröuden erwerben.
> sîstu im holt, sô lâ dînen wunschlîchen lîp niht verderben!
>
> Biut im daz zêren, lâ wider clâren
> dîniu ougen, diu wange, dîn kinne! wie stêt alsô iunclîchen iâren,
> op sô liehtez vel dâ bî verlischet?
> dû hâst in die kurzlîchen fröude vil sorge alze sêre gemischet."
> (T 129, 2–130, 4)

[If after all she [i.e. Anflise] did not give her advice in bad faith, which affected you so painfully, then you give him [i.e. Schionatulander] much joy and he you. If you are devoted to him, then do not permit your desirable body to spoil.

Do this in his honor: let your eyes, your cheeks and your chin clear up! How is it befitting to such youth, if such radiant skin loses its glow? You managed only too well to mix much sorrow into this recent joy.]

She reassures Sigune that each lover can bring much joy to the other, that if she favors him, she should make herself beautiful again, that is, make herself physically desirable to a man again, just as the Winsbeckin advised her daughter. It is Sigune's outward, bodily beauty alone that matters to bring joy in *minne* to them, and it is honorable for her and an honor to him, if she does not spoil her physical beauty. It is her "alze vil sorge" [excessive worrying] that diminished her recent joy of *minne* and ruined her beauty. Bound up in these words is an implicit rebuking of Sigune, who by failing to conduct herself according to such courtly virtues as "mâze" [measure/humility] and "zuht" [good manners/proper conduct], neglects her "êre" [honor], which for a woman is irrevocably tied to being sexually desirable to a man, as the Winsbeckin so poignantly tells her daughter. Here Herzeloyde speaks in the representative voice of courtly society, by reminding Sigune of her responsibilities to make herself desirable to a man, to become the object of men's sexual desire; though at the same time she would have to guard her virtue, her reputation and especially her virginity.

In contrast, Albrecht's less compassionate Herzeloyde questions Sigune more strongly in the corresponding passage about whether this is indeed what Sigune wants:

"durch triegens under windel   gab si licht rat, der dich unsanfte rûrte
wiltu im vreuden vil und dir erwerben,
sistu im holt, so ziere   den lip mit vreud und la in nicht verderben.

Biut im daz *zu wirde*   und la di werden claren
kinne, ougen, wange *mit girde*.   wie stet iz also kintlichen jaren,
ob so liechtez vel da bi erlischet?
du hast den last der sorgen   zevrû in din kintlich vrucht gemischet."
(JT 807, 2–808, 4, emphasis mine)

[In bad faith and with deception, she [i.e. Anflise] gave easy advice, which affected you so painfully. If you want to acquire many joys for him [i.e. Schionatulander] and yourself, and if you are devoted to him, then adorn your body with joy and do not let it spoil. Offer that to him *in dignity*, and let your chin, eyes and cheeks become clear *with desire*. How is it befitting to such youth, if such radiant skin loses its glow? You encountered the weight of sorrow too soon because of your naïve manner; emphasis mine].

By changing the statement from Wolfram's "dû maht im, er dir vil vreuden erwerben" [then you give him much joy and he you] to "wiltu im vreuden vil und dir erwerben" [should you want to acquire many joys for him and yourself], Albrecht gives Herzeloyde's speech a much more doubtful tone by employing the formula: "should you really want this . . ., only then . . .". The advice of Albrecht's Herzeloyde to Sigune is laced with questions, probing, and doubts about whether Sigune knows or perhaps can know what she is doing and perhaps she intends to inspire doubt in Sigune herself. Only if she is really sure, then should she adorn her body with joy and make it beautiful again. In Wolfram's version, Sigune is instructed to transform her body back to its beauty exclusively as a sign of honor to Schionatulander and as a tool to restore her own honor by means of making herself sexually desirable to him, willingly placing herself into an object position for a man's desire. By contrast, in Albrecht's version, Sigune is instructed to restore her physical beauty out of dignity for him ("zu wirde") and out of her own sexual desire ("mit girde"). It is thus Sigune's desire for Schionatulander which not only will heighten her physical beauty but also reverse the physical impact of her lovesickness. The tables have been turned here, for Albrecht's Herzeloyde posits female desire for a man as part of the cure to regain her bodily beauty, as she tells Sigune to use her sexually desirable body and its beauty as an asset to attract and hold on to Schionatulander for herself. Albrecht's Herzeloyde thus is much closer to the willful figure the audience knew from *Parzival*, a female figure fiercely desiring control over men and her own pleasure, and to the one at the beginning of this conversation, who exploded into anger, because of the harmful and restrictive nature of the conventions of courtly love. But here too, Herzeloyde appends the negative thought "du hast den last der sorgen zevrů in din *kintlich* vrucht gemischet" [you encountered the weight of sorrow too soon because of your *naïve* manner; emphasis mine] which shifts the focus away from *minne*'s joys and Sigune's active desire for a man to the burden of sorrow caused by *minne*. By adding "kintlich" [naïve] and deleting Wolfram's "die kurzlîchen fröude" [your recent joy], this sentence conveys an entirely different message than Wolfram's Herzeloyde, who focuses on Sigune's inability to hold on to *minne*'s greater joy when faced with *minne*'s sorrow. Albrecht's Herzeloyde may very well be telling Sigune that because she is "kintlich" [naïve], she is not ready to play an active role in desiring men and therefore encountered the weight of sorrow, and because of her naiveté, too early in her life. Here, in sharp contrast to Wolfram's Herzeloyde, Albrecht's Herzeloyde speaks with a private voice throughout, to express her personal opinion that women as subjects and agents can and should desire men, but also that they require maturity to do so. Not once does she speak in support of normative courtly expectations.

This difference in the two renditions of Herzeloyde's position on desire is maintained throughout their respective talks, as is the voice with which she speaks: Wolfram's Herzeloyde speaks with a public, courtly voice by representing normative courtly views, by advising Sigune about that which is socially expected of her in this situation, whereas Albrecht's Herzeloyde speaks with a private, almost anti-courtly voice which expresses her personal views that do not (fully) conform to public, courtly expectations. In an effort to give Sigune some hope that *minne* results not only in sorrow, Wolfram's Herzeloyde assures her that if Schionatulander robbed her of joy and wounded her, then "der mac dich wol an fröuden gerîchen" [T 131, 2; he can nonetheless make you rich in joys]. Sigune's joy depends on Schionatulander's action. He is the agent of her happiness. Herzeloyde does not prepare Sigune in any practical terms for what may be involved in said happiness, perhaps because of her own ambivalence towards courtly conventions surrounding *minne*, perhaps because she does not deem it courtly to discuss matters of sex, or because she thinks Sigune too young to be taught more specifically about sex, desire and fulfilled love. This Herzeloyde speaks in a representative, public voice of courtly society, which advocates for women's sexuality depending on male agency and male desire. By contrast, Albrecht's Herzeloyde, who promotes women as desiring subjects, is far more explicit in what she says to Sigune: "in vreude wider setzet dich sin lip" (JT 809, 2), that is, Schionatulander and/or his body ("sin lip") will delight her again. While this simply may mean that Schionatulander will lift her gloomy spirits when he returns to her, this certainly plays off the notion of sexual desire and longing ("mit girde") which Herzeloyde earlier instructed Sigune to use to reverse the effects of lovesickness by actively desiring Schionatulander. Furthermore, she comments explicitly that through the physicality of his body, that is through sex, Sigune will experience "vreude": joy, fulfillment, and happiness. Thus Albrecht's Herzeloyde continues to suffuse her advice to Sigune with a personal message expressed through an individual, private voice, which validates female sexual desire and control over it, as well as the joy of sex.

Herzeloyde's individuality and subjectivity are further consolidated by means of her final piece of advice for Sigune in which she most clearly links the joy of *minne* to the sorrow of chivalry. Wolfram's Herzeloyde says: "nu halt dâ ze im die trœstlîchen frôude, und er *der sorge* über dich niht verhenge!" [T 133, 4; Help him now to preserve happy anticipation, so that he not impose *sorrow* onto you; emphasis mine], whereas Albrecht's Herzeloyde says: "nu hilf, daz im sin vreude icht *ander sorgen* uber dich verhenge!" [JT 811, 4; Now help him so that his joy not impose *other/further sorrows* on you; emphasis mine]. Wolfram's Herzeloyde again presents male agency and male control as the norm: only if the man is happy, then will he not inflict sorrow onto a woman. A woman's happiness fully depends on a man being happy with her. Albrecht's Herzeloyde however places greater agency, and here perhaps also greater responsibility, onto the woman. She can prevent the imposition of additional sorrows onto herself, by helping the man. While it is possible to read different forms of joy and sorrow into these statements, and the multiplicity of meaning is intentional, in the context of that which precedes this vague advice, namely that Schionatulander because of his "zuht" [education/breeding] must focus on increasing his honor and reputation through knightly deeds, I believe she refers with "sorgen" [sorrows] especially to the fear of the ultimate sacrifice of *minnedienst*, the knight's death in battle, that which triggered her explosion into anger at the beginning of this conversation. The only logical way to avoid this particular sorrow, then, is to avoid the relationship altogether, but at the same time, Sigune should offer him "vreude" [joy/happiness/fulfillment] as a means to prevent the ultimate sorrow from occurring, and thus participate in this relationship. It is as if Herzeloyde advises Sigune to do something impossible: to fully participate in the joys of *minne*, but also to avoid the sorrow of required *minnedienst*, that results either in his absence or death or her loss of honor, should she engage, for example, in pre-marital sex.

In both *Titurel* and *Jüngerer Titurel*, Herzeloyde is depicted as a deeply conflicted female figure, torn between her role as surrogate mother to Sigune in matters of courtly expectations and love lore and her personal aversion and anger for the link between chivalry and *minne* that not only deprives her of her own beloved's company, but especially reminds her that she cannot fully be in control. Sager already observed this duality and conflict in Herzeloyde in Wolfram's *Titurel*. He writes:

> Diese Ambivalenz – man könnte fast meinen: Schizophrenie – im Charakter Herzeloydes drückt die Dualität ihrer Rolle gegenüber Sigune aus. In ihren Ausfällen gegen Anphlise und ihren "Bedenken" gegen die Verfrühtheit der Liebe spricht Herzeloyde in ihrer "Individualität."
> (Sager 2003, 284–85)

> [This ambivalence – one could even call it: schizophrenia – in Herzeloyde's character expresses the duality of her role towards Sigune. In her sallies against Anflise and in her 'concerns' about the prematurity of love, Herzeloyde speaks from a position of 'individuality.']

I would argue that Herzeloyde's ambivalence and the duality of her role go even further. Her speech reveals her deeply divided feelings about *minne* more broadly and its "real," contrary effects on lovers. It also discloses her inner conflict regarding societal expectations that the aristocracy participate in *minne* and that women accept being objects of male desire while being deprived of actively desiring men themselves. Throughout her speech, Wolfram's Herzeloyde continually fluctuates between her personal opinions which represent her private voice, and expected public position about *minne*, to safely direct a young noble woman towards marriage, there speaking with a representative, public voice of courtly society. The text signals Herzeloyde's private voice by means of rhetorical or actual questions, and interjections such as "owê", many I-statements that refer to Herzeloyde, and the use of subjunctive to express Herzeloyde's heightened emotional state and her frustration over the effects of *minne* and *minnedienst*. These are entirely absent when she uses the public voice, where in sharp contrast she appears calm and rational, uses imperatives to instruct, and focuses on describing *minnedienst* in a "factual" manner, such as listing qualities a man ought to have, or how a woman's beauty attracts a man. Albrecht reshapes this fluctuation between private and public voices from which Herzeloyde speaks in *Titurel* to one in which Herzeloyde speaks almost exclusively in a private voice, by increasing the use of subjunctive, rendering much as hypothetical and conditional, along the lines of "if he were to love you, . . ." or "are you sure this is what you really want?" This voice criticizes the public position that defines sexual passion in terms of male desire and agency, and assigns to woman a place of passivity, whereby being beautiful and therewith sexually desirable, she only becomes worthy, if men desire her. Instead, this voice advises Signue to desire a man and to enjoy the pleasures of his body and expresses anguish and anger over the pain caused by linking *minne* and chivalry by means of *minnedienst*.

Though Sigune asked for Herzeloyde's advice on how to cope with her lovesickness as well as her love for Schionatulander, she gets very little *practical* advice. This is unusual, as according to the dominant view expressed in medieval medical and theological theories, women were perceived to be physically inferior to men and their physical inferiority contributed directly to intellectual inferiority.[14] Because of their assumed intellectual inferiority, women could not understand abstract thought, and

---

14 For a convincing analysis of such gendered theories on educating medieval boys and girls, see Dronzek's (2001) study of fifteenth-century conduct books in England, in which she compares conduct books written for boys to those written for girls and can convincingly show: (1) how medieval ideas about gender dictated authors' understanding of how to educate children; (2) that boys and girls needed to be presented with information differently: boys visually, girls aurally; (3) that boys and girls had different capacities for absorbing information: boys could handle abstract concepts, whereas girls were taught through practical experience in the form of a parent's life wisdom; (4) that female honor was similarly tied to the body, and was inextricably linked to sexual conduct and the realm of the private and domestic, whereas male honor was determined not by the body's sexual conduct, but by the perception of a boy's bodily behavior; and (5) that girls required threats of

instead, as Anna Dronzek convincingly argues, had to be, and in fact were, instructed differently than boys, by means of "information presented in a tangible, physical way, through the use of examples or the experiential model of a parent imparting life wisdom" (Dronzek 2001, 151). This is the model followed generally in other medieval (German) mother-daughter advice conversations, but one that neither Wolfram nor Albrecht employ. Instead, Herzeloyde remains primarily abstract in her teaching of Sigune and only gives her one tangible piece of advice: namely, to restore and maintain her physical beauty, as is appropriate for a young noble lady. But even this piece of advice is delivered in a fairly abstract form. Herzeloyde underpins this advice with vague comments validating sexual desire either by placing women as an object under the umbrella of male desire, or as an active subject desiring a man. What is noticeably absent in Herzeloyde's reply are explicit instructions for how to cope with lovesickness which would automatically lead to the restoration of Sigune's physical beauty, what virtuous behavior consists of in a young noble lady in love, or how to maintain her reputation and to enhance his. Herzeloyde's personal inner conflict and anger about chivalry linked to *minne* stand in the foreground despite her efforts to speak in the representative voice of courtly society. Despite the emotional intensity of her response, she cannot reach Sigune, who in the end only hears the approval for her love relationship with Schionatulander.

As with Parzival, in the end, Herzeloyde fails to mentor Sigune well, for she can neither reach through her own despair, nor through her intense longing and love for Gahmuret. Not only do Wolfram and Albrecht provide us insights into Herzeloyde's deep inner conflict about chivalry in this conversation with Sigune, but through Herzeloyde they also provide us with another view on courtly love and its ties to chivalry, a critical voice that comes through loud and clear through the chatter of voices expressing the expected. Courtly norms stipulate that *minne* needs to be earned through chivalric service, that a woman must be beautiful in order to make herself a desirable object, and that thereby the honor of courtly lovers is increased. Even though Herzeloyde in the end gives her approval for this relationship, the anguish that shapes her instructions for Sigune makes her memorable, and even more so in Albrecht's version, by turning the tables on social expectations around women's sexual desire.

The different, often conflicting models of expectations of women and the roles mothers and daughters play "reveal themselves" most frequently by comparing narrative advice sections throughout a variety of medieval literary texts, as Ann Marie Rasmussen did in *Mothers and Daughters* (1997). Here, however, we encountered conflicting models in two adaptations of the *same* narrative. Neither Wolfram nor Albrecht follow the convention of conduct literature for women in which mothers teach their daughters about *minne*, how to obtain and maintain their honor despite

---

corporeal punishment to enforce moral lessons, whereas boys needed no examples of violence to ensure their obedience.

being the objects of men's sexual desire, and how to conduct themselves in virtuous and courtly ways. Wolfram and Albrecht play with the narrative conventions of conduct literature, but also refute them by allowing us instead to eavesdrop on a pseudo-advice conversation which memorably and strikingly presents us with a woman deeply conflicted about the advice she owes her charge. Herzeloyde questions the ideality of the triad of *minne*, marriage, and chivalry for members of the aristocracy, especially where women's sexual pleasure is objectified by male desire and privilege. This advice-conversation absorbed elements of traditional teachings, in particular that women are objects of men's sexual desire and must be beautiful to arouse a man's desire. Although it may not match up with the behavior of real or literary female figures, it is the dominant advice that a mother was expected to pass along to her daughter. Again, this does not mean that every mother did just that and passed on the expected, normative advice – many other literary examples show how medieval people imagined other options. And as we have seen, this advice-conversation also contains and creates space for new interpretations of these teachings, in this instance specifically around the issue of female sexual desire and agency. As I have shown here, these conversations not only debate them, but transform them into new ones, especially in Albrecht's version. This change was triggered most likely by "a new era of literary tastes" (Krueger 2009, x), as well as by the expanding literacy during the later Middle Ages whereby "instructional literature moved beyond the courts to bourgeois households to reach new audiences of girls and women" (Krueger 2009, xviii). Just as likely, this change reflects how the author may have *wished* social life to be in sharp contrast to reality. Accordingly, I suggest that Albrecht's Herzeloyde advocates that, like lower class or peasant women in conduct literature, noble women also have or should have choices about sexual activities and sexual partners, to be able to act from a subject position in the area of love and sex instead of having to wait passively for a man to find them sexually attractive and desirable as a marriage partner. These side-by-side examples of a mother figure initiating the daughter in sexual desire and "love lore" even in its less than perfect form expose this shift, this space for potential transformation, this space to renegotiate women's "proper" conduct around female sexual desire and agency and a man's place therein.

It was equally important to both authors to stay true to the figure of Herzeloyde, as we know her from Wolfram's *Parzival*, a woman who did not conduct herself according to courtly expectations when securing her marriage to Gahmuret and who repeatedly challenges social norms of proper courtly female conduct, be that in her dealings with her own husband – in the manner in which she raises her son Parzival in the isolation of Soltane away from life at court and without giving him the proper education due a noble son – or in her angry outburst when Sigune seeks to be mentored in love lore. Herzeloyde cannot fulfill the role of passing on social expectations of proper courtly conduct for women to Sigune. Instead, she instructs her about the suffering generated by *minnedienst* that frequently leaves the woman behind, longing for her beloved without any certainty that he will return from his chivalric expeditions. As the "law" of *minne* requires women to occupy a passive role, their "only" option for agency within its framework is to make herself so beautiful that she attracts a man, arouses his sexual desire for her, and allows him to win her. Herzeloyde, angry that her bid for agency in matters of love failed and wishing that her own sexual desire for Gahmuret would make him want to stay with her instead of participating in chivalric adventures, therefore teaches Sigune about the necessity of challenging the objectification of women's sexual desires within medieval courtly society by desiring a man for herself and her pleasure. Herzeloyde tells Sigune that she herself is to blame for her own misery, for "du hast in die kurzlîchen fröude vil sorge alze sere gemischet" [T 130, 4 // JT 808, 4; you managed only too well to mix much sorrow into this recent joy], but if she now is proactive about making herself beautiful again, about expressing her desire for Schionatulander, she will make sure that he will make her rich in joys, that her sexual desire for him will be satisfied. Herzeloyde is no model mentor to Sigune, not because she is not her biological mother, but because of her own dissatisfaction with her lack of control over her husband and over her own sexual desires, as well as her own inability to be so desirable to Gahmuret that he would want to stay at home with her. As a woman who herself does not conform to many social norms, she finds herself unable to teach Sigune socially acceptable forms of sexual desire and love lore.

Works Cited

Albrecht von Scharfenberg. *Jüngerer Titurel*. Edited by Werner Wolf. Berlin: Akademie Verlag, 1955.
Ashley, Kathleen and Robert L. A. Clark. "Introduction: Medieval Conduct: Texts, Theories, Practices." In Ashley and Clark, *Medieval Conduct*, ix–xx.
Ashley, Kathleen and Robert L. A. Clark, eds. *Medieval Conduct*. Minneapolis: University of Minnesota Press, 2001.
Classen, Albrecht. "*The Winsbeckin* – Female Discourse or Male Projection? New Questions to a Middle High German Gendered Didactic Text in Comparison with Christine de Pizan. What do we make out of female voice within a male dominated textual genre?" In *The Power of a Woman's Voice in Medieval and Early Modern Literatures. New Approaches to German and European Women Writers and to Violence Against Women in Premodern Times*, edited by Albrecht Classen, 159–86. Berlin/New York: De Gruyter, 2007.
Dronzek, Anna. "Gendered Theories of Education in Fifteenth-Century Conduct Books." In Ashley and Clark, *Medieval Conduct*, 135–59.
Johnston, Mark D., ed. *Medieval Conduct Literature: An Anthology of Vernacular Guides to Behaviour for Youths, with English Translations*, with an introduction by Roberta L. Krueger and texts edited and translated by Kathleen Ashley, Emily C. Francomano, Mark D. Johnston, Ann Marie Rasmussen, Claire Sponsler, Eleonora Stoppino, and Olga Trokhimenko. Toronto: University of Toronto Press, 2009.
König Tirol, Winsbecke und Winsbeckin. Edited by Albrecht Leitzmann. Halle: Niemeyer, 1988.

Krueger, Roberta L. "Introduction: Teach Your Children Well: Medieval Conduct Guides for Youths." In Johnston, ed., *Medieval Conduct Literature*, ix–xxxiii.

Orme, Nicholas. *Medieval Children*. New Haven, CT: Yale University Press, 2001.

Rasmussen, Ann Marie. *Mothers and Daughters in Medieval German Literature*. Syracuse, NY: Syracuse University Press, 1997.

Rasmussen, Ann Marie. "Fathers to Think Back Through: The Middle High German Mother-Daughter and Father-Son Advice Poems Known as *Die Winsbeckin* and *Der Winsbecke*." In Ashley and Clark, *Medieval Conduct*, 106–34.

Rasmussen, Ann Marie, and Olga V. Trokhimenko, eds. and trans. "The German *Winsbecke, Winsbeckin,* and *Winsbecke* Parodies (Selections)." In Johnston, *Medieval Conduct Literature*, 61–125.

Ruh, Kurt. "Bemerkungen zur Liebessprache in Wolframs *Titurel*." In *Studien zu Wolfram von Eschenbach: Festschrift für Werner Schröder zum 75. Geburtstag*, edited by Kurt Gärtner and Joachim Heinzle, 501–12. Tübingen: Max Niemeyer, 1989.

Sager, Alexander. "Geheimnis und Subjekt in Wolframs *Titurel*." *Beiträge zur Geschichte der deutschen Sprache und Literatur* 125 (2003): 267–91.

Sager, Alexander. *minne von mæren. On Wolfram's* Titurel. Göttingen: V&R unipress, 2006.

Slitt, Rebecca. n.d. "Medieval Childhood in England: The Case of William Marshal." http://ultimatehistoryproject.com/medieval-childhood-the-life-of-william-marshal.html (accessed June 27, 2018).

Trokhimenko, Olga V. "*Gedanken sind vrî?*: Proverbs and Socialization of Genders in the Middle High German Didactic Poems *Die Winsbeckin* and *Der Winsbecke*." In *Res humanae proverbiorum et sententiarum: Ad honorem Wolfgangi Mieder*, edited by Csaba Földes, 327–50. Tübingen: Gunter Narr, 2004.

Trokhimenko, Olga V. "On the Dignity of Women: The 'Ethical Reading' of *Winsbeckin* in mgf 474, Staatsbibliothek zu Berlin-Preussischer Kulturbesitz." *Journal of English and Germanic Philology* 107, no. 1 (2008): 490–505.

Wolfram von Eschenbach. *Parzival*. 6th edition. Edited by Karl Lachmann. Translated by Peter Knecht. Introduction and commentary by Bernd Schirock. Berlin: De Gruyter, 2003.

Wolfram von Eschenbach. *Titurel*. Edited, translated, and introduction and commentary by Helmut Brackert and Stephan Fuchs-Jolie. Berlin: De Gruyter, 2003.

Ingrid Bennewitz

6 Mothers and Daughters Revisited: The Mother-Daughter Songs in the Context of the Later Neidhart Tradition

1 Introduction

If we are to believe the evidence of the manuscript tradition, the Neidhart songs enjoyed an unparalleled popularity in the later Middle Ages. Their success, unmatched anywhere in the history of medieval poetry, extended from the second, third, and fourth decades of the thirteenth century – the period when the author's biography laid down its faint traces – to the 1566 printing of *Neithart Fuchs* by Martin Lechler. Only the transmission of the Walther von der Vogelweide corpus is at all comparable, although those poems failed to make the same transition from manuscript to print (cf. Schweikle 1990, 1–2; Müller, Bennewitz, Spechtler 2007 vol. 3, 497–537;[1] Springeth and Spechtler 2018). Of course, the evidence of that manuscript tradition has always been in conflict with the athetizations undertaken in (older) *Minnesang* scholarship, which recognized not even a third of the songs and strophes transmitted under Neidhart's name as genuine compositions. That circumstance would prove to have critical consequences for both the editorial history and, especially, the interpretive history of the medieval song, consequences that have remained significant to the present day: even recent scholarship appears to fall again and again into the temptation of reconstructing an "authentic" corpus (e.g., Warning 2007; see also Bennewitz 2010). In what follows, I focus on the late medieval transmission of the songs; in keeping with the manuscript tradition, I treat the Neidhart song as a distinct genre, a concept clearly reflected in the term used by the late medieval scribes and compilers, "ain neithart" [a Neidhart].

Ann Marie Rasmussen is among the few medievalists who, early on, recognized the significance of the late medieval Neidhart tradition and who took it into account in her work. In her 1997 book *Mothers and Daughters in Medieval German Literature*, she treats not only the mother-daughter debates about dancing and "minne" [love] transmitted in the Riedegger and Manesse manuscripts (usually referred to as Ms. R and Ms. C, respectively), familiar from the so-called "little" edition of the Neidhart songs (Wießner and Fischer 1999) and inextricably bound up with the literary figure

---

[1] This edition will be referred to hereafter as SNE volume number, page number; when relevant, song number, strophe number, and line numbers will also be supplied.

Translated by Aaron E. Wright

of the Singer from "Riuwental," but also those found only in manuscript B or in manuscript c, which preserve the most extensive number of Neidhart songs.[2]

In this essay, I offer a first look at *all* the late medieval mother-daughter songs in the Neidhart genre, inquiring into how the songs and strophes that survive only in the late medieval witnesses differ from those found in more canonical manuscripts R and C as edited by Haupt/Wiessner. I make direct use of contextual materials (including manuscript associations, commentaries, and so on) that have recently become available in the most comprehensive edition of Neidhart material, known in the scholarship as the Salzburg Neidhart Edition (SNE). This edition has as its goal to bring together for the first time in a comprehensive and readily accessible form all of the texts and melodies transmitted under the name "Neidhart"/"Nithart" or in a clear "Neidhart" context. Volume 1 contains all of the Neidhart songs from the parchment manuscripts and their parallel transmission; Volume 2 offers the Neidhart songs from the paper manuscripts and their parallel transmission; and Volume 3 provides commentaries on the transmission and editions of the texts and melodies in the first two volumes, together with bibliographies, a discography, indexes, and concordances. Wherever possible, my discussions below of the textual transmission of the songs are furnished with references to the SNE.

2 The Mother-Daughter Conversations in Manuscripts R, C, and c

In 1858, Moriz Haupt placed a total of eight "Sommerlieder" [summer songs] at the beginning of his edition, songs transmitted only in the Manesse Manuscript (Ms. C) and, in some cases, in manuscript c. Among them are five mother-daughter debates: Sommerlied 1 (found only in C), Sommerlied 2 (C, c), Sommerlied 6 (C, c), Sommerlied 7 (only C), and Sommerlied 8 (C, c).[3] What is immediately striking is the extensive agreement between the texts as preserved in the Manesse Manuscript, credited with such great authority and accorded great editorial significance, and their counterparts in the younger manuscript c, which has historically been far less

---

[2] For a complete list of Neidhart manuscripts referred to in this essay, see below, Works Cited. For a complete list of Neidhart manuscripts, see SNE 1, XI–XII. The songs mentioned here are: c 30: "Der mai hat menig hercz hoch erstaiget/ Ein wechsel" (Ms. c, fol.160v–161v; SNE 2: 75–77); c 36: "Winter dir zu laide / Die pfann. ein wechsel" (Ms. c, fol. 166v–167; SNE 2, 93–97); and c 64: "Frewet euch, kinder ubéral" (Ms. c, fol. 190r-191r; SNE 1, 394–398). Until recently, we owed the only trustworthy translations from Ms. c into English to Rasmussen 1997, chapter six. An extensive translation and edition of Neidhart songs from Manuscript R into English by Kathryn Starkey and Edith Wenzel appeared in 2016.

[3] See below, Appendix I for a complete list.

highly regarded in the editorial enterprise. The strophes of Sommerlieder 2, 6, and 8 are found in the same order in both manuscripts c and C, and, except for Sommerlied 2 – to which c adds two strophes – in the same number. The additional strophes of Sommerlied 2 in manuscript c (SNE 1, 474, c 55, strophes VI–VII) clearly accentuate certain aspects of the song's content, namely, the unmistakably sexual connotation given female desire ("ich belig den knaben werden" [SNE 1, 474, c 55, strophe VI, line 5; I lie with the worthy boy]) and the geographically localized setting ("von Bayern uncz in Francken"[SNE 1, 474, c 55, strophe VII, line 5; from Bavaria to Franconia]).

The Sommerlieder from Ms. R that follow in the Haupt/Wießner edition vary the pattern found in Ms. C. For example, in Sommerlied 9 (SNE 1, 90), the mother and the daughter are replaced by the figures of a young woman ("ein stolziu magt" [SNE 1, 90, strophe V, line 3; a proud woman]) and an old woman ("ein altiu in ir gæile" [SNE 1, 90, strophe IV, line 6; an old woman in her exuberance]), neither of whom are identified further. Manuscripts R and c largely agree in the number and sequence of strophes for Sommerlieder 15, 16, 18, 19, and 20, with additional strophes in c (and f). The case of Sommerlied 17 is similar: in the two manuscripts, it has the same number of strophes but in a different sequence (See Appendices I and II). Exceptions are found in Sommerlied 21, where Haupt's athetizations apply to both manuscript R and c, and in Sommerlieder 23 and 27, for which manuscripts R, c, and f provide four or five additional strophes: in Sommerlied 23, the additions include the call to the dance (unclear whether issued by the girl or by the singer) and the physical confrontation between mother and daughter. In the course of this exchange, the mother, armed with her distaff ("kunchel" [SNE 1, 364: C 108, strophe IX, line 1]), confronts her daughter and accuses her of having lost her virginity ("bind auff dein har!" [SNE 1, 365: c 29, strophe X, line 4, and f 13, strophe IX, line 4; tie up your hair!]), while the daughter insists on the putatively "honorable" intentions of her admirer:

> es wirbet einer umb mich, des habt ir ymer eree,
> dovon lost trawren uberall.
> hin gein Rewental,
> da wil er mich wirdtenlichen seczen.
>   (SNE 1, 365, f 13, strophe X, lines 2–5)

> [you will gain honor evermore from the man who is wooing me and so abandon all your grieving. He will take me to Reuental in a dignified way.][4]

In Sommerlied 27, there are a total of seven additional strophes, which map the political situation of the country ("Fromut ist auß Osterrich entrunnen" [SNE 1, 87, c

---

[4] All translations by Aaron E. Wright, unless otherwise noted.

39 (38), strophe VIII, 1; joy has fled from Austria],[5] onto the domestic disaster of a mother who cannot provide her daughter with suitable festival attire, a failure tantamount to excluding her from the festivities of rustic ("dörperlichen") society:

> "Nun we," sprach mir ein alte, "meiner swere.
> ich han ein kindt daheim, das ist so recht und mynnepere.
> denn das ich nicht klaider han,
> und soll es mir hie heym bestan,
> das ist ein hertes mere."
> (SNE 1, 87, c 39 [38], strophe XI)

> ["Alas," said an old woman to me, "alas, my pain. I have a girl at home, so neat and lovely. But I do not have the garments, and if she has to stay at home with me, that will be a bitter thing."]

This fact, however, does not appear to present a significant obstacle to the daughter ("han ich nicht gute claider an, so han ich doch mein ere"[SNE 1, 87, c 39 (38), strophe XII, line 2; even if I am not wearing fine garments, I still have my honor], similarly to the daughter in the "Winsbeckin" (cf. Bennewitz 1996, Rasmussen 1997). While the daughter dwells on the value of waiting ("lang beit flos ir nye wert" [SNE 1, 87, c 39 (38), strophe XIV, line 3; long waiting was never valued by her], the concluding strophe, also preserved only in manuscript c, makes plain the political consequences of waiting too long:

> Herr Neithart, ewer kaiser ist zu lange,
> den bringet ir uns alle jar mit ewrm newen gesange.
> des wer auch den pawren nott,
> die sind vil nahendt hungers todt
> und dúnnent yne die wange.
> (SNE 1, 87, c 39 [38], strophe XV)

> [Sir Neithart, your emperor is taking too long; every year you bring him to us in a new song. The peasants need him; they are very nearly starved and their cheeks are growing gaunt.]

Once again, manuscript c dispenses with the customary roles: While it is normally the daughter lamenting her mother's command to wait on a partner for the dance and for love, here the mother herself assumes this perspective to defend female autonomy *in eroticis* against the daughter's demand that social convention be observed; that demand is indirectly reinforced by the political statement of this "Trutzstrophe," [defensive stanza] which unmasks as a facile literary illusion the hopes for political stability after the arrival of the emperor.

---

[5] This strophe concludes the song in Ms R (R 8, strophe VIII); the seven additional strophes in c 39 follow this strophe.

3 The Mother-Daughter Conversations in the Neidhart Manuscripts C, f, and w, and in the Early Prints z, z_1, and z_2

As Rasmussen has shown in connection with the so-called "genuine" Neidhart songs, it is precisely the "interchangeability of the mother-daughter roles" and "the sexualized continuity between women characterizing Neidhart's poetry" that reveals that "the roles of [both] the sexually active, socially rebellious women and the sexually restrained, socially conformist women are tied neither to age nor to marital station" (Rasmussen 1997, 174). The "pseudo" Neidhart songs c 64 and c 46 she investigated, on the other hand, exhibit a new apportionment of roles: mother and daughter "have become versions of each other," and it is in particular the mother "who, at the end of the poem, turns the equality of rivalry into the equality of solidarity" (Rasmussen 1997, 188; Bennewitz 1994).

In fact, the text of manuscript c makes it more than clear that the mother-daughter exchanges were integral to the success of the Neidhart songs in the late Middle Ages. Manuscript c transmits twenty-seven songs of this genre, out of its total of 131; thirteen were declared "genuine" by Haupt and fourteen "spurious." We will look more closely at just a few of the numerous developments in the genre shown in the texts preserved only in Ms. c and in such later manuscripts as f, s, st, and w – some also in C (c 32; c 52) – developments that in some cases belie the phenomenon of female solidarity between mother and daughter pointed out by Rasmussen. Such is the case, for example, in c 30, where the daughter accuses her mother of being desirable to young men only because of her money, or when the daughter suddenly invokes the role of the absent (deceived, or punishing) husband ("mein vater der ist ewer man/ der euch des nicht gemaistern kan,/ ir tragt das lenger messer" [SNE 2, 97, c 36, strophe VIII, lines 4–6; my father is your husband, but he cannot be your master so long as you are holding the longer knife]; "West ir, muter, wes mich zwen baten,/ da wir in dem hirs vast gaten/ mein vater hett mich einem gegeben," [SNE 2, 104, c 40, strophe IV, lines 1–3; do you know, mother, what two asked me for when we met intimately in the field? My father would have given me to one]). This theme appears to have maintained its appeal into the early modern period: the early prints z, z_1, and z_2 transmit c 36 and c 40, some of them with woodcuts that leave nothing to the erotic imagination (See Rasmussen 1997, 170 and 178). The mother's control over the daughter's sexuality also makes her the antagonist not just of the daughter but, unsurprisingly, of the singer as well, both of whom hurl imprecations at her even outside the genre of the mother-daughter dialogue. For example:

> Weliche alte hewer das ir tochter weret,
> das sie mit andern kinden an den raien nicht enferet,

> die sei von mir verfluchet und verwachsen
> umb ir unnútze dro!
>> (SNE 2, 129, c 47, strophe IV, lines 1–4)

[whatever old woman keeps her daughter from joining the other girls in the dance, let her be accursed for her pointless threats]

and:

> Sie sprach: "es tut mein muter
> mit mir nichcz wan wagen.
> sie ist des teufels lotter:
> iedoch will ich es bagen."
>> (SNE 2, 132, c 48, strophe IX, lines 1–4)

[she said, "my mother does nothing but scold. She is the devil's whore: but I will risk it")].

The popularity of the genre is likewise attested by the presence in manuscript c of new hybrid forms linking mother-daughter strophes with the *Gespielinnenlied* (playmate song) (c 32), or even with the crusade song (c 35) and singer's monologue (c 95).[6] Last but not least, with just one exception (c 35),[7] it is only manuscript c that in at least some cases has preserved Neidhart's mother-daughter songs with both text and music (Figure 6.1) – that is, in such a way that they can be performed in the same way that they first found success with a medieval audience.[8]

That a gender-focused analysis of Neidhart's songs in Mss. C and R can prove to be rewarding has already been shown by Rasmussen. In this essay, I have offered a brief account of what such an analysis might yield when brought to bear on the full transmission of the songs. My hope is that this might be motivation for a more intensive investigation of the mother-daughter songs in the later Neidhart tradition.

---

6 For c 32, c 35, and c 95, see SNE 1, 492–494; SNE 2, 89–91 and 177–180 respectively.

7 The melody for this song is not preserved in manuscript c, but is present in manuscript w (w 7). See SNE 2, 88.

8 For the melody for c 29, see SNE 1, 361; for those of c 30, c 36, c 38, and c 95; see SNE 2, pages 75, 94, 99, and 176 respectively.

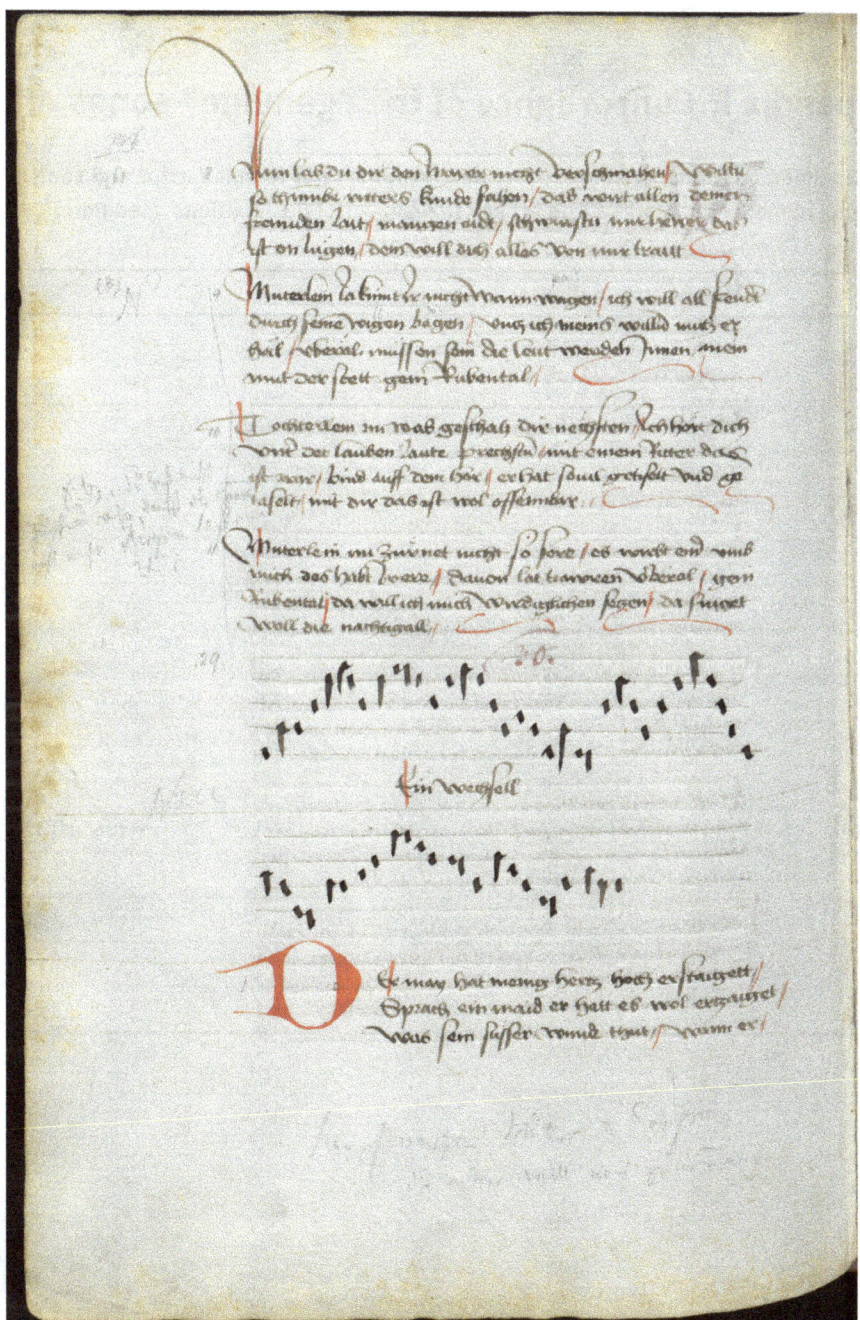

Figure 6.1: Ms c, showing text with notes. Berlin, Staatsbibliothek zu Berlin – Preußischer Kulturbesitz, mgf 779, fol. 160v.

Appendices

Appendix I: Concordance of the "genuine" songs

SL=Sommerlied [Summer song]; other designations refer to manuscript and song or strophe number (see Works Cited for key to manuscript designations used here)[9]

SL	C	R	c	other
SL 1	C 210	–	–	–
SL 2	C 222	–	c 55 (+ 2)	–
SL 6	C 260 a	–	c 68	–
SL 7	C 266	–	–	–
SL 8	C 280	–	c 67	–
SL 9	–	R 9	–	A 2
SL 15	–	R 22	c 21 [20] – c 49	m
SL 16	–	R 23	c 24	–
SL 17	–	R 50	c 57	B 35
SL 18	C 276	R 56	c 71	–
SL 19	–	R 25	c 74	–
SL 20	–	R 48	c 50	A (Gedrut) 32[10]
SL 21	C 109	R 51	c 23	–
SL 23	C 100	R 53	c 29 [28]	f 13
SL 24	C 173	R 57	c 25 [24]	–
SL 27	–	R 8	c 39 [38]	–

---

9 See SNE, volumes 1 and 2, pages IX–X and VII–IX respectively, which list songs by manuscript designation and page number in volumes. The charts here reproduce the information collated in the entries for each song in the SNE.

10 Gedrut is the name to which these strophes are attributed in Ms. A.

Appendix II: Strophe concordance

The following tables show the order of strophes for the Sommerlieder across the main manuscripts and the various Neidhart editions, which are also listed with abbreviations in Works Cited.

SL 1: Ein altú dú begunde springen (SNE 1, C str. 210–212)

C	MS	HW	Bg	ATB
I	22,1	3,1	L 70,I	SL 1,I
II	2	3,8	II	II
III	3	3,15	III	III

SL 2: Der meie der ist riche (SNE 1, C str. 222–226)

C	c	MS	HW	Bg	ATB
I (222)	I	25,1	3,22	L 63,I	SL 2,I
II (223)	II	2	4,1	II	II
III (224)	III	3	4,6	III	III
IV (225)	IV	4	4,11	IV	IV
V (226)	V	5	4,16	V	V
–	VI	6	4,21	VI	VI
–	VII	7	4,26	VII	VII

SL 6: In dem tal (SNE 1, C str. 260a-265)

C	c	MS	HW	Bg	ATB
I (260a)	I	34,1	6,19	L 62,I	SL 6,I
II (261)	II	2	6,24	II	II
III (262)	III	3	6,29	III	III
IV (263)	IV	4	6,34	IV	IV
V (264)	V	5	7,1	V	V
VI (265)	VI	6	7,6	VI	VI

SL 7: Es meiet hiure aber als ê (SNE 1, C str. 266–271)

C	MS	HW	Bg	ATB
I	35,1	7,11	L 65,I	SL 7,I
II	2	7,19	II	II
III	3	7,27	III	III
IV	4	7,35	IV	IV
V	5	8,4	V	V
VI	6	p. 106f.	VI	Va

SL 8: Ir froeit úch, iunge und alte (SNE 1, C str. 280–284)

C	c	MS	HW	Bg	ATB
I (280)	I	38,1	8,12	L 64,I	SL 8,I
II (281)	II	2	8,20	II	II
III (282)	III	3	8,28	III	III
IV (283)	IV	4	8,36	IV	IV
V (284)	V	5	9,5	V	V

SL 9: Sumer, wis enphangen (SNE 1, R 9)

R	A	MS (R)	MS (A)	HW	Bg	ATB
I	–	92,1		9,13	L 16,I	SL 9,I
II	–	2		9,19	II	II
III	–	3		9,25	III	III
IV	–	4		9,31	IV	IV
V	–	5		9,37	V	V
VI	I (2)	6	S. 313	10,4	VI	VI
VII	–	7		10,10	VII	VII
VIII	–	8		10,16	VIII	VIII

SL 15: Alle di den sumer lobelich wellent enphahen (SNE 1, R 22)

R	c	c	m	MS	HW	Bg	ATB
I	21,IV	49,I	–	20,4	16,38	L 14,I	SL 15, I
II	I	II	–	1	17,4	II	II
III	II	III	I	2	17,9 / p. 115	III	III
IV	III	IV	–	3	17,14	IV	IV
V	V	V	II	5	17,19 / p. 115	V	V
–	VI,1–2	VI,1–2	III,1–2	6,1–2	p. 114 / p. 115	–	Va,1–2
–	VI,3–4	VI,3–4	–	6,3–4	p. 114	–	Va,3–4
VI,1–2	VII,1–2	VII,1–2	–	7,1–2	17,24	VI,1–2	VI,1–2
VI,3–4	VII,3–4	VII,3–4	III,3–4	7,3–4	17,26 / p. 115	VI,3–4	VI,3–4
VII,1–2	VIII,1–2	VIII,1–2	IV,1–2	8,1–2	17,29 / p. 115	VII,1–2	VII,1–2
–	–	–	IV,3–4	–	p. 115	–	–
–	–	–	V,1–2	–	p. 115	–	–
VII,3–4	VIII,3–4	VIII,3–4	V,3–4	8,3–4	17,31 / p. 115	VII,3–4	VII,3–4
VIII	IX	IX	VI	9	17,34 / p. 115	VIII	VIII
IX	X	X	–	10	17,39	IX	IX
–	–	–	VII	–	p. 115	–	–

SL 16: Schon als ein golt grunet der hagen (SNE 1, R 23)

R	c	MS	HW	Bg	ATB
–	I, 1–5	23,1	p. 116	–	SL 16, I*
I	I, 6–10	2	18,4	L 11,I	I
II	II, 6–10	3	18,10	II	II
III	II, 1–5	4	18,16	III	III
–	III, 1–5	5	p. 116	–	IIa
IV	III, 6–10	6	18,22	IV	IV
V	IV, 1–5	7	18,28	V	V
VI	IV, 6–10	8	18,34	VI	VI
VII	V, 1–5	9	19,1	VII	VII
–	V, 6–10	10	p. 117	–	VIIa

SL 17: Schowet an den walt, wi er niwes loubes reichet (SNE 1, R 50)

R	B	c	MS	HW	Bg	ATB
I	IV (38)	IV	57,4	19,7	L 15,I	SL 17,I
II	II (36)	II	2	19,17	II	II
III	III (37)	III	3	19,27	III	III
IV	I (35)	I	1	19,37	IV	IV
V	V (39)	V	5	20,8	V	V
VI	VI (40)	VI	6	20,18	VI	VI
VII	VII (41)	VII	7	20,28	VII	VII

SL 18: Uns wil ein sumer chomen (SNE 1, R 56)

R	C	c	MS	HW	Bg	ATB
–	–	I	37,1	20,38	L 12,I	SL 18,I
I	I (276)	(vgl. VI)			–	
II	II (277)	II	2	21,6	II	II
III	III (278)	III	3	21,13	III	III
IV	IV (279)	V	5	21,20	IV	IV
V	–	IV	6	21,27	V	V
–	–	VI	4	20,38 App.	–	I App.

SL 19: Wol dem tage (SNE 1, R 25)

R	c	MS	HW	Bg	ATB
I	II	74,2	21,34	L 9,I	SL 19,I
N	–	–	22,3	II	III
II	I	1	22,10	III	II
III	III	3	22,17	IV	IV
IV	IV	4	22,24	V	V
V	V	5	22,31	VI	VI

SL 20: Ich gesach den walt und all die heide (SNE 1, R 48)

R	A (Gedrut)	c	MS	HW	Bg	ATB
I	I (13)	I	50,1	22,38	L 6, I	SL 20, I
II	–	II	2	23,5	II	II
III	II (14)	III	3	23,11	III	III
IV	III (15)	IV	4	23,17	IV	IV
V	IV (16)	V	5	23,23	V	V
VI	V (17)	VI	6	23,29	VI	VI
VII	VI (18)	VII	7	23,35	VII	VII
VIII	–	VIII	8	24,1	VIII	VIII
IX	–	IX	9	24,7	IX	IX

SL 21: Nu ist der chule winder gar zergangen (SNE 1, R 51)

R	C	c	MS	HW	Bg	ATB
I	II (110)	I	8,1	24,13	L 13,I	SL 21, I
II	I (109)	II	2	24,18	II	II
–	–	III	3	p. 121	–	IIa
III	III (111)	IV	4	24,23	III	III
IV	IV (112)	V	5	24,28	IV	IV
V	V (113)	VI	6	24,33	V	V
–	VI (114)	–	7	p. 121	Va	Va
VI	VII (115)	VII	8	24,38	VI	VI
VII	VIII (116)	VIII	9	25,3	VII	VII
VIII	–	IX	10	25,9	VIII	VIIa

SL 23: Losa, wie di vogel alle donent (SNE 1, R 53)

R	C	c	f	MS II	MS III	HW	Bg	ATB	Bey
I	I (100)	II	II	7,1	28,2	27,3	L 10,IV	SL 23,IV	2,IV
II	III (102)	III	III	3	3	27,9	V	V	V
-	-	IV	IV	-	4	p. 127	-	Va	-
III	VII (106)	V	V	7	5	27,15	VI	VI	VI
IV,1-2	II,1-2 (101)	I,1-2	I,1-2	2,1-2	1,1-2	26,23	I,1-2	I,1-2	I,1-2
IV,3-6	II,3-6	-	-	2,3-6	-	26,25	I,3-6	I,3-6	I,3-6
V	-	-	-	-	26,29	II	II	II	
VI,1-2	V,1-2 (104)	-	-	5,1-2	-	26,35	III,1-2	III,1-2	III,1-2
VI,3-6	V,3-6	I,3-6	I,3-6	5,3-6	1,3-6	26,37	III,3-6	III,3-6	III,3-6
VII	IV (103)	VI	VI	4	6	27,21	VII	VII	VII
-	-	VII	-	-	7	p. 128	-	VIIa	-
VIII	VI (105)	VIII	VII	6	8	27,27	VIII	VIII	VIII
IX	VIII (107)	IX	VIII	8	9	27,33	IX	IX	IX
-	IX (108)	-	-	9	-	p. 128	X	IXa	Zusatz
-	-	X	IX	-	10	p. 129	-	IXb	-
-	-	XI	X	-	11	p. 129	-	IXc	-

SL 24: Der walt aber mit maniger chleinen voglin stimme erhillet (SNE 1, R 57)

R	C	c	MS	HW	Bg	ATB
I	VII (179)	I	14,1	28,1	L 2,I	SL 24,I
II	IX (181)	IV	4	28,8	II	II
III	I (173)	V	5	28,15	III	III
-	II (174)	-	6	p. 130	IIIa	IIIa
IV	III (175)	VI	7	28,22	IV	IV
V	VI (178)	VII	9	28,29	V	V
VI	IV (176)	II	2	p. 130,1	VI	Va
-	V (177)	-	8	p. 130	VIa	Vb
VII	VIII (180)	III	3	p. 130,8	VII	Vc

SL 27: Chomen ist ein wunnechlicher maie (SNE 1, R 8)

R	c	MS	HW	Bg	ATB
I	I	38,1	31,5	L 19, I	SL 27, I
II	II	2	31,10	II	II
III	III	3	31,15	III	III
IV	IV	4	31,20	IV	IV
V	V	5	31,25	V	V
VI	VI	6	31,30	VI	VI
VII	VII	7	31,35	VII	VII
VIII	VIII	8	32,1	VIII	VIII
–	IX	9	p. 135,1	–	VIIIa
–	X	10	p. 136,6	–	VIIIb
–	XI	11	p. 136,11	–	VIIIc
–	XII	12	p. 136,16	–	VIIId
–	XIII	13	p. 136,21	–	VIIIe
–	XIV	14	p. 136,26	–	VIIIf
–	XV	15	p. 134	Tr.	VIIIg

Appendix III: Concordance of "spurious" songs

c	C	F	other
c 30 (29)[11]	–	f 14	–
c 32 (31)	C 255	f 15	–
c 35	–	f 6	s 1, st 1, w 7
c 36 (35)	–	–	z 9
c 37 (36)	–	–	–
c 38 (37)	–	–	–
c 40	–	–	z 32
c 52	C 232	–	–
c 58	–	–	–
c 63	–	–	–
c 64	–	–	B 42, z 30
c 66	–	–	C (von Stamhein)
c 69	–	–	–
c 95	–	–	s 11, z 16

Appendix IV: Strophe concordance for "spurious songs"

(indicates variation of strophe order across manuscripts and editions)

Der mai hat menig hercz hoch erstaiget (SNE 2, c 30 (29))
    c 30 (29)
    f 14
    [This song is transmitted in manuscripts c and f with the same number of strophes in the same sequence.]

---

[11] The songs in Ms. c were numbered in red by the medieval rubricator. The number in parentheses following the song number refers to Friedrich von der Hagen's separate numbering (in pencil) of the songs in the manuscript. See Figure 6.1 for an image of this manuscript.

Auff und hin (SNE 1, c 32 (31))

C	c	f	MS	HW	Bg
I (255)	I	I	32,1	LI,1	L 68, I
–	II	II	2	LI,14	II
II (256)	III	III	3	LI,27	III
III (257)	IV	IV	4	LII,8	IV
–	V	V	5	LII,21	V
–	VI	VI	6	LIII,5	VI
–	VII	VII	7	LIII,18	VII

Do man den gúmpel gempel sanck (SNE 2, c 35)

c/MS	f	s	st	w
I	I	I	–	I
II	II	II	–	II
III	III	III	–	III
IV	IV	IV	–	IV
V	V	V	–	V
VI	VI	VI	–	VI
VII	VII	VII	I	VII
VIII	VIII	VIII	II	VIII
IX	IX	IX	III	IX
X	X	X	IV	X
XI	XI	XI	V	XI
XII	XII	XII	VI	XII
XIII	XIII	–	VII	XIII
XIV	XIV	–	VIII	XIV

Winter, dir zu laide (SNE 2, c 36 (35))

c	$z/z_1/z_2$/Bo	MS
I	I	I
–	II	(II)
–	III	(III)
–	IV	(IV)
II	V	V
III	VII	VI
IV	–	VII
–	VIII	–
–	IX	–
–	X	–
V	XI	VIII
–	XII	–
VI	VI	IX
VII	XIII	X
X	XIV	XI
IX	XV	XII
X	XVI	XIII
XI	–	XIV
–	XVII	–

Uns will der liebe sumer aber pringen (SNE 2, c 37 (36))

Tochter, spinn den rocken (SNE 2, c 38 (37))

Der summer ist kumen (SNE 2, c 40)

c/MS	$z/z_1/z_2$/Bo
I	I, 1–2
II	I, 3–7
III	II
IV	III

(continued)

c/MS	z/z₁/z₂/Bo
V	IV
VI	V
VII	–

Ein alte vor den rayen trat (SNE 1, c 52)

C	c	MS	HW	Bg
I (232)	I	27,1	L,6	L 71, I
II (233)	II	2	L,10	II
III (234)	III	3	L,14	III
IV (235)	IV	4	L,18	IV
V (236)	V	5	L,22	V

Es grunet in dem walde (SNE 2, c 58)

Owe, das ich nicht entar (SNE 2, c 63)

Frewet euch, kinder, ubéral (SNE 1, c 64)

B	c	z/z₁/z₂	MS	Bo	HW	Bg
I (42)	I	I	64, 1	30, 1	XIV,1	L 67, I
II (43),1–4	–	–	–	–	–	–
–	II,1–4	II,1–4	2,1–4	2,1–4	XIV,10	II,1–4
II (43),5–9	II,5–9	II,5–9	2,5–9	2,1–4	XIV,14	II,5–9
III (44)	V	IV	5	4	XV,7	IV
IV (45)	III	III	3	3	XIV,19	III
V (46)	IV	V	4	5	XIV,16	V
–	VI	–	6	–	XV,24 (Anm.)	–

Wol dann raien fúr den waldt (SNE 2, c 66)

Wo sind nu die alten und die jungen (SNE 2, c 69)

Kinder, ir habt einen winter an der handt (SNE 2, c 95)

c	s	z	MS	BO
I	I	I	95 a I	16a I
II	II	II	II	II
III	III	III	III	III
IV	IV	V	IV	V
V	V	VI	VI	VI
VI	VI	IV	V	VI
VII	VII	VII	95 b I	16b I
VIII	VIII	VIII	II	II
IX	IX	IX	III	III
X	X	X	IV	IV
XI	XI	XI	V	V
XII	XII	XII	VI	VI
XIII	XIII	XIII	VII	VII
–	XIV	XIV	–	VIII
XIV	XV	XV	VIII	IX
XV	XVI	XVI	IX	X
XVI	XVII*	XVII	X	XI
XVII	XVIII*	XVIII	XI	XII

Works Cited

Manuscripts

A: Heidelberg, Universitätsbibliothek Heidelberg, cpg 357 ("Kleine Heidelberger Liederhandshrift")
B: Stuttgart, Württembergische Landesbibliothek Stuttgart, HB XIII poetae germanici 1, (Weingartner/ Stuttgarter Liederhandschrift), on-line at: http://digital.wlb-stuttgart.de/sammlungen/sammlungsliste/werksansicht/?no_cache=1&tx_dlf%5Bid%5D=3919&tx_dlf%5Bpage%5D=1 (accessed December 18, 2020).
C: Heidelberg, Universitätsbibliothek Heidelberg cpg 848, ("Große Heidelberger" or "Manessische," previously "Pariser Liederhandschrift"), on-line at: https://digi.ub.uni-heidelberg.de/diglit/cpg848 (accessed December 18, 2020).
c: Berlin, Staatsbibliothek zu Berlin – Preußischer Kulturbesitz, mgf 779, (previously also known as the "Riedsche Handschrift"), online at: https://digital.staatsbibliothek-berlin.de/werkansicht?PPN=PPN721568572&PHYSID=PHYS_0001&DMDID= (accessed December 18, 2020).
f: Berlin, Staatsbibliothek zu Berlin – Preußischer Kulturbesitz, mgq 764 ("Neidhart-Sammlung Brentanos").
m: Munich, Bayerische Staatsbibliothek, clm 3576 ("Augsburger Codex").
R: Berlin, Staatsbibliothek zu Berlin – Preußischer Kulturbesitz, mfg. 1062, (also "Riedegger Handschrift"), online at: https://digital.staatsbibliothek-berlin.de/werkansicht?PPN=PPN721570089&PHYSID=PHYS_0001&DMDID (accessed December 18, 2020).
s: Sterzing, Stadtarchiv, no shelf mark ("Sterzinger Miszellaneen-Handschrift"), on-line at: http://www.literature.at/viewer.alo?objid=14101&page=1&viewmode=fullscreen (accessed December 18, 2020).
st: Stockholm, Kungliga Biblioteka, Vu 85:2
w: Vienna, Österreichische Nationalbibliothek, series nova 3344 ("Eghenveldersches Liederbuch," previously also known as "Schratsche Handschrift").

Early Prints

z: Neithart-Fuchs-Druck, Augsburg: Johann Schaur, um 1495; Staats- und Universitätsbibliothek Hamburg, in scrinio 229°. Also Germanisches Nationalmuseum Nürnberg, 8° Inc. 100996.
z_1: Nürnberger Neithart-Fuchs-Druck; 1537, wahrscheinlich Nürnberg. Ratschulbibliothek Zwickau, 30.5.22.
z_2: Frankfurter Neithart-Fuchs-Druck; Verlag von Sigmund Feyerabend und Simon Hüter, Frankfurt am Main. 1566, hergestellt in der Offizin von Martin Lechler. Staatsbibliothek zu Berlin – Preußischer Kulturbesitz, Yg 3851. Also, Germanisches Nationalmuseum Nürnberg, 8° L. 1878f.

Primary Sources

Die Berliner Neidhart-Handschrift c (mgf 779): Transkription der Texte und Melodien. Edited by Ingrid Bennewitz-Behr and Ulrich Müller. Göppingen: Kümmerle, 1981.
Neidhart. *Neidharts Lieder*. Unrevised reprint of 1858 and 1923 editions by Moriz Haupt and Edmund Wießner, with new Afterword and Bibliography. Edited by Ingrid Bennewitz-Behr, Ulrich Müller, and Franz Viktor Spechtler. Stuttgart: Hirzel, 1986 (**HW**).

Neidhart. *Neidhart-Lieder: Texte und Melodien sämtlicher Handschriften und Drucke*. Edited by Ingrid Bennewitz-Behr, Ulrich Müller, and Franz Viktor Spechtler. 3 vols. Berlin/New York: De Gruyter, 2007 (**SNE**).

Beyschlag, Siegfried, ed. *Die Lieder Neidharts: Der Textbestand der Pergament-Handschriften und die Melodien*. Edition of Melodies by Horst Brunner. Darmstadt: Wissenschaftliche Buchgesellschaft, 1975 (**Bg**).

Bobertag, Felix, ed. *Narrenbuch: Der Pfarrer von Kalenberg. Peter Leu. Neithart Fuchs. Salamon und Markolf. Bruder Rausch*. Reprint of the Berlin Edition (Stuttgart 1884). Darmstadt: Wissenschaftliche Buchgesellschaft, 1964 (**Bo**).

Neidhart von Reuenthal. *Neidhart: Selected Songs from the Riedegg Manuscript (Staatsbibliothek Preussischer Kulturbesitz, Berlin, mgf 1062)*. Translated and edited by Kathryn Starkey and Edith Wenzel. Kalamazoo, MI: Medieval Institute Publications, 2016.

Reiffenstein, Ingo, ed. *Winsbeckische Gedichte nebst Tirol und Fridebrant*. Tübingen: Max Niemeyer, 1962.

Wackernagel, Wilhelm, ed. "Neidhartlieder der Berliner Neidhart Handschrift c u.a." In *Minnesinger: Deutsche Liederdichter des zwölften, dreizehnten und vierzehnten Jahrhunderts aus allen bekannten Handschriften und früheren Drucken gesammelt und berichtigt, mit den Lesarten derselben, Geschichte des Lebens der Dichter und ihrer Werke, Sangweisen der Lieder, Reimverzeichnis der Anfänge und Abbildungen sämtlicher Handschriften*, edited by Friedrich Heinrich von der Hagen, 5 parts in 4 volumes, 3: 183–313 and 757–801. Leipzig: J. A. Barth, 1838–1861 (Reprint 1962) (**MS**).

Wießner, Edmund and Hanns Fischer, eds. *Die Lieder Neidharts*. 5th rev. ed. Edited by Paul Sappler, with an appendix of melodies by Helmut Lomnitzer. Tübingen: Max Niemeyer, 1999 (**ATB**).

Secondary Sources

Bennewitz, Ingrid. "'Frauen'-Gespräche: Zur Inszenierung des Frauendialogs in der mittelhochdeutschen Literatur." *Das Mittelalter* 1, no. 2 (1996): 11–26.

Bennewitz, Ingrid. "Quarrelling Women as Seen by a Man: The 'Women's Dialogues' in Neidhart's Summer Songs." In *New Texts, Methodologies, and Interpretations in Medieval German Literature*, edited by Sybille Jefferis, 107–25. Göppingen: Kümmerle, 1999.

Bennewitz, Ingrid. "Review of Jessika Warning, *Neidharts Sommerlieder: Überlieferungsvarianz und Autoridentität*." *Zeitschrift für deutsches Altertum und deutsche Literatur* 139 (2010): 106–108.

Bennewitz, Ingrid. "'Wie ihre Mütter?' Zur männlichen Inszenierung des weiblichen Streitgesprächs in Neidharts Sommerliedern." In *Sprachspiel und Lachkultur: Beiträge zur Literatur- und Sprachgeschichte. Festschrift für Rolf Bräuer*, edited by Angela Bader et al., 178–93. Stuttgart: Akademie Verlag, 1994.

Rasmussen, Ann Marie. *Mothers and Daughters in Medieval German Literature*. Syracuse, NY: Syracuse University Press, 1997.

Schweikle, Günther. *Neidhart*. Stuttgart: Metzler, 1990.

Springeth, Margarete und Franz Viktor Spechtler, eds. *Neidhart und die Neidhart-Lieder. Ein Handbuch*. Berlin: De Gruyter, 2018.

Warning, Jessica. *Neidharts Sommerlieder: Überlieferungsvarianz und Autoridentität*. Tübingen: Max Niemeyer Verlag, 2007.

Discography

Kummer, Eberhard. *Lieder und Reigen des Mittelalters – Neidhart von Reuental*. Vienna: Pan-Verlag, 1986.
Ensemble für Frühe Musik, Augsburg. *Neidhart von Reuental*. Heidelberg: Christophorus 2002.
Lewon, Marc. *Neidhart: A Minnesinger and his 'Vale of Tears' – Songs and Interludes*. Hong Kong: Naxos, 2012.

Andreas Kraß
7 Rivalrous Masculinities: Competing Concepts of Knighthood in Bernard of Clairvaux's Sermon *In Praise of the New Knighthood* and Hartmann von Aue's Novella *Gregorius*

This essay grew out of the parallel seminars "Rivalrous Masculinities/Rivalisierende Männlichkeiten" conducted in the winter term of 2013/2014 together with Ann Marie Rasmussen at Duke University and Claudia Benthien at the University of Hamburg. The course, held at the Humboldt-University Berlin, focused on competing concepts of masculinity in medieval German literature, including a section on the tension of chivalry and sanctity in Bernard of Clairvaux's sermon *In Praise of the New Knighthood* as well as Hartmann von Aue's novella *Gregorius*. Following the methodological premises of New Historicism, the comparison between Bernard's and Hartmann's texts aims at reconstructing the "social energy" (Greenblatt 1989) circulating in medieval discourses on Christian knighthood rather than examining to what extent Hartmann's novella – or, respectively the French original it is based on (*La vie du pape saint Grégoire*) – may have been familiar with Bernard's sermon. As this essay will show, the competing concepts of masculinity as constructed in the respective texts is closely connected to the issue of gender difference on an external (relationship between knights and ladies) as well as internal ('effeminate' knights) level. The different genres will also be taken into account: while Bernard wrote a propagandistic clerical treatise, Hartmann composes a fictitious courtly narrative.

1 Competing Images of Knighthood

Two tendencies characterized the image of knighthood in the High Middle Ages: its Christianization in the course of the crusades and the Pax Dei movement (Brennecke 2002; Althoff 1981; Erdmann 1965), and its courtly transformation in connection with the establishment and dissemination of aristocratic courtly culture (Laudage and Leiverkus 2006; Paravicini 1994; Bumke 1986). The Christian knight was to place himself in God's service, the courtly knight in the service of the lady. These two tendencies, Christianization and the courtly metamorphosis, were by no means unrelated: the secular ethos of courtly and chivalrous society was derived largely from the spiritual

---

Translated by Aaron E. Wright

ethos of Christianity, while the princes of the church participated in the courtly life of the secular nobility (Jaeger 1985). The courtly knight conceived of himself always as a Christian knight; he went to church and he believed in God. At the same time, his efforts to do justice to both the courtly and the Christian ideals of knighthood could be the source of considerable conflict. This is made especially striking in the courtly crusade song, a genre that thematizes the conflict between Christian service to God and secular service to the lady.

With knighthood no longer defined as merely a warrior class but rather also as a force for the advocacy of ethical values, the confrontation of the demands made by Christianity with those made by courtly culture results in four possible combinations: (1) the knight who is neither courtly nor Christian, (2) the knight who is Christian but not courtly, (3) the knight who is courtly but not Christian, and (4) the knight who is both courtly and Christian. These four "options" are played out in the courtly literature of the twelfth century. The first can be found in the vernacular heroic literature of the early Middle Ages, which, although partially Christianized, draws on pre-Christian Germanic materials and traditions; examples include the warriors of the *Hildebrandslied* and *Beowulf*. High medieval literature also preserves remnants of this type, among them the depiction in the *Nibelungenlied* of Siegfried as victor over dragons, dwarves, and giants, the Amazon-like Brunhild, and the Saxons and Danes. The second case is found in the heroic epic of French provenance (*chanson de geste*), for example, the *Rolandslied*, which shows the Christian knight doing battle against the pagans in a world still largely untouched by courtly culture and in which the courtly lady still plays no role. The third occurs in courtly literature only as the opponent of the chivalrous hero, as the courtly knight is usually a Christian knight as well. One can take as an example Etzel, king of the Huns, depicted in the *Nibelungenlied* as a courtly but pagan prince (who, however, keeps company with Christian knights and considers being baptized before marrying Kriemhild). The fourth is the default case in the courtly literature of the high Middle Ages; this category includes both the knights of the Arthurian romance and the courtly Siegfried who woos Kriemhild in the *Nibelungenlied*. The type of the courtly and Christian knight is encountered in heightened form in those epics that approach the genre of the hagiographic legend; they tell the stories of knights like Oswald or Orendel, attended by an odor of sanctity even before their deaths.

In what follows, I compare the two afore-mentioned texts of the twelfth century that approach the problem of reconciling knighthood and Christianity from different points of view. The first is Bernard of Clairvaux's *In Praise of the New Knighthood*, composed by the Cistercian abbot as a propaganda piece for the religious order of the Knights Templar (Bernard of Clairvaux 1990; Fleckenstein 1991). Bernard's work was written before the death, in May 1136, of its addressee, Hugues de Payens, a relative of Bernard of Clairvaux and the co-founder and first Grand Master of the Templars. This text reflects on the beginnings of courtly culture by sketching the image of a fashionably dressed knight, at the same time taking a sideswipe at the enterprise of courtly literature (282: "fabulatores, scurrilesque cantilenas" [romanciers, bawdy songs]).[1] Bernard presents the courtly knight and the Christian knight as strictly antithetical: courtly knights cannot be Christian, and Christian knights (meaning the Knights Templar) renounce courtly culture.

The second text is the work of a courtly author who presents himself in the prologues to his epics as a knight, a *ministerialis*, and a scholar; he certainly had the benefit of an education in a cloister or cathedral school (Cormeau 1981, 502). This is *Gregorius* by Hartmann von Aue, a novella of chivalry with aspects of the hagiographic legend; it is based on a French source, *La vie du pape saint Grégoire*, composed around 1150, just a few years before Bernard's *In Praise of the New Knighthood* (Kasten 1991). Hartmann produced his German reworking some decades later; consequently, it is more strongly influenced by courtly culture and literature (of which it is itself a part) than was its source. Where Bernard places the Christian knight in opposition to the courtly knight, Hartmann stages a narrative climax that assembles three types of Christian knighthood in succession, each supplanting and complementing the one before: the courtly, the monastic, and the saintly knight.

In both texts, the figure of the admonishing abbot and the metaphors of pen and lance play a central role. Bernard of Clairvaux is himself the admonishing abbot, rebuking secular knights and encouraging Christian ones. He makes a point of the fact that he has at his disposal not the knight's lance but only the monk's stylus: it is his duty, he writes, to "fling my pen [*stilum vibrarem*], since I am not allowed a lance [*lanceam non liceret*], against your tyrannical enemy" (269). When Bernard writes that he will brandish his stylus like a lance, he evokes the image of a knightly monk, thus anticipating the image of the monastic knight, the Templar.

In Hartmann von Aue's case, the admonishing abbot appears in the narrative as the ruler of an island monastery, who tries to keep his pupil Gregorius from devoting himself to knighthood. Gregorius, however, insists that he is destined not for the stylus but for the lance: "ouch was mir ie vil ger / vür den griffel zuo dem sper, / vür die veder ze dem swerte: / daz ist des ich ie gerte" [The spear was always my desire and not the stylus, the sword and not the quill; that is what I always really wanted].[2]

---

[1] Page numbers refer to the Latin/German edition by Gerard B. Winkler. Bernard von Clairvaux, "Ad milites templi. De laude novae militiae. An die Tempelritter. Lobrede auf das neue Rittertum," in *Sämtliche Werke: lateinisch/deutsch,* edited by Gerhard B. Winkler, (Innsbruck: Tyrolia-Verlag, 1990), 1: 268–85. English translations are those of David Carbon available at: http://www.mgr.org/Bernard_Clarivaux_Military_Theology.html [sic] (Accessed December 18, 2020). Carbon translates the main parts; for a complete English translation, see Bernard of Clairvaux, "In Praise of Knighthood," in *Treatises III, The Works of Bernard of Clairvaux*, translated by Conrad Greenia, (Kalamazoo: Cistercian Publicatons, 1977) 7: 127–67.

[2] References to Hartmann's *Gregorius* will be referred to parenthetically first by the line numbers of the Middle High German version, followed by page number of the English translation listed below in Works Cited; e.g.: (lines 1589–1592; 187).

2 Bernard of Clairvaux, *In Praise of the New Knighthood*

The rhetoric of the exhortatory sermon (*sermo exhortationis*; cf. Fleckenstein 1991, 381) Bernard composed for the Knights Templar is characterized by contrast and opposition: God vs. the devil, monk vs. knight, Christianity vs. paganism, spiritual vs. secular knighthood. While God and the devil, Christianity and paganism, and spiritual and secular knighthood are each an irreconcilable pair, the boundary between the monk and the knight is permeable. The spiritual knights of the Templars are to fuse their knightly way of life with the monastic, living austerely like monks but also doing battle as valiant knights against the 'heathen foe.' The fundamental opposition based in social categories is thus transformed into an internal opposition: no longer is the monk contrasted with the knight (even if Bernard does hint at this at the beginning of *The New Knighthood*), but rather the monastic knight with the courtly knight. The monastic knight knows that he has God and Christendom behind him, while the courtly knight falls victim to the devil and paganism.

To reinforce this opposition between the two forms of knighthood, Bernard adduces the Pauline doctrine of the old and the new man. Secular knights represent the old (courtly) knighthood, while spiritual knights represent the new (monastic) knighthood. Paul calls on Christians to lay down the old man like a garment and to clothe themselves with the new man (Eph 4:22–24):

> To put off, according to former conversation, the old man, who is corrupted according to the desire of error. And be renewed in the spirit of your mind: And put on the new man, who according to God is created in justice and holiness of truth.[3]

The contrast between the old and the new man has an ethical overlay. The old man stands for blindness and desire, the new man for justice and holiness. Projecting this concept onto knighthood, Bernard succeeds in carrying out a rhetorical inversion. In the first half of the twelfth century, when he was writing his *New Knighthood*, courtly knighthood was a new phenomenon; the transformation of the mounted warrior into a courtly knight had just begun. For instance, in his ecclesiastical history of 1140, the Norman monk Ordericus Vitalis bemoans the "nouis adinuentionibus" [new ideas] of young knights, which represented a break with the "honestus patrum mos antiquorum" [honorable practices of their forefathers] (Bumke 1986, 109).[4] For Ordericus, the old is good and the new is bad; for Bernard, the old is bad and the new is good. The two agree in their rejection of courtly-secular knighthood; they simply strike a different chord in rejecting it as new or as old.

---

[3] Quoted from the Douay-Rheims 1899 American Edition (DRA).
[4] On the clergy's criticism of courtly life, see Jaeger 1985, 176–94.

2.1 The Courtly Knight

Bernard adopts from Paul not just the antithesis of the old and the new man, but also the motif of dressing, which he understands not as metaphorical but literal. Like Ordericus, he reproaches secular knights for wearing fashionable clothes and hair styles:

> You wear [. . .] your hair after the fashion of women, impeding your vision; trip up your own feet with your long overhanging overgarments; bury your delicate, tender hands in sleeves cut long and flowing. (274)

Courtly dress and hairstyles impede the freedom of movement the knight needs to succeed in battle. Long hair interferes with his vision, long garments hinder the movements of his arms and legs. But the true knight, he continues, must satisfy three conditions; he is to "be careful [*circumspectus*] in shielding himself; unencumbered [*expeditus*] for movement on the field, and quick [*promptus*] to strike his adversary" (ibid.). What is true for the rider should also be true for his horse. Bernard expresses himself vehemently about the way that courtly knights adorn their mounts:

> You cover your horses in silks and dress your armor with swatches of flowing cloth; you figure your lances, shields and saddles; your bridles and your spurs you adorn with gold and silver and jewels; and with all this display, you rush only towards death, in shameful madness and shameless idiocy. Are these the tokens of chivalry or the trappings of women? Perhaps you imagine that your adversary's sword will reverence the gold, be gentle with you because of your jewels, be unable to pierce your silks? (ibid.)

When Bernard derides the knight's hairstyle as "*ritu feminea*" [a feminine fashion] and the adornment of his horses as "the trappings of women," he denies the courtly knight his masculinity. In Bernard's eyes, men who value a fashionable appearance are effeminate; they have made themselves resemble women. Bernard also appears to present the view that contact with women can "rub off" onto the knight; he emphasizes that spiritual knights, unlike secular knights, live "*absque uxoribus*" [without women] (Kraß 2011). Bernard does not address the courtly cult of *minne*, but the connection between courtly clothing and courtly love is more than hinted at in his assertions. Whoever dresses like a woman and surrounds himself with women, he implies, loses his masculinity and becomes like a woman himself.

There is a further point. Bernard insinuates that the secular knight seeks to counter the mortal danger of combat against the enemy by ornamenting his horse. The courtly knight rushes heedless into death and imagines that gold and silk can protect him from the weapons of his opponent. Whoever enters battle like this, Bernard continues, will bring death, death of the body and of the soul, not just to his enemy but to himself:

> What then is the end or issue of this secular chivalry, which I should probably just call wickedness outright, if its murderers sin mortally and its victims perish forever? To use the words of the Apostle, "he who plows should plow in hope, and he who threshes should thresh in hope of gain of some fruit." What error, knights, so incredible, what madness so unbearable draws

you to chivalrous deeds at such expense and labor, all for no return but death or crime? [. . .] Every time you who live in the ways of worldly chivalry gather to fight among yourselves, you need fear killing your adversary in body and yourself in soul; even more, you need fear finding yourself killed by him, both in body as well as soul. (272, 274)

Once again Bernard employs a rhetorical inversion, in this case based on a pun. Secular knighthood is not *militia* but *malitia*, not true knighthood but wickedness. Thus, whenever the secular knight fells an opponent, he is killing not just the enemy but himself as well. Whoever kills for lowly motives is guilty of a violation of the fifth commandment, a mortal sin. When he dies, it is not as a martyr but as a murderer.

2.2 The Monkish Knight

For Bernard, the picture of the secular knight is the dark background against which the image of the spiritual knight shines that much the brighter. In his view, the Knights Templar have a different relationship to clothing, to women, and to death. In their strong rejection of courtly culture, they do without beautiful clothing, long hair, and regular personal hygiene:

> They keep their hair short, having learned from the Apostle that it is shameful for a man to wear his hair like a woman. Never do they set and rarely do they wash their hair, preferring to go about disheveled and unkempt, covered in dust and blackened by the sun and their armor. (282)

This disdain for a courtly appearance is concomitant with a refusal to join in courtly leisure activities:

> They swear off dice and gaming; they detest hunting, and take no pleasure in the absurd cruelty of falconry, as it is practiced. They renounce and abominate mimes and magicians and romanciers, bawdy songs and the spectacle of the joust as vanity and dangerous folly. (ibid.)

Instead, they use the time when they are not in combat preparing for the next battle, and "repair the wear and tear that their clothes and armor have suffered" (ibid.). The reversion to a pre-courtly set of behaviors is here assessed as ethical progress.

Unlike courtly knights, the Knights Templar in Bernard's depiction want nothing to do with women and children. Bound by oath as brothers in arms ("commilitones"), they prefer each other's company:

> They have a joyous and sober life in their community, without women and without children. That they might lack no evangelical perfection, they live without private property, in one house, in one way, eager to safeguard spiritual oneness within the bounds of their peace. You could say that all their multitude has but one heart and one spirit. (ibid.)

The Templars are a masculine-homosocial society that strictly avoids any proximity to women or anything that is considered feminine. Contrasting themselves with courtly knights, whom they despise as effeminate men, they see themselves as masculine men.⁵ This does not mean that women play no role in their lives. The Templars venerate women – but only those who claim to maintain their virginal state, following the example of such allegorical figures as the Virgin Israel who is seen to personify the Christian church. Indeed, the Knights Templar place themselves in the service of the Virgin Israel, helping her rise again after her fall:

> O Virgin Israel, you had fallen and there was no one to raise you up. Rise now, shake off the dust, virgin, captive daughter of Sion. Rise and stand tall, and see the pleasure which comes [to] you from your God. (278)

They believe firmly, too, that the city of Jerusalem is an allegorical prefiguration of the Virgin Mother of God: "We do not falter in our assertion that the one is but a figure of another, which is our mother in heaven" (280).

Their relationship to death also distinguishes them from the courtly knights. While those knights gamble away the salvation of their souls when they kill and are killed, the Templars' conduct of a holy war makes them martyrs. As *"milites Christi"* [knights of Christ] they need not fear killing or death:

> But Christ's knights can fight their Lord's fight in safety, fearless of sin in slaughter of their adversaries and fearless of danger at their own deaths, since death suffered or dealt out on Christ's behalf holds no crime and merits great glory.. . . Christ's knight deals out death in safety, as I said, and suffers death in even greater safety. He benefits himself when he suffers death, and benefits Christ when he deals out death.. . . Clearly, when he kills an evil-doer, he is not a homicide, but, if you will allow me the term, a malicide, and is plainly Christ's vengeance on those who work evil and the defense Christ provides for Christians. When such a knight is himself killed, we know that he has not simply perished but has won through to the end of this life. The death he inflicts accrues to Christ's profit; the death he receives accrues to his own. (276)

Because they are fighting for Christ, they are protected not just by armor of iron but a spiritual armor as well: "his soul is dressed in an armor of faith just as his body is dressed in an armor of steel. Since he is well protected by both kinds of arms, he fears neither the demon nor man" (270).

3 Hartmann von Aue, *Gregorius*

Hartmann addresses the relationship of the courtly and the Christian knight by recounting the path of a knightly hero, a path strewn with repeated changes of location, clothing, and role.⁶ Born the son of an Aquitaine prince, Gregorius undergoes four

---

5 One might speak of a hegemonic masculinity, in Raewyn Connell's sense, that seeks to marginalize the masculinity of the courtly knights; see Connell 2005; German edition: Connell 1999.
6 On the central issues of *Gregorius* see Strohschneider 2000; on the clothing motif in *Gregorius* see Kraß 2006, 83–92.

phases: spiritual life as a pupil in a cloister school; secular life as a knightly sovereign; spiritual life as an ascetic penitent; and finally life as pope, simultaneously spiritual and secular. These repeated shifts between the spiritual and the secular life result in an accumulation of identities, and in his role as pope, Gregorius combines the qualities that he has attained in his earlier stages of life: education, sovereignty, and sanctity.

The relationship between the secular and the spiritual way of life is such that the former leads to supreme sin and the latter to supreme grace. That exorbitant sin is incest; incest is Gregorius's origin as a princely scion and it is his destination, too, as a knightly sovereign. He obtains equally extraordinary grace as a penitent and pope. Unlike their presentation in Bernard's *New Knighthood*, the secular and the spiritual ways of life are shown here to be related not antithetically but dialectically. In each of these phases, Gregorius is a knight: his knighthood is potential when he lives as a cloister school pupil, manifest when he lives as a sovereign, negated when he lives as a recluse, and sublimated when he lives as pope.

3.1 The Courtly Knight

Conceived in incest, Gregorius cannot embark on the life as knight and sovereign that would otherwise be socially appropriate; instead, he is exposed by his parents. Divine providence leads the infant to an island cloister, where the noble foundling is reared by a family of fishermen and then accepted by the abbot into the cloister school. The boy develops into a talented scholar, quickly mastering grammar, law, and theology. The abbot expects Gregorius to take up a spiritual career, but Gregorius wants to follow his inner yearning for knighthood. Finally yielding, the abbot reveals to Gregorius his princely origins and uses the gold and silk his parents had set afloat with him to outfit the young man. Thus, Gregorius commences his life as a courtly knight supplied with worldly accoutrements and with spiritual socialization. Even as a courtly knight, he remains a good Christian. He renounces life in the cloister but not his faith. The abbot – like Bernard of Clairvaux had once done – warns Gregorius of the moral perils of knighthood, but finally grants him his blessing:

> dû bist, daz merke ich wol dar an,
> des muotes niht ein klôsterman.
> nû wil ich dichs niht wenden mê.
> got gebe daz ez dir wol ergê
> und gebe dir durch sîne kraft
> heil ze dîner ritterschaft.
>   (lines 1635–40; 187–88)

["your disposition is not, as I can tell from all this, that of a monk. Now I shall no longer keep you from it. May God grant that things go well for you and give you through His might all the best for knighthood."]

Gregorius sets off on his journey with a prayer; just as God once led him to the island cloister, so he should guide him to his new destination:

> Nû bôt der ellende
> herze unde hende
> ze himele und bat vil verre
> daz in unser herrre
> sande in etelîchez lant
> dâ sîn vart wære bewant.
> (lines 1825–30; 190)

> [Now the stranger raised up heart and hands to heaven and beseeched Our Lord repeatedly to send him to some land where his journey would find an end].

Every day Gregorius rereads the story of his origins, written on the tablet that his mother had sent with him as an infant and that the abbot had given him so that he might beseech God on behalf of his parents. These daily readings recall the prayers of the monastic hours; thus, Gregorius takes an element of life in the cloister with him into his knightly life. He uses his knightly weapons in a good cause when he liberates a desperate queen from occupation. Gregorius leads an exemplary Christian life as a knight. Bernard of Clairvaux's reproach of courtly knighthood does not apply to him.

The criteria by which Bernard rejects knighthood are accordingly re-evaluated. This takes place first with regard to the courtly knight's focus on women. In his first knightly adventure, Gregorius gives his heart to the besieged queen ("sîn herze lie er bî ir dâ" [line 1966; 191; his heart he left with her there]), liberates her, and marries her. Only when Gregorius learns that the woman he has married is his mother does conflict arise. He has assumed the office of sovereign over Aquitaine, the role his birth entitled him to, but at the same time he has repeated the incest of his origin. This incest, however, is not a personal sin, but rather a token of the fundamental sinfulness of man. It does not imply any condemnation of courtly knighthood.

The motif of courtly clothing is also revalued. Admission to knighthood is marked by a change of clothing and thus highlighted as an act of investiture. Just as the abbot had once furnished his pupil with a monk's habit ("und kleidetez mit selher wât / diu phäflîchen stât" [lines 1161–62; 182; and dressed it in such an outfit that befitted a cleric]), now he dresses the knight in the silk that had been given the child when it was abandoned:

> Nû schuof er daz man im sneit
> von dem selben phelle kleit
> den er dâ bî im vant:
> ez enkam nie bezzer in daz lant.
> (lines, 1641–44; 188)

> [Now he arranged that someone cut for him clothing from the same silk material that he had once found with him. Never had better come into that land.]

Hartmann refrains from any more detailed description of Gregorius's clothing so long as he is a knight and sovereign, minimizing the impression of courtly splendor, perhaps taking into account the objections to courtly knighthood raised by clerical critics.

3.2 The Monkish Knight

When Gregorius again embarks on a spiritual life, it is as an ascetic hermit. He goes to an island cliff, a topographic designation that alludes to the island cloister. As the Rule of St. Benedict explicitly affirms, life as a hermit is a form of monasticism.[7] Gregorius is portrayed as a monastic knight, or a knightly monk, to the extent that his ascetic way of life is depicted as contrasting with his previous life as a knight. After leaving Aquitaine as a beggar to do penance for his incest, he asks a fisherman for shelter for the night. The fisherman mocks Gregorius for his good looks ("schœnen lîp" [line 2785; 201; his fair body]), well-fed appearance ("dich vrâz" [line 2790; 201; you glutton]), and ruddy-cheeked good health ("sô veiz und sô rôt" [line 2908; 202; so chubby and so red]). His well-proportioned body, clean fingernails, and neatly combed hair still lend Gregorius the appearance of a courtly knight:

> dû bist gemestet harte wol,
> dîn schenkel sint sleht, dîn vüeze hol,
> dîn zêhen gelîmet unde lanc,
> dîn nagel lûter unde blanc.
> [. . .]
> sleht und unzevüeret
> ist dîn hâr und dîn lîch
> eim gemasten vrâze gelîch.
> dîn arme und dîn hende
> stânt âne missewende:
> die sint sô sleht und sô wîz.
> (lines 2913–2916 and 2926–2931; 202)

[You have been fattened quite nicely. Your thighs are sleek, your feet well-arched, your toes close together and long, your nails clean and shiny. . . . Smooth and not disheveled is your hair, and your figure is like that of a fattened glutton. Your arms and your hands are without a blemish; they are so smooth and so white.]

Just as in Bernard's *New Knighthood*, the knight is clearly deprecated for his courtly appearance; that disapproval, however, is not the narrator's, but rather that of a figure within the narrative, the suspicious fisherman, and the mockery is in fact directed at him. Gregorius changes his clothes, and his way of life is changed with them.

---

7 See the Rule of St. Benedict, Ch. 1.

When he left the island cloister, Gregorius had promised to put on the monk's habit again if knighthood should bring him harm ("und lege die kutten wider an" [line 1562; 186; (I) shall put the cowl back on]). And now it has happened. Gregorius dons the garment of a penitent, even more austere than the habit of a monk:

> im wâren kleider vremede,
> niuwan ein hærîn hemede:
> im wâren bein und arme blôz.
>   (lines 3111–13; 204)

[Clothing he lacked, save for a hair shirt. His arms and legs were bare].

Gregorius's penance is depicted as the gradual fading of his knightly identity. When legates come to take him to Rome, as the pope elected by God, Hartmann describes the penitent in terms of how he did *not* look after seventeen years of ascetic life:

> ein harte schœner man
> dem vil lützel iender an
> hunger oder vrost schein
> oder armuot dehein,
> von zierlîchem geræte
> an lîbe und an der wæte,
> daz niemen deheine
> von edelem gesteine,
> von sîden und von golde
> bezzer haben solde,
> wol ze wunsche gesniten,
> der mit lachenden siten
> mit gelphen ougen gienge
> und liebe vriunt emphienge,
> mit goltvarwen hâre,
> daz iuch in zewâre
> ze sehenne luste harte,
> mit wol geschornem barte,
> in allen wîs alsô getân
> als er ze tanze solde gân,
> mit sô gelîmter beinwât
> sô sî zer werlde beste stât
> den envunden sie niender dâ:
> er mohte wol wesen anderswâ.
>   (lines 3379–402; 207)

[a very handsome man on whom was hardly visible anywhere any trace from hunger or freezing weather, or any kind of want; with graceful jewelry on his body and his clothes so that no one could be said to have any better precious stones, or silk and gold, made well to order; who went with a cheerful air, with sparkling eyes, and received dear friends; with gold-colored hair, so that he was a joy for you to behold; with well-trimmed beard, well-groomed in every way as though he were going dancing; with such tight leggings that were the best in the world. In no way did they find this there. Maybe he was somewhere else.]

It is as a gesture of irony that Hartmann provides this description of the well-dressed, well-groomed knight who knows how to comport himself in courtly society. The motif of the courtier going to a dance in close-fitting leggings ("als er ze tanze solde gân" [line 3398; 207; as though he were going dancing]) recalls the effeminacy for which Bernard rebukes the courtly knight. But this implicit criticism no longer applies to Gregorius, who has long since relinquished his knightly beauty. Hartmann succeeds in alluding to the cleric's reproach of courtly culture without affirming it. The critical words are transformed into their opposite; they no longer fit the one whom they ostensibly describe.

After seventeen years of penance, the hermit is a piteous sight:

> Der arme was zewâre
> erwahsen von dem hâre,
> verwalken zuo der swarte,
> an houbet unde an barte:
> ê was ez ze rehte reit,
> nû ruozvar von der arbeit,
> ê wâren im diu wangen
> mit roete bevangen
> mit gemischeter wîze
> mit werdeclichem vlîze,
> nû swarz und in gewichen,
> daz antlütze erblichen,
> ê wâren im vür wâr
> diu ougen gelph unde klâr,
> der munt ze vreuden gestalt,
> nû bleich unde kalt,
> diu ougen tief trüebe rôt,
> als ez der mangel gebot,
> mit brâwen behangen
> rûhen unde langen;
> ê grôz ze den liden allen
> daz vleisch, nû zuo gevallen.
> unz an daz gebeine:
> er was sô glîche kleine
> an beinen und an armen,
> ez möhte got erbarmen.
>   (lines 3423–48; 208)

[The wretched man was totally overgrown with hair, matted to his skin, on his head, and in his beard. Once it had been fashionably curled, now soot-colored from his troubles. Once his cheeks had been touched with red, mixed with white, and filled out – color and plumpness vying with each other – now black and sunken, his face bleached. Once his eyes had been, alas, truly sparkling and clear, his mouth formed for joy, now pale and cold, his eyes deep-set, dull, and red, as privation had rendered them, with overhanging brows, coarse and long. His flesh, once filled out on all his limbs, was now wasted away down to the bone. He was so thin everywhere on his legs and arms that God might have felt pity.]

The squalid appearance of the penitent recalls Bernard's characterization of the Templar: "Never do they set and rarely do they wash their hair, preferring to go about disheveled and unkempt, covered in dust and blackened by the sun . . . " (282). There are further parallels: like the Templars, Gregorius avoids the company of women, separated as he is from his mother and wife. Like the Templars, Gregorius has a special relationship to death. He is a martyr, too, but a martyr in his own lifetime, before his death. He does battle against enemies that are internal, not external. He mortifies himself, and is dead to the secular world. He is the "living martyr" (line 3378; 207).

3.3 The Holy Knight

At the end of Hartmann's novella, an alternative arises that Bernard of Clairvaux had not anticipated: the fusing of spiritual and secular knighthood. When he becomes pope, Gregorius enters into a life that combines both elements. Hartmann's depiction of the Roman families' striving for papal office makes clear that from their point of view this is a lucrative position, bringing with it both power ("gewalt") and wealth ("guot"):

> ein ieglich Rômære warp
> besunder sînem künne
> durch des guotes wünne
> umbe den selben gewalt.
>   (lines 3146–49; 205)

[every Roman tried to gain that very power for his kith and kin because of the magnificent benefice.]

The pope occupies a spiritual office, but his position as a secular sovereign necessarily also brings with it some participation in courtly pleasures ("wünne"), as the topographic-semantic structure of the novella suggests. While the island cloister and the island cliff are associated with each other as spiritual spaces, Rome provides a counterpart to Aquitaine. Italy, as a peninsula, simultaneously recalls the spiritual spaces, thus geographically fusing both dimensions.

The transformation from life as a penitent to life as pope is once again marked by a change of attire. The Roman legates share their clerical garments with the naked penitent: "dô teilten die alten / mit im ir phäflîchiu kleit" [3654–3655; 210; Then the aged men shared their priestly robes with him]. This anticipates Gregorius's formal investiture as pope, a proceeding that is itself not narrated. As pope, Gregorius embodies all of the positive qualities of his earlier ways of life: the learning of the cloister school pupil, the power of the sovereign, and the sanctity of the penitent. His papacy is a synthesis of his earlier identities, a synthesis that is characterized as an ideal state and identified as sanctity, "heilikeit," in the text (line 3762; 211).

Pope Gregorius once again has a woman at his side. He takes in his mother (his former wife), who has sought him out to beg forgiveness for her sins. Hartmann invokes a Trinitarian formulation to sum up the incestuous relationship, identifying her as "[s]în muoter, sîn base, sîn wîp / (diu driu heten einen lîp)" [3831–12; 212; His mother, his aunt, and his wife – these three were one]. There is a fourth component to their relationship: she is now also his spiritual daughter. Thus, as pope, Gregorius once again takes up the heterosocial aspect of his former life as a knightly sovereign, now, though, elevated to a new spiritual significance.

4 Knighthood and Christianity

In their works, Bernard of Clairvaux and Hartmann von Aue address a question of fundamental importance to courtly knighthood of the twelfth century: can a courtly knight be a Christian knight at the same time? Bernard's answer is a negative one. In his eyes, courtly knighthood and Christianity cannot be reconciled. He dismisses courtly knights as effeminate men who affect a lifestyle marked by their clothing, hairstyles, and horses – and keep company with women. Any secular knight who kills is a murderer, and any secular knight who is killed loses both his life and his soul. Bernard demands that spiritual knighthood abjure courtly culture to assimilate itself to monastic life. In his opinion, only the Knights Templar are genuine men, as they lead a simple life, forgoing contact with women and preferring only male company. It is accounted a work of virtue if the Templar kills those who are considered enemies of God, and if he himself falls in presumably just battle, he can hope to attain salvation as a martyr.

The situation appears different from the perspective of Hartmann's *Gregorius*. Hartmann is treating exactly the same problem, but as a member of courtly-knightly society himself, he comes to a different conclusion. For him, courtly knighthood and Christianity are entirely reconcilable. Hartmann delineates three types of Christian knight: the courtly, the monastic, and the holy knight. Hartmann finds the masculinity of each knightly type beyond question. The courtly knight is distinguished by a life that is indeed secular, but is conducted in accord with Christian faith. He conducts himself according to Christian values, says his daily prayers, intervenes on behalf of the oppressed, and unites service to his lady with service to God. Though Gregorius is caught up in the sin of his parents, this sin does not attach to him personally, as he commits incest with his mother only unknowingly and unwillingly. Rather, the incest is used here to address a basic dilemma in courtly knighthood, appearing as an aristocratic variation on the basic anthropological dilemma that grounds Christian theology in man's fall from grace.

The monastic knight in the sense of Hartmann's novella withdraws from the world as a hermit to do battle against himself as a penitent. He nevertheless remains a knight, for his identity is innate, as was made clear earlier in the cloister schoolboy's dreams of knighthood even before he learned of his knightly background. The knight does penance, but he is still a knight– even after seventeen years of penance has reduced him to a picture of naked misery. The extravagant nature of his penance, in a sense an overdetermined rite of transformation, anticipates the third form of Christian knighthood: the holy knight, incarnated by Gregorius as pope. As pope, he is not simply the head of the Christian church but also the Roman sovereign. In his role as pope, he builds on the education he received in the cloister school; as sovereign, he builds on the experience gained as ruler of Aquitaine. Hartmann suggests that the pope, as a spiritual prince, leads a courtly life; thus, Gregorius does not return to the monastic life he had assumed as a pupil in the cloister school and as a hermit.

The complexity of Hartmann's position on what it means to be a courtly knight stands out even more clearly when compared to the propagandistic position taken by Bernard of Clairvaux in his *New Knighthood*. In a bold attempt to redeem the Christian honor of courtly knighthood, Hartmann tells the story of a courtly knight who attains the papacy – and a reputation for sanctity in his own lifetime. While Bernard's sermon is bound by patterns of antithesis, Hartmann's novella provides a more differentiated response to the question of how knighthood and Christianity may be reconciled.

Works Cited

Althoff, Gert. "Nunc fiant christi milites, qui dudum extiterunt raptores: Zur Entstehung von Rittertum und Ritterethos." *Saeculum* 32 (1981): 317–33.

Bernard von Clairvaux. "Ad milites templi. De laude novae militiae. An die Tempelritter. Lobrede auf das neue Rittertum." In *Bernard von Clairvaux. Sämtliche Werke: lateinisch/deutsch*, edited by Gerhard B. Winkler, 1: 268–85. Innsbruck: Tyrolia-Verlag, 1990.

Bernard von Clairvaux. "De laude novae militia." Translated by David Carbon. The M+G+R Foundation, 2011–2016. http://www.mgr.org/Bernard_Clarivaux_Military_Theology.html [Clarivaux, sic] (accessed December 18, 2020).

Bernard von Clairvaux. "In Praise of Knighthood." In *Treatises III, The Works of Bernard of Clairvaux*, translated by Conrad Greenia, 7: 127–67. Kalamazoo, MI: Cistercian Publications, 1977.

Betz, Hans Dieter. *Handwörterbuch für Theologie und Religionswissenschaft*. Tübingen: Mohr Siebeck, 1998.

Brennecke, Hans Christof. "Militia Christi." In *Religion in Geschichte und Gegenwart: Handwörterbuch für Theologie und Religionswissenschaft*, edited by Hans Dieter Betz, 5: 1231–33. Tübingen: Mohr Siebeck, 2002.

Bumke, Joachim. *Höfische Kultur: Literatur und Gesellschaft im hohen Mittelalter*. Munich: Deutscher Taschenbuch Verlag, 1986.

Connell, Raewyn. *Der gemachte Mann*. Edited by Ursula Müller and translated by Christian Stahl. Opladen: Leske & Budrich, 1999.
Connell, Raewyn. *Masculinities*. 2nd ed. Cambridge: Polity Press, 2005.
Cormeau, Christoph. "Hartmann von Aue." In *Die deutsche Literatur des Mittelalters: Verfasserlexikon*, 2nd ed., edited by Kurt Ruh, 3: 500–20. Berlin: De Gruyter, 1981.
Erdmann, Carl. *Die Enstehung des Kreuzzugsgedankens*. Stuttgart: Kohlhammer, 1965.
Fleckenstein, Josef. "Die Rechtfertigung der geistlichen Ritterorden nach der Schrift 'De laude novae militiae' Bernhards von Clairvaux." In *Ordnungen und formende Kräfte des Mittelalters: Ausgewählte Beiträge*, 2nd ed., edited by Josef Fleckenstein, 377–92. Göttingen: Vandenhoeck & Ruprecht, 1991.
Greenblatt, Stephen. *Shakespearean Negotiations: The Circulation of Social Energy in Renaissance England*. Berkeley and Los Angeles: University of California Press, 1989.
Hartmann von Aue. *Gregorius*. 15th ed. Edited by Hermann Paul and Burghart Wachinger. Tübingen: Niemeyer, 2004.
Hartmann von Aue. *Gregorius*. In *Arthurian Romances, Tales, and Lyric Poetry: The Complete Works of Hartmann von Aue*, translated and commentary by Frank Tobin, Kim Vivian, and Richard H. Lawson, 165–214. University Park: Pennsylvania State University Press. 2001.
Jaeger, C. Stephen. *The Origins of Courtliness: Civilizing Trends and the Formation of Courtly Ideals, 939–1210*. Philadelphia: University of Pennsylvania Press, 1985.
Kasten, Ingrid, ed. *La vie du pape Saint Grégoire, ou La légende du bon pécheur = Das Leben des heiligen Papstes Gregorius, oder Die Legende vom guten Sünder / Text nach der Ausgabe von Hendrik Bastiaan Sol mit Übersetzung und Vorwort von Ingrid Kasten*. Munich: W. Fink, 1991.
Kraß, Andreas. "Der Effeminierte Mann: Eine Diskursgeschichtliche Skizze." In *Hard Bodies*, edited by Ralph J. Poole et al., 35–52. Münster: LIT, 2011.
Kraß, Andreas. *Geschriebene Kleider: Höfische Identität als literarisches Spiel*. Tübingen: Francke, 2006.
Laudage, Johannes, and Yvonne Leiverkus, eds. *Rittertum und höfische Kultur der Stauferzeit*. Cologne: Böhlau, 2006.
Paravicini, Werner. *Die ritterlich-höfische Kultur des Mittelalters*. Munich: Oldenbourg, 1994.
Rule of St. Benedict. https://www.solesmes.com/sites/default/files/upload/pdf/rule_of_st_benedict.pdf. (Accessed, February 28, 2021).
Strohschneider, Peter. "Inzest-Heiligkeit: Krise und Aufhebung der Unterschiede in Hartmanns 'Gregorius.'" In *Geistliches in weltlicher und Weltliches in geistlicher Literatur des Mittelalters*, edited by Christoph Huber, 105–33. Tübingen: Niemeyer, 2000.

Alison L. Beringer
8 A Fate Worse than Death? Virgil's "steinîn wîp" in Jans der Enikel's *Weltchronik*

The stories of Pygmalion, with his ivory statue that comes to life, and of Medusa, whose petrifying glance turns the living into stone, have long been represented in literary and artistic media, evincing an ongoing human fascination with the metamorphosis from inanimate to animate and vice versa. Less frequent, however, are stories in which a transformation from animate to inanimate is presented metaphorically: that is to say, where a figure in a story is treated as if inanimate by all the other characters even though this figure remains human and alive, not stone and dead.

Such a story is included among the tales told about Virgil in the *Weltchronik* by the Viennese author Jans der Enikel, which was completed about 1272.[1] By reading this story against the broader context of Virgilian tales that Jans der Enikel selects for his work, and by concentrating on the chronicler's presentation of the character Virgil, particularly that character's relationship to language, I will demonstrate how Virgil transforms the woman who has rejected his love into a living statue. A woman's rejection of a man's love is nothing new – one thinks of the *Nibelungenlied* and Kriemhild's negative response to her mother's interpretation of her dream as symbolic of a noble maiden and her outright rejection of the love of any man[2] – but significant in the Virgilian tale is that the woman in question is not an untouched maiden, but rather a married woman. Her behavior in rejecting her suitor is entirely socially appropriate, indeed expected: as a married woman, her "no," prompted neither by maidenly shame nor by provocative coyness, is the proper answer if she wishes to keep her own – and her husband's – honor.

The tale, which culminates in the woman's utter humiliation, offers a startling example of how a woman is defined and controlled by male desire, and how, in effect, she is trapped by that desire and cannot escape its consequences. Though in many ways very different, nonetheless this tale resonates with Ann Marie Rasmussen's discussion of *Die Winsbeckin* in her *Mothers and Daughters in Medieval German Literature* (135–59). In analyzing *Die Winsbeckin*, a dialogue between a noblewoman and her daughter which was probably produced in the first half of the thirteenth

---

[1] On Jans der Enikel see Geith 1980, and Dunphy 2010. The use of "Enikel" as a surname is a mistake made since the seventeenth century; the word is simply a form of the medieval German word for grandson. Dunphy 2003, 17. I therefore adopt the more recent appellation, Jans der Enikel. The standard edition of Jans's *Weltchronik* remains that by Philipp Strauch 1891; this edition forms the basis of the online text provided by Graeme Dunphy and Angus Graham http://www.dunphy.de/ac/je/jehome.htm (Accessed December 18, 2020). Line numbers refer to this edition.
[2] *Nibelungenlied* Stanzas 14–17; see also, chapter two of this volume.

century, Rasmussen notes that "the noblewomen's world is narrow, entirely focused on dealing with social consequences of love as sexual passion, which is defined in terms of male desire" (139). In our tale, the woman is "ein burgærinn" [line 23786; a citizen] yet for her, too, life becomes increasingly structured by male desire and by the consequences of the sexual passion of two men: her unwanted suitor and her husband.[3] In rejecting the former and trying to keep the latter, the woman is made ever more passive. In *Die Winsbeckin*, the mother insists that virtuous behavior will secure the daughter's appeal among men as well as provide the key to a happy and fortunate old age: according to the mother, the daughter's happiness depends on her acceptance of her role as object in an economy of sexual politics. In contrast, in our tale, the conviction that being virtuous will bring you happiness is proven completely false. Here being virtuous leads the woman into an increasingly isolated state in which she eventually loses her humanity and ends up as an inanimate object, as a tool used for the welfare of the community.

Virtue is not rewarded. The unnamed female protagonist initially has agency, an agency she expresses in her refusal of Virgil's dishonorable advances: her action is a refusal to act. Paradoxically that refusal leads to punishment, instead of honor and respect. Undoubtedly, the extreme situation of this tale evoked laughter from a medieval audience; indeed, Jans der Enikel's style, compared to that of one of his sources, is "often more reminiscent of the *Schwank* [comic tale], with its scurrilous, bawdy humor" (Dunphy 2003, 18).[4] But beyond the humor that this tale elicits, its inclusion in the *Weltchronik* and also its illustration in one manuscript, as I discuss below, guides a reader or audience to ponder the untenable situation of the female protagonist. Tapping into humankind's fascination with the inanimate and with metamorphoses into (or out of) inanimate states, Jans der Enikel's narrative effectively draws attention to the plight of the unnamed female. The tale is inarguably misogynistic: the husband, despite being the mastermind of the plan for his wife's actions is not explicitly punished by the events. What one remembers from this tale is the woman, the injustice done her, and the price of virtue.

1 Virgil and the *Weltchronik*

Jans der Enikel's *Weltchronik* is the third of the three major Middle High German world chronicles produced in verse in the thirteenth century – the other two are

---

3 The Virgil stories are lines 23695–4224 of Strauch (1891). William Carroll's English translation of these lines is found on pages 926–32 in Putnam and Ziolkowski, *The Virgilian Tradition*. Translations of Jans der Enikel's text in my essay are my own, unless otherwise noted.
4 For a brief discussion of the term *Schwank*, see Eming, chapter nine in this volume, esp. 200–01.

Rudolf von Ems's *Weltchronik* and the anonymous *Christherre-Chronik*.[5] In almost 30,000 verses of rhymed couplets, Jans der Enikel's *Weltchronik* records selected events of world history – from God's creation of heaven, earth, and the angels, up to the death of Emperor Frederick II in 1250. As Graeme Dunphy observes in his introduction to translated selections of Jans der Enikel's text, the work reveals an interest in "urban perspectives" which is lacking in both the *Christherre-Chronik* and Rudolf's *Weltchronik*.[6]

Both Rudolf's *Weltchronik* and the *Christherre-Chronik* were left unfinished by their authors: Rudolf "died while working on Solomon," and the *Christherre-Chronik* stops in the Book of Judges; thus neither reaches the time of Virgil.[7] Jans der Enikel, then, is alone among the three chroniclers to reach the time of Virgil; he is also credited with being the first author to name Virgil as protagonist in the revenge against the virtuous woman and to narrate this story in the vernacular.[8]

Virgil is of course primarily known as the author of the *Aeneid* and as such his identity as a vengeful and lustful character is initially surprising. However, in the Middle Ages, the venerable Roman poet had a second identity as a magician, and though Jans der Enikel did not invent this tradition, the chronicler nonetheless holds an important position in its vernacular German branch. His was the first extensive German account to cast Virgil as a sorcerer and to associate the author of the *Aeneid* with diabolism, an identification absent from earlier Latin works.[9] As Jans der Enikel writes, Virgil acquired his magical skill from demons: digging in a garden one day, Virgil came upon a glass in which seventy-two devils were trapped.

---

[5] On Rudolf von Ems see Walliczek 1992 and Klein 2010. On the *Christherre-Chronik* see Ott 1977, 1: 1213–17, Ott 2004, 11: 317, and, more recently, Plate 2010, 1: 270–72.

[6] Dunphy 2003, 18. One example Dunphy cites is that instead of a tent, Abraham has a townhouse with courtyard.

[7] Rudolf von Ems, *Weltchronik*, line 33491, quoted by Dunphy 2003, 7. The text was continued by another writer but only for a few hundred lines. The *Christherre-Chronik* is often continued by drawing on Rudolf's text: Ott 1977, 1215. The transmission of German world chronicles is notoriously complicated; Gärtner 1985 remains an excellent introduction.

[8] See Mierke 2014, 118 and references there. Spargo, in his seminal study of the tradition of Virgil in the Middle Ages also credits Jans der Enikel with expanding the legends in an attempt to portray Virgil as necromancer, although he is scathing in his evaluation of Jans's ability: "Instead of merely referring fleetingly to the legends, as his predecessors did, he [Jans] devotes some five hundred lines of very bad verse to spinning the yarns into stories of a sort, and thus he is the first individual to attempt a sustained account of the legends or a consistent characterization of Virgil the necromancer." Spargo 1934, 25.

[9] The best place to start for the medieval tradition of Virgil as magician is Ziolkowski and Putnam 2008, 825–1024 and 457–63. See also Spargo 1934, (23 for Jans der Enikel and diabolism); and Comparetti 1966. See also Petzoldt 1995. Reference articles include: Worstbrock 2001, 10: 247–84, especially 274–79 and 284 and Ziolkowski 2014, 2: 737–40. Wolfram von Eschenbach in his *Parzival* casts the evil sorcerer Clinschor as Virgil's nephew, but does not *explicitly* link Virgil to the devil. Book 13, stanza 656, lines 14–18.

Virgil shattered the glass and released the demons in exchange for knowledge of all of the devils' "zouberlist" [line 23749; magic]. With his newly acquired skills, Virgil heads to where an unrequited love will eventually lead to the act of vengeance at the core of the metaphorical metamorphosis of a living human into a stone artifact.

The story of Virgil's unlucky love is commonly referred to as the "basket" episode, and its elements existed long before the protagonist was identified as Virgil. John Webster Spargo discusses oriental tales, the Old French romance of *Floire et Blancheflor*,[10] and a version recounted in the sixteenth-century *L'estoire del Saint Gral*; in this last text, the unlucky lover is the philosopher and physician Hippocrates.[11] In what is probably the earliest attestation of Virgil in the role, transmitted in a thirteenth-century Latin manuscript[12] his desire is for the daughter of Nero, but the identity of the female love object also changes over time.[13]

In Jans der Enikel's account, Virgil, living in Rome, becomes enamored of a female "burgaerinn" [citizen], married and described as a "stæt" [constant] woman who refuses his advances. Despite this discouragement, Virgil persists; in response, the woman assures him that: "Ez müesten ê bresten all stein, / ê ich iuch wærlîch wolt gewern, / des ir wolt an mich gern" [lines 23802–04; all stones would break before [she] would let him have his way with her]. Refusing Virgil's proffered silver and gold, the woman seeks her husband's advice on how to deal with him. The woman is highly conscious of her honor, emphasizing that she has guarded it carefully since childhood, and that she plans to grow old with it, if it is her husband's will.[14]

Her husband, recognizing that her shame and ignominy would cause him to suffer, hatches a plan to shame Virgil: his wife is to tell Virgil she will acquiesce in his wishes this very evening. She is to tell him that her husband has departed from her in anger, that she has lost his good will, and that Virgil should come to her immediately. She is furthermore to tell Virgil that she will lower a basket in which he should sit "ân schal" [line 23852; without cover or noise (or perhaps both?)] and which she will then hoist up into her tower, where she will do his bidding – a motif familiar from other stories, as discussed below. The husband is confident that Virgil, hearing the woman's scheme, will believe her and have no fear.

All goes according to the husband's plan, which the wife embellishes with the claim that her husband has beaten her, an act that adds vehemence to her statement

---

10 The source text for *Flôre und Blanscheflûr* discussed in chapter four of this volume.
11 Spargo 1934, 137–44; here 144. For earlier association of the name Hippocrates with the male protagonist in the basket story, see Roth, 1859, 274. See also Putnam and Ziolkowski, (2008), 874–89.
12 Spargo's suggestion that this may be the earliest example remains current. Spargo 1934, 145, and Putnam and Ziolkowski 2008, 876. The manuscript is Paris, Bibliothèque nationale, MS lat. 6186.
13 In select fifteenth-century manuscripts of the *Indulgentiae ecclesiarum urbis Romae*, the woman is identified as Kriemhild. See Mierke 2016, 432–35.
14 ahtet, wie ich behalt / mîn wîplîch êr, / die ich von miner kintheit her / mit zühten hân behalten. / mit êren muoz ich alten, / ob ez nu iuwer will ist. (lines 23818–23).

that there is nothing in the entire country that has caused her more suffering than her husband.¹⁵ In the evening, the woman lowers the basket, Virgil climbs in, and she begins to draw him up. However, she stops before the basket reaches the window, for "si was ein reinez wîp; / kiusch und schœn was ir lîp," [lines 23912–14; she was a pure woman, chaste and beautiful was her body]. On the following day, hearing the news that Virgil has been left hanging from the tower, many go to see for themselves.

The husband, pretending to just now be returning to town, arrives and asks Virgil how he comes to be suspended in a basket beneath his tower window. Virgil simply says it was his own desire, and the husband, feigning sympathy with his experience of shame, lowers him again. The episode ends with Virgil suffering greatly from his shame.¹⁶

The basket episode became well known particularly in its incorporation into the Power of Women topos. Virgil joins an illustrious company of wise or heroic men – among them Samson, Aristotle, and Holofernes – who are undone by a woman.¹⁷ The depiction of Virgil suspended in the basket thus enjoys a visual life independent of textual witnesses and appears in a range of media, including a small bronze medallion and a capital in Saint Pierre in Caen, Normandy.¹⁸ Sometimes, such as in the fourteenth-century Malterer Tapestry, more than one scene of this episode is depicted – in that case, an illustration of the wife's meeting with Virgil to discuss the plan precedes the iconic basket scene. Yet while the dominant visual tradition emphasizes Virgil's folly and entrapment, textual versions often continue with a story of Virgil's revenge, a scene less frequently found in visual representations.¹⁹

In Jans der Enikel's account, we learn that Virgil, eager for revenge on those who have ridiculed him, extinguishes all the fires in Rome, thereby bringing all cooking and brewing to a halt. The Romans are full of "riuwe" [regret] and close to starvation; eventually, one of them suggests asking Virgil for advice. The people willingly swear an oath to Virgil that they will do whatever he commands and that they will respect him if he returns fire to them. Although the citizens do ask Virgil not to harbor any resentment if one of them has in some way offended him, that request

---

15 Mir ist [niht] in den landen wît / niht sô leides sô mîn man. (lines 23874–75).
16 The basket episode ends at line 23960; the vengeance is narrated in lines 23961–24138.
17 See Smith 1995.
18 Koch 1959, 107–8, illustrations 1 and 2. The motif of a man hanging in a basket, associated with Virgil, is also used for other figures, e.g. the Codex Manesse's author portrait for Kristan von Hamle. Koch 1959, 108, and the brief discussion and more recent bibliography in Ziolkowski and Putnam 2008, 457–59.
19 With regard to the uneven illustration of the two stories, see Koch 1959, 106. A glance at Spargo's list of tales from John of Salisbury's *Policraticus*, c. 1159, to the mid-sixteenth-century *Deceyte of Women* shows that of the sixteen texts relating the basket episode, in ten it is followed by the story of revenge. Ziolkowski observes that probably the first attestation of the revenge motif is in Guiraut de Calanson's Occitan *Fadet Joglar* (c. 1215–1220). Putnam and Ziolkowski 2008, 875.

seems to fall on deaf ears. Quite the contrary, the reader realizes that Virgil is entirely motivated by anger and his desire for revenge.

Virgil reveals that the only one who can relieve their suffering is the woman from the tower. Eventually and reluctantly, her husband yields to the Romans' cajoling and sends her to Virgil. Virgil tells the woman that if she does not want her country and her people to be destroyed, she must act as he commands to win the return of fire to the city's hearths.

The initial response of the wife is a request that Virgil offer "ein ander spil" [a different game], as she has already suffered greatly because of him.[20] Though Jans der Enikel's choice of *spil* here was undoubtedly dictated by rhyme, it is nonetheless worth noting that the term can mean intercourse, thus reminding the reader of Virgil's original desire.[21] Unsurprisingly Virgil dismisses this request. In the next twenty lines, Virgil reveals to the wife what her fate is to be:

> "frou, seht ir disen stein?
> dâ sült ir ûf stên alein.
> daz gewant sült ir ab ziehen.
> ab dem stein sült ir niht fliehen
> ir sült niht haben wan ein hemd.
> ander kleider sîn iu fremd;
> und sült daz aftermuoder zwâr
> hinden ûf lesen gar
> und an allen vieren stân.
> zehant sô sol wîp und man
> zünden vor dem hindern teil.
> swer danne gewinnet daz unheil,
> der zuo dem andern zünden wil,
> sô wirt in beiden niht ze vil,
> wan si erleschent beid daz lieht,
> daz man ez nimmer brinnen siht.
> wellent si aber fiur hân,
> sô müezen si hin wider gân
> und müezen wider zünden,
> so beginnet der after lünden."
> (lines 24075–94)

["Lady, do you see this stone? / You shall stand on it alone. / And you shall take off your clothing. / You shall not leave the stone, / And you shall wear nothing but your slip. / You shall have no other clothing; / And you shall raise the back of your slip / Completely and go down on all fours. / The men and women will / Light fires from your behind. / If anyone fails / And tries to

---

20 Si sprach: "lieber herr mîn, / möht ez in iuwern hulden sîn, / sô bæt ich iuch gern, / ob ir mich wolt gewern, / sô liezt ez sîn ein ander spil / ich hân doch von iu leides vil" (lines 24061–66).
21 Benecke, Müller, and Zarncke 1854–66: the seventh definition reads, "verhüllend für beischlaf." Given the wife's steadfast loyalty, it is highly unlikely that she is actually offering her body to him, but the lexical choice does admit such a reading.

light his fire from another, / Neither will gain anything, / For both their lights will go out / And not burn at all. / And if they want fire again, / They will need to go behind you again / And light their fire again / When your rear end begins to flame."]

Such an absurd demand by Virgil is, of course, meant to elicit shock and disbelief in the reader or audience: just like a modern audience, presumably a medieval one would have recognized the burlesque humor of this passage with its reference to flatulence, but which also engages misogynistic tropes in humiliating and de-humanizing the wife. However, there is more to it than humor or misogyny. For the impetus behind Virgil's demand for this de-humanization was the wife's rejection of an extramarital affair with the sorcerer: in other words, her inexcusable action in his eyes was her refusal to act. In his subsequent demand, Virgil punishes the wife's inaction by demanding that she become a stationary object, thereby making her inaction permanent and eternal. Moreover, she must serve as an instrument to others. The responsibility for restoring fire to the city thus rests entirely on the wife's shoulders – she alone is to stand on the stone – regardless of the fact that Virgil's humiliation was the brain child of her husband. Indeed, the husband is explicitly left out of Virgil's plan of revenge, even though the sorcerer aims to shame the wife's relatives through his treatment of her. Again, the wife serves as an instrument used by others:

> Do man Virgilium her ab geliez,
> . . .
> do begun der sêr trachten
> und in dem herzen ahten,
> wie er dem getæte,
> daz diu frou stæte
> von im leit gewunne
> und ouch alz ir kunne
> von dem leid geschant wurde.
>   (lines 23951–59)

[When Virgil was let down [from the wall] / . . . / then he pondered greatly / and considered in his heart / how he could act / so that the loyal wife / received pain from him / and that also her relatives / were shamed by her pain]

Virgil's plan is thus to expose the wife to the public in a state of undress where she is not to move from the stone. Finally, she is required to be on all fours so that the whole picture – the elevation of the stone she is required to mount and her static pose atop it – call to mind a statue and its pedestal: the posture she must assume transforms her into a four-legged beast, evoking the ultimate animal statue, the Golden Calf.

The wife rejects Virgil's commands, asserting she would rather die than experience such shame,[22] but Virgil merely responds that it will be up to the people to

---

[22] "ê wolt ich den lîp lân / ê ich hêt sölich schant" (lines 24096–97).

force her acquiescence. When word of her refusal reaches her relatives, they turn to her husband, who immediately sees that there is no escape from the situation. Relatives plead with her, but she remains unwilling, and claims that she would rather be killed than comply with Virgil's demands.[23] It is the husband who then takes control: ordering his wife bound and her clothing removed, he places her atop the stone. There, she must give fire to all: "dâ muost diu frou mit schal / daz fiur geben über al" (lines 24123–24). The use of the phrase "mit schal" – noisily – admits of two readings. More prominent, given the scatological undertones of the story, the phrase suggests that flatulence accompanies or perhaps even sparks her production of fire. Less humorous is to understand the phrase as indicative of the continued vocal objections of the woman: they are not coherent words, but rather simply noise and thus another way in which the wife loses her human status. At this point the poet reiterates a third time that she must stand on the stone.[24] Following six lines listing the types of kindling the people light, the episode ends by emphasizing how bitter the position was for the woman, but that it was inescapable that she endure the shame and suffering – "Si was nâhen tôt" [line 24138; she was nearly dead].

As Gesine Mierke has argued in her reading of this episode, the treatment of the wife is equivalent to a display of a public and repeated rape. The wife must submit to Virgil's demands in order to save the Roman people and no one, including her husband, comes to her aid. The woman's body suffers, and because she is married, Mierke and others suggest that her shame will also affect her relatives.[25] This is certainly plausible, although the text does not record any reaction of the husband to his wife's ordeal. Under the pressure exerted by his relatives and the citizens of Rome, the husband facilitates the public humiliation of his wife – he, too, becomes an instrument of Virgil – but once she is in place and restoring fire, the husband disappears from the narrative. In fact, the episode ends abruptly with the information that Virgil leaves Rome and heads to Naples (lines 24139–42).

Though still alive – she is only *near* death – the wife has been made into what is as close to an inanimate being as possible. Placed on a pedestal and ordered not to move, subjected to public scrutiny, she has become a statue. All the characters in the story know that she is alive, yet their desperate need for fire – and their own survival – has erased any respect for her dignity as a person; she has been reduced to a utility.

The wife, then, has been increasingly instrumentalized. In the first instance, she became an instrument of – or perhaps for – her husband by following his instructions to avoid their mutual loss of honor. Here the wife exercised (a modicum

---

[23] "ich lâz mich tœten ê, / ê es also an mir ergê" (lines 24113–14).
[24] Wan si muost ûf dem stein stân (line 24125).
[25] Mierke 2014, 119. On male relatives as intentional targets when women are raped, see also Bennewitz 1989, 142, whom Mierke cites. As quoted above, Virgil shaming the relatives is part of Virgil's plan, lines 23958–59.

of) agency as she decided to approach her husband for help. In subsequently executing her husband's plan, the wife is active but as her actions are prescribed by him, she is not projecting independence: "swaz ir der wirt vor sprach, / diue frouwe tet ez allez nâch" [lines 23861–62; whatever her husband advised her to do / the wife did all of this accordingly.] Virgil's frustration at the wife's lack of fulfillment of his desire provides the second manifestation of the wife as instrument, if we assume that her shame will reflect badly on her relatives: she becomes the means to shame others. Finally, in the completion of his vengeance, Virgil makes the wife into the instrument required – and used – by all members of the community for their survival. The wife, who began the tale as a woman whose desirability put a well-known male authority figure in her power, increasingly loses her ability to direct her actions and finally even to act at all until she is reduced to a mere object – a fate worse than death, as she herself asserts. Her downward spiral from respected wife to community tool is paradoxically fueled by her choices to be true, to be a good woman/wife: that is, her refusal to commit adultery and her determination to defend her (and her husband's) honor. We might say that for the woman in this story, no good deed goes unpunished.

2 Magic and Materials

In his depiction of Virgil's revenge, Jans der Enikel draws the sorcerer as a character who concretizes and manipulates language, a character who takes the figurative and makes it literal. This is most clearly seen in the role of fire in the woman's humiliation. Desire has always been described as a metaphoric fire. Such ardor is disappointingly absent in the lady when she spurns Virgil. Having failed to ignite a metaphoric fire, the sorcerer instead creates a literal fire in her. That he has extinguished all fires in Rome well in advance of igniting the lady ensures that all the Romans will be desperate and will go to the lady to light their various inflammables. As she did not burn privately and metaphorically for Virgil, she will now burn publically and concretely for all of Rome.

A more subtle example of the sorcerer's manipulation of figurative language is seen when we reconsider the language of the lady's initial rejection of his advances. As noted above, she remarks that "ez müesten ê bresten all stein, / ê ich iuch wærlich wolt gewern, / des ir wolt an mich gern" [lines 23802–04; all stones would break before I would grant you what you want with me]. The revenge that Virgil takes on the woman resonates with this adynaton. In light of his rejection and his humiliation, Virgil decides that the lady whose affections he cannot force (there is a certain irony in the limitation of Virgil's magic power here as it falls short of manipulating his beloved into adultery) shall nonetheless be forced to perform in a manner against her wishes. By thus imposing his will on her – forcing her to disrobe, to stand on a stone, and to expose her flaming behind to all of Rome – Virgil breaks her, like an unruly filly: the wife loses her agency, she is no longer in control of her actions, and is placed and positioned according to the magician's orders. That Virgil's initial desire remains unfulfilled is of no importance; what the sorcerer has succeeded in doing is transforming the intractable woman into a controlled and utilitarian substance: he has broken her will and ensured her obedience.

In this new role, the woman's body is no longer an object of desire for Virgil, but instead has become material to be manipulated and controlled. Virgil here becomes a sculptor and an artist. His art consists in the magical transformation of figurative language. The woman no longer exists for the sorcerer (or indeed for any of the Roman citizens) as a living, breathing, and attractive woman: her body has become the equivalent of stone – eventually that stone will be shaped into a conduit of fire – with the result that he transforms her into a symbolic statue. By acting in this way – breaking the woman and treating her as stone – Virgil may reveal that his approach to language is linguistically naïve, grounded in the individual words and not allowing for interpretation of a figurative expression. More likely, however, given Virgil's double identity as sorcerer and as highly-respected poet of the *Aeneid* is that Virgil is magically aware of the power of language and chooses to manipulate words to his advantage. What he extracts from the wife's original adynaton is not its intended meaning (that she will *never* welcome his advances), an extraction which would require simply the ability to translate her figurative expression, but rather he chooses to focus on the act of breaking and the material of stone. Grounded in literalness, but creative in interpretation, Virgil breaks the woman by making her into stone; needless to say, neither of these actions were the intent of the original adynaton.

Jans der Enikel's connection of Virgil with such idiosyncratic interpretation of language is no surprise. As the greatest poet of antiquity, Virgil's most important tools were linguistic; as a magician, too, words are essential for him. Indeed, both a poet and a magician work with words in the way that a sculptor works with stone, forming raw material into creations. Raw material in the form of words for a magician and stone for a sculptor is critical for the successful production of spells and sculpture respectively. Words failed the magician Virgil in his attempts at seducing the wife: the raw material proved useless in creating the desired effect. Instead of accepting defeat, Virgil changes his raw material and his art form: from words to stone, from magician to sculptor. Once the female has become stone, Virgil is able to shape her into a statue; upon having completed his "art work," he leaves Rome. Virgil thus succeeds in overpowering or conquering the wife and at least partially vindicating his wounded pride, though he does not conquer her in the way he initially wanted and his desire is never fulfilled. Unwittingly, the woman has inspired Virgil – first to lust and then to vengeance – and she is transformed, quite literally, into raw material. What is interesting here is that Virgil seems unable to leave her – even when he has been rejected, shamed in the basket, and then set free by the husband. His determination to revenge himself on the wife suggests a certain dependence on her, albeit one motivated by shame. He is unable to walk away before re-asserting his own power and importance, and the only way that he thinks he can do this is by transforming the woman into an inanimate being. She – and she alone – must be the raw material through which he will re-establish himself as a subject, as in control; in his inability to walk away from the situation, in his using her as raw material, Virgil shows that he remains affected by her. It is only once Virgil has completed his vengeance – completed his statue – that he can leave.

3 Virgil and Statues

It may be worth remembering here that Virgil is a pagan in a text that is overtly Christian, relating as it does the history of the world in a salvific framework. When Jans der Enikel introduces Virgil, he makes Virgil's religious affiliation quite clear:

> er [Virgil] was ein rehter heiden.
> an rehtem glouben was er blint.
> Er was gar der helle kint. (lines 23700–702)
> [He [Virgil] was a true pagan. / To true faith he was blind. / He was a child of hell.]

The triple description – he is a true pagan, blind to the true faith, a child of hell – leaves no doubt in the reader's mind. In the basket episode, Virgil is further maligned when the lady, refusing his advances, asserts that even if he were more handsome than Absalom – that biblical paradigm of physical beauty – she would reject him. In addition to his beauty, Absalom is known for his vengeance against his half-brother for that man's rape of Tamar, Absalom's sister.[26] Unlike Virgil in the basket episode, Absalom showed respect toward women. Virgil's magical manipulation of literal language coupled with the unfavorable comparison to Absalom and his unequivocal identification as a pagan cast him strongly as an "other" – that is to say, unlike the Christian reader of the *Weltchronik*.

Given that the defining characteristic of pagans is their adoration of idols, one would expect that Virgil, as a pagan, be associated with statues. Indeed, even a cursory familiarity with the medieval tradition of Virgil as magician reveals that statues, including mechanical statues, are a recurring motif.[27] Ranging from a bronze horse that, as long as it remained undamaged, would ensure the durability of all equine backs[28] to the famous *bocca della verità*, a stone image with a mouth that purportedly bit the fingers of adulteresses, Virgil's name was repeatedly coupled with these creations. Jans der Enikel recounts neither of these stories in his Virgil selections,[29] but he

---

26 2 Samuel 20: 22–33
27 Ziolkowski 2014, 738.
28 This is first described as Virgil's manufacture by the German, Conrad of Querfurt, but the idea of such a talisman goes back to antiquity. See Spargo 1934, 84–86.
29 The Virgil selections under discussion are from lines 23695–4223.

does include a less well-known story, one that in his chronicle immediately precedes, and gains particular resonance from, the story of Virgil and the basket. In that story, a stone woman serves to extinguish the metaphoric fire of male desire.

This less frequent story narrates the very first action Virgil undertakes using the magical skills received from the devils which he released from the glass; in fact, Jans der Enikel informs his readership that Virgil is testing his power, to see whether the promise of these devils was true.[30] According to the chronicler, Virgil uses the powers to create a "steinîn wîp," a stone woman, which has the unusual feature of seeming to be a real woman whenever a "schalc" [bad man] approaches it, desiring a woman:

> Virgilius der selb man
> begund zu Rôm gân.
> und versuocht sîn meisterschaft,
> ob ez wær wâr der tiufel kraft.
> er macht zu Rôm ein steinîn wîp
> von kunst,
> diu hêt einen lîp,
> swanne ein schalc, ein bœser man
> wolde ze einem wîp gân,
> daz er gie zuo dem steine,
> der bœs, der unreine,
> daz im was bî des steines lîp,
> reht als ez wær von art ein wîp
> niht fürbaz ich iu sagen sol,
> mîn meinung wizt ir alle wol.
>   (lines 23765–78)

[Virgil himself / went to Rome / to practice his skills / and to determine whether the powers the devils had granted him were real. / In Rome he used his abilities to create a woman of stone, / her body formed in such a way that whenever a wicked rascal / wanted a woman / he could go to the stone one, / and the stone body would be for that wicked, impure man / just like a woman's. / I will not tell you any more; / you know what I mean.]

By choosing to begin the Virgil section of the chronicle with this story, Jans der Enikel places the image of a female statue at the forefront, thus preparing the audience for the symbolic female statue that will be the result of the subsequent story about the sorcerer and the faithful *burgærinn*. The first two stories, then, are chiastic: in the first, a statue appears to be a woman and in the second, a woman a statue.

In this first story the inanimate stone statue appears to be alive and to satisfy those men who are unfaithful: a "schalc" is a person whose character is, among other things, faithless.[31] That the men are performing a sexual act with the statue is

---

[30] Virgilius . . . versuocht sîn meisterschaft, / ob ez wær wâr der tiufel kraft. (lines 23767–68)
[31] Benecke, Müller, and Zarncke 1854–66: the second entry reads: "mensch von knechtisch bösem, ungetreuem, schadenfrohem charakter."

emphasized in the final two lines, in which the narrator asserts that he need say no more, as everyone understands his meaning. By downplaying the line between the inanimate and the animate, the story foregrounds women as objects while at the same time establishing the faithlessness of men. As we have seen, the story of Virgil and the *burgærinn*[32] that follows exploits the notion of women as objects, but it also explores the second motif (the faithlessness of men), albeit in a less direct way.

Whereas honor and faithfulness are what drives the wife in the second story, faithlessness increasingly defines the husband. When Virgil's attentions become too much, she, a model wife, turns to her husband and seeks his aid. *He* is the one who plans to shame Virgil, and yet, as noted above, the end of "Virgil's Revenge" narrates no discomfort for him. Apart from the narrator's words indicating the husband's recognition of the inevitability of the execution of Virgil's plan, and the information that the wife's laments were ignored (the formulation is impersonal: "dô niht half weder drô noch bet" [line 24115; neither threat nor pleading helped]), the reader learns nothing of the husband's emotional reaction, let alone any type of support for his beleaguered wife. On the contrary, the husband becomes Virgil's chisel, ordering his wife bound and undressed and himself placing her on the stone. In acting in this manner, the husband helps the community, but collaborates in the shaming of his wife. He fails her, neither comforting nor protecting her, but instead breaking faith with her and showing himself to be the faithless one.

The first story of Virgil's "steinîn wîp," then, provides a brief (the whole episode is only twelve lines) but pointed introduction to the basket and revenge episodes. Nor is this the only statue included in Jans der Enikel's Virgil as sorcerer selection. Just nineteen lines later, after Virgil has left Rome (and the "burgærinn" is "near death"), we encounter yet another Virgil statue story (lines 24157–224). In this subsequent tale, Virgil makes a golden statue with an inscription stating that the statue indicates the location of treasure. As one hand of the statue rests on its stomach and the other points in the direction of a mountain opposite, numerous treasure hunters go off to try their luck by digging in the mountain. Finally, a drunken person determines that the image has been mocking the people enough and he will wreak vengeance on it, by smashing it.[33] Once shattered, the statue reveals its treasure was inside all along (under the hand on the stomach) – gold – and the drunken man becomes wealthy. This final Virgil story reminds the reader of the central role of statues in the Virgilian episodes; in particular, the act of destruction directs the reader specifically to think about the materiality of the statue. In

---

32 This sequel to the "Virgil and the Basket" story is designated in scholarship as "Virgil's Revenge." As with "Virgil and the Basket," the identity of the woman is fluid.
33 The drunken man asks rhetorically, "wie lang sol uns daz bilde / effen an dem wilde [Philipp Strauch's critical apparatus to Jans der Enikel's *Weltchronik* suggests *in* and *velde*, which I use in my translation] / ich wil die liut an im rechen / und wil ez zerbrechen [lines 24197–200; how long must that image mock us in the meadow / I want to avenge the people on it and break it].

destroying the statue, the drunkard destroys the physical creation made by a pagan (Virgil) and the symbolic representation of pagan religion (an idol). Pagans and their religion are erased from the text, to be replaced by the religion of the contemporary world: Christianity. To ensure that the reader grasps the ultimate victory of Christianity over Paganism, the narrator includes both a moral and an allegorical interpretation of this episode, lines 24209–19 and 24220–24 respectively. In the former, the narrator notes that one becomes wealthy through luck (as the drunk man did). In the allegorical interpretation, we learn that as wealth is a matter of chance, salvation is a matter of God's grace:

> daz golt viel nider ûf daz gras.
> dar an sol man besehen wol,
> wer grôzez guot haben sol,
> dem muoz ez werden beschaffen,
> ez sîn leien oder pfaffen,
> als dem trunken man geschach,
> der daz bilde brach –
> 'diz bild sol nieman effent sîn' –;
> der west niht, daz daz golt was sîn,
> unz er daz golt truoc von dan.
> dô wart er ein rîch man.
> im wart beschert grôzez guot.
> ôwê, wie sanft ez manigem tut,
> daz er gewinnet sæld und heil!
> ôwê, wurd uns noch des ein teil!
> des helf uns got von himelrîch!
> zwâr sô wurden wir freudenrîch.
> (lines 24208–19)

[The gold fell onto the grass. / In this one can see that / Whoever is going to have lots of wealth / Whether a layman or a cleric / It will happen to him / In the same way as it happened to the drunk man / Who broke the statue – 'this statue ought to mock no one' – / And didn't know that the gold was his, / Until he carried the gold away. / Then he became a rich man. / He was given great wealth. / Alas how easy it is for many people to gain happiness and salvation! / Alas, if we could only have some of that! / May god in heaven help us with that / Then we would be very happy.]

Jans der Enikel includes six tales about the pagan sorcerer: the discovery and release of the 72 devils trapped in the glass, the creation of a "steinîn wîp," the basket episode, the revenge episode, the building of Naples,[34] and the creation and destruction of the golden statue. Statues (real or symbolic) are central to the second, fourth, and sixth episodes. The material of the statue varies each time and yet each time it holds particular narrative significance. In the first example, Jans der Enikel draws attention

---

[34] This story occurs between Virgil leaving Rome and his building of the golden statue (lines 24139–56).

to the material simply by using the term "steinîn wîp," denoting that the woman is *of stone* and by emphasizing men's inability to tell the difference between living, human body and cold stone. In the last example, the chronicler writes that "daz bild muost von gold sîn" [line 24610; the image should be of gold] and the return of the statue to its basic material form through the drunken man's attack results in changing his life from one of poverty to one of wealth, thus emphasizing the monetary value of the statue. Positioned between these two traditional statues, the inanimate wife must be seen as a symbolic statue. As in the first story, there is a blurring of the line between animate and inanimate, though with the significant difference that everyone in the story *knows* the woman is alive and animate but, following their own best interest and their instinct for survival, choose to *treat* her as if she were inanimate. Her existence as statue will provide the people with life-changing circumstances, they will go from dire straits to a comfortable existence again. Such a critical shift in fortune is echoed in the last tale's change of status of the drunken man.

By narrating his selection of Virgilian tales in this sequence, Jans der Enikel ensures that statues are never far from the reader's imagination. This continued presence of statues is significant as it provides a subtle reminder of the importance of statues to pagans: the adoration of statues, for example, was a simple and quick way to contrast the misguided pagans with the enlightened Christians.

4 Depicting Metamorphosis

It has already been observed that "Virgil's Revenge" is not as well represented in visual forms as "Virgil and the Basket". In his 1902 study of the iconography of Virgil as a magician, M. Eugène Müntz even limits his re-telling of the revenge episode, avoiding the base corporeal details of the woman's fate, and "hasten[s] to add that the scene was rarely depicted."[35] Nonetheless, the scene is illustrated in select German world chronicle manuscripts.[36] Jörn-Uwe Günther, in his iconographic charts

---

[35] The full quotation reads: "Mais la comédie a un second acte et des plus scabreux, tel qu'il est difficile de le raconter ici. Qu'il nous suffise de dire que Virgile, délivré enfin, tira une vengeance terrible de la fille de l'Empereur. Il éteignit d'un coup tous les feux de Rome et décida qu'ils ne pourraient être rallumés que si chaque Romain approchait un tison de la personne de la princesse. J'ai hâte d'ajouter que cette scène a été rarement représentée." [But the comedy has a second act, one of the most shocking, one so shocking that it is difficult to recount here. Suffice it to say that Virgil, finally released, exacted terrible vengeance on the daughter of the emperor. He extinguished with one stroke all the fires in Rome and determined that they could be lit anew only once each Roman approached the person of the princess with a glowing coal. I hasten to add that this scene was rarely depicted.] Müntz 1902, 85.
[36] For comparative work on the pictorial material in the manuscripts, Günther 1993 is the best place to start. Günther lists 56 illustrated manuscripts and fragments of rhymed Middle High German world chronicles.

for illustrated manuscripts of Middle High German world chronicles in verse, lists five manuscripts with illustrations for the revenge episode; one in particular evokes a statue in the viewer's imagination.[37] This manuscript, now housed in the Herzog August Bibliothek in Wolfenbüttel (cod. Guelf. 1.5.2. Aug. 2°), is a world chronicle compilation that includes the Virgilian tales from Jans der Enikel.[38] For this Bavarian manuscript, Günther notes that some illustrations were produced already in the late fourteenth century, while others not until the second half of the fifteenth; these latter include four that depict the Virgilian episodes.[39] The last of these four shows the revenge scene in a framed miniature that extends over the width of two thirds of the page (Figure 8.1). In the center of the picture the viewer is faced with the exposed behind of the woman, who leans over as if into the picture. Very clearly she is standing on a stone pedestal. In accordance with the textual description, the woman is not completely naked: her back is covered by a simple blue garment; her head is covered by a turban. Kneeling in the foreground of the picture and extending some sort of flammable object (a twig or a bundle of twigs) into the woman's behind, from which small flames can be seen to be emerging, the first of seven people is seen. Following the description in the text very closely and unlike the other four illustrations of this scene, the Wolfenbüttel manuscript artist has drawn men and women, the scene clearly depicts a *public* humiliation.[40]

Lastly, and again unique to this illustration, the artist has included the city in the background, but connects it to the woman and her public through a bridge that joins the grassy landscape where the woman stands with an open gate of the city. The urban setting of the picture reinforces that the woman is made to act for the salvation of all of Rome.

To depict a statue in a painting raises peculiar challenges, most notably how to distinguish a statue from a living person in a medium that is entirely static. To depict

---

37 NB: Günther's iconographic charts only include the manuscripts which have more than twenty illustrations in total.
38 See below, n40, for the other four manuscripts.
39 The Virgilian episodes depicted are: Virgil breaking glass with devils (142ra), Virgil in the basket (142va), Virgil mocked by Romans (142vb), the revenge (143vab).
40 The other four miniatures that I have seen for this iconography show from one to three people of one sex. (Regensburg, Fürstl. Thurn und Taxissche Hofbibliothek, Ms. Perg. III, fol. 137ra, shows three women; Vienna, Österreichische Nationalbibliothek, cod. 2921, fol. 243r, shows half of one man (?) emerging from the miniature frame; Heidelberg, Universitätsbibliothek, cpg 336, fol. 233r, shows three men; Munich, Bayerische Staatsbibliothek, cgm 250, fol. 258v shows two figures, very probably both men. The Regensburg illustration is reproduced in Mierke, pl. 7; the Heidelberg one is available online http://digi.ub.uni-heidelberg.de/diglit/cpg336/0479?sid=be5dae6da28 f99a5e44f8000c0cc2e7f (Accessed December 18, 2020), as is the Munich one http://daten.digitale-sammlungen.de/~db/0004/bsb00048175/images/index.html?id=00048175&groesser=&fip= xsxdsydxsyztsxdsydfsdreayaxdsyd&no=13&seite=436 (Accessed December 18, 2020). I thank the Hill Monastic Manuscript Library for scans of their microfilm of the Vienna manuscript.

8 A Fate Worse than Death? Virgil's "steinîn wîp" in Jans der Enikel's *Weltchronik* — 193

Figure 8.1: "Virgil's Revenge" Jans der Enikel, Weltchronik, Herzog August Bibliothek, Wolfenbüttel: Cod. Guelf. 1.5.2 Aug. 2°, fol. 143v.
Photo: Herzog August Library, Wolfenbüttel

a living person who is being treated *as* a statue yet is still animate would appear to be an impossibility. Yet the artist here, I posit, subtly suggests that the woman is a statue, most particularly in the use of a similar neutral shade for both the exposed woman's legs and the pedestal. By thus decreasing the visual distinction between human flesh and inanimate stone, the artist hints at a merging of human with stone, while at the same time, through the figure's white turban and the strong blue shift ("hemd"), reminding the viewer of the human nature of his creation. That the artist uses the same neutral color for the buildings of the city strengthens the association of stone with human, too.

In a roughly contemporary copper engraving, the artist goes even further and makes the identification of the woman as statue explicit. The engraving is attributed to the Italian Baccio Baldini and dated to 1460/63.[41] It shows an elaborate scene set in Rome, a civic identification made by the inclusion of both the colosseum and the arch of Constantine. Crowded with people, the left portion of the engraving shows Virgil, dressed in contemporary clothing, suspended in the basket, while on the right,

---

41 The engraving is reproduced in Koch 1959, 110, illustration 6. The attribution to Baldini is cited by Koch, who follows John Goldsmith Philipps. Koch 1959, 118n11. On Baldo Baldini, see Whitaker 2003. The engraving is also visible at: https://collections.artsmia.org/art/44010/virgil-the-sorcerer-baccio-baldini (Accessed December 18, 2020).

we see his revenge. A naked female figure is shown standing on two feet and directly facing a large crowd. She stands on an exceptionally elaborate pedestal, while the crowd below raise poles towards her genitals; farther away, some poles are already lit and burning. Her hands folded at her breast, as if she were at prayer, this figure clearly evokes a pagan idol. That the artist has placed her close to the reliefs in the arch of Constantine solidifies her identity as a statue, not a living woman.

The engraving is produced in Italy and the visual emphasis given architecture and sculpture in the picture reflects the renaissance love of the monuments of antiquity as well as its engagement with the medieval tradition of Virgil as unlucky lover and vicious avenger. Those two contemporary interests come together in the depiction of the woman as statue, thus concretizing an image that Jans der Enikel had described in his *Weltchronik* over one hundred and fifty years earlier. This should not be viewed as an act of direct translation of text into picture – such an oversimplification belies the rich and complex relationships between word and image in the Middle Ages and Renaissance. But it does draw the reader and viewer's attention to the different modes of verbal and non-verbal communication, the tools – be they words or chisels – and materials – be they ink, stone, or human body – required for each.

This tale of Virgil's revenge narrates an impossible situation for a married woman and ends with a fate for her which is worse than death. The wife's agency, which she first exercises by rejecting Virgil and then by enlisting her husband's aid, is ultimately removed from her first by Virgil and then, more disturbingly, by her husband. The very acts of protecting her virtue, of saying no, of *not* acting in an adulterous manner – all of which should make her appealing to men as we saw in the mother's words to her daughter in *Die Winsbeckin* – lead to her loss of status, her loss of agency, and her degradation to an object.

In seeking to understand the ideological import of this tale, two details bear consideration: first, the husband's attempts to protect his wife falter once the pagan Virgil has harnessed his powers of magic. Surprisingly, Virgil had not used his magic in his seduction attempts; only after he had been publically shamed did he turn to the supernatural. The husband and wife were successful in their initial response to Virgil's unwanted advances: as long as Virgil behaved in the manner of an ordinary – albeit annoying – human, wife and husband communicate and succeed. It is the introduction of magic, an introduction which underscores Virgil's identity as pagan that alters the trajectory of the story. Viewed this way, the tale posits that the insurmountable danger in married life is not the potential infidelity of married women accosted by admirers, nor even a lack of communication and support between spouses: the true danger is pagans and their magic.[42]

---

[42] The pagans are, of course, representative of the devil, though my point here is more that the pagans are not Christian and therefore practitioners of magic, not religion. Of course, such magic must come from the devil (which it does for Virgil in the initial tale of the seventy-two devils).

The second detail to recall is that the husband turns against his wife after the involvement of "mâge" [line 24105; relatives]. The point is not to suggest that his switch of allegiance is justified, but rather that it takes the community's pressure for the husband to cease protecting his wife and to enact her petrification. The community was always present – it saw Virgil hanging from the basket, it had been suffering Virgil's vengeance – but now it becomes active and its action emphasizes that what began as a situation among wife, husband, and Virgil, and thus was a private one, albeit one that had been open to their voyeuristic pleasure, has become public. Now it is a matter of life and death for the entire city. It is ultimately the relatives' questions that compel the husband to act:

> Dô daz[43] erhôrten ir mâge
> dô heten si manig frage.
> Ouch sach ez zehant ir man,
> Daz ez niht anders moht ergân.
> (lines 24105–08)
>
> [When her relatives heard this / then they had many questions. / Her husband also saw immediately / that it would not work in any other way.]

The community is under the spell of the pagan Virgil who has removed all fire, but more sinister is that they view Virgil as the one who can save them: they turn to him as a man who will be able and willing to help them.[44] The pagan and his magic have succeeded in utterly duping the community which then pressures the husband to break his allegiance with his wife and to participate in de-humanizing her. The ability to destroy the husband's will to protect his wife is rooted in pagan magic and required the force of the community behind it. The one on whom pagan magic appears to have no effect is the wife: she, too, must be suffering from the general absence of fire, but she would rather die than concede to Virgil's plan. She alone is immune to Virgil's charms.

The plot ends with the petrification of the woman, with her reduction to an inanimate, statuesque state, despite – or rather because – she was "stæte" [constant]. The tale hereby offers the unpalatable conclusions that a woman should maintain her virtue even in the face of drastic consequences and that as an object – in this case as a conduit of fire – a woman can serve a salvific function. In addition, the tale suggests that marriage does not offer safety or stability for a woman, nor even much agency. Yet the tale also suggests that the woman provides Virgil with a real obstacle: she does not submit to his advances and she is transformed by him only through the help of her husband and the community. When faced by the woman alone, Virgil is in fact powerless; he admits as much when he asserts that others will have to force the

---

43 [Virgil's assertion that the wife will have to be forced to obey if the citizens want happiness.]
44 lines 23978–83.

woman to concede to his plan. The clear identification of Virgil as pagan – through the descriptive words introducing him, through his magic powers of diabolical origin, and through his consistent association with statues and statue-making – mark him as fundamentally evil in the eyes of Jans der Enikel's medieval Christian audience. That the woman does not capitulate to him of her own accord and that he is dependent upon others for the execution of his vengeance casts the woman as an exceptionally and uniquely powerful figure. She withstands the pagan; she remains "stæte."

Works Cited

Benecke, Georg Friedrich, Wilhelm Müller, and Friedrich Zarncke. *Mittelhochdeutsches Wörterbuch*. 3 vols. Leipzig: 1854–66. http://www.woerterbuchnetz.de/BMZ (Accessed December 18, 2020).

Bennewitz, Ingrid. "Lukretia, oder: Über die literarischen Projektionen von der Macht der Männer und der Ohnmacht der Frauen. Darstellung und Bewertung von Vergewaltigung in der 'Kaiserchronik' und im 'Ritter vom Thurn'." In *Der frauwen buoch. Versuche zu einer feministischen Mediävistik*, edited by Ingrid Bennewitz, 113–34. Göppingen: Kümmerle, 1989.

Comparetti, Domenico. *Vergil in the Middle Ages*. Translated by E.F.M. Benecke. London: George Allen & Unwin, Ltd., 1966.

Das Nibelungenlied. Edited by Helmut de Boor, according to the edition by Karl Bartsch, 22nd edition, revised and expanded by Roswitha Wisniewski. Mannheim: Brockhaus, 1988.

Dunphy, Graeme. *History as Literature: German World Chronicles of the Thirteenth Century in Verse*. Kalamazoo, MI: Medieval Institute Publications, 2003.

Dunphy, Graeme. "Jans [der] Enikel (Jans the Grandson)." In *The Encyclopedia of the Medieval Chronicle*, edited by Graeme Dunphy, 2: 905. Leiden: Koninklijke Brill NV, 2010.

Dunphy, Graeme, and Angus Graham. *Jansen Enikels Weltchronik*. http://www.dunphy.de/ac/je/je home.htm (Accessed December 18, 2020). Edited by Philipp Strauch, Hannover and Leipzig: 1891–1900. Reprinted Munich: 1980.

Gärtner, Kurt. "Überlieferungstypen mittelhochdeutscher Weltchroniken." In *Geschichtsbewußtsein in der deutschen Literatur des Mittelalters: Tübinger Colloquium 1983*, edited by Christoph Gerhardt, Nigel F. Palmer, and Burghart Wachinger, 110–18. Tübingen: Niemeyer, 1985.

Geith, Karl-Ernst. "Enikel, Jans." In *Die deutsche Literatur des Mittelalters: Verfasserlexikon*, 2nd ed., edited by Kurt Ruh and Wolfgang Stammler, 2: 565–69. Berlin: De Gruyter, 1980.

Günther, Jörn-Uwe. *Die illustrierten mittelhochdeutschen Weltchronikhandschriften in Versen: Katalog der Handschriften und Einordnung der Illustrationen in die Bildüberlieferung*. Munich: tuduv, 1993.

Jans der Enikel. *Jansen Enikels Weltchronik*. Edited by Philipp Strauch. Hannover & Leipzig: Hahn'sche Buchhandlung, 1891–1900.

Klein, Dorothea. "Rudolf von Ems." In *The Encyclopedia of the Medieval Chronicle*, edited by Graeme Dunphy, 2: 1307–9. Leiden: Koninklijke Brill NV, 2010.

Koch, Georg Friedrich. "Virgil im Korbe." In *Festschrift für Erich Meyer zum 60. Geburtstag, 29. Oktober 1957: Studien zu Werken in den Sammlungen des Museums für Kunst und Gewerbe Hamburg*, edited by Werner Gramberg et al., 105–121. Hamburg: Hauswedell, 1959.

Mierke, Gesine. *Riskante Ordnungen: von der Kaiserchronik zu Jans von Wien*. Berlin: De Gruyter, 2014.

Mierke, Gesine. "Transformationen Vergils in der spätmittelalterlichen Literatur: Sangspruchdichtung und Ablassverzeichnisse." *Daphnis* 44 (2016): 425–63.

Müntz, M. Eugène. "La Légende du Sorcier Virgile dans l'Art des XIVe, XVe, et XVIe siècles." *Monatsberichte über Kunst und Kunstwissenschaft* 2 (1902): 85–91.

Ott, Norbert. "Christerre-Chronik." In *Die deutsche Literatur des Mittelalters: Verfasserlexikon*, 2nd ed., edited by Kurt Ruh and Wolfgang Stammler, 1: 1213–17, 11: 317. Berlin: De Gruyter, 1977 and 2004.

Petzoldt, Leander. "Virgilius Magus. Der Zauberer Virgil in der literarischen Tradition des Mittelalters." In *Hören, Sagen, Lesen, Lernen: Bausteine zu einer Geschichte der kommunikativen Kultur. Festschrift für Rudolf Schenda zum 65. Geburtstag*, edited by Ursula Brunold-Bigler and Hermann Bausinger, 549–68. Bern/New York: Peter Lang, 1995.

Plate, Ralph. "Christherre-Chronik." In *The Encyclopedia of the Medieval Chronicle*, edited by Graeme Dunphy, 1: 270–72. Leiden: Koninklijke Brill NV, 2010.

Rasmussen, Ann Marie. *Mothers and Daughters in Medieval German Literature*. Syracuse, N.Y.: Syracuse University Press, 1997.

Roth, K. L. "Über den Zauberer Virgilius." *Germania* 4 (1859): 257–98.

Spargo, John Webster. *Virgil the Necromancer: Studies in Virgilian Legends*. Cambridge, MA: Harvard University Press, 1934.

Smith, Susan L. *The Power of Women. A topos in Medieval Art and Literature*. Philadelphia: University of Pennsylvania Press, 1995.

Walliczek, Wolfgang. "Rudolf von Ems." In *Die deutsche Literatur des Mittelalters: Verfasserlexikon*, 2nd ed., edited by Kurt Ruh and Wolfgang Stammler, 8: 322–45. Berlin: De Gruyter, 1992.

Whitaker, Lucy. "Baldini, Baccio." *Grove Art Online*. 2003. Oxford University Press.

Wolfram von Eschenbach. *Parzival*. Edited by Gottfried Weber. Darmstadt: Wissenschaftliche Buchgesellschaft, 1967.

Worstbrock, Franz J. "Vergil." In *Die deutsche Literatur des Mittelalters: Verfasserlexikon*, 2nd ed., edited by Kurt Ruh and Wolfgang Stammler, 10: 247–84. Berlin: De Gruyter, 2001.

Ziolkowski, Jan C., and Michael C. J. Putnam, eds. *The Virgilian Tradition. The First Fifteen Hundred Years*. New Haven, CT: Yale University Press, 2008.

Ziolkowski, Jan C. "Legends." In *The Virgil Encyclopedia*, edited by Richard F. Thomas and Jan M. Ziolkowski, 2: 737–40. Chichester, West Sussex: Wiley Blackwell, 2014.

Jutta Eming
9 Love and Disgust: Ambiguous Genres and Ambivalent Feelings in *Herzmäre*

The medieval genre of *Schwankmären* [comic tales][1] is not usually classified together with love poetry of the Middle Ages. Although these tales deal with relationships between the sexes, love itself frequently remains in the background. As Ann Marie Rasmussen has so convincingly shown, it is especially the married couples in these stories who are preoccupied with humiliating, dominating, besting, and even destroying one another.[2] Although it was not uncommon for such tales to include some form of edifying moral – especially as the genre was first developing – Christian teachings were given little prominence in the narratives. Scandalous portrayals of religious figures often featured deceiving clerics who were lascivious and corrupt, while their female counterparts were characterized as promiscuous and oversexed.

With regard to religious interpretations of reality, sacred practices, and logic, Christian teaching did indeed play a role in the power struggle between the sexes. However, it developed into a form that was often breathtakingly funny and ribald, using its own unique logic to manipulate elements of the Christian faith. A good example is the story of the tradesman. After a year of traveling, the merchant returns home to find his wife with a newborn child. She would have him believe that during the previous winter, while she was sitting in the garden – thinking of him – two snowflakes made their way into her open mouth and caused something akin to an immaculate conception. It was a Mary-like miracle which yielded a "Snow Child" (the usual title of the story). Who would dare question such a miracle? Certainly not the husband, who is held helplessly in check by this explanation, and is forced to put a good face on a contemptible situation. The child grows up, is educated, and finally goes on his first business trip with the father. When the tradesman returns home alone, he must answer to the wife about their son's whereabouts. He explains

---

[1] German scholarship differentiates between *Mären* (short rhymed couplet tales written in German) and *Fabliaux* (their French precursors). Anglo-American research tends to use 'Fabliaux.' According to Sebastian Coxon, one may generalize: "In contrast with several other types of medieval short narrative that have proved tremendously difficult to define, the comic tale, whether it be in German, French, English or Italian, is quite distinctive. These stories revolve around tricks and deception often in an overtly sexual context, most commonly pitching the clever against the stupid to reveal the hilarious and shocking extent of human folly" (Coxon 2002, 21n6). Because aspects of the form play a role in relationships to other genres, I will be using the German term.
[2] See especially Rasmussen 2005.

Translated by Bill C. Ray

that crashing waves during their sea voyage melted away their Snow Child. In reality, he had actually sold the boy.[3]

At this juncture, further questions about the parents' feelings are of little consequence. The husband has clearly reciprocated; his act of revenge was successful; and there is little left to tell. In past examinations of this tale, some have wished to further analyze the story with questions about the fate of the child. Klaus Grubmüller dismisses such efforts as follows:

> This story is not meant to be a portrait of society. Instead, it has the structure of a callous joke, and is cruel as only this kind of humor can be.[4] It is confined to a narrow but intense view of the characters' actions and reactions. There is even a certain charm to the total lack of regard for normal concerns, for example, human sympathy.[5]

In other words, it is exactly the cold-bloodedness, and the ironclad resolve with which the man vengefully sells the child which provides the surprise ending and an enjoyable shock for the reader. This corresponds to Freud's theory – often cited in research on the *Schwankmären* – that jokes are the gateway to aggression.[6] There are many other examples of this sort of merciless drive to extract revenge and do damage to others.[7]

1 Climax Structure and Body Fragmentation in *Schwankmären*

While *Mären* [short rhymed couplet tales] are generally structured similarly to medieval short stories, a *Schwank* does not actually belong to a specific genre. Instead, it constitutes a form of storytelling, which can be adapted to a number of different genres. According to Erich Straßner, they employ a brand of humor with very specific qualities, including: ridiculing the less fortunate, obscenity, touching on taboos, a

---

[3] Grubmüller 1996a, 82–93. Grubmüller's edition and translation contains both versions of the story. This represents the ending of the earlier version (A) of the story, which is transmitted in several different manuscripts. According to another version (B), which is known only from the fifteenth century's *Donaueschinger Liederhandschrift*, the Snow Child melted in the heat of the brutal Egyptian sun.
[4] For a recent discussion of ways to differentiate medieval comical narratives, see Velten 2014.
[5] "Sie ist kein Gesellschaftsgemälde, sie hat die Struktur des Witzes und ist grausam wie dieser nur je, weil sie den Blick in aller einseitigen Prägnanz nur auf Handlung und Gegenhandlung richtet und vielleicht sogar noch einen gewissen Reiz aus der Vernachlässigung aller Umstände (z.B. menschlichen Mitgefühls) bezieht" (Grubmüller 1996b, 345).
[6] See Grubmüller 1996a, and also isolated in Grubmüller 2006; Röcke 1987; and Freud's classic study, Freud 1978a.
[7] For example, from the collection of fifteenth century *Mären* by der Stricker, *Der begrabene Ehemann* and especially Heinrich Kaufringer's *Die Rache des Ehemanns*, both in Grubmüller 1996a, 30–43 and 738–67 respectively.

tendency toward conflict, treating serious subjects profanely, and exaggerating reality (Straßner 1978, 4–5). Formal attributes include the use of a punch line or climax (which usually involves getting the better of an opponent), the concentration on a single story line, and the use of a few important images within the story and dialogue (Straßner 1978, 6–7).

Since Hanns Fischer's fundamental studies, it has become accepted that German *Mären* constitute a specific genre.[8] According to Fischer, about 80% of these are *Schwankmären*. In addition to the above-mentioned characteristics, they can also be recognized by their comic qualities and a plot line which finds the "tumben" [seemingly slow-witted character] somehow winning out over the "wîsen" [seemingly intelligent character] through some clever trick. Ultimately, it varies as to whether one turns out to be the clever one or the dupe. The inevitable punch line is usually about turning the tables – with a seemingly weaker character taking advantage of an apparently stronger one. It is this upheaval of the normal hierarchy which gives the tale its surprise effect. The wife wins out over the husband, the knave takes advantage of his master, or the farmer fools the priest. Such a twist might be clear at the start of the tale, or the reversal can happen during the course of the story, as in the story of the Snow Child (*Schneekind*).[9] *Schwankmären* employ humor to relate a variety of transgressions, whether social, class-oriented, sexual, or dealing with gender hierarchy. How to evaluate these gender issues is the subject of much ongoing debate. Research tends to stress the potential for subversion in these stories, especially when it comes to reordering gender hierarchy. Others insist that violent and obscene speech as well as contrary behavior is meant to didactically reinforce and support gender roles.[10] These two opposing positions have hardened over time. Even in the case of the *Priapeia*, a subgroup of ribald, anarchic tales, which emphasize the vulnerabilities of the sexes, there is still no agreement. This special class of farcical tale often features male or female genitalia as the central focus of the story – whether attached or detached from their hosts. For example, in the late medieval tale of the *Nonnenturnier*, convent nuns hold a tournament featuring an oversized phallus as the prize. Some believe that the importance placed on the male genitalia clearly reaffirms the cultural power of traditional patriarchal hierarchy.[11]

---

[8] Grubmüller 2006, 90. A discussion about the *Märe* as genre per se is beyond the scope of this essay. I will only broach the subject when the topic of genre is directly related to the specific *Märe* under discussion.
[9] Nina Nowakowski has conducted an exemplary analysis of the narrative versatility of *Schwankmären* with regard to revenge and retribution (2014).
[10] Cf., additionally, the differentiating discussion in Schallenberg 2012.
[11] This, however, has rightly been put into question by Rasmussen 2009: "This is the paradox: the penis's presence in the convent is so hyper-masculine that it sets off chaos, but on the other hand its way of being in the world is [. . .] instrumentalized" (14). See also Rasmussen's analysis of fragmented genitalia on medieval badges (Rasmussen 2017).

The fragmentation of bodies and the isolation and emancipation of its parts is a theme that extends well beyond the *Priapeia*. Characterizations of independent body parts – whether genitalia, teeth, or an exposed belly – appear in a large number of tales. They support the ever-present connections between sexuality, power, and violence (Grubmüller 2006, 201–12), and are reminiscent of such historical cultural patterns as the dismembered body parts displayed in religious reliquaries. Not least, they hold a special position as power-objects in storytelling (See, especially, Bloch 1986; Klinger 2001, 221–26; and Kiening 2008).

A body part is also at the center of the next text under discussion in this essay. It is again the story of a husband's revenge, but would not be categorized as a *Schwankmäre*. Instead, *Herzmäre* by Konrad von Würzburg belongs to a very specific subgroup of *Mären*, the courtly tale of gallantry. In the following, I would like to examine and also question this conventional classification.

2 *Herzmäre* as Paradigm for the Courtly Tale of Gallantry

According to Fischer's accepted definition, a courtly tale of gallantry is not humorous, it stresses the themes of chivalry and love (similar to courtly romances), it is driven by sentimentality and it tends toward emotionality (Straßner 1978, 109). Fischer calculates that only about 15% of surviving *Mären* belong to this group, and according to Grubmüller, only *Herzmäre* actually fulfills Fischer's generic criteria (2006, 155–56).[12] He has also given *Herzmäre* a new classification, grouping it together with a series of thirteenth-century tales that deal in one way or another with the theme of passionate love (2006, 156–58). I will return to this aspect later.

In *Herzmäre*, which was presumably written sometime before 1260, a pair of lovers carry on a virtuous and chaste love affair, but are not actually married to each other. As in *Tristan*, the fact that the woman is married to another man does not inhibit the ardor felt between the two lovers. Indeed, Konrad von Würzburg openly admits to emulating the writing of Gottfried von Strassburg, and tries to recreate some of his concepts and style.

> Ein ritter unde ein frouwe guot
> diu hæten leben unde muot
> in einander sô verweben,
> daz beide ir muot unde ir leben
> ein dinc was worden alsô gar:
> swaz der frouwen arges war,

---

[12] This only applies to a purely formal view of verse length and range.

daz war ouch deme ritter;
dâ von ze jungest bitter
wart ir ende leider;
diu minne was ir beider
worden sô gewaltec,
daz si vil manicvaltec
mahte in herzesmerzen.
grôz smerze wart ir herzen
von der süezen minne kunt.[13]

[A knight and a fine lady / loved each other with body and soul, / and were so intertwined,/ that their thoughts and feelings became as one. / All the lady's adversities / troubled the knight as well, / For this reason / they chose a tragic end. / Their overwhelming love / brought endless heartache. / Knowing the sweetness of love / broke their hearts.]

The rhetorical phrasing which describes the lovers as joined together in unity is as much a reference to Gottfried as is the relationship between love and suffering. Similarly, the way in which the husband discovers the secret affair is clearly inspired by *Tristan*. At a certain point, he can no longer ignore the signs of love between the two and he decides to take action. His plan is to take his wife on a pilgrimage to Jerusalem with the hope that enough physical distance between the two will cause their love to fade away. When the knight hears of the plan, "der muotsieche man" [line 124; the tormented man] immediately decides to follow them, since he would not be able to endure the pain of separation for so long. The lady believes the plan would work better in reverse order, and she encourages the knight to voluntarily depart immediately in order to convince the husband that he had no special feelings for the wife, "sus wirt der zwîvel im benomen / den wider mich sîn herze treit" [line 164f; This will ease the doubt that he (the husband) has in his heart for me].

The knight reluctantly agrees "ûz trüebes herzen sinne," [with a heavy heart] and expresses the fear that he might perish from longing (line 195). Both lovers experience great pain ("marter," line 217) upon parting. As expected, the knight cannot endure the separation for long, and during the voyage to the Holy Land his emotional pain manifests itself as physical pain:

[. . .] wart sîn leit sô rehte starc
daz im der jâmer durch daz marc
dranc biz an der sêle grunt;
er wart viel tiefer sorgen wunt
und inneclicher swære.
         (lines 255–59)

---

13 Konrad von Würzburg, *Herzmäre*, in Grubmüller 1996a, 262. Hereafter citations to this text will appear parenthetically with line numbers. For critical remarks on Konrad's indebtedness to Gottfried based on manuscript evidence, see Jones 2017. All translations by Bill C. Ray, unless otherwise noted.

[He was so lovesick / that it pained him to the marrow / and reached to the bottom of his soul. / He was injured by great sorrow / and penetrating agony.]

Here, one must consider the context of the medieval concept of love, which was characterized as a violent external intervention. In the quote above, "sorgen" [sorrow] is depicted as a force, capable of physically gripping a person all the way to the marrow, reaching to the bottom of the soul, and permanently damaging it ("wunt" [wounded]). The concept is a tightly woven mix of mental and emotional pain, combined with the metaphoric and material integrity of the suffering person, which prepares the way for the unusual turn in the plot that the knight decides to take. When he realizes that he is about to die from his affliction, he calls for his page and gives the following instructions:

> swenne ich sî verdorben
> unde ich lige erstorben
> durch daz keiserlîche wîp,
> sô heiz mir snîden ûf den lîp
> und nim dar ûz mîn herze gar,
> bluotic unde riuwevar;
> daz soltu denne salben
> mit balsam allenthalben,
> durch daz ez lange frisch bestê.
> vernim waz ich dir sage mê:
> frum eine lade cleine
> von golde und von gesteine,
> dar în mîn tôtez herze tuo,
> und lege daz vingerlîn dar zuo
> daz mir gab diu frouwe mîn;
> sô diu zwei bî einander sîn
> verslozzen und versigelet,
> sô bring alsô verrigelet
> si beidiu mîner frouwen,
> durch daz si müge schouwen
> waz ich von ir habe erliten,
> und wie mîn herze sî versniten
> nâch ir vil süezen minne.
>   (lines 295–317)

[When I am dead / And lying there / because of this wonderful woman / cut me open and remove my heart, / sad and bloodied / then cover it in balm / to preserve it. / Now listen closely, / prepare a small box / made of gold and jewels, / lay my dead heart within, / along with the ring / that my lady gave to me. / When all is together, / closed and sealed, / then bring them safely / to my lady / so that she can see / how I suffered because of her, / and how my heart wasted away for her love.]

The knight has prepared a very unconventional gift for the lover he has left behind: his preserved heart should serve as both a sign of his love and the torment it caused him. The embalming of his heart and its storage in a bejeweled container bring to mind the context of reliquary cults and the concept of holy bodies, fragments of which are thought to work miracles, especially through contact (Angenendt 1997). The heart, given (literally) as a gift, takes a semantic swing between the religious and the profane, corresponding to the play on its metaphoric and material qualities. The metaphoric "giving of one's heart," or the "exchange of hearts" are found quite often in medieval literature and serve as effective substitutes for abstract terms.[14] In *Herzmäre*, the metaphoric concept is made concrete by the materiality of the physical broken heart, suggesting that upon receiving it, the lady will see the knight's desire and the pain of separation he suffered. This parting gesture by the knight is usually interpreted as an integral part of the main story, and not as a separate act unto itself. In fact, one can indeed see it as a spectacular twist to the main story – the climax. Nonetheless, there is also merit to a two-part interpretation and an attempt to analyze how the knight's gift fits with the tale's concept of love.

3 The Gift

To date, only a few scholars have found the embalmed heart worthy of comment. Florian Kragl has posed a series of questions (308–9), several of which I would like to quote:

> [. . .] why does the knight send his physical heart to his lover? In the customary communication of courtly love, sending a letter or note would usually suffice. Is he somehow signaling a wish for her death as well?[15]

It is difficult to argue whether or not the accepted rules of expression have been broken, especially since literary conventions of communication were constantly changing and developing. A more pertinent question would be: how appropriate is the gift relative to the rest of the story line. Does it provide balanced reciprocity or create imbalanced asymmetry?[16] For her part, the lady's parting gift to the knight was a ring:

> nu genc, vil lieber herre, her,
> enpfâch von mir diz vingerlîn:
> dâ bî soltû der swære mîn
> gedenken under stunden

---

[14] For a demonstration and further literary sources, see Linden 2007.
[15] "[. . .] weshalb lässt der Ritter sein körperliches Herz zu seiner Geliebten bringen? Selbst im Diskurshoriziont der Hohen Minne wäre hier ein Brief oder dergleichen wohl das adäquatere Mittel gewesen [. . .] Wünscht er ihr damit tatsächlich den Tod?" (Kragl 2008, 309). Kragl thoroughly examines the scholarly debate surrounding *Herzmäre*.
[16] Susanne Reichlin examines the variety of possible combinations for exchanges (2009).

> dâ mite ich bin gebunden,
> sô dich mîn ouge niht ensiht:
> wan zwâre swaz sô mir geschiht,
> ich muoz an dich gedenken,
> dîn vart diu kan mir senken
> jâmer in mîns herzen grunt.
> (lines 180–89)

[Now, come to me dear sir / and take this ring from me, / so that you are reminded of / my suffering from time to time / which binds me to you. / Truly, should I not see you again, / regardless of my fate, / I will think of you, / and the pain of your leaving will / sink to the bottom of my heart.]

The ring is a relatively conventional symbol for the inner bond between lovers, which in this case may well be a variation on the separation scene in *Tristan*. Isolde also gave her lover a ring as a parting gift. Not only does the lady in this story use the ring to symbolize her connection to the knight, it also signals her condition. She is without her lover, in pain, and held prisoner by thoughts of him. The unspoken message also suggests that she will not let herself be distracted from her plight; she will not forget him; and she will not permit any substitute happiness in her life (See also Eming 2008).

Might placing the ring together with the heart be a reciprocal gesture to indicate their bond, and how it will survive even after death? Claire Taylor Jones has argued in a recent article that the composite object is to be understood in the framework of contemporary relic culture. According to her reading, the ring "functions as an *authentic*, the document or seal that confirmed the identity of a relic and validated it for veneration" (Jones 2017, 306). However, this function is not included in the instructions given to his pages, in which he asserts that his lover will see and feel his pain:

> si hât sô reine sinne
> und alsô ganze triuwe
> daz ir mîn jâmer niuwe
> lît iemer an ir herzen,
> bevindet si den smerzen
> den ich durch si lîden sol.
> dar umbe tuo sô rehte wol
> unde erfülle mîn gebot.
> (lines 318–25)

[She is so pure in her thoughts / And so perfectly devoted / That she will hold my recent pain / forever in her heart / When she sees the pain / That I had to suffer because of her. / For this reason, kindly / fulfill my wish.]

It apparently never occurs to the knight to release his lover from her commitment to him upon his death, or to send her some sort of liberating note to this effect. Quite the opposite, even when deceased, he intends to force his presence upon her life and ensure further pain. Whether intentional or not, this is reminiscent of the asymmetry in the parting of the lovers in Gottfried's *Tristan* – taking into account the reversed gender of the characters. In his farewell monologue, Tristan expresses the belief that – to a certain degree – it is possible to hold the absent (former) lover in one's thoughts, even if the separation or break is forever. Isolde, on the other hand, insists that the bond between them is impossible to break, and as a symbolic gesture, she gives Tristan a ring (Eming 2008).

In the relationship between the knight and the lady, it is clear that he explicitly does not wish her an untimely death. On the contrary, he says:

> der reine und der vil süeze got,
> der kein edel herze nie
> mit der helfe sîn verlie,
> der ruoche sich erbarmen
> über mich vil armen,
> und müeze der vil lieben geben,
> fröud unde ein wünneclichez leben,
> von der ich hie muoz ligen tôt.
> (lines 326–33)

[The perfect and loving God, / who has never forsaken / the pure of heart, / should show his mercy / to poor me, / and grant my most beloved one / joy and a happy life / for which I go to my death.]

The express wish that his lady should live a long and happy life is part of a fairly conventional *ars moriendi* practice. However, one wonders how this squares with the knight's earlier wish for her to feel the pain of his loss upon seeing his lifeless heart. The rest of the story gives no actual indication that the embalmed heart was meant to urge the lady to follow him into death. Nonetheless, it was clearly intended to maintain her unhappiness after the knight's passing, despite his poetic plea to God on her behalf. Structurally, the gift was a unilateral act of aggression with no chance for reciprocity. With regard to content, the direct, unwavering message given is that the lady is required to suffer because of her lover's death. This form of aggression is apparently not associated with Freud's definition of the kind of comic aggression found in jokes. One can nonetheless assess the incident from a psychoanalytic viewpoint.[17]

---

[17] In a recent essay, Christiane Ackermann has characterized psychoanalytical approaches to interpreting literary protagonists and their emotions as 'problematic.' Without explaining exactly what the problem might be, she insists that literary heroes should not be treated as 'real persons.' Ackermann 2007, 10. I would argue instead that the figures in medieval literature are invested with exemplary emotions, which are not meant to individualize a character. Especially in a highly stylized genre such as the *Märe*, descriptions of conflicts, practices, actions, and emotions are not in accordance with those of real persons. At the same time, however, they are clearly related to them – or they would not be comprehensible. Psychoanalytical literary criticism, among other things, aims at

The knight did indeed make a significantly aggressive gesture to the lady – the literal giving of his heart – insisting that his desire be acknowledged at exactly the ultimate moment of futility – his death.[18]

But the story is far from over.

4 The Meal

The tale continues with a description of how the knight's page removes and prepares the heart according to his master's wishes, and then brings it back to his homeland for presentation to the lady. There, the gift is intercepted by the lady's husband, who immediately understands its significance. He gives the heart to his cook, and has it prepared as a meal for his unsuspecting wife. While unknowingly consuming her lover's heart, the lady even comments on how she has never eaten anything so sweet in her life. In complete control of the situation, the husband takes his full revenge and delivers the "punch line": "du hâst des ritters herze gâz / daz er in sîme lîbe truoc" [lines 466–67; You have eaten the knight's heart / that he had carried in his body]. He then witnesses her reaction:

> Von disem leiden mære
> wart diu sældenbære
> als ein tôtez wîp gestalt,
> ir wart in deme lîbe kalt
> daz herze, daz geloubent mir.
> ir blanken hende enphielen ir
> beide für sich in die schôz,
> daz bluot ir ûz dem munde dôz,
> als ir diu wâre schult gebôt.[19]
> "jâ", sprach si dô mit maneger nôt,
> "hân ich sîn herze denne gâz
> der mir hât ân underlâz

---

explanations for seemingly contradictory emotional patterns and behavior, such as: humor and aggression, violence and love, anger and shame. In examining such ambivalent qualities, it can "expose something of the 'sub-text,' which, like an unconscious wish, the work both conceals and reveals. It can attend, in other words, not only to what the text says, but how it *works*" (Eagleton 2003, 158). This is the heart of the matter. It makes no difference if the psychoanalytical framework is Freudian and rooted in a model of operations of the psyche, or Lacanian, and based on a model of operations of language.

18 See the corresponding Lacanian analysis of a scene in Heinrich von Kleist's *Michael Kohlhaas*, specifically of the final scene in which Kohlhaas triumphantly dines on the object most desired by his enemy, the prince, in the moment before his execution (Gallas 1981, 86–89).

19 Grubmüller comments on the frequency with which Konrad von Würzburg employs the formulation *wâre schulde* and translates it as "grausames Schicksal" [horrible fate] (Grubmüller 1996a, 1132; 289, line 485).

> von grunde ie holden muot getragen,
> sô wil ich iu benamen sagen,
> daz ich nâch dirre spîse hêr
> dekeiner trahte niemer mêr
> mich fürbaz wil genieten."
>
> (lines 477–93)

[From this terrible news / the otherwise happy lady / turned deathly pale, and / her heart truly froze in her breast. / Her white hands fell into her lap, / blood shot from her mouth, / a result of her penance. / "So," she said in her misery, / "if I have eaten the heart of the man / Who gave me unwavering love / from the depths of his soul, / Then I assure you, / After this noble repast / I will never take another bite.]

Her speech continues, elaborating on the extraordinary nature of her meal, and how her loyalty forbids all further consumption. She expires almost immediately after uttering these words, and suffers intense internal writhing in her struggle with death.

> sus wart ir nôt sô rehte starc
> daz si von herzenleide
> ir blanken hende beide
> mit grimme zuo einander vielt.
> daz herze ir in dem lîbe spielt
> von sender jâmerunge.
>
> (lines 516–21)

[Then her suffering was overwhelming / and in deepest pain, / twisting and pressing / her two white hands together, / her lovesick heart broke / from yearning and sorrow.]

In his tale, Konrad von Würzburg uses a familiar motif of world literature, which has been applied in a broad variety of ways. In general, this involves an adulterous pair being castigated by having one of the two (usually the woman) eat a body part of the other, either the heart or the genitalia. This is commonly viewed as the appropriate vengeance for the transgression (Cf. Grubmüller 1996a, 1124). In Konrad's version of the story, however, the theme of revenge is less obvious. Indeed, Ursula Schulze has interpreted the tale as featuring the transformation of revenge into an expression of love, since the heart is the center of affection (Cf. Schulze 1971). The use of language similar to Gottfried's lends support to this concept.[20] Before I spell out some reservations about this interpretation, however, I would like to turn to a discussion about *Schwänke* and novellas that, to some degree, revolves around *Herzmäre* and one of its French variations, and that will factor into my final points.

---

20 See, in support of Schulze's argument, Wachinger 1975, 71–76.

5 A Few Remarks Concerning the Discussion About *Märe* and Novellas

How does a novella differ from a *Schwankmäre*? They are both short stories with plot lines leading up to a "Höhepunkt" [climax] or "outrageous occurrence" (Goethe). Further, the structure of the climax itself is also comparable in both forms. However, the novella does not employ the same kind of entertaining and forceful dialog.[21]

In his influential book, the Romance studies scholar Hans-Jürgen Neuschäfer takes the position that Boccaccio's use of the novelistic style in the *Decameron* introduced a momentous change to the style used in short works of European literature. The earlier stories upon which Boccaccio's novellas are based were grounded in still earlier medieval (and even older) texts (*Fabliau, Exemplum, Stories from a Thousand and One Nights*, Saints' Lives and Miracle Tales, Lays). Subsequently, Neuschäfer emphasizes the special nature of Boccaccio's novellas by comparing each of them to their earlier source. In short, he concludes that the Renaissance novellas are more complex than their medieval predecessors. Further, he argues that, whereas the medieval stories tend to be simple and direct, Boccaccio's novellas are more ambivalent and open to interpretation (with regard to both the characters and the plots). Instead of generalized models, they relate unique and discrete examples. While the medieval texts reflect legitimate, general norms, the novella makes specific value references. The older texts stress rules and laws, while the newer texts stress the exceptions. Themes of divine guidance give way to coincidence and chance. Singular solutions are replaced by unsolvable problems and open endings. Finally, characters are no longer driven by fate, but are instead free and autonomous (Neuschäfer 1969).

Neuschäfer's assertions that Boccaccio's novellas constitute a literary sea change are based on his characterization of medieval stories as simplistic and one-dimensional. This assumption clearly had consequences beyond Romance literature, and not surprisingly, also ignited much discussion within German studies. Neuschäfer's comparison of the ninth novella of the fourth day to the medieval "Vida" by Guillem de Cabestaing is a good example, since the latter is essentially a French version of *Herzmäre*. Here, Neuschäfer finds clearly drawn contrasts among the main characters: "The lovers are portrayed as having only good qualities, while the jealous husband has only bad ones" (35).[22] It is thus, for him, an extreme example meant to illustrate the fateful nature of love.

According to Neuschäfer, Boccaccio's story is, by comparison, much more complex. For example, it turns out that the husband is initially good friends with his wife's lover: "The husband's nature was to be generally unsuspecting, which makes

---

21 See, in general, Aust 1995, and on the *Herzmäre*, Aust 1995, 58.
22 "die Liebenden haben nur gute, der eifersüchtige Ehemann nur schlechte Eigenschaften."

the adultery that much more troubling. And when he finally discovers the lovers, they must bear all the blame; getting caught was not so much an 'inevitability' as it was chance" (39).[23] The husband is ultimately a sympathetic character, despite his being fully aware of the "monstrous nature" of his revenge (40). There are also further important differences in Boccaccio's approach, Neuschäfer argues. First, in this version it is the husband who actually kills his wife's lover and cuts out his heart. Secondly, at the end, the wife leaps to her death from a window instead of dying from a broken heart. Finally, out of shame for what he has done, the husband leaves his homeland. According to Neuschäfer, Boccaccio has made the plot especially complex, so that each reader must make an effort to fully understand it (42): "[. . .] here it is [. . .] no longer about a *typical* case of maleficent jealousy, but a complicated, *unique* [. . .] entanglement with a variety of causes; whose horrific ending is the fault of no single person" (43).[24] Joachim Heinzle, a leading critic of Neuschäfer, finds that the examples of medieval texts used in the comparisons are not representative, and that attempting to contrast the Middle Ages and the Renaissance is a questionable undertaking (1979).[25] To explore this question further, I will return to the story.

6 Shock, Disgust, and Cannibalism

The exemplary nature of the relationship between the two lovers is a consistent element in a large majority of *Herzmäre* variations. At the same time, however, there is no doubt that the husband's drastic retaliation more closely follows the kind of storyline found in *Schwankmären*. Nevertheless, Christian Kiening has observed that it varies from this form in the way the climax of the story is constructed: the act of revenge sets up an opportunity for the lady and the knight to achieve a paradoxical form of union as each tragically goes to a lover's death (Kiening 2008, 188 and Bonnemann 2008, 65). The paradox lies in the switching of the heart's usual role from being a representative symbol to being a physical presence. At first, the

---

[23] "Der Ehemann ist hier also prinzipiell guten Glaubens, was den Ehebruch um so bedenklicher macht, und wenn er die Liebenden trotzdem entdeckt, so ist dies nur ihre eigene Schuld; auch die Entdeckung erscheint damit nicht mehr 'notwendig', sondern ist kontingent."
[24] "[. . .] hier handelt es sich [. . .] nicht mehr um einen *typischen* Fall von bösartiger Eifersucht, sondern um eine *einmalige*, komplizierte, auf mannigfachen Voraussetzungen beruhende [. . .] Verwicklung, deren häßlicher Ausgang nicht mehr einer Person allein zur Last gelegt werden kann" (emphasis in original).
[25] Jan-Dirk Müller continued the discussion (2004), which had been revisited by Heinzle (1992). See also Kasten 1999. Grubmüller (2006, 257–60) discusses the "Vida," *Herzmäre*, and Boccaccio's novella once again, and with a few modifications, comes to the same conclusion as Neuschäfer (1969). However, Grubmüller does question the judgment of Boccaccio's general narrative style as innovative (260–67).

heart is conceptualized as a relic that gives special powers to its host, who then has the ability to pass this power on to others, as is the case with relics from the bodies of saints. However, this transference model implodes at the point when the heart is no longer an object to be touched, but is instead incorporated (Kiening 2008, 188) – that is, eaten. Kiening's term "Einverleibung" (physical incorporation) refers to the act of cannibalism in which one person is eaten by another in part or entirely. The audience is clearly meant to see this as a barbaric aspect of the story. Less clear is to what degree this practice was intentionally being connected to the wider discourse about love, and further, how the concept of cannibalism should be understood within the context of desire.

Again, we can turn to psychoanalysis for possible answers to these questions. Cannibalism or introjection was considered by Freud to be part of an early stage of sexual organization during which associations exist between the desire for nourishment and sexual activity (1978b, 98). A fundamental ambivalence occurs when one identifies with an object that is consumed for the purpose of incorporation, but is also simultaneously destroyed by the same act (Freud 1978c, 116). As with all developmental phases in early childhood, vestiges of this wish for physical incorporation can have an influence on the love lives of adults. With this theory in mind, we return to the questions about the materiality of the heart in *Herzmäre* and to the reactions caused by its consumption.

Why does the lady turn pale when she finds out what she has eaten? Why does she suffer hemorrhaging? What does her extreme inner turmoil signify as she attempts to forcefully suppress its expression with the twisting and knotting of her hands? Might she even die from her imploding emotions? Beatrice Trînca points out that the gestures and emotions she shows create a broad circle of associations that switch back and forth between anger and helplessness (2014, 148–49). The text provides no specific answers to any of these questions. The wave of emotion is self-inflicted, reinforcing and compounding the aggressive treatment the lady has just experienced. It could also be that her reactions are simply caused by hearing of her lover's death and the awful realization that she has just eaten his heart. The fact that she then vomits up blood alludes to a common religious convention that holds blood to be a sign of truth.[26] Viewing this link in light of the earlier discussion about love and desire, we can say that such an extreme expression would certainly validate and authenticate the lady's love and passion. Nevertheless, this sort of physical expulsion – vomiting – is also a reminder of what she has just eaten. Therefore, in contrast to most past readings

---

[26] Recently, Silvan Wagner has put forth a bold, yet for me, not entirely plausible religious interpretation of the events in *Herzmäre*. It is based on the perspective of a God who has been constructed within courtly culture and transcends the suffering found in courtly love poetry (Wagner 2007; see also Wagner 2011).

of this moment, it seems plausible that the lady's extreme reactions are due to "horror" (Jones 2017, 288), revulsion, and disgust because of what she has consumed.[27]

Disgust is usually categorized as a basic human emotion, which shows itself primarily through facial expressions (Eckman and Friesen 1975). To capture the literary essence of this emotion in historical texts, however, is especially difficult. One approach might be to examine how disgust fits into complex historical concepts of beauty and ugliness, in short, through medieval aesthetics (Menninghaus and Schnell 2005, 70). Of particular interest is whether specific time periods had their own triggers for disgust, or if disgust has emotional characteristics that transcend all eras. If the latter is the case, it may be possible to better comprehend disgust, at least to some degree, with the help of psychoanalytic methods.[28]

As with all emotional reactions, it is possible to misinterpret and draw false conclusions about disgust, or that which appears to be disgusting, if viewed only through a modern lens. Caroline Walker Bynum's notable discussion of mysticism and mystical practices delves into the motives behind the consumption of body parts and fluids, and the especially important role this played for female mystics. In a religious context, such activities belong to asceticism, in which the intent is not to overcome disgust but rather to transform it.[29]

In the eating scene, the allusions to religious practices are meant entirely for the reading or listening audience.[30] The lady is completely unaware of what she is eating, and takes special enjoyment in such a delicious meal. Indeed, the enjoyment is completely dependent on her ignorance of what it is that she is eating. In this case, one might conclude that the transformation from disgust into enjoyment is set up to occur in reverse order: as the husband reveals his deceit, the intent is to subsequently shatter her pleasure and to cruelly convert it to horror. At the moment of realization, and afterwards while hemorrhaging, the sweet taste in the lady's mouth turns to disgust. Had she been informed of what was on her plate before

---

27 Scholars, most recently (again) Müller, have consistently denied that what happens here is about disgust. They find that she reacts this way because she has lost her beloved, because they love each other so intimately, because she is so faithful and true, because she does not want to live without him. Nowhere is it acknowledged, except marginally by Kragl, that she is the victim of an aggressive attack and that this is what is expressed in her reaction.
28 For more on this complex comparison, see, especially, Schnell 2005.
29 On Catherine of Siena: "Several of her biographers report that she twice forced herself to overcome nausea by thrusting her mouth onto the putrefying breast of a dying woman or by drinking pus, and the reports stress these incidents as turning points [. . .] She told Raymond: 'Never in my life have I tasted any food and drink sweeter or more exquisite [. . .]'" (Bynum 1987, 172). See also Wagner 2011, 312–13, regarding the conventional idea of the sweetness of the host, as mentioned in *Herzmäre* and the discussion in Schnell (2005, 425–27).
30 Kragl's thesis that the narrator projects a metaphoric meaning to the material heart through a sweet flavor, seems only somewhat convincing to me. Why shouldn't the heart be generally very flavorful? (326).

eating, she would have felt disgust from the beginning. In this case, too, the husband's revenge would have consisted in shocking his wife, thereby extracting delayed retribution for her having turned to another. And he probably would not have expected his actions to lead to a tragic "lover's death." But could that have been the knight's expectation? Again one wonders, why is the heart given such conspicuous prominence in the story?

As indicated earlier, the knight's gift to his lover can be interpreted as an act of aggression. To understand the heart's role, we need to see that the initial shift toward the organ's materiality is not with the husband's intervention, as Kiening would have it, but actually with the knight's decision to send the heart to his lover, as Kragl believes.[31] It is not only an expression of his love, but also a protestation of his anguish. Thus, the lady can very literally witness his suffering and somehow compensate him with her own grief. Does he also count on her being shocked by this macabre gift? Will she be dismayed? Will she feel regret? Whatever the case, he explicitly wishes for her to feel pain. And yet, despite all of the above, his intent is not for her to die, but to live, and live a long time.

Fundamentally, the structure and core theme of the tale lies with neither the love story nor the death of the central pair, but with the revenge of the husband.[32] The narrative logic of *Schwankmäre* is more prominent than the rhetoric of love or added layers of religious meaning.[33] Consistent with the husband in *Schneekind*, the husband in *Herzmäre* seizes the opportunity to take revenge on his wife without hesitation. However, his cold-bloodedness does not mean that his actions were particularly well thought out. While he certainly wants to shock his wife, he probably has no wish for her to die. With the escalation of tension, which is typical for the genre, the husband understands that the knight's gift to the lady is both an act of love and an act of aggression. His response is not to hinder the action but to enhance its effect and greatly amplify its shock value. That the lady should find her

---

31 In this respect, I disagree with Katharina Philipowski's view that metaphorical and material meanings are present throughout the story (2013).

32 Kragl mentions the perversion of the *Minne* content (316). He considers the story to be "odd" especially due to its "idealized escalation," which is fundamentally uncharacteristic of *Schwänke* (309).

33 Grubmüller's commentary cites the absence of a formal stringency and concludes, due to the primacy of thematic consistency: "[. . .] nicht eine konsequent inszenierte List-Handlung des Ehemannes treibt das Paar auseinander und in den Tod, sondern das Leid in der Welt und die immer schon vorweggenommene unauflösliche Bindung von Liebe und Schmerz" [Grubmüller 1996a, 1127; (. . .) it is not the usual setup in which the husband's trickery drives the pair apart. Instead, it is the suffering in the world and the ever present and irresolvable connection between love and pain]. However, the "fragility" (1126) of the tale is a result of the *Schwank* structure being combined with an elaborate love story. As argued above, traditionally, this aspect of the tale is an unconventional addition that is both misplaced and ultimately weakened by the motifs of aggression and revenge.

meal so "sweet" makes her discovery even more appalling, and her own feelings of guilt that much stronger. She is described as being consumed by a storm of emotional ambivalence and confusion: how could she possibly enjoy eating the flesh of her dead lover? From a psychoanalytical perspective, when a taboo forbids something we find desirable, then an association is formed between disgust and that which gives us pleasure.[34] The cannibalistic act and its revelation dramatize just this sort of emotional ambivalence. The idea that "love will somehow triumph" does not apply here. Instead, we have a patriarchal ranking of the sexes that makes it possible for one man to hijack the violent actions of another and expand on them. Targeted by both men, the woman ends up assaulted twice over.

Attempts to extract such a single, clear, gender-theoretical statement from *Herzmäre*, however, would fail as much as the traditional message of 'true love.' While there are various references to this theme in the story, they are open to interpretation, which leaves the overall message of the narrative ambivalent. There is ambiguity among the emotions of love, aggression, and disgust on many levels: in their manifest expressions, between text and cultural or psychological subtexts, and within the contours of the genres of courtly and comic tales. A more comprehensive analysis of such stories is possible when taking the following factors under consideration. How do courtly motifs and themes, along with a variety of characters, interact with the structure of the *Schwankmäre* and its many points of view and semantic allusions?[35] Compared to *Herzmäre*, Boccaccio's variation of this tale is significantly more coherent. He has turned the husband into a murderer whose aggression exceeds the knight's bloody gift-giving, and he interprets the wife's self-destruction as a willful act when she leaps to her death. This was not the only time, nor will it be the last, that the allusion-rich, multifaceted literary works of the High Middle Ages were abridged in the Late Middle Ages, the early modern age, and modernity.

Works Cited

Ackermann, Christiane. "Mediävistik und psychoanalytische Literaturtheorie (mit einer Annäherung an den 'Armen Heinrich' Hartmanns von Aue)." *Literaturwissenschaftliches Jahrbuch N.F.* 48 (2007): 9–44.
Angenendt, Arnold. *Heilige und Reliquien: Die Geschichte ihres Kultes vom frühen Christentum bis zur Gegenwart*. 2nd ed. Munich: C. H. Beck, 1997.
Aust, Hugo. *Novelle*. 2nd ed. Stuttgart: Metzler, 1995.
Bloch, Howard R. *The Scandal of the Fabliaux*. Chicago, IL: University of Chicago Press, 1986.
Bonnemann, Jens. *Die wirkungsästhetische Interaktion zwischen Text und Leser: Wolfgang Isers impliziter Leser im Herzmaere Konrads von Würzburg*. Frankfurt am Main: Peter Lang, 2008.

---

34 See also the discussion in Menninghaus and Schnell 2005, 420–25.
35 This is made especially clear in Schallenberg 2012.

Bynum, Caroline Walker. *Holy Feast and Holy Fast: The Religious Significance of Food to Medieval Women*. Berkeley: University of California Press, 1987.

Coxon, Sebastian. "'schrîber kunnen liste vil': Literate Protagonists and Literary Antics in the Medieval German Comic Tale." *Oxford German Studies* 31 (2002): 17–62.

Eagleton, Terry. *Literary Theory: An Introduction*. 2nd ed. Minneapolis: University of Minnesota Press, 2003.

Ekman, Paul and W. V. Friesen. *Unmasking the Face: A Guide to Recognizing Emotions from Facial Clues*. Englewood Cliffs, N.J.: Prentice-Hall, 1975.

Eming, Jutta. "Weiterlieben, weitererzählen. Der Abschiedsmonolog Isoldes und die Verwerfung der poetologischen Alternative." In *Der Tod der Nachtigall: Liebe als Reflexion von Kunst*, edited by Martin Baisch and Beatrice Trînca, 189–211. Göttingen: Vandenhoek & Ruprecht, 2008.

Freud, Sigmund. "Der Witz und seine Beziehung zum Unbewussten." In *Gesammelte Werke in achtzehn Bänden mit einem Nachtragsband*, 6th ed., edited by Anna Freud et. al, vol. 6. Frankfurt am Main: Fischer, 1978a.

Freud, Sigmund. "Drei Abhandlungen zur Sexualtheorie." In *Gesammelte Werke in achtzehn Bänden mit einem Nachtragsband*. 6th ed., edited by Anna Freud et. al. 5: 27–145. Frankfurt am Main: Fischer, 1978b.

Freud, Sigmund. *Massenpsychologie und Ich-Analyse*. In *Gesammelte Werke in achtzehn Bänden mit einem Nachtragsband*, 6th ed., edited by Anna Freud et. al. 13: 71–161. Frankfurt am Main: Fischer, 1978c.

Gallas, Helga. *Das Textbegehren des 'Michael Kohlhaas': Die Sprache des Unbewussten und der Sinn der Literatur*. Reinbek: Rowohlt, 1981.

Grubmüller, Klaus. "Der Tor und der Tod: Anmerkungen zur Gewalt in der Märendichtung." In *Spannungen und Konflikte menschlichen Zusammenlebens in der deutschen Literatur des Mittelalters. Bristoler Colloquium 1993*, edited by Kurt Gärtner, Ingrid Kasten, and Frank Shaw, 340–47. Tübingen: Niemeyer, 1996b.

Grubmüller, Klaus. *Die Ordnung, der Witz und das Chaos: Eine Geschichte der europäischen Novellistik im Mittelalter: Fabliau – Märe – Novelle*. Tübingen: Niemeyer, 2006.

Grubmüller, Klaus, ed. and trans. *Novellistik des Mittelalters: Märendichtung*. Frankfurt am Main: Deutscher Klassiker Verlag, 1996a.

Heinzle, Joachim. "Boccaccio und die Tradition der Novelle. Zur Strukturanalyse und Gattungsbestimmung kleinepischer Formen zwischen Mittelalter und Neuzeit," in *Wolfram-Studien* 5 (1979): 41–62.

Heinzle, Joachim. "Vom Mittelalter zur Neuzeit: Weiteres zum Thema Boccaccio und die Tradition der Novelle." In *Festschrift Walter Haug und Burghart Wachinger*, edited by Johannes Janota et al., 2: 661–70. Tübingen: Niemeyer, 1992.

Jones, Claire Taylor. "Relics and the Anxiety of Exposure in Konrad von Würzburg's *Herzmaere*." *Journal of English and Germanic Philology* 116, no. 3 (2017): 286–309.

Kasten, Ingrid. "Erzählen an einer Epochenschwelle: Boccaccio und die deutsche Novellistik im 15. Jahrhundert." In *Mittelalter und frühe Neuzeit: Übergänge, Umbrüche und Neuansätze*, edited by Walter Haug, 164–86. Tübingen: Niemeyer, 1999.

Kiening, Christian. "Verletzende Worte – verstümmelte Körper: Zur doppelten Logik spätmittelalterlicher Kurzerzählungen." *Zeitschrift für deutsche Philologie* 127 (2008): 321–35.

Klinger, Judith. "Aus der Haut gekritzelt: Zur sexuellen Poetik im 'Rädlein' Johannes von Freiberg." In *'Worüber man (noch) nicht reden kann, davon kann die Kunst ein Lied singen': Texte und Lektüren. Beiträge zur Kunst-, Literatur- und Sprachkritik*, edited by Hans-Christian Stillmark and Brigitte Krüger, 221–26. Berlin: Peter Lang, 2001.

Konrad von Würzburg. *Herzmäre*. In *Novellistik des Mittelalters: Märendichtung*, edited and translated by Klaus Grubmüller, 262–95. Frankfurt am Main: Deutscher Klassiker Verlag, 1996.

Kragl, Florian. "Wie man in Furten ertrinkt und warum Herzen süß schmecken." *Euphorion* 102 (2008): 289–330.

Linden, Sandra. "Körperkonzepte jenseits der Rationalität: Die Herzenstauschmetaphorik im *Iwein* Hartmanns von Aue." In *Körperkonzepte im arthurischen Roman*, edited by Friedrich Wolfzettel, 3–20. Tübingen: Niemeyer, 2007.

Menninghaus, Winfried and Rüdiger Schnell. "Die höfische Kultur des Mittelalters zwischen Ekel und Ästhetik." *Frühmittelalterliche Studien* 39 (2005): 1–100.

Müller, Jan-Dirk. "Formen literarischer Kommunikation im Übergang vom Mittelalter zur Neuzeit." In *Die Literatur im Übergang vom Mittelalter zur Neuzeit*, edited by Werner Röcke und Marina Münkler, 21–53. Munich: Hanser, 2004.

Neuschäfer, Hans-Jürgen. *Boccaccio und der Beginn der Novelle: Strukturen der Kurzerzählung auf der Schwelle zwischen Mittelalter und Neuzeit*. Munich: Fink, 1969.

Nowakowski, Nina. "Alternativen der Vergeltung: Rache, Revanche und die Logik des Wiedererzählens in schwankhaften mittelhochdeutschen Kurzerzählungen." In *Rache – Zorn – Neid: Zur Faszination negativer Emotionen in der Kultur und Literatur des Mittelalters*, edited by Martin Baisch, Evamaria Freienhofer, and Eva Lieberich, 74–100. Göttingen: Vandenhoeck & Ruprecht, 2014.

Philipowski, Katharina. *Die Gestalt des Unsichtbaren: Narrative Konzeptionen des Inneren in der höfischen Erzählliteratur*. Berlin: De Gruyter, 2013.

Rasmussen, Ann Marie. "Gender und Subjektivität im Märe *Die zwei Beichten* (A und B)." In *Inszenierungen von Subjektivität in der Literatur des Mittelalters*, edited by Martin Baisch, Jutta Eming, Hendrikje Haufe and Andrea Sieber, 271–87. Königstein/Taunus: Helmer, 2005.

Rasmussen, Ann Marie. *Wandering Genitalia: Sexuality & the Body in German Culture between the Late Middle Ages & Early Modernity*. King's College London Centre for Antique & Medieval Studies Occasional Publications, 2 (2009).

Rasmussen, Ann Marie. "*Badges*: Abzeichen als sprechende Objekte." In *Stimme und Performanz in der mittelalterlichen Literatur*, edited by Monika Unzeitig, Angela Schrott, and Nine Miedema, 469–87. Berlin: De Gruyter, 2017.

Reichlin, Susanne. *Mären, Ökonomien des Begehrens, Ökonomien des Erzählens: Zur poetologischen Dimension des Tauschens in Mären*. Göttingen: Vandenhoeck and Ruprecht, 2009.

Röcke, Werner. *Die Freude am Bösen: Studien zu einer Poetik des deutschen Schwankromans im Spätmittelalter*. Munich: Finck, 1987.

Schallenberg, Andrea. *Spiel mit Grenzen: Zur Geschlechterdifferenz in mittelhochdeutschen Verserzählungen*. Berlin: Akademie-Verlag, 2012.

Schnell, Rüdiger. "Ekel und Emotionsforschung: Mediävistische Überlegungen zur 'Aisthetik des Hässlichen'." *Deutsche Vierteljahrsschrift für Literatur- und Geistesgeschichte* 79 (2005): 359–432.

Schulze, Ursula. "Konrads von Würzburg novellistische Gestaltungskunst im 'Herzmære'." *Mediaevalia litteraria: Festschrift für Helmut de Boor*, edited by Ursula Hennig and Herbert Kolb, 451–84. Munich: C. H. Beck, 1971.

Straßner, Erich. *Schwank*. 2nd ed. Stuttgart: Metzler, 1978.

Trînca, Beatrice. "Der Zorn der Ohnmächtigen: Zum *Laüstic*, *Tristan* von Thomas und zum *Herzmaere*." In *Rache – Zorn – Neid: Zur Faszination negativer Emotionen in der Kultur und Literatur des Mittelalters*, edited by Martin Baisch, Evamaria Freienhofer and Eva Lieberich, 135–51. Göttingen: Vandenhoeck & Ruprecht, 2014.

Velten, Hans Rudolf. "Poetik des Lachens? – Zur gegenwärtigen Lach- und Komikforschung in der germanistischen Mediävistik." *Zeitschrift für deutsche Philologie* 133 (2014): 439–50.

Wachinger, Burghart. "Zur Rezeption Gottfrieds von Straßburg im 13. Jahrhundert." In *Deutsche Literatur des späten Mittelalters: Hamburger Colloquium 1973*, edited by Wolfgang Harms and Peter L. Johnson, 56–82. Berlin: Erich Schmidt, 1975.

Wagner, Silvan. *Gottesbilder in höfischen Mären des Hochmittelalters: Höfische Paradoxie und religiöse Kontingenzbewältigung durch die Grammatik des christlichen Glaubens*. Frankfurt am Main: Peter Lang, 2007.

Wagner, Silvan. "Sterben als Eintritt in höfisches Heil: Gott und der Tod in Mären des 13. Jahrhunderts (*Herzmaere, Der nackte Kaiser, Die eingemauerte Frau*)." In *Gott und Tod: Tod und Sterben in der höfischen Kultur des Mittelalters*, edited by Susanne Knaeble, Silvan Wagner and Viola Wittmann, 309–30. Berlin: LIT, 2011.

Index

Absalom 187
advice 7–8, 10, 27, 44, 79–80, 84, 86, 95, 118–35, 181; *see also*: conduct literature
Aeneas/Eneas (*Aeneid, Eneasroman*) 10, 16
Aeneid 10, 179, 186
agency 4, 8, 26–27, 28, 30, 59–60, 47, 55, 97, 99–100, 119, 127, 130, 132, 134–35, 178, 184–85, 194, 195
Agnes of Werdenberg, see: Oettingen family
Alberich 56–57
Albertus Magnus 42
Albrecht von Scharfenberg (*Jüngerer Titurel*) 7–8, 118–19, 123, 129–31, 132–34
amiral [ruler] 106
Amoryus and Cleopes 43; *see also*: John Metham
Aquitaine 167, 170, 173, 175
Aristotle 181
Augustine 42n
Augustinians 41; *see also*: monk

badges 3, 11, 201n
Baldini, Baccio 193–94
Balmung 56–57
Begrabene Ehemann, Der (der Stricker) 200n
Beowulf 162
Bernard of Clairvaux 9–10, 161–70, 172, 173, 174–75
Blanscheflûr 6–7, 12, 103–14, 180n
Boccaccio, Giovanni 11–12, 210–11, 215
bridal quest 4–5, 16, 50–51, 55, 66–68, 105
brother 31, 50, 60n, 61, 62, 63, 65, 68, 78n, 80, 88, 96, 98, 166, 187
– lay 41
– in-law 96; *see also*: monk
Brother Hermann of Veldenz (*Das Leben der Gräfin Iolande von Vianden*) 25–26
Brunhild 5, 49, 61, 63–68, 162; *see also*: Nibelungenlied
Burgundy 5, 50, 53, 59–64; *see also*: Gunther

Carthusian order 28, 29n, 31; *see also*: monk
Catherine of Siena 213n
chanson de geste 162
Charlemagne 103

Christherre-Chronik (anonymous) 179
Christianity 7, 10, 97, 103, 105–109, 111–12, 117, 121, 160–77, 187, 190, 191, 194n, 196, 199; *see also*: Observance Reform, monasticism, convent, cloister, monk, nun
Cistercian order 4, 25, 27, 29, 162
cloister 4, 28, 44, 163, 168–69, 17071, 173, 175; *see also*: convent
clothing 8, 35, 70, 165–172, 174, 182, 184, 186, 193; *see also*: headdress
conduct literature 4, 18–19, 34n, 78, 87n, 92–96, 100, 117–19, 120, 121n 122n, 124–28, 132–35; *see also*: advice
Constantine 60n
– arch of 194
convent 3, 27, 29–30, 32, 201; *see also*: cloister
crusade 10
crusade song 142, 162

Dancwart 63, 65; *see also*: Nibelungenlied
Danes/Danish 5, 62, 63, 65, 67, 103, 162
Frauchen von 21 Jahren, Das 44
daughter 1–2, 3, 5–9, 15–20, 25–26, 28–32, 42–44, 48, 79–81, 84, 85, 97–89, 91–96, 98, 99, 117, 118–19, 122n 124, 127–28, 133–34, 138–42, 167, 177–78, 194, of Nero 180, spiritual 174; *see also*: mother-daughter-relationship
Decameron (Boccaccio) 210
Deceyte of Women 181n
"De mineralibus" 42
"De virtutibus lapidum" 42
desire
– sexual 6, 8, 10, 18, 28, 34, 35, 39-40, 42–44, 78, 82, 88, 90-93, 96, 100, 105, 106, 117, 119, 122, 124–25, 128–35, 139, 164, 177–78, 180, 181–82, 185, 185–86, 188, 205, 208, 212
– to error (sin) 164
– for religious life 15, 26, 28
– for knightly life 163
– for wealth/property/material gain 17, 38, 41, 106
– for status 25, 41, 44

– for home [Xanten] 62
– for vengeance 84, 182
Dominican order 3, 25, 27, 41, 43n; *see also*: monk
Duchess of Arundel 5, 78–87, 91–95, 98–99
dream 5, 16, 47–48, 59, 92, 175, 177

Eckhart, Meister 43n
Eilhart von Oberge 6, 78, 81, 100
Elisabeth of Württemberg 31, 32, 42
Eneasroman (Heinrich von Veldeke) 1, 16, 19
enclosure, see: cloister
êre 50, 59, 67, 84, 89, 128, 139–140, 180; *see also*: honor
Erec (Hartmann von Aue) 70n, 91
L'estoire del Saint Gral 180
Etzel 162; *see also*: Nibelungenlied
Exemplum 210

Fabliau 210
Fadet Joglar (Guiraut de Calanson) 181n
father 6–7, 11, 17, 18, 50, 54, 55, 57, 79–89, 103, 106, 110, 118, 120, 121, 122, 141, 199
femininity 1, 6, 10, 16n, 47–48, 51–53, 55–56, 59, 68, 77, 91, 92, 98, 167
Fênix, King 105–6, 108–11
Fleck, Konrad 6, 103–14
Floire et Blancheflor 180
Flôre und Blanscheflûr 6, 12, 103–14
Flôre 6–7, 12, 103–14, 180n
foster (parenting) 7, 15, 16 –17, 19, 118–20, 122–23
Frauchen von 21 Jahren, Das, 44
Freud, Sigmund 11–12, 57n 200, 207, 212
friendship 7, 80, 87, 88–89, 93, 95–96, 104, 107–8, 210–11

"Geistliches Gespräch zwischen einer Fürstin und einer Krämerin von einem Rosenkranz aus Edelsteinen" 4, 30–31, 32–43
gemstones (and lore) 28, 33–42, 165, 204; *see also*: jewelry
gender 1–11, 15–20, 20, 26–27, 47–49, 51–53, 55, 56, 59, 67, 77–78, 86–87, 109n 117, 121–22, 132n 142, 161, 201, 215; *see also*: agency, femininity, masculinity, patriarchy
gender hierarchy, see: patriarchy

Gernot 63; *see also*: Nibelungenlied
Gottfried von Strassburg 1, 5–6, 9, 11, 17–18, 43, 78–80, 86, 92, 95, 98–100, 118, 202–3, 207, 209
grandfather 17
Gregorius (Hartmann von Aue) 9–10, 11, 161–63, 167–75
Guillem de Cabestaing (*Vida*) 210
Guiraut de Calanson (*Fadet Joglar*) 181n
Gunther 5, 50–51, 53, 56, 59–68; *see also*: Nibelungenlied
guote Gêrhart, Der (Rudolf von Ems) 103
Güterstein 31, 44

Hagen 48, 56–59, 60n 61, 63, 65, 67n, 70–71; *see also*: Nibelungenlied
Hagen (*Kudrun*) 17
Hagen, Friedrich von der 152n
Hartmann von Aue 9–10, 70n 91, 161, 163, 167–75
headdress 41, 44, 89, 93n
hermit 170–73, 175
Heinrich von Freiberg (*Tristan und Isolde*) 5, 78–80, 86–87, 91–100
Heinrich von Veldeke 1, 16, 48n; *see also*: Eneasroman
Herzeloyde 7–8, 12, 117–35
Herzmaere (Konrad von Würzburg) 11–12, 199–215
Hilde (*Kudrun*) 16
Hildebrandslied 160
Hippocrates 180
Holofernes 181
honor 8, 10, 19, 50, 59, 67, 78, 82, 84, 89–91, 96, 99, 103, 20, 125, 128–29, 131–33, 139–40, 164, 175, 177–78, 180, 184–85, 189; *see also*: êre
hortus conclusus 94
Hugo von Trimberg (*Der Renner*) 118
husband
– advice of 10, 180, 185
– betrothed/proposed 3, 18, 48, 98, 105
– jealous/vengeful 11, 199–200, 202–3, 208–11, 214–15
– marital duty of 89–93, 95, 99
– mistreatment by 11, 98, 180–81, 195
– securing a 119, 126–34, 178 (*see also: Die Winsbeckin*)

– unfaithful/faithless 82, 189, 194–95
– wife speaking for/political power through 6, 80, 84, 98, 109–10; *see also*: marriage

Iceland 63–64, 103
In Praise of New Knighthood (Bernard of Clairvaux) 9–10, 161, 163–68, 170, 175
incest 168–70, 174
Isenstein 5, 64–65, 66–67
Isolde of the White Hands 5–6, 7, 77–100
Isolde (Queen) 5, 17–18, 43, 78, 80, 84–85, 90, 92, 95, 99
Isolde the Blonde (Princess) 5–6, 7, 17–18, 77–100, 103, 206, 207
Italy 171, 173, 194

Jans der Enikel (*Weltchronik*) 110–11, 177–96
Jerusalem 167, 203
jewelry 34, 41, 171; *see also*: gemstones
John of Salisbury (*Policraticus*) 181n
Jüngerer Titurel (Albrecht von Scharfenberg) 7–8, 118–35

Karsie, see: Duchess of Arundel
Kaufringer, Heinrich 200n
kinship 3, 118; *see also*: mother-daughter-relationship
Kirchheim am Ries 27, 29, 31–32, 44
Kleist, Heinrich von (*Michael Kohlhaas*) 208n
Konrad von Würzburg (*Herzmaere*) 11, 202–3, 208n, 209
Kriemhild 5, 16, 47–51, 54–56, 59–63, 65–71, 77, 162, 177, 180n; *see also*: *Nibelungenlied*

Lauretis, Teresa de 48, 51–55
La vie du pape saint Grégoire 161, 163
Lavinia (*Eneasroman*) 16, 19
Leben der Gräfin Yolande von Vianden, Das (Brother Hermann) 25
Lechler, Martin (*Neithart Fuchs*) 138
Leipzig 41
locus amoenus 69–70
lovesickness 7, 120–33
Ludwig I of Württemberg 31, 32
Ludwig XI of Oettingen, see: Oettingen family

Magdalena of Oettingen, abbess of Kirchheim, see: Oettingen family
magic
– and Virgil 179–80, 185–91, 194–96
– of love potion 43, 95; *see also*: gemstones (and lore)
Märe [short rhymed tale] 70n, 71n, 77, 199n, 200; *see also*: Schwank
Marbode of Rennes 38n, 40–41
Margaret of Courtenay 15, 25–26
marriage 51n 64, 66, 77, 82, 88, 97–98, 121, 134, 169, 195
– deceit in 199–201, 202
– political 6, 15–16, 18, 25, 43, 79–81, 90–92, 95, 111, 118–19
– related by 4, 31
– women's control in 126, 131–32, 134–35
masculinity/masculinities 1, 9–10, 12, 48–49, 51–53, 59, 69–71, 161–75, 201n
material culture 10
– of devotion 27
Mechthild, Countess of the Rhine Palatinate 4, 31, 42
Medusa 177
Metham, John (*Amoryus and Cleopes*) 43
minne [courtly love] 50–51, 68, 77, 99, 119–28, 130–35, 137, 165, 202–5
minnedienst [love-service] 7–8, 62–65, 120–22, 127, 131–32, 134–34
Minnesang [courtly love lyric] 137
misogyny 34, 42–43, 94n, 112
monastery 163, 168–69; *see also*: Güterstein, cloister, monasticism
monasticism 28–29, 163–64, 169, 170, 174–75
monk 10, 28, 31, 42–43, 44, 163–64, 166–67, 168, 169
mother 1–9, 12, 15–20, 25–27, 29–32, 47–48, 78–84, 87–100, 103, 108–9, 111–14, 117–19, 122–23, 127, 131, 133–35, 137–42, 169, 174, 177, 194
Mothers and Daughters in Medieval German Literature 1–9, 11, 15–20, 25–26, 34n, 43, 47–49, 51, 79, 84, 87–88, 90, 94–95, 98–99, 103, 108, 110, 113–14, 117, 118–19, 127–28, 133, 137, 140–42, 177–78; *see also*: Rasmussen, Ann Marie

mother-daughter-relationship 3–9, 11, 12, 15–20, 25–26, 27, 29–32, 47–48, 79, 83–84, 87–91, 94–95, 103, 108–9, 113–14, 117, 118, 124, 127, 133, 137, 141–42
myth 48, 52–53

Naples 184, 190
Neidhart (von Reuenthal) 1, 8–9, 18–19, 137–156
Neithart Fuchs (Martin Fechler) 137
Nero 180
Nibelungenlied 1, 4–5, 16, 47–71, 77, 118, 162, 177n
Nonnenturnier 201
nun 4, 31–32, 201; see also, cloister, convent

Observance Reform 3–4, 27, 28–29, 30, 43–44
Oettingen family
- Agnes of Werdenberg, Countess (ca. 1400–ca. 1471) (m. Ludwig XI 1420) 4, 27–28, 29–32
- Anna (abbess of Kirchheim 1535–1545) 29n
- Ludwig XI, Count (1361–1440) 29
- Magdalena (abbess of Kirchheim 1446–1496, daughter of Agnes) 4, 27, 29–32
- Margarethe (abbess of Kirchheim 1505–1535) 29n
Order of Preachers, see: Dominican order

Parzival (Wolfram von Eschenbach) 12, 118, 126, 129, 133–35, 179n
paternoster 28, 31–32, 33, 36, 37, 41
patriarchy 2, 7, 18, 25, 27, 33, 44, 48–49, 54, 57, 59, 62, 65, 70n, 71, 77, 87, 94–95, 98–100, 114, 117
- gender hierarchy in 86, 99, 201, 215
penance 170–72, 175, 209
Policraticus 181n
pope 10, 168, 171–75
Priapeia 202
psychoanalysis 11, 207–8, 212–15
Pygmalion 177

Rache des Ehemanns, Die (Heinrich Kaufringer) 200n
Rasmussen, Ann Marie 1–12, 15–23, 25–26, 27, 34n 43, 47–49, 51, 78–79, 84, 87, 88, 90, 92, 94–96, 98–99, 104, 108–11, 114, 117–19, 121, 127, 128, 133, 137, 138n, 140–42, 161, 177–78, 199, 201n; see also: *Mothers and Daughters in Medieval German Literature*
Renner, Der (Hugo von Trimberg) 118
Rolandslied 162
Rome 10, 171, 173, 180, 181, 184–86, 188–93
rosary 4, 27, 31, 33–42, 44; see also: paternoster
Rudolf von Ems, *Der guote Gêrhart* 103
- *Weltchronik* 179
- *Ruodlieb* 60n

saint 10, 12, 163
- relics of 212
saints' lives/legends 26, 58, 162, 163, 210
- female 77
Samson 181
Saxo, Arnoldo (*De virtutibus lapidum*) 42
Saxony 5, 62, 65, 67n, 162
Schneekind 11, 199–200, 214
Schwank, (*Schwänke*, *Schwankmäre*) 77, 178, 199–202, 209, 211, 214, 215
sculpture 186, 194
sexuality
- female 8–9, 19, 114, 117, 139, 141–42, 199
- and gender 51n, 87–88, 90–95, 122, 124–25, 128–31, 132–35, 177–78, 199
- and Muslim stereotypes 106
- and procreation 10
- and psychoanalysis 212; see also: desire
Siegfried 4–5, 12, 16, 47–71, 162; see also: *Nibelungenlied*
Siegmund 49, 54, 56, 65, 66n; see also: *Nibelungenlied*
Sigune 7–8, 12, 118–35
sin 12, 35, 40–41, 43, 165–66, 167, 168, 169, 174
sister 32, 41, 62, 63, 64, 65, 66n 78, 79, 81, 87, 94n, 96, 187
- in-law 31; see also: nun
Snow Child, see: *Schneekind*
Solomon 179
Sommerlieder [summer songs] 18, 138–41, 143–52
son 6, 7, 17, 18, 49, 54, 56, 57, 65, 79, 80, 81, 84, 85, 86, 88, 105, 109, 110–14, 121, 134, 167, 199
- in-law 88, 96
- foster 119, 120

Spain 10, 151, 154
statue 11, 177, 183–96
Stiefmutter und Tochter [Stepmother and Daughter] 1, 7, 18, 19
Stricker, der (*Der begrabene Ehemann*) 200n

Tale of the Heart, see: *Herzmaere*
Tamar (sister of Absalom) 187
Templars 10, 163, 166–67, 173, 174; *see also*: crusade
Thomasin von Zerklaere (*Der Wälsche Gast*) 118
Tristan (character) 5, 77–100, 103, 207
Tristan (Gottfried von Strassburg) 1, 5, 9, 11, 17–18, 43, 77–100, 118, 202–3, 206–7
Tristan und Isolde, see: Ulrich von Türheim, Heinrich von Freiberg
Tristrant, see: Eilhart von Oberge
Titurel (Wolfram von Eschenbach) 7–8, 118–35

Ulrich von Türheim (*Tristan und Isolde*) 5, 78–91, 94–100
Uote 16, 47–48; *see also*: *Nibelungenlied*

"Vida" (Guillem de Cabestaing) 210–211
Virgil 10–11, 177–96
Virgin Mary 34, 38, 39, 199
virginity 19, 94, 128, 13
voice 34, 43, 120, 121n, 127
– private vs. public 122, 128, 130, 132–33,
– women's 20, 83

Wälsche Gast, Der (Thomasin von Zerklaere) 118
Walther von der Vogelweide 55n, 137
Weltchronik (Rudolf von Ems) 179
Weltchronik (Jans der Enikel) 10, 177–96

Werdenberg family
– Agnes, Countess of Oettingen, see: Oettingen family
– Eberhard III 29, 32
– Johann II 31, 32
wife
– adulterous 11, 98, 199, 201, 203, 208–11, 214–15
– co-wife 106
– instrumentalization of 183–86, 191, 194, 195
– jealous 11, 78, 89, 96
– model (submissive) 77, 91, 96, 98, 180–83, 185, 189
– as object of bridal quest 17, 48, 68, 105–6,
– as partner 194–95
– political function of 6, 18, 59, 65, 67n, 79, 80, 88, 95, 109–10, 195
– wronged 6, 83–84, 95–96, 98–100, 178, 183, 184; *see also*: marriage
Wigalois (Wirnt von Grafenberg) 58
Winsbecke, Der 18, 118, 121n
Winsbeckin, Die 1, 7, 15, 18 19, 92–94, 95–96, 100, 118, 119, 122n, 127–28, 140, 177–78, 194
Wolfram von Eschenbach 7–8, 118–19, 120n, 123, 124n, 152n, 126–34
Worms 5, 49–51, 53–56, 62–68, 71; *see also*: *Nibelungenlied*

Xanten 50, 62; *see also*: *Nibelungenlied*

Yolande of Vianden 25, 38–40

zuht [good/courtly behavior] 92, 94, 128, 131, 180; *see also*: conduct literature

www.ingramcontent.com/pod-product-compliance
Lightning Source LLC
Chambersburg PA
CBHW080223170426
43192CB00015B/2738